Romy Schneider

Romy Schneider

A Star Across Europe

Marion Hallet

BLOOMSBURY ACADEMIC
NEW YORK • LONDON • OXFORD • NEW DELHI • SYDNEY

BLOOMSBURY ACADEMIC
Bloomsbury Publishing Inc
1385 Broadway, New York, NY 10018, USA
50 Bedford Square, London, WC1B 3DP, UK
29 Earlsfort Terrace, Dublin 2, Ireland

BLOOMSBURY, BLOOMSBURY ACADEMIC and the Diana logo are trademarks of
Bloomsbury Publishing Plc

First published in the United States of America 2022
Paperback edition published 2023

Cover design: Eleanor Rose
Cover image: Romy Schneider on the set of 1971 movie *Max et les Ferrailleurs*.
Photograph by Jean-Pierre Bonnotte © Gamma-Legends / Getty Images

Library of Congress Cataloging-in-Publication Data
Names: Hallet, Marion, author.
Title: Romy Schneider : a star across Europe / Marion Hallet.
Description: New York : Bloomsbury Academic, 2022. |
Includes bibliographical references and index. |
Summary: "This book explores the star image of Austrian born actress
Romy Schneider (1938-1982), with her evolving cinema roles together with
her acting choices and events in her private life, led her career
into varied and fascinating directions within European and
Hollywood cinemas"– Provided by publisher.
Identifiers: LCCN 2021048073 (print) | LCCN 2021048074 (ebook) | ISBN 9781501378850
(hardback) | ISBN 9781501378843 (epub) | ISBN 9781501378836 (ebook other)
Subjects: LCSH: Schneider, Romy, 1938-1982. | Motion picture actors and
actresses–Austria–Biography. | Motion picture actors and actresses–France–Biography. |
Motion pictures– History– 20th century.
Classification: LCC PN2618.S34 H35 2022 (print) | LCC PN2618.S34 (ebook) |
DDC 791.4302/8092 [B]–dc23/eng/20211027
LC record available at https://lccn.loc.gov/2021048073
LC ebook record available at https://lccn.loc.gov/2021048074

ISBN: HB: 978-1-5013-7885-0
          PB: 978-1-5013-7882-9
          ePDF: 978-1-5013-7883-6
          eBook: 978-1-5013-7884-3

Typeset by Integra Software Services Pvt. Ltd.

To find out more about our authors and books visit www.bloomsbury.com
and sign up for our newsletters.

For Pierran.

CONTENTS

Conclusion: The legacy of Romy Schneider   217

FIGURES

ACKNOWLEDGEMENTS

I would like to extend my deepest gratitude and most sincere thanks to my mentor at King's College London, Professor Ginette Vincendeau. Her brilliance, motivation and encouragement have inspired me and taught me to be a better researcher, writer, teacher and feminist. I also thank Professor Erica Carter, whose advice and guidance were paramount in my study of Schneider's Austrianness, and the academic staff and PhD students in the Film Studies department at KCL. Special thanks to the always great Elizabeth, Tessa, Alice, Jenny, Anna, Jen, Eleonora, Joe A., Simon, Karolina and Joe J. for being pillars of laughter and support.

Massive thanks to the fantastic Jen Wallace (and Kiki) for hosting me in Paris for research and patisseries, and for proofreading my manuscript.

I would also like to thank Régis Robert and his team of archivists at the bibliothèque du film and the espace chercheurs of the Cinémathèque française, as well as Anne Andreu.

Thank you to my girlfriends Amandine, Camille, Loulou and Carolane, for being the greatest confidantes and listening to me perorate about Schneider, films and feminism.

Thank you to my dear grandparents: Monique and Jean, for their love and words of wisdom, and Joseph and Lucie for introducing me to *Sissi* before I could walk. And my final thanks go to my wonderful parents, Benoît and Viviane, and my sisters Camille and Clotilde (and our Poppy) for being my rock and first cheerleaders.

Note

Some parts of my chapter on Schneider's Occupation films have been published previously, in: Marion Hallet (2021) Beautiful victim: Romy Schneider in French Occupation cinema, *French Screen Studies*, 21:2, 166–83, DOI: 10.1080/26438941.2020.1864198.

with attention paid to performance[2] and other mise-en-scène elements (costume, lighting, composition, production design, makeup and hairstyle), dialogue and music. By analysing the form of Schneider's films, as well as their narrative and character construction, I look at how a feminine image is established on screen, and how Schneider's characters within her films construct different ideologies of womanhood at particular historical moments. The corpus of films analysed in my study consists of Schneider's complete filmography, that is sixty-three films released from 1953 to 1982, which includes two TV films and one documentary. While every film has been viewed, some are briefly considered while others have been selected for deeper analysis as the most representative of the star's evolution. I also refer to films outside Schneider's filmography, from the 1920s to the present day, such as the original versions of the remakes in which Schneider starred in the 1950s, and the films (and star personas) of European female stars contemporaneous with Schneider along the years (in particular Hildegard Knef, Brigitte Bardot, Anna Karina, Jeanne Moreau, Catherine Deneuve, Annie Girardot, Hannah Schygulla, Isabelle Adjani), for comparative purposes in order to historicize Schneider's career and persona within the canon of European film history. I look at other films by European and Hollywood directors with whom Schneider worked in order to evaluate her impact as a performer and as a star on their collaborations, as well as other auteur and popular films to situate and contextualize Schneider's work and representation of femininity over time (the evolution of Occupation films in France since the end of the Second World War, for example).

Beyond the films, the printed media coverage that built Schneider's star image is amply analysed throughout this book (promotional material, reviews, articles and photographs published in the press at the time), with material from Austria, Germany, France, Belgium, Netherlands, Italy, Spain, the UK and the United States. I also made use of archival material such as private correspondence, production notes and original drafts of scripts. I have found a substantial amount of such material in libraries and archives in film institutes in Paris, Berlin, Vienna, London and Lausanne and at the Bibliothèque nationale de France in Paris. In addition, many radio and television interviews with Schneider, as well as journalistic comments and TV documentaries about her are available on the internet (on video-sharing

---

[2]In *Stars* (1979), Richard Dyer stresses how a star possesses a particular performance style that 'through its familiarity will inform the performance s/he gives in any particular film' (1998, p. 142). Following Dyer's analytical methodology of 'performance signs' (facial expression, voice, gestures, body posture and body movement, pp. 134–50) and the development of a systematic methodology by James Naremore (1988), I am, for my study of Schneider, directly concerned with the semiotics and stylistics of film acting. That is the actor's repertory of gestures, postures, expression and speech that compose a 'field of discourse', an ensemble of signs established by a star over a number of films, that expresses meaning for audience.

and audio-visual archives websites such as YouTube and Dailymotion, and the Ina[3] website). Other audio-visual material were only available in archives such as some of her lesser-known films (*L'Amour à la mer*, Guy Gilles, 1964; *My Lover, My Son*, John Newland, 1970; *Tausend Lieder ohne Ton*, 1977, Claudia Holldack). I also examined a plethora of websites dedicated to Schneider and administrated by her fans, but bearing in mind their variable degree of reliability, they were rigorously cross-checked with primary sources when possible.

I have also relied on established scholarship in several academic fields (theories and paradigms developed in Anglo-American film star studies from the 1970s onwards, including German and French star studies, European and transnational film stardom). Considering the importance of stars and films as pillars of identification for male and female audiences and representations of sexual 'norms', one can see the critical importance of adopting a gender perspective when studying stars. I study Schneider in terms of her construction of gender (as well as from a feminist point of view), in the context of the traditional German society of the 1950s and of the rise of women's rights and radical cultural changes in the 1960s and 1970s, as well as notions of female beauty, their historical and cultural anchorage and ideological ambiguities. This is helpful in understanding the appeal of Schneider's image as a woman, as well as the media construction of her as an emanation of the 'eternal feminine'.

Curiously, as already mentioned, there have been very few scholarly studies of Schneider. Yet there has been a lot of published material about her. However, as is common to other major popular stars, large amounts of writing on Schneider consist of biographical and autobiographical material of different value. Those works often lack originality, reliability or analytical perspective and their sources are rarely cited. Nevertheless, they contribute to the promotion and the construction of the star's image. Therefore, these works on Schneider are useful as raw material, for they are symptomatic of discourses on the star.

There is a so-called 'autobiography' by Renate Seydel, *Ich, Romy: Tagebuch eines Lebens* (1988), that has been published several times and translated into French (1989). The book is a compilation of Schneider's own diary of her early life and of second-hand writing; therefore, it is not exactly the 'diary' that the title suggests. It assembles excerpts from a series of articles published by Schneider's mother Magda Schneider in the *München Illustrierte* in early 1957, excerpts from articles published in magazines such as *Abendzeitung* (1958) and *Quick* (1965) and fragments from interviews given by Schneider to the German and French magazines *Stern* and *Paris Match* in 1981 and 1982. Seydel writes that all other comments

---

[3]Institut national de l'audiovisuel.

by Schneider come from publications between 1957 and 1982 and are reproduced with the intention to present a coherent autobiography, but she does not provide specific references. While it is a fascinating document, *Ich, Romy* has to be considered with caution regarding the accuracy of timeline, events and the comments on them. As far as possible I double-checked this source with others, such as reviews, and radio and television interviews although these too are not necessarily reliable as there are particular biases attached to specific contexts (for example, in the 1970s, the New German Cinema practitioners' dislike of popular post-war German cinema cemented Schneider's own rejection of the *Sissis*). I try to be alert to exaggerations, contradictions and changes present in those discourses.

Another point of interest in those types of 'memoirs' is the stars' perception of their own image. Several protagonists in Schneider's entourage – friends, parents, celebrity colleagues, the star herself – keep repeating the same anecdotes and stories, using sometimes the exact same words, yet years apart (in that regard the 1983 biography of Schneider by fellow actress Hildegard Knef who alleged she had known and understood Schneider intimately is both fascinating in its details yet patronizing in its tone). The stars' own discourses, however truthful they may aim to be, are inevitably distorted by what they read, saw and have been told about themselves by journalists or agents. As a result, it is not unusual for the stars and those close to them to spread clichés about their life and career. Schneider is no exception to this process and this is the case too for Delon, for instance, who wrote the preface to *Delon-Romy, ils se sont tant aimés* (Barbier, Dureau and Pommier, 2009) and to the second edition (2017) of David Lelait-Helo's *Romy*. More recently, Romy Schneider's daughter, Sarah Biasini (2020), who rarely speaks publicly about her mother, wrote her own memoirs about herself becoming a mother while she grew up without one (Biasini was about to turn five when Schneider died). Although her mother's career and acting choices are briefly evoked, as contextual background, and Schneider's presence (or absence rather) is felt throughout, the book is first and foremost about Biasini's life.

Much writing on Schneider is composed of annotated collections of photographs (Renate Seydel, 1987; Hanna Schygulla, 1988; Will McBride, 2002), biographies and novels (Evelyne Bloch-Dano, 2007; Olaf Kraemer, 2008) – there are even 'astro-biographies' that purport to relate Schneider's life and character through the zodiac at the moment of her birth. Most of the works presented as biographies (Catherine Hermary-Vieille, 1988; Emmanuel Bonini, 2001; Sophie Guillou, 2006) contain romanticized elements and it is sometimes difficult for the reader to separate fact from fiction. As well as repeating previous accounts, those works draw heavily on the lexical fields of 'passion', 'myth', 'destiny', 'tragedy' and 'death' – as is perceptible in their titles (*La double mort de Romy* by Bernard Pascuito in 2002, *Des lilacs blancs en enfer*, by Christian Dureau in 2010). They are written in a colloquial or hyperbolic style, and they all rely on and relay the same 'mythemes',[4] the basic elements that once reassembled build the Schneider myth. One extreme example is Marco Innocenti's 2009 Italian book about twenty-three famous 'tragic' women (including Schneider, Marilyn Monroe, Françoise Sagan, Vivien Leigh, Virginia Woolf, Jean Seberg, Janis Joplin and Sylvia Plath) entitled *La malattia chiamata Donna. Erano belle, famose e depresse* (*The disease called Woman. They were beautiful, famous and depressed*). Nonetheless, this massive amount of international writing on Schneider and its popularity – most of the books were published more than once, and have been translated into several languages – signpost the actress's wide impact on audiences and of her continuing media presence.

The best-documented biographies of Schneider, and ones that adopt some critical and analytical perspective, are by Michael Jürgs (1991) and Günter Krenn (2013a) – only available in German. They develop their discussion in a more scientific manner and in a more refined language. Krenn also wrote *Romy & Alain. Eine Amour fou* (2013b), a detailed account of the personal and professional relationship between Schneider and Delon.

I approach Schneider's life and career chronologically and therefore divide this book into three parts, each one corresponding to a major period in the star's career. The first part focuses on her Germanic[5] phase in the 1950s – when she embodied the ingénue and became a screen icon as Sissi in continental Europe. Here, I dissect her relationship with German-speaking cinema and media. The second part is dedicated to what I call her 'international phase' in the 1960s when she develops a new identity as a sensual and sophisticated woman. Finally, the third part is on her French career in the 1970s and early 1980s. During this phase, which corresponded to important social and cultural changes in women's lives and identities with the rise of the women's movement, Schneider's persona was constructed in relation to a paradoxical image of ostensibly 'modern' yet vulnerable womanhood, crystallized in Claude Sautet's films; this image then developed into that of a 'tragic victim' in *rétro* and Occupation films, and, in turn, evolved into a more extreme, at times morbid identity in a set of films that drew on, and foregrounded, her highly regarded melodramatic performance. Her film roles during this last phase were increasingly perceived as echoing her personal life, at the time and ever since.

---

[4]The term 'mytheme' was coined by Claude Lévi-Strauss in his 1955 essay 'La structure des mythes', edited in his book *Anthropologie structurale* (1958, pp. 227–55).
[5]I will sometimes use the term 'Germanic' (as in Germanic cultures) to cover both West German and Austrian cinemas as Schneider moved from one to the other during the 1950s, although those are distinct film industries (I talk about this distinction in more details in Part I, Chapter 1).

Through examining Schneider's changing depictions of femininity – examining what types of gender dynamics and relationships are at play – the figure of the star in terms of her biography and of the social and cultural context surrounding her, I seek to understand how a female star persona such as Schneider's contributes to the history of women's representation. Furthermore, owing to the actress working in various national film industries and being perceived through different national media and acting in different languages, this book deals with the history and experiences of women in Western European cultures from the 1950s to the early 1980s – and brings her legacy to the present day in the conclusion. By studying the historical implications of Schneider's image spanning her filmic and extra-filmic persona and by reflecting through a feminist lens on her career and legacy, I hope to contribute to a critical understanding of a major star who has so far been neglected, as well as to a key period of the post-war European star-system.

PART ONE

Romy Schneider's Germanic career: 1953–1959

1

Romy before *Sissi*

Introduction

This first chapter discusses the ways in which Romy Schneider's star image developed with regards to three core aspects – an on- and off-screen mother-daughter relationship, her identification with historical costume films and the ideological component of her persona in relation to the context of post-war West Germany and Austria. Throughout these main features runs the notion of submission – to her mother and to a nation – with the important question being how and why the young actress ended up embodying such a successful image of the modern young woman in films that appeared, even at the time, outdated.

* * *

Romy Schneider started as a young starlet in 1953 in mainstream German-speaking cinema. From early on two major themes emerged and shaped her acting career – family and history. Schneider's Germanic phase is mainly associated with a juvenile image that is, beyond her age, related to her family background and her mother's career in particular, and to her portrayals of young and romantic royal figures, the most iconic of which being Empress Elisabeth of Austria, known as Sissi. When we look deeper into Schneider's pre-*Sissi* films period, we see that the Sissi character and what it represented in 1950s West Germany and Austria were the culmination of Schneider's previous character arcs and film narratives.

Between 1953 and 1955 Schneider made five films: *Wenn der weiße Flieder wieder blüht / When the White Lilacs Bloom Again* (Hans Deppe, 1953), *Feuerwerk / Fireworks* (Kurt Hoffmann, 1954), *Mädchenjahre einer Königin / Victoria in Dover* (Ernst Marischka, 1954), *Die Deutschmeister / A March for the Emperor* (Ernst Marischka, 1955) and *Der letzte Mann / The Last Man*

(Harald Braun, 1955). These films from Schneider's early career were distributed only in West Germany and Austria, with a couple of exceptions for Belgium, the Netherlands and Sweden. Therefore, Schneider's star image construction began on a national, even local level. These early films, however, were all distributed European-wide (and worldwide for *Mädchenjahre einer Königin*) after the release and the immense success of *Sissi* (Ernst Marischka, 1955).

Schneider's first films span a large spectrum of genres although some dominate – the musical and the historical film – and because some overlap with others it is useful to consider them in terms of several subtypes. The musical films include *Wenn der weiße Flieder wieder blüht* and *Feuerwerk*; yet, they cannot be considered as musicals *per se* – that is according to our understanding of musicals in the sense of the classical Hollywood musical as both the 'backstage' and the 'integrated' type (Altman, 1987; Feuer, 1993). The narratives of *Wenn der weiße Flieder wieder blüht* and *Feuerwerk* do not progress through songs or dance. Both are built around musical success though: the eponymous song in *Wenn der weiße Flieder wieder blüht* was a popular hit in the 1920s, and 'O mein Papa' sung by Lilli Palmer in *Feuerwerk* was written for a 1939 musical. The operetta film ('Operettenfilm') is also worth mentioning in regard to these two films but also to Schneider's mother's background. Mainly associated with German language cinema, the operetta film (Traubner, 2007) is a subgenre of the musical film whose roots stretch back to the tradition of nineteenth-century Viennese operettas, a genre of 'light' Opera – light in terms of both music and subject matter. Many operetta films are adaptations of stage operettas, as was the case for *Feuerwerk*. With these distinctions in mind, I nevertheless refer to *Wenn der weiße Flieder wieder blüht* and *Feuerwerk* as musical films.

Schneider's historical films are *Mädchenjahre einer Königin* and *Die Deutschmeister*, and also cover several subgenres. Natalie Zemon Davis (2000) defines the historical genre as being composed of dramatic films in which the primary plot is based on historical events, or in which an imagined plot unfolds in such a way that historical events are central to the narrative (see also Sorlin, 1980; Carnes, 1995; and Sobchack, 1996). For *Mädchenjahre einer Königin* the historical genre overlaps with other well-established subgenres – the biopic (see Custen, 1992; Altman, 1999; Brown and Vidal, 2014), which includes royalty films (biographically based films about royal families).

As for *Die Deutschmeister*, Schneider's fourth film, it is considered one of the last examples of Wiener film (literally 'Viennese film'). The genre was popular in Austria, especially during the 1930s, and consisted of a combination of comedy, romance and melodrama in an historical setting, mostly Vienna of the late nineteenth/early twentieth century (Kramer and Prucha, 1994). It is also worth mentioning the Heimat[1] film in relation to

---

[1] The German word 'Heimat' can be translated as home, homeland, home soil or fatherland.

Die Deutschmeister, a genre that had an important resonance in Germany, Austria and Switzerland, and was popular from the 1920s to the early 1970s, with renewed enthusiasm in the 1950s. Heimat films were noted for their rural settings, sentimental tone and simplistic morality, and centred on love, friendship, family and rural life. Also important to the genre is the polarity between old and young, tradition and progress, and rural and urban life (Von Moltke, 2002 and 2005).

Apart from the popular genres of films that prevailed at the beginning of Schneider's career, another major influence on its direction was her mother. From all the aspects that resonated in the young Schneider's image and later expressed through her Sissi character, the most eloquent one would be the passéist viewpoint channelled through the historical settings of the films (mostly remakes), and especially by the presence of her mother Magda Schneider. The latter appeared in three of the five Romy Schneider films of that period: *Wenn der weiße Flieder wieder blüht*, *Mädchenjahre einer Königin* and *Die Deutschmeister*. One of the ways the Schneiders developed their on- and off-screen collaboration was by playing mother (or a related maternal figure) and daughter in eight films. The mother figure is essential to understand the foundation of Romy Schneider's star image. Indeed, Schneider's persona revolved around maternal bonds: the actress began her career as 'the daughter of', and ended it as a wounded mother herself.

1. Magda Schneider's daughter on and off screen

Romy Schneider was born Rosemarie Magdalena Albach on 23 September 1938 in Vienna, Austria, a few months after the capital became a Nazi Third Reich city due to the *Anschluss*. She lived there only a few weeks, as she mostly grew up in the Bavarian Alps, in her parents' isolated property named 'Mariengrund' in Schönau am Königssee, Germany. This was near Nazism's hotbed Berchtesgaden, where the 'Berghof' was located: Adolf Hitler's second residence from 1924 and one of his headquarters during the Second World War. The reference to Germany's modern history comes early in this book because Germany's historical past was and still is omnipresent when one approaches Schneider's star image.

Romy Schneider's mother, Magda Schneider, was an emblematic figure of German cinema in the 1930s as a young starlet with ballet training who sang operetta in romantic, light-hearted comedies. She became popular in 1933 when she starred in Max Ophüls's romantic drama *Liebelei*. She married Wolfgang Albach-Retty, also an actor and son of stage actress Rosa Retty, resident and then honorary member of the Burgtheater in Vienna. Romy's paternal great-grandparents were also itinerant actors. Her parents met on the set of *Kind, ich freu' mich auf dein Kommen* (Kurt Gerron, 1933) and married in Berlin in February 1936. Magda was German (she was born in Augsburg in 1909) and Wolf was Austrian, and together they starred in several romantic films before divorcing in 1945 when Romy was seven. Being the daughter of two prominent actors with busy schedules, Romy and her younger brother Wolf (born in 1941) were mainly raised by their maternal grandparents in the 'Mariengrund' chalet.

Later in the 1960s it was discovered that Romy Schneider's parents were exempted from tax by the Nazi Propaganda Ministry during the Second World War and that Magda was a close acquaintance of Gerda Buch, the wife of the Nazi Party Chancellery's head and Hitler's private secretary Martin Bormann, whose children played with the little Romy. Hitler himself was an admirer of Magda and they met probably more than once – there is film footage of at least one meeting that was recently discovered and is frequently used in documentaries about the star, especially French portraits. Magda's unclear connection with the Nazi regime impacted her daughter's perception of Germany; it also influenced how Romy Schneider's persona was polarized and differently received in Germanic and Francophone territories.

Magda Schneider's film career suffered from her divorce and the aftermath of the Second World War (it took a little while for the German cinema industry to recover), but in what was considered by the German-speaking press as an attempt to 'revive her success', she became increasingly known from 1953 as the ambitious mother who turned her attention to her beautiful teenage daughter, and decided to focus on promoting Romy in major productions rather than herself. When Magda did not appear alongside Romy on screen, she supervised her daughter's acting choices and negotiated contracts. This control over her daughter's career and wages was considered natural since Romy was still underage, but it continued beyond her majority, and not without tension, as we shall see.

Romy Schneider's first role in *Wenn der weiße Flieder wieder blüht*, a West German musical film, was secured by her mother who introduced her to director Hans Deppe. Schneider, who had just graduated from Goldenstein boarding school, a Catholic establishment for young girls near Salzburg, turned fifteen while filming the role of Eva 'Evchen' Forster, the daughter of a character played by her mother. Set in Wiesbaden, West Germany, the film narrates the story of single mother Therese Forster (Magda Schneider) who, after another argument about their financial situation, is left by her singer husband Willy (Willy Fritsch), while he is unaware that she is pregnant. Fifteen years later and crowned with success, Willy comes back on his European tour under the stage name of Bill Perry of whom Evchen is a fan; the two meet without knowing each other's identity. This leads Therese to face the past – should she marry Peter, her best friend who helped her to raise her daughter after Willy's departure, or go back to her ex-husband who claims that he still loves her?

In December 1953 the press described *Wenn der weiße Flieder wieder blüht* as Magda Schneider's comeback (her last film had been Jürgen von Alten's *Die Sterne lügen nicht* in 1950), and not as her daughter's 'first breakthrough' as it was retrospectively suggested. At the film's release only a few German-speaking critics pointed out the amusing fact that mother and daughter appeared together on screen, the focus being on Magda's return, and not particularly on Romy's acting ('Magda Schneider back on screen after years', *Österreichische Film und Kino Zeitung*, 19/12/1953). The film was a success in West Germany and Austria.

Romy Schneider first appears thirty-three minutes into the film, as the grown-up Evchen, a supporting role, but nevertheless a pivotal one in terms of both film narrative and star image construction. The notions of purity, naturalness and chastity became key to the young Schneider image, and all of them found their origins in this first film. Evchen is a naive and sweet teenager who has a good relationship with her mother and her mother's fiancé Peter. She is a modern character – a teenager who hangs out with her friends and does not particularly stand out. Schneider appears in the film with a girlish, conventional look. She wears tartan and pastels such as blue (a nightgown with Peter Pan collar and short puffed sleeves, a cocktail dress with floral pattern details and a modest décolleté and a woollen sweater), yellow (a turtleneck sweater) and grey (a calf-length skirt), and wears her curly hair up. In the last sequence, Schneider wears an elegant camel trench coat, but this more grown-up look is cancelled out by her desperate, crying face and farewell gesture to her father ('Vati!'). This weepy moment is emphasized by one of Schneider's first close-ups, a composition that became a pattern used to display her characters' moments of authenticity by emphasizing her tears.

As Evchen is a supporting role, the character's arc is not particularly developed: she is defined through her relationship with the adults on whom she depends and there is no room for a teenage romance. She supports her mother, acts as a groupie vis-à-vis her father, expresses the desire to be a popular singer 'just like him', and once he is gone, she replaces him with the comforting Peter, the 'real' father who taught her how to ride a bicycle. Although Schneider's womanly features were already alluring (her straight posture enhances her chest), in accordance to her character's age in this film she adopted the girlish traits that would influence her acting style for years – talking in a soft high-pitched voice, looking cheerful, giggling and smiling profusely.

Evchen shows nonetheless a great deal of maturity and depth, linked to the film's unusual view, for its time, on divorce – though there is no mention that Therese and Willy are actually divorced. Instead of pushing her mother back into her father's arms in what would be the classic and expected happy ending to a family film, Evchen urges her father to leave for her mother's sake and for the happiness of the real family they form with

Peter. Nevertheless, the traditional family model – biological father, mother and daughter – had the press's preference: the photos attached to articles and reviews of the film showed the smiling trio reunited, a choice that had to do with the popularity of major star Willy Fritsch, who embraced mostly paternal roles in his late career.

As previously said, *Wenn der weiße Flieder wieder blüht* was not about Romy Schneider's stardom, but about Magda's, especially since Therese's personal narrative strikingly shared elements with Magda's biography: divorce from an actor entertainer, being a single mother and what it implies, such as struggling financially and projecting the forsaken wife image. Fifteen years later, Therese's position has much improved in that regard: she has become a successful fashion designer and runs her own salon, and when Willy asks her to choose him and to quit her flourishing business, she refuses. These elements, mingling fictional narrative and private sphere – in a typical feature of stardom formation – were promoting Magda as an exemplary, courageous and strong woman, the maternal strength behind her daughter. This positive and supporting mother image would recur in all of the films shared by the Schneiders. Romy was credited as 'Romy Schneider-Albach' in *Wenn der weiße Flieder wieder blüht*, Albach being her father's name, but by her second film she was credited as 'Romy Schneider', stressing her maternal parentage. The strength of the maternal bond provoked a backlash when Romy Schneider left for France, a point that I will examine later.

Although Evchen was her first and a supporting role, between *Wenn der weiße Flieder wieder blüht* and the release of *Feuerwerk*, Schneider was portrayed on a few magazine covers – alongside her mother, but also on her own – and was nicknamed 'kleine Krabbe' ('sweetheart'; *Mein Film*, 25/12/1953). This term of endearment that refers to a small animal is telling of the way Schneider was presented by the press to the German-speaking public as the face of innocence and unspoilt childhood. Some covers even showed her in the company of pets: a short-haired dachshund (possibly hers that would also make an appearance in *Sissi*) or a white kid goat.

Schneider had another supporting role in her second musical film *Feuerwerk* (1954). Here two further components to the young Schneider's image were introduced: romance (Schneider and her partner Claus Biederstaedt were featured on many magazines' covers) and period setting – *Feuerwerk* is set over the summer of 1909. If Magda Schneider did not have a part in the film she unofficially stepped in as Romy's manager, negotiating her contract and having the right to inspect the script and her daughter's performance. She kept that role for several years, until her daughter moved to France in 1958.

The star of *Feuerwerk* was Lilli Palmer who had just returned from Hollywood (the two would work together again in 1958). Schneider portrays Anna Oberholzer, a teenager from a German upper-class family whose adult members snub Anna's uncle, the long-lost brother of the respectful head of the family who comes back in town as the director of a circus. Unlike the adults, especially the women anxious to maintain appearances, Anna is more open to her uncle's unorthodox career as an entertainer. Anna is a properly educated young woman of approximately sixteen who develops her skills, notably her 'grace', 'in order to find a husband' (the first scene shows Schneider during a dancing and poise lesson). In honour of her father's birthday she sings a poem of her own composition (as in her first film, Schneider's singing was dubbed) and executes a ballet routine. The character appears so young and innocent dressed up with shimmery fairy wings and a flower crown that it is surprising to see her engaged to a man. Anna is in love with gardener Robert who is eager to start a family with her. Although Anna is brought up in this conservative – and misogynist – environment, her personality is a little more developed than Schneider's Evchen: Anna has a sense of humour, and like Evchen she is cheerful and smiles a lot, but she can also be impertinent and occasionally raises her voice.

Each new role added new elements that constructed and enriched what became, two years later, Schneider's massively successful Sissi image. In *Feuerwerk* that element was her rebel temperament, as Anna wishes to pursue her dream to join her uncle's troupe and leave home. Anna's trajectory is ultimately a conventional one: something is not right with her circus wish (an uncomfortable, almost incestuous relationship with her uncle), and after she has a nightmare in which she fails her act and finds herself trapped in the lion's cage from where Robert saves her, Anna realizes that the circus is not a place for her. Although her fiancé belittles her as soon as she expresses the desire for more than 'what life has to offer' – he calls her 'a young madcap' and feels apparently threatened by her (modestly expressed) sexual potential if she keeps 'exhibiting herself as a ballerina' – she realizes that she 'belongs' to him and returns to her 'rightful place', which is becoming a wife and a mother. In a parallel subplot, her uncle's partner Iduna (Palmer) intervenes to stop him chasing other women, including Anna. Once again, Schneider's character, while displaying a degree of independence, is chaste and righteous, within the narrative in accordance to the puritan social and family values of 1909 Germany but also to those of the time of the film's making, the 1950s' 'reactionary ideology' as Johannes Von Molke rightly puts it (2002, p. 19). 'Conventional' describes well the ideology permeating the 1950s Germanic territories. As Erica Carter (1997) argues, the experience of National Socialism left Germany seeking security in economic stability and family relations,[2] which was one explanation for Germany's return to models of tradition, propriety and celebration of domestic labour, that had previously risen to the fore only thirty years earlier in the 1920s (see Nolan, 1994).

---

[2] Federal Ministry for Family Affairs Franz-Josef Wuermeling (in office from 1953 to 1962), of the Adenauer Chancery, was well-known for his 'strengthen the will for children' policy.

2. 'Yesterday a starlet, today a Queen'

After these two supporting roles Schneider could have been typecast as the ingénue in operetta films, like her mother on her debut, but the importance of the 'princess' roles that she went on to play and the dynamism of the duo formed with her mother would have a greater impact on her whole career.

2.1. From innocent child to submissive wife:
Mädchenjahre einer Königin

Schneider's first major film role was as a young Queen Victoria in her third film *Mädchenjahre einer Königin* in 1954 in which her mother played governess Baroness Lehzen. This biopic with elements of romantic comedy narrates the early reign of the Queen, from her ascension to the throne in 1837, to her fortuitous love encounter with her cousin Prince Albert in a Dover inn on her way to Paris and their subsequent engagement.

One may wonder why an Austrian film was made about a British Queen. A few elements could provide a response: in 1954 Austria was still occupied by allied troops, including British ones; additionally, Prince consort Albert was German, as was Queen Victoria's mother, and they all spoke German. It also appears that the British monarchy was a source of fascination at the time: this has in part to do with the collapse of both the Hohenzollern and Habsburg dynasties in Germany and Austria in 1918, and with a nostalgia for the Empire that was displaced onto images of other European monarchies (Giloi, 2011). Thus, the dynastic film families, of which the Schneider mother and daughter duo are an example, could be seen as a republican replacement for the lost Germanic monarchies after 1918.[3] Still, Maria Fritsche argues that *Mädchenjahre einer Königin* '[implies] Austrianness through the use of Austrian stars and settings, the Austrian mode of speaking and the foregrounding of characteristics such as sensitivity, musicality or sanguinity, which are presented as Austrian traits' (2013, p. 62). More precisely, the film was redolent of Viennese romanticism (light humour, piano music, waltzes, glorious costumes, soft pastel colours, pastries), thus cementing a foundation in Schneider's star image construction.

At the release of *Mädchenjahre einer Königin* over the Christmas holidays in Austria and West Germany, the parallel drawn by the press between Victoria's immature but innocent personality and the 'charming and graceful performance' of the actress – is manifest. Putting an emphasis

---

[3]For more on this topic, see Rachel Dwyer's chapter 'A star is born? Rishi Kapoor and dynastic charisma' in Shelley Cobb and Neil Ewen (eds.) (2015), *First Comes Love: Power Couples, Celebrity Kinship and Cultural Politics*, pp. 96–115.

on the film's success, Schneider's character and what it brought her in terms of stardom, the *Illustriertre Woche* stated on its 4 December 1954 cover: 'Yesterday a starlet, today a Queen'. Victoria is presented as a playful and loving young Princess, easily distracted, and who often has to be reminded of court etiquette. She has great appetite and is at first only interested in frivolous things, such as her outfit for her confirmation ceremony. Her uncle Leopold of Belgium says of her that she is 'light-hearted', and her mother the Duchess of Kent calls her an 'innocent child', unaware of her role as heir to the throne until the last moment. Victoria has to be guided step by step, closely advised and watched over by an entourage of adults, including one played by the actress's own mother.

Schneider's comedy skills in the pre-*Sissi* years evolved around a naivety register – it is her characters' innocence and artlessness that make them funny and appealing. There was no sassiness and Victoria was a character detached from sexual desire. The young Queen is related to notions of chastity, authenticity, purity and spontaneity (when she takes the oath, she does not read the intended speech, she goes off-track and speaks with her heart), notions that are highlighted by her relationship with Lehzen, her 'only friend', a compassionate, understanding and supportive motherly figure. Lehzen (Magda Schneider) is Victoria's 'good' mother, without the negative qualities of her real mother: the Duchess of Kent (Christl Mardayn) is authoritarian, difficult, easily shocked and demanding, whilst Lehzen is her confidante, adviser and accomplice.

Particularly eloquent is the scene where Lehzen, with tact and gentleness, guides Victoria through the House of Hanover's genealogy, making her understand that she is to be Queen. Later on, Victoria insists that the protocol's severity shall not come between their relationship. The soothing presence of Magda Schneider as a mother figure to her debutante daughter is visually translated through physical contact. In *Mädchenjahre einer Königin*, but also in *Die Deutschmeister* (and later the *Sissi* films), Magda frequently touches her daughter's face and grasps her hands or arms when she comforts Romy's character, they walk arm in arm, embrace each other or talk forehead to forehead in a gesture of complicity and intimacy.

Strangely enough, the two women's performance styles, or even their looks were never compared in the media – although their family connection was stressed. Yet, the films themselves do so: the dissimilarities between the two actresses and particularly their roles in the films' narratives were visually transposed. Whilst Romy wore a lot of pink clothing with a plunging neckline, Magda was dressed in blue, and buttoned up or with a more modest décolleté. Also, their performance styles differed: the mother adopted more severe postures and a series of domineering gestures (fists on hips, scolding forefinger, rubbing hands), while Romy's facial expressions and gestures spoke of her youth: hands crossed on her heart, candid smiles and laughter, which had the particularity of making her eyes smaller in a very childish way. Some features and expressions in evidence in *Mädchenjahre einer Königin* would endure and become characteristic of Romy Schneider's acting later in her career: an impish expression, for instance, followed by a repressed smile, and her recurrent performance sign of lifting her chin and looking up towards her partner seductively. There is an interesting play on this particular gesture and its 'opposite' – looking up with her eyes while her face is down, as discussed later. It appears that the actress made the most of her short height, and learned to use it in her characters' composition.

This protective, on-screen relationship between the maternal figure and the child as seen in *Mädchenjahre einer Königin* echoed the off-screen one. Magda was known for managing her daughter's career at that time and they appeared together in public events and other numerous promotion tours where they were seen as a perfect duo: the obedient and proper daughter, her promising career supported and protected by her mother who had experience of the film business and progressively made way for her daughter, nicknamed the 'second-generation market', as did a number of other German and Austrian stars[4] (Siegfried Breuer, Paul Hörbiger, Paula Wessely) as pointed out by an article by the *Spiegel*.[5]

But the notion that Romy Schneider also helped her mother improve her image was simultaneously clear from the start, after the release of *Wenn der weiße Flieder wieder blüht* ('She facilitated her mother's return to film', *Österreichische Film und Kino Zeitung*, 19/12/1953; 'Romy helped me greatly in an important step', *Mein Film*, 25/12/1953). Magda and Romy were seen as a team who worked better together than apart. This (lucrative) mother-daughter combination was overseen by Magda's second husband and businessman Hans Herbert Blatzheim who managed Romy's and the family's fortune and emerged in media discourses about the young star in the mid-1950s and early 1960s. I will consider the imposing presence of her stepfather later on.

When she learns that her family plans to submit to her a selection of pretenders, Victoria flees her birthday party along with her governess and her valet. If the Queen is of age to be married, the question of love and sex arises. But Victoria's attitude to sex is presented as almost inexistent. On their way to Paris, 'the city of love' (where she plans a 'thorough study of youth'), Victoria asks Lehzen how a 'girl knows that she has fallen in love'. To which the governess says that love cannot be explained. In another scene where Victoria is asked by Lord Melbourne to endorse a law that would reduce the death penalty to extreme cases, she asks him the meaning of the

---

[4]Other children of stars appeared alongside Romy Schneider in *Wenn der weiße Flieder wieder blüht*: Nina von Porembsky, the daughter of Alexa von Porembsky and Götz George, the son of Heinrich George and Berta Drews.
[5]Romy Schneider. Die Tocher-Gesellschaft, *Der Spiegel*, 07/03/1956, pp. 34–41.

word 'rape'. Embarrassed, her PM attempts to explain but cuts it short and says that the law will be 'put aside' for the time being.

The femininity of Schneider's early characters, in accordance with her stereotypically feminine looks, especially in *Mädchenjahre einer Königin*, was tame. As soon as she displays a temper, tries to assert her authority or a desire for reforms, the paternal figure in her life, Lord Melbourne, responds to her outbursts with plans of marriage. In the film Melbourne, who visually appears above Victoria, talking over her shoulders, acts as a father figure to the Queen. By the middle of the film, Melbourne's patriarchal authority is replaced by Prince Albert's. Although he does not initially know that he is talking to the Queen of England he still belittles the sovereign, pointing out her physique and her alleged inability to rule. But, once she has fallen in love, Victoria realizes that she actually needed a husband all along, 'a strong and bossy man' by her side, 'someone who keeps things under control'. A pattern is emerging: from innocent children, Schneider's characters tend to grow into passive women. Albert describes her as a 'charming young lady', and so did the critics in 1954: there was a connection between Schneider's physical appearance – generous smile, classical and fine facial features, full lips, dewy complexion, short height, thin waist, girlish voice, soft brunette hair – and the submissive characters that she portrayed. The association of her characters' beautiful appearance, explicitly talked about in the films, and the inferiority associated with her status as a woman would be particularly exposed in the *Sissi* films.

2.2. Just a sweet girl?: *Die Deutschmeister*

Schneider's fourth film and second collaboration with writer-director Marischka right after *Mädchenjahre einer Königin* was *Die Deutschmeister* (1955). This romantic comedy is a good example of generic hybridity in Austrian cinema of the time as a Wiener film that begins as a Heimat film. This combination seems to have been designed to convey the narrative of a naive country girl who comes to the city to 'meet her destiny'. The film, promoted on its original poster as 'a colourful motion picture for those who are happy to live', fitted the tradition of 1950s Viennese light comedies.

The film was a hit in Austria (Fritsche, 2013, p. 60) but did not reach a wider audience: it stars many well-known theatre and film actors of the time (Susi Nicoletti, Gunther Philipp, Adrienne Gessner, Hans Moser, Josef Meinrad, Paul Hörbiger) and displays Viennese dialect, slang and accent that play an important role in the comic aspect of the film. *Die Deutschmeister* was yet another film connected to Schneider's 'pedigree' – a term used several times in the press at the time and in Schneider's biographies – and to Austrian cinema history: it was the second remake of *Frühjahrsparade* (Géza von Bolváry, 1934), the first was written by Marischka and Schneider's father

Wolf Albach-Retty had played the role of Jurek, the dashing soldier and love interest of the heroine.

Twenty-one years later, Schneider portrayed Constanze 'Stanzi' Hübner, the country girl who comes to Vienna to work for her aunt Therese (Magda Schneider) in her bakery. Stanzi meets Jurek, a would-be composer and soldier in Die Deutschmeister regiment, and she plots to encourage Therese's flirtation with an Imperial Court Councillor who stops by the shop every morning to pick two 'Salzstangerl' (salt sticks) for Emperor Franz Josef. Stanzi hides the sheet music of a new March composed by Jurek in one of the Emperor's rolls that ends up being served at a State dinner in honour of the visiting German Kaiser Wilhelm II. Stanzi's audacity alarms Therese and Jurek, but is ultimately rewarded when she is granted a hearing with the Austrian Emperor who falls for her charm. At the end, the two Emperors praise Jurek, his new March is played during the Spring Parade, Therese is appointed official supplier of the court and she marries the Councillor.

Schneider's casting as a pastry cook fitted and reinforced her budding star image that, since Wenn der weiße Flieder wieder blüht, fell within the lexical field of sweetness. Even more than for Mädchenjahre einer Königin the press deployed girly adjectives, praising the actress's 'freshness', 'spontaneity', her 'charm and grace', her performance combining 'sincerity and naivety, humour and cheerfulness' (Evangelischer Presseverband München, 1955). Most striking is the emphasis on her unaffectedness. A notion of 'innate gift' is now attached to Schneider, and critics assign the term 'easiness' to her performance style. These qualifiers first applied to her youth, but progressively would designate the fact that 'she did not act, she simply was [the character]' – a paramount component of her French star image in the 1970s but also of stardom in general.[6] At this early stage, Schneider's much-talked-about naturalness was in fact highly constructed by mise-en-scène, with emphasis on her milky complexion, rosy cheeks and bright red lips. She also wears clothing with soft tones – for instance in Die Deutschmeister, a muslin light pink and white dress adorned with lace apron, and a muslin white and red polka-dot dress with a matching bow on her straw hat (Figure 1).

This is a salient moment to focus on Schneider's performance of the young girl – a specific, contradictory combination of freshness, sprightliness and innocence, but with a hint of sexuality, expressed through her play on the gaze, as aforementioned and succinctly illustrated in the date scene between Stanzi and Jurek. The latter says: 'I've always dreamed to meet a young girl like you'. Her reaction is to look up, her round face is luminous, then she candidly smiles, embodying the childish side of her character,

---

[6]On stardom and authenticity see Richard Dyer (1991), 'A Star Is Born and and the Construction of Authenticity' (in Gledhill, ed.), pp. 132–40; and on the distinction between 'star acting' (personification) and the ability for the star to 'become' a character (impersonation) see Barry King (1985), Articulating Stardom, Screen, 26:5, pp. 27–51.

FIGURE 1 *Schneider's play on the childish/sexual gaze in* Die Deutschmeister.

the 'perfect young girl'. Then she looks down, blushing, and looks at him through a sidelong glance, a look that carries a sexual knowingness, and the hint that she is more than an innocent girl (Figure 1). Simultaneously in the narrative Stanzi shows she is not just a child as she manipulates her aunt. This play on the gaze would become recurrent and a characteristic Schneider performance sign.

3. Historical settings

Feuerwerk, *Die Deutschmeister* and *Mädchenjahre einer Königin* are historical films and their popularity would be significant for Schneider's career. *Die Deutschmeister* was what could be called a 'local blockbuster'. In Vienna, it ranked second and *Mädchenjahre einer Königin* fourth of all films released that year. This is an impressive score for Schneider, who thus was in two films in the top five out of 1,000 films exhibited that year in 107 Viennese cinemas (including 55 Austrian films, 585 American, 176 West German and 59 French). These figures show the popularity of a 'formula' that already by 1955, only two years after her debut, encased Schneider's core image for German-speaking audience in romantic costume drama. Additionally, the fact that Schneider's commercial successes were films set in the past shows that those historical times carried a resonant cultural value for the 1950s public.

In *Feuerwerk*'s opening sequence, a narrator sets the date of 8 August 1909, pointing out that it was the 'good old times', the Belle Époque. The first decade of the twentieth century in the German and Austro-Hungarian Empires was a time of industrial progress and faith in the future, a time where both Empires were at an economic and political peak, the most powerful nations in continental Europe. But the historical relevance of these films also relates to the time of their making. As many scholars have argued, the Germanic nations' politics and public opinion remained relatively stable in the aftermath of the Second World War, and part of this stability resulted from a near total oblivion of their Nazi past – the defeated nations and their populations who had known humiliation and destruction were not ready to engage with the acknowledgement process yet. In their seminal book *The Inability to Mourn* (*Unfähigkeit zu trauern. Grundlagen kollektiven Verhaltens*, 1967), Alexander and Margarete Mitscherlich noted that neither contrition nor a desire to remember were prominent in post-war German society. People repressed the unpleasant past and instead looked back to their golden years of strength, pride and fulfilment. See also Santner (1990) and Sabine Hake, who talks about a 'culture of amnesia after the Second World War' (2008, p. 92). I will come back to this specific context in the following chapter on the *Sissi* films.

Schneider's emerging stardom in the mid-1950s answered to a critical time for that wounded territory, and she gradually became a polarized symbol. On the one hand, as a starlet, and the face of light-hearted comedies, she was the meeting point of hopeful and promising perspectives for Germanic nations, and in some sense of modernity – as Melbourne says in *Mädchenjahre einer Königin*, Victoria/Romy 'is the radiant youth, who does not need old age'. On the other hand, her persona was shaped by the inferior status and lack of power of her characters: her film roles and what was known of her private life and her relationship with her mother evolved around the notion that Schneider was an obedient child who must, and did, toe the line. These binary oppositions – strength/independence/the future vs. weakness/submissiveness/the past – established the first paradox of the early Schneider's star image: youth, freshness and modernity cohabitated with patriarchy and a reactionary mindset whose values became progressively 'weakened' in regard to the status of women in the post-war sociocultural context of (the) 'Wirtschaftswunder' ('economic miracle') in West Germany and Austria. This perspective has been thoroughly studied by Erica Carter (1997) and Nadja Krämer (2012) who consider the 'Wirtschaftswunder' a time of paradoxes, characterized by both dynamism and anxiety, echoing the equivocal female status in the 1950s. Carter argues that woman functioned as the compromise formation of apparently irreconcilable opposites: the rational and respectable housewife, and the irrationally consuming woman whose excess threatened the process of nation building. Evchen, Anna, Victoria, Stanzi and Niddy (Schneider's character in *Der letzte Mann,* which I consider later) are all female characters who express a desire to witness change in their own life and to be part of a renewal – on a personal, familial or public level – but their wishful thinking threatens the status quo, the tacit order established by older generations. Ultimately their longings are fulfilled but never in their initial state, considered excessive, and the adults gently redirect the young women towards a more suitable path that appears like *their* choice and restores the status quo. As we will see, the *Sissi* films exacerbate this paradox whilst at the same time, to some extent, reconciling it.

3.1. Of the importance of costumes

If costume films seemed to suit audiences, costumes also suited Schneider in a literal sense. Particularly striking in *Mädchenjahre einer Königin* and another founding element to her 'princess' star image, was the actress's historical wardrobe and the fact that it fit her perfectly. The costumes, their colour palette and their shimmery details played – and still play – an important part in the attraction of the Sissi image, and this was set in motion in the earlier films. In *Wenn der weiße Flieder wieder blüht* and *Feuerwerk*, and even more so in *Die Deutschmeister*, and *Mädchenjahre einer Königin*, Schneider's wardrobe is mostly designed with pale colours, with pink dominating. Stanzi is an insouciant Salzburger maiden, the very image of the young country girl: dressed in a pink and soft red dirndl, her hair braided in a crown on top of her head. For the character of Queen Victoria, Schneider's dresses were loosely inspired by British fashion in the 1830s, but adaptations were clearly made to fit the actress and the fashion of the 1950s – the hour-glass figure with pointed bust and rounded shoulder line inspired by Christian Dior's New Look (Bigelow, 1979, p. 309; Steele, 1997, pp. 1–48). These adaptations emphasized the juvenile aspect of her physique (she was sixteen and slim).

In *Mädchenjahre einer Königin*, Schneider wore almost exclusively evening gowns, even in scenes set during the daytime. This technicality is significant as it lengthened her silhouette; indeed, it could be argued that the full-length costumes covered her only 'weakness'[7] – her short legs. Although fashion in the 1830s favoured wide puffed sleeves, the Schneider silhouette was highlighted by puffed but very short sleeves from a dropped shoulder, which were historically inaccurate, but had the particularity to accentuate the shape of her (small) breasts and to reveal an important

---

[7]By 'weakness' I mean departure from conventional Western norms of white female beauty.

amount of pale skin (neckline, shoulders, arms, hands and face). Schneider's
pale complexion carried concepts of nobility, sensitivity and refinement (see
Dyer, 1997), enhanced by her full red lips – fashionable in the 1950s but
not in the Victorian era where no one at court wore makeup. Schneider also
wore crinolines, which widened her skirts (another historical error from the
film as the crinoline superseded the petticoat in the 1850s).

Schneider's gowns – the style of which was referred to as a 'princess
line', possibly after Queen Consort Alexandra of Denmark (Lewandowski,
2011, p. 238) – presented fashionable details that enhanced the character's
romantic image: such as pale roses in the pink belt knot, at the bottom of
the skirt or in her hair, realistic flower trimming and panels of lace arranged
horizontally over her bust and around the shoulders. Romanticism was
without a doubt the key word in *Mädchenjahre einer Königin* and another
component to add to the young Schneider's star image. Schneider's gowns
were made of satin, silk or taffeta, with trimmings of lace or sequins, but the
designs were kept simple – no ruffles, nor ruching, and the patterns on the
fabrics (stripes, dots) remain so thin that they are barely noticeable so as not
detract from the 'natural' persona already attached to the star. Schneider's
costumes in *Mädchenjahre einer Königin* prefigured the ones in the *Sissi*
films; they certainly shared the same aura of romanticism and luxury, both
visually with wide skirts and full-length ball gowns, and aurally (the sound
of rustling fabric can be heard when the dress passes a door).

This brings me to a second element explaining the appeal and the
success of Schneider in costume – the multi-sensorial pleasure found in the
costume itself, the texture and the opulent and shimmering beauty of her
clothing. This is an aspect of the costume film that has attracted scholarly
attention in recent years, although not in the German-Austrian context.
Nevertheless, the pleasure principle applied to historical film has been
considered – predominantly in the Anglo-American context – by scholars
such as Pam Cook (1996), Andrew Higson (2006), Julianne Pidduck (2004)
and Belén Vidal (2012a and b). The latter qualifies the 'temporality of the
period film' as an *'emotionally* charged space' that 'shows a preference for
affective rather than intellectual histories' (p. 21, my emphasis). As for Jean-
Louis Comolli he considered, in a famous 1978 analysis, that historical film
articulates spectatorship as 'a kind of dialectic between a "realist" quest
for the referential, and a certain simultaneous spectatorial awareness of
and *pleasure in the artifice* of the film' (cited in Rosen, 2001, p. 181, my
emphasis). Drawing from Vidal and Comolli, I would stress the enjoyment
and the intimate, affective, relationship engendered and fostered between
the visual spectacle of Schneider in costumes and its audience.

Schneider's hairstyle in the *Sissi* films, which had an equal impact to that
of her costumes, also finds its roots in *Mädchenjahre einer Königin*. The
film roughly respected the 1830s hairstyle: women's hair was parted in the
centre and dressed in elaborate curls, loops and knots extending out to both

sides and up from the crown of the head. Braids were fashionable and were likewise looped over both ears and gathered into a topknot. Schneider's hairstyle was therefore much more complicated than her costumes, but the wig's hair mass kept it uniform, harmonious – her abundant hair was never flat, hence making her taller, an outcome also used in the narrative (when Victoria considers a high hairdo to match Albert's stature). Schneider's hairstyle changes throughout the film: in the first scene she wears a simple and pale pink dress and her hair is loose, the wavy locks simply falling over her shoulders, frizzy hair framing her face. When she becomes Queen, the character trades her looseness – her freedom in some way – for a sophisticated hairstyle (high and thick coiffures, ringlets, elaborated plaits in the form of a crown on top of her head) and precious jewellery (diamond necklaces, tiaras and crowns).

After the success of *Mädchenjahre einer Königin* Schneider became renowned as the fresh starlet whose beauty and poise were selected, once again by Marischka, for playing historical figures. 'Freshness' was indeed the word: for the role of Victoria, Marischka had first cast Sonja Ziemann who was a well-established actress by the mid-1950s, but changed his mind for a 'fresher' face (Krenn, 2013a, p. 53). Paradoxically, costume also bolstered Schneider's 'fresh' and 'natural' persona (*Der Spiegel*, 07/03/1956, p. 36; *Libelle*, 05/02/1955, cover and pp. 30–1). From early on the depictions of Schneider's 'naturalness' in the press blurred the line between the actress's physique and her acting style, naturalness being a notion that described both in a positive way. And from *Mädchenjahre einer Königin* onwards, these adjectives used to depict her look and screen performances reached a level that intertwined Schneider's roles and private life via, notably, the use of costumes. The 'first Schneider paradox' as I call it – embodying the fresh young girl while performing characters from the past – soon set in motion a repeated and normalized image of the actress at premieres, galas and balls wearing film costumes instead of modern and couture dresses.

At the press conference for the premiere of *Wenn der weiße Flieder wieder blüht* on 24 November 1953 in Stuttgart, Schneider wore the blue cocktail dress from the film. But more eloquent examples occurred after the release of *Mädchenjahre einer Königin*. Schneider attended the fifth Berlin International Film Festival, and video footage shows her kissing a crowned teddy bear (the bear being the emblem of the Berlinale). Even more telling was the 'Bal de la Monnaie' in Brussels (also known as the 'Bal du cinéma') on the 14 February 1956, where she wore the gown and the crown from the birthday ball scene in *Mädchenjahre einer Königin*, and was awarded the 'Queen of the Ball' title; the film was released in Belgium in December 1955, three months prior to *Sissi*. There is a film from 'Les Actualités françaises' that shows some highlights of the event, including the moment when Schneider pulled on a stole in a way that recalled beauty pageants' coronation.

3.2. Dress rehearsals for *Sissi*

With their winning combination of a Viennese setting with the image of the sweet princess on the point of becoming queen, Schneider's early films presented an open path to the *Sissi* trilogy's success (the René Chateau DVD edition of the *Sissi*s presents *Mädchenjahre einer Königin* as the 'fourth *Sissi* film'). Ernst Marischka worked efficiently with collaborator and distributor Herzog-Filmverleih, reinforcing the close connection of *Mädchenjahre einer Königin* to *Sissi* (1955) and *Sissi, Die junge Kaiserin* (1956) by using the same illustrations for the films' opening credits. *Sissi* also reunited the crew who worked on *Mädchenjahre einer Königin* and *Die Deutschmeister*: producer Karl Ehrlich, director and writer Marischka, cinematographer Bruno Mondi, editor Alfred Srp (on *Die Deutschmeister* and the *Sissi* films), production managers Fritz Andraschko and Karl Ehrlich, costume designers Leo Bei and Gerda Gottstein, art director and set decorator Fritz Jüptner-Jonstorff and assistant Alexander Sawczynski, composer Anto Profes (on *Mädchenjahre einer Königin* and the *Sissi*s), camera operator Herbert Geier, etc. The audience could also recognize actors from film to film: Romy and Magda Schneider of course, but also in supporting roles Josef Meinrad, Rudolf Vogel, Peter Weck and Paul Hörbiger. Even (an old) Franz Joseph and his Hofburg Palace (in particular the Redoutensaaltrakt, where the wedding banquet takes place in *Sissi*) already appeared in *Die Deutschmeister*. Additionally, a few scene compositions from *Mädchenjahre einer Königin* were visually transferred to Sissi, notably the in-between shots of pages trumpeting an official ceremony. These shots show the palace of Schönbrunn in Vienna, and not Kensington Palace or Buckingham Palace.

This continuity throughout Marischka's films instilled warmth and cosiness: the audience became used to seeing Schneider evolving in a familiar ambiance, in which the costumes, the hairstyle and the music had a great impact, especially Viennese waltzes by Johann Strauss I. One of the musical themes of *Mädchenjahre einer Königin* is 'Lorelei Rhein Klänge Opus 154' composed by Strauss in 1843, and the character of Strauss makes an appearance in the film (the composer attended the Queen's coronation in London in 1838). Waltz was essential to both the romantic mood and Schneider's persona: the young actress's first waltz on film was also her character's, and the moment Victoria fell in love for the first time. The Viennese waltz is a graceful and smooth dance, performed by couples in closed formation (the male partner clasped his arm around the female partner's waist), and on a light rhythm of string instruments. As a German character says in *Mädchenjahre einer Königin*: '[Strauss's] Waltzes [are] sparkling like champagne. English society is too uptight, it needs to be shaken', and '[the waltz] is good preparation for marital emotions'. After *Mädchenjahre einer Königin* and *Sissi*, ball scenes in the two sequels were much anticipated.

3.3. A Minor setback: *Der letzte Mann*

Der letzte Mann (a remake of Friedrich Wilhelm Murnau's 1924 eponymous film) was Schneider's last project before *Sissi*, and in several ways a film 'out of sequence' with the rest of her early career – it is a black-and-white film, in contemporary settings, and one that was not successful.

Schneider portrays Niddy, the seventeen-year-old daughter of a five-star hotel owner in the spa town of Badenau. Karl the butler runs the hotel with an iron fist and takes care of Niddy, who is courted by the clumsy intern Helmut. When Niddy's mother dies, the hotel is in jeopardy as the heirs wish to sell. Cousin Alwin, one of the heirs, takes advantage of the situation by acting as the new manager and reconciling the family's appetite for money and Niddy's attachment to her hotel. Karl and Alwin do not see eye to eye, especially since the dashing young man courts his cousin, who in turn is dazzled that someone 'finally treats her like a woman'. The butler is demoted to the lavatories, humiliated. Once Niddy and Alwin are engaged he threatens to sell the hotel if they do not marry quickly. At the end, a rich businessman buys the hotel and Karl returns to his manager role, stops the wedding and Niddy falls into Helmut's arms.

At its release in October 1955 the film gathered mostly negative reviews, and despite heavy promotion and press coverage (which had to do with the presence of major star Hans Albers as the butler), it was not a success. The film can be seen as a 'regression' in the progression of Schneider's career insofar as she has a supporting role compared to Albers. Probably disappointing for audiences was the treatment of Schneider's character. Niddy is a modern, head-turning girl – when boys call her a 'bombshell', she contemptuously replies that she 'wants more [...], a grown-up man' – but as we have seen it seems that 1950s German-speaking audiences preferred to see Schneider performing 'the modern girl' in historical settings and confined to princess-like costumes. Schneider's attempted move towards modernity is echoed in the film's modern setting – the white and clear-cut design of the hotel, Schneider's form-fitting dresses (though embellished with girlish little bows), including a gingham skirt (in a pattern and fabric popular in the mid-1950s and made fashionable by the epitome of modernity at the time, French star Brigitte Bardot). Additionally, Schneider went blonde for the first time on screen, which was a significant move in the context of the mid-1950s when the 'Hollywood blonde [was] clearly residing at the pinnacle of the new celebrity culture' (Gundle, 2011, p. 170). Vincendeau (2015a) too, makes a compelling argument for the connection between blondness, Americanness and modernity for European stars. But the 'American' modernity symbolized by Schneider's blond hair was incongruent with her overall image primarily linked to costume films.

In *Der letzte Mann*, Schneider's character was ultimately – again – wrong to aspire for more than what she already had: she is the sexy blonde who makes a fool of herself. The character's opposing traits of personality – gullibility and modernity – induce a tension that could confuse the spectator. Niddy overtly claims her modern woman status and intends to take responsibility, but she is relieved to find a loophole – her cousin who will take charge. This is where the absence of a motherly figure in *Der letzte Mann*'s narrative – contrary to the other Schneider's films – appears patent. Niddy is adrift (her mother is never seen and dies early on, and her two aunts are portrayed as 'wicked witches') and she has no one to guide her or to turn to for solace. That person should have been Karl, the fatherly figure in Niddy's life, but his harshness puts her off. Ultimately *her* lack of discernment and maturity is to blame for the butler's downfall – and running down a hill in a wedding dress to meet Helmut in her last scene emphasizes the film's fairy-tale style.

The film was a small bump in the road of Schneider's star image construction in the mid-1950s that was soon forgotten with the release of *Sissi* two months later, which triumphantly and permanently cemented her romantic/historical persona.

Conclusion

Between 1953 and 1955, Schneider's film roles and appearances in the media established solid foundations for the successful development of her star image. The Sissi character associated with Schneider could have been construed as a princess from some distant world, but instead, and because of the actress's previous roles, the Empress-to-be appeared to filmgoers as both a familiar figure and a fresh character, displaying youthful enthusiasm, liveliness and vibrancy. The defining elements of the Sissi image can be traced back to *Mädchenjahre einer Königin*: the relationship with a mother figure (yet again portrayed by the actress's mother in the *Sissis*), the girlish status of a young queen, a first true love, the escape motif and the connection between love and reason of State.

Before embarking on the *Sissi* trilogy, Schneider was already pinpointed as a child who relied on adults: she followed in her mother's footsteps while benefiting from her experience, and director Ernst Marischka's assumed the role of a Pygmalion in the actress's early career. Schneider's star image figures the actress as an emblem of a widespread Germanic womanhood, to which the Romy-Magda dyad is crucial, yet in a paradoxical way. As in the case of other Germanic acting dynasties, Magda Schneider (a former Ufa star) lent cachet to her daughter, but on the other hand, she tainted Romy's star image because of her association with the Nazi elite. Thus, from the beginning of Schneider's career two major tendencies emerged and increasingly appropriated the actress's private life into her persona: family narratives, that were played on and off screen, and the importance of costume films with compelling music. Both trends were then combined and developed tenfold in the *Sissi* films, which revealed to a wider international public the image of the young Schneider.

2

Sissi: Romy becomes European

Introduction

At the age of seventeen, between August and November 1955, Schneider filmed *Sissi*. At the time, she proudly wrote in her journal that a 'German magazine's survey ranked her second place of the most popular actors' (between Maria Schell and Ruth Leuwerik), only two years and five films after her debuts (Schneider and Seydel, 1989, p. 97). *Sissi* was a phenomenal success with German-speaking audiences in the year following its release over the 1955 Christmas holidays in Austria and West Germany, and was subsequently well-received in other European countries, making it the most successful German-speaking film of the 1950s on the continent. The role of *Sissi* and what it represented in 1950s Austria and West Germany was the culmination of Schneider's previous characters and film narratives. After their hits of *Mädchenjahre einer Königin* and *Die Deutschmeister*, *Sissi*'s production company Erma-Film and producer Karl Ehrlich expected the film to do well, but they had not anticipated the overwhelmingly positive audience response to it. Two successful sequels followed: *Sissi, Die junge Kaiserin/Sissi, the young Empress* (1956) and *Sissi, Schicksalsjahre einer Kaiserin/Sissi, the fateful years of an Empress* (1957).[1] Production plans for a fourth film was abandoned, because, as I shall explore later, Schneider refused to be cast again despite a sensational salary offer of 1 million Deutschmarks[2] (Krämer, 2012, p. 342).

This chapter considers Schneider crossing borders, and explores the evidence that attests to her development into a trans-European star. The Sissi period in Schneider's early career in German-speaking cinema is of vital importance, for it lays the foundation of a significant aspect of her changeable

---

[1] In the following, I shall refer to the respective films of the trilogy as *Sissi 1*, *Sissi 2*, and *Sissi 3*.
[2] The average equivalent of 6,220,630 US dollars in 2022.

star image that would continue to resonate throughout her career. There
was a confluence between Schneider's national and transnational images:
the period of 1955–7 was the moment she emerged as a European star, and
yet she became attached to a specific national culture, notably the costume
film, a genre very popular in post-war Austria.[3]

1. The reception of the *Sissi* trilogy

Like *Mädchenjahre einer Königin* and *Die Deutschmeister*, the *Sissi* films
were written and directed by Austrian filmmaker Ernst Marischka, who had
nurtured the project for many years (Krenn, 2013a, p. 67). Although the films
clearly belong to the historical costume genre (see Fritsche, 2013), they are
also a combination of several other genres – romantic film, family drama,
Heimatfilm (see Von Molke, 2002, 2005), and even fairy tale (Korte and
Lowry, 2000, p. 113). The films dismiss most, if not all, of the negative aspects
of the life of the real Elisabeth of Austria (which ended tragically[4]). Although
they touch on the Empress's taste for travel, her tendency to flee and hint at
her deep dissatisfaction and depression, her life is heavily romanticized in the
narrative. *Sissi 1* presents the romantic fortuitous encounter in 1853 in Bad
Ischl (Upper Austria) and the courtship between young Princess Elisabeth of
Bavaria (Sissi) and Habsburg Emperor Franz Joseph (Karlheinz Böhm), who
is at first promised to become engaged to Sissi's elder sister Helene (nicknamed
Nene and played by Uta Franz). The film ends with their wedding at the
Augustinerkirche in Vienna on 24 April 1854. The second instalment focuses
on Elisabeth's struggles to adjust to her new life at the Vienna imperial court
after her wedding, then centres on the tense relationship with her mother-in-
law Archduchess Sophie (Vilma Degischer), the birth of her first child, her
attempts to make peace with Hungarian dissidents on behalf of her husband
and the imperial couple's final coronation as King and Queen of Hungary. The
third film narrates Sissi's illness, her recuperation in Madeira and Corfu in
the company of her supportive mother Duchess Ludovika (Magda Schneider)
and an official visit to Italian territories, where a hostile crowd in Venice
begins to cheer, won over by the touching reunion of Sissi and her daughter
Gisela (Helga Jesch).

---

[3]For a thorough analysis of the genre and its role in the process of building a new national
identity in post-Second World War Austria see the chapter 'The Historical costume film' in
Maria Fritsche (2013), *Homemade Men in Postwar Austrian Cinema: Nationhood, Genre and
Masculinity*, pp. 59–99. For a discussion on the interchangeable terms 'costume', 'historical' or
'heritage' see Sue Harper (1994), *Picturing the Past: The Rise and Fall of the British Costume
Film*; and Andrew Higson (2003), *English Heritage, English Cinema: Costume Drama since
1980*, pp. 9–11.
[4]Elisabeth of Austria (1837–98) was stabbed to death by an Italian anarchist in Geneva,
Switzerland.

1.1. A Variety of approaches

While the films were embraced by contemporary audiences, at the time of their original release they were rejected by most German-speaking critics who disapproved of the trilogy's alleged aesthetic irrelevance (its glossiness and kitsch aspect), its shallowness and its sugar-coated and mendacious distortion of History. This rejection probably explains why, for many years, scholarly attention was generally limited to plot descriptions in German and Austrian film historiographies (e.g. Barthel, 1986, pp. 239–49; Bessen, 1989, pp. 319–28; Jary, 1993, pp. 143–52). Even when the films were the objects of more in-depth analysis, they have mostly been considered as indicating the regressive and traditional politics attributed to the Heimat genre of the 1950s, with its representations of an idyllic pastoral Germanic nation as a gentle 'cure' for contemporary and distressing national histories. One could argue at length against this scholarly trend, especially the pairing of 1950s German and Austrian cinemas (Seidl, 1987; Bergfelder, 2006, pp. 31, 40; Wauchope, 2007), and the inaccurate tendency to consider the latter a subcategory, or a 'variation' (Fritsche, 2013, p. 11) of the former. This is tangential to the goals of this book and strays too far from the core subject.

There are now substantial scholarly works in German and English that expand the investigation and cover many aspects of the *Sissi* trilogy. Amongst them, studies by Gerhard Bliersbach (1985) and Susanne Marschall (1997) offer more comprehensive readings, pointing out that the films' depictions of the Habsburg family set during the 1850s examine complex family structures and dynamics that are more germane to the social situation in post-war West Germany and Austria. Other research focuses largely on the popular title protagonist. In these studies, Sissi is usually seen as young and vulnerable, fighting the traditional power structures of the Vienna court through her spontaneity, innocence and authenticity (Korte and Lowry, 2000, p. 117). Georg Seeßlen (1992a, 1992b) points to the character's significance in the 1950s in light of post-war destruction and Holocaust guilt. Sissi plays a 'central role as a "figure of salvation"' who operates through her 'innocence and energy to "deliver" men from their guilt and at the same time give new glory to qualities necessary for reconstruction' (1992a, p. 12). In other words, the character represents the 'promise of regeneration', a concept suggested by Heide Fehrenbach (1995) in her seminal study of popular German cinema of the 1950s (which nonetheless neglects the *Sissi* series). Some more recent publications on 1950s German cinema, such as Sabine Hake's *German National Cinema* (2002, p. 114) and the anthology *Take Two: Fifties Cinema in a Divided Germany* (Davidson and Hake, 2007), hardly mention the *Sissi*s. Mary Wauchope (2002), however, suggests a positive reading of the films, highlighting their popular quality on behalf of Austria's national image, and Erica Carter (2010) analyses the films through the lens of victimhood and nostalgia. Focusing on the Sissi character, she conducts a formal analysis of colour palette, composition and camera movement, which she sees as signalling an aesthetic memory of the Austrian Empire and its imperial past through the 'representational models' of the Biedermeier period (1815–48) and Third Reich films (p. 93).

In other significant works, Heidi Schlipphacke (2010) suggests a queer reading of the trilogy, Nadja Krämer (2012) considers models of masculinity in post-war Germany in relation to the films, and so does Maria Fritsche (2013) who focuses on the complex Austrian 'process of social reorganisation' (p. 5) and nationhood reconstruction. Although I will come back to these contrasted readings of the character, often calling them forth to support my own analysis, the object of my examination through the films remains Romy Schneider as a star. My approach to the image of Schneider in the *Sissi* trilogy and the star's European appeal is multifaceted. By analysing the narratives (character's development), themes (my examination of the films has to be embedded in their social, political and economic contexts,[5] and with regard to post-war gender discourses, especially the role of women) and the aesthetics (performance and costume analyses) of Schneider's presence in the films, I demonstrate that the seventeen-year-old actress's stardom in the mid-1950s was not only part of the dominant identity and gender discourse on nationhood, but that her image was key to the films' successful European export.

Although there was a Europe-wide interest in the *Sissi* trilogy from 1956 – with the notable exception of the UK – there is little work on exportability and reception discourses on the films outside of the German-speaking film markets.[6] I fill this gap here, since an understanding of Schneider's status as a European star and the strong resonance of her image in France is instrumental to my argument. Considering the paucity of film data available across continental Europe, I have limited my reception analysis to German-speaking countries and francophone regions. I use two sets of sources: statistical film data such as box-office figures, and works on reception markets and on national and popular film markets in Austria, West Germany, France and Belgium. All point to the films' massive popularity with filmgoers, an observation that is corroborated by scholarly works (Albrecht, 1985, pp. 80–1, Garncarz, 1994, p. 125, Carter, 2010, p. 81, Schlipphacke, 2010, p. 232 and Krämer, 2012, p. 370, Hametz and Schlipphacke, 2018, to name a few).

---

[5]Historical films are significant indicators of the socio-political context in which they were made: Pierre Sorlin states that 'nearly all films refer, if indirectly, to current events' (1980, p. 18). See also Derek Elley (1984), *The Epic Film: Myth and History*, p. 6; and Fritsche, 2013, pp. 59–60.
[6]Fei-Hsien Wang and Ke-chin Hsia's chapters (in Hametz and Schlipphacke, 2018, pp. 181–214) on the *Sissi* films' reception in China represent a welcome contribution, though also an exception.

1.2. Sissi at home

With the exception of France, for which there are precise box-office and attendance records from 1945, it is much more difficult to obtain these numbers for other countries, including Austria and West Germany. Yet, some comprehensive studies offer useful indications.[7] Although I have no way of knowing the exact domestic attendance records of the screening of the *Sissis*,[8] there are grounds for suggesting that the trilogy was the most successful German-speaking film of the 1950s in Austria and West Germany since the end of the Second World War (Krämer, 2012, p. 341). My methodology follows Joseph Garncarz (1994, pp. 94–135) in using Top Ten figures, which I correlate with secondary sources, and also includes readings that hypothesize about the relationship between the *Sissi* films and larger processes of national identity formation and *Vergangenheitsbewältigung* (see later). My research shows that the first film is the most popular one of the cycle. *Sissi 1* gained the first place in *Film-Echo*'s 1955/1956 'Top Ten' in West Germany (Garncarz, 1994, p. 125), with, according to Heidi Schlipphacke (2010, p. 232), ten million tickets sold for the film premiere in December 1955. Erica Carter (2010, p. 81), citing the film distributor Herzog-Film's press pack of *Sissi 2* reflecting on the success of their first opus, advances the number to 12 million. One indicator frequently mentioned to illustrate the success of *Sissi 1* in West Germany is that it exceeded the box-office record held in the new Republic by *Gone with the Wind* (Victor Fleming, 1939) (Albrecht, 1985, p. 80).[9] *Sissi 2* and *Sissi 3* ranked respectively in second and third place in the 'Top Ten' for 1956/1957 and 1957/1958 (Garncarz, 1994, pp. 125–6) in West Germany.

The reasons for this Germanic success have been thoroughly and expansively analysed. The 1950s was a period of historical significance for two reasons: firstly, it constitutes the heyday of Austrian popular cinema, and secondly, the concept of Austria as the nation that we know today emerged during the post-war decade (Fritsche, 2013, p. 3). It is crucial to detail the historical context to understand the meaning of Marischka's trilogy. Austria

---

[7]Joseph Garncarz (1994, pp. 94–135) calculated and reassembled the lists of the most popular films (the 'Top Ten') distributed in West Germany and usually published in magazines such as *Film-Echo* for the period 1952/53–72. Therefore, there are no tangible attendance numbers for the *Sissi* trilogy in West Germany, but rather, and according to the cinema owners who rated the commercial success of the films on a scale of 1 to 7, indicators of their immense popularity (p. 120).

[8]It is worth noting that records may in fact exist for screenings of the *Sissi* trilogy that could be found for instance in local archives with documents on local cinemas. In that regard, regional research by local history and media history scholars are paramount as they contribute to paint a bigger and more detailed picture of a nation's cinematic history (see Knut, 1993).

[9]Although, as previously said, substantial numbers to compare those 'records' are either non-existent or lost.

came out of the Second World War defeated and, right after the end of the war, there emerged what is commonly known as the victimhood narrative (Austrians citizens and soldiers were the 'first victims' of German Nazis), which after the Waldheim debate in 1986[10] was denounced as a 'historical lie' (Uhl, 2011, p. 185). But from 1947 onwards, for many Austrians the victim thesis gave way to a heroism counter-narrative that lasted nearly a decade, until the 'liberation' from the Allied 'Occupation' with the ratification of the Austrian State Treaty in May 1955 (Uhl, pp. 186–9) when Austria regained its national independence (shortly before the premiere of *Sissi 1* in December).

During those uncertain times, political elites sought to absolve Austria from any involvement in Nazi war crimes (Bruckmüller, 1985, p. 520). In order to do so, they attempted to *distance* Austria from Germany (in contrary to most scholarship on Austrian cinema, which rather too eagerly puts Austrian and German cinema under the same banner, Fritsche, 2013, p. 4). Political and later popular discourses claimed fundamental intellectual and cultural differences between Austrian and German people, making ample use of popular national stereotypes. The creation of a new national identity required more than negating the German element, but an arsenal of positive features that could evoke pride (Hanisch, 1994, p. 161–3), such as the 'felix Austria' myth[11] (Bischof, 1997) and the nation's imperial history and cultural heritage, which were extensively featured in historical costume film.

Historical costume film regularly topped the lists of the most successful films at the time in Austria. Moreover, Austrian costume films (*Kaiserwalzer*, 1953, *Der Feldherrnhügel*, 1953, *Kaisermanöver*, 1954, and *Mädchenjahre einer Königin* and *Die Deutschmeister* with Schneider) proved to be highly exportable to other German-speaking countries (Fritsche, 2013, p. 61). Several factors explain the appeal of the genre: first, it provided escape and spectacle through its music, sumptuous costumes and splendid settings (shot on location in the case of Schneider's films) of the imperial palaces of Vienna and the countryside. Secondly, historical costume films offered reassurance and a source of identification: they depicted people living happily and in harmony, barely disturbed by violent conflicts or politics, safe in the knowledge that their nation was grand and powerful. The genre also exalted the values and life of the lower middle class and eulogized sacrifice

---

[10]Kurt Josef Waldheim was President of Austria from 1986 to 1992, and while he was running for president in 1985 the revelation of his service as an intelligence officer in the Wehrmacht raised international controversy; it is since then that 'the public commemoration of the fallen soldiers became an issue of public debate again' (Uhl, 2011, p. 196).

[11]'Allii gerant bella, tu felix Austria nube' is a founder myth of Austrian historical memory – its pacifism. This idea, forged during the Cold War, considered Austria the child prodigy of neutrality, an 'island of the blessed' between the two powerful and antagonist blocks (Bischof, 1997).

(the character of Sissi is a telling example: she sacrifices her freedom and her lively personality in favour of her husband). It argued that true happiness lies in a simple life and not in the pursuit of a higher social status (again, the *Sissi* films epitomize this perspective, with Sissi's childhood home in peaceful Possenhofen, and her father's simple lifestyle and easy-going philosophy). These narratives reverberated with an Austrian society that had experienced two decades of political turmoil and war, and was now confronted with an uncertain future, wishing for stability and harmony.

Historical films offer an interpretation of the historical past that shapes our views of History, and the choice of historical periods is meaningful (Sorlin, 1980, p. 21). The reign of Franz Joseph (Emperor of Austria from 1848 to 1916) still evokes memories of glory, especially the last decades of the Austria-Hungarian Empire (though marred by social and ethnic conflicts, see Fritsche, 2013, pp. 70–1). In the light of the atrocities committed by the Nazi regime, the post-war Austrian film industry revived the memory of former greatness, inventing a past of imperial splendour and civic harmony that spoke to Austrian *and* German audiences, who had *both* experienced a painful loss of status as citizens of a once-powerful nation. Thus, with primary motifs such as innocence, filial love and youth, associated with glorious landscapes, the *Sissi* films were in line with a pattern followed by many Germanic post-war films: the beneficial, almost healing depiction of a 'lost' era transfigured into a beautiful world by nostalgia[12] and the means of fictional cinema.

Moreover, this evocative pattern is commonly considered part of the 1950s' Germanic political and cultural process of *Vergangenheitsbewältigung*, which can be roughly translated by 'coming to terms with the past' (Seeßlen, 1992a, pp. 10–14; Seeßlen, 1992b, pp. 65–79; Korte and Lowry, 2000, pp. 113–19). From this perspective, the figure of the innocent girl, in this instance Sissi, has significant resonance in 1950s Austria *and* West Germany. During those sensitive times, Sissi could be read as the face of redemption. With her youthful energy she 'redeems' men and bears the burden of the fathers' generation with the qualities necessary to rebuild new nations, especially via her positive influence on Franz Joseph as the modern vision of the moderate new man (Bliersbach, 1985, p. 172; Seeßlen, 1992a, p. 12; Fritsche, 2013, p. 83). She revitalizes the man in charge of the nation and thus secures the perpetuation of the Empire by giving an heir to the crown (Seeßlen, 1992b, p. 74).

I concur also with the interpretation of Susanne Marschall, who emphasizes the familial and national significations attributed to the Sissi figure and who sees the role of the 'innocent angel' as the symbol of a 'new ethical foundation for a new social order' (1997, p. 382). Unlike Gerhard Bliersbach and Georg Seeßlen, who considered the character a sign of

---

[12]For more on nostalgia see Svetlana Boym's book *The Future of Nostalgia* (2001).

compensation, Marschall's approach is more favourably nuanced: in her insightful essay she regards Sissi and the 'childlike' Schneider as a model of virtue who projected long-neglected high moral standards such as 'grief, hope, sacrifice, pacifism, progressive view, and gentleness' (p. 382).

1.3. Sissi in Europe

The *Sissi* trilogy had an equally successful run in the other continental European film markets (see Appendix 2). According to my research, *Sissi 1* was one of the most successful films distributed in continental Europe at the time. *Sissi 1* was the second most popular film in France in 1957 with a total number of 6,497,043 spectators (Simsi, 2012, p. 22), but *Sissi 2* dropped down to 1,275,021[13] to rise back up to 5,149,522 for *Sissi 3* in 1958, ranking fourth place in the most popular films of the year (p. 23). *Sissi 1* was a blockbuster also in the Netherlands, Denmark and Belgium (especially in Brussels and Antwerp), where excellent box-office results were reported by *La Cinégraphie belge* (see also Albrecht, 1985, p. 80). In other countries, such as Spain, Italy, Portugal, Greece, Ireland, Sweden and Finland, where German-speaking films had hitherto failed to gain a foothold so far, *Sissi 1* had impressively long cinema runs that were only comparable to the most successful US films (Albrecht, p. 80; Schneider and Seydel, 1989, p. 115). This tremendous popularity is confirmed by the extensive press coverage and the numerous magazine covers featuring Schneider at the time, with a clear preference for photos of the young star dressed in her character's costumes. It also appears that in countries where Schneider's previous films were released, they had established a solid fan base, especially *Mädchenjahre einer Königin*, which confirms my assumption that the appeal of Schneider as a star resides in the romantic persona that was developed early on in her career and was further consolidated in *Sissi 1*.

Although *Sissi 2* and *Sissi 3* were selected to represent Austria at the Cannes Film Festival in 1957 and 1958, and box-office results were still high, domestically and abroad, the trilogy's success had slightly dwindled by the release of *Sissi 3*. For example, according to the Norwegian cinema association Film & Kino and the Instituto de la Cinematografía y la Artes audiovisuales, the last film was never distributed in Norway, nor was it released in Spain until 1974. The explanation for *Sissi 1*'s popular preference over the last two films might lie, on the one hand, in the 'novelty effect' that might consist of Schneider's star quality (her freshness), and on the other hand with the film narrative that revolves around a classic 'fairy-tale story'

---

[13]This surprising 'drop' (despite that more than one million viewers was still an impressive number for the time) could be due to some kind of 'oversaturation' as both *Sissi 1* and *Sissi 2* were released in French cinemas only five months apart in 1957.

(Fritsche, 2013, pp. 80, 83). The second and last films tend to leave aside the spontaneity of the princess and instead show her struggle to find her place and fit into a rather hostile environment (the strict ceremonial of the court personified by Archduchess Sophie), and address Sissi's motherly issues and other 'adult' topics such as politics.

The trilogy's common ground with fairy-tale traditions sheds further light on its post-war success in West Germany. According to Jack Zipes (2002), fairy tales are a reference in German culture 'for self-comprehension and *Weltanschauung*' ('philosophy of life') (p. 121), it is a national institution based on 'compensatory images of reconciliation' (p. 118); and he argues that there is a German disposition to resolve social conflicts 'within art, within subjectively constructed realms' (p. 121). When adding the overall 'continuing, conservative longing for order' (Giloi, 2011, p. 360) that was prevailing in Western Europe in the 1950s, we can comprehend the appeal of cultural products such as the *Sissi* films that offered the (alleged) glamour of court life. *Sissi*s' fairy-tale narrative combines different classical motifs (a royal family, scheming matchmakers, mistaken identities, the heroine becomes a wife in a romantic ascent, she has to overcome forces that oppose her love) which appear to create optimum conditions to appeal to audiences' emotions, especially through Sissi's difficult relation with her mother-in-law, rendering her more relatable. Thus the nostalgic inclination that I have examined regarding Austrian audiences seemed to speak to audiences in other European countries as well.

Whilst the films were successful in Austria and West Germany – both newly independent republics – and in France a year later, the absence of a royal family at the head of the state in these nations and therefore an audience inclination for royalty nostalgia[14] are not the sole explanation for the trilogy's phenomenal success. The *Sissi* trilogy was as much celebrated in monarchies, that is, Belgium, Netherlands, Denmark, Spain and Greece where Schneider was received by the King and the Queen at the premiere of *Sissi 2* in Athens (Schneider and Seydel, 1989, p. 129). Nonetheless, the films were not distributed in the UK, which explains why Schneider remains unknown there. What could have been the reason considering their success on the continent? A look at the British trade press does not shed light on this exception. It might have been the chauvinistic attitude adopted by the British film industry in the post-war decade that mirrored public opinion where West Germany was still not viewed as an ally (Hennessy, 1992, p. 261; Geraghty, 2000a, p. 95). It could also have been that the prominent place already occupied in 1950s media by the newly crowned Queen Elizabeth II would have made redundant an extended cinematic narrative on the golden

---

[14]European monarchs were a major source of coverage and gossip in the popular press with figures such as Queen Elizabeth II and Princess Margaret in the UK, Queen Fabiola and Princess Paola of Belgium, and Princess Grace of Monaco.

years of the Austro-Hungarian Empire. Viewing habits could also explain the absence of the trilogy on British soil, where audiences were never keen on films with subtitles (those that crossed the border were usually auteur films, a market to which the *Sissis* do not belong) nor on dubbing (the films were dubbed in continental Europe, a technical trait that made them more accessible and pushed forward their success).

Still, the story told in the *Sissi* cycle is one that travelled effectively. My empirical analysis of box-office figures correlated with textual analysis has established that Schneider started to move beyond a persona as Germanic star and captivated European audiences. I will now examine the diverse reasons for this popular fascination by analysing how Schneider embodied the Empress and why her casting was so successful.

2. Coming-of-age narratives

Beyond the context of the aftermath of the Second World War and the thesis of nationhood reconstruction, I identify three ways in which Schneider's border-crossing from German-speaking countries to Europe was enabled. First, it occurred through a narrative development that established the actress as a sexual being; secondly, through the development of a repertoire of gestures and idiosyncrasies that would become her performance signature; and finally, via her appeal to European popular memory through the visual transition she made in the *Sissi* series, establishing an iconography (particularly through costume), from Princess, to Queen and Empress.

2.1. More than an ingénue: a future wife

It is worth establishing briefly what I mean by the concept of the 'ingénue'. The term carries a semantic weight, and considering its extensive usage in common language and the popularity of the role of the ingénue in theatre, it is surprising that there are so few academic studies dedicated to the ingénue *per se*. Susan Weiner's comments on the eighteenth and nineteenth centuries' concept of the 'jeune fille' (girl) in her book *Enfants Terribles: Youth and Femininity in the Mass Media in France, 1945–1968* (2001) help to redress this imbalance, especially in reference to the 'intactness', the 'cultural imperative of female purity' and the '[place of] the female trajectory [...] within earthly patriarchal control' that particularly resonate with Schneider (p. 2). The ingénue is the artistic adaptation of the *jeune fille* as a category of identity – sexually ignorant, and 'the image of angelic femininity' (p. 3). There are studies of the *jeune fille*, beginning with Simone de Beauvoir in 1958, and Marcel Bernon et al. in 1983 (both in French), followed by Katherine Dalsmier's psychoanalytic approach to literature about female adolescence (1986); an entire category of gender studies is now dedicated to what is commonly referred to as 'girlhood' and the whole process of growing up (Johnson, 1993; Handyside and Taylor-Jones, 2016).

Patricia Meyer Spacks defines 'coming-of-age' and adolescence as the transition from childhood to adulthood, 'the time of life when the individual has developed full sexual capacity but has not yet assumed a full adult role in society' (1982, p. 7). Through film roles such as Queen Victoria and Stanzi (in *Die Deutschmeister*), and media representation, Schneider had already developed an ingénue persona, and, in *Sissi 1*, the Bavarian Princess is the epitome of such characterization. From *Sissi 2* Elisabeth began to acquire an erotic image and potentiality as a sexual figure. The ambivalent combination of the ingénue and the eroticized female is, I argue, the source of the character's trans-European and transgenerational appeal. There were two coming-of-age narratives outlined by the *Sissi* films: that of the Sissi character, and that of Schneider as an actress and a star.

Sissi's coming-of-age

Romy Schneider's first appearance characterizes Elisabeth in a single stroke. Against a triumphant, joyful, brass soundtrack, she enters the scene on horseback; she rides skilfully, laughing and cheering. After stepping down, Sissi heads for an aviary and feeds her birds. She chats with an old groom about her animals in a joyous tone. Then, surrounded by three dogs, she enters a paddock and bottle-feeds a fawn. This image (Figure 2) of the young Princess crouched in the grass, with her smiling, sunlit face, endowing a rescued forest creature with maternal affection (the baby bottle is the evident link), is the epitome of devotion and sweetness, and her interest in animal well-being relates to the preservation and love of nature, which connect her to ideas of purity and health. Sissi the girl is spontaneous, pleasant (she expresses genuine concern for her staff) and overflowing with energy; she remains the sweet figure that had already become familiar both in Schneider's star image and to German-speaking audiences.

Moving on from the opening sequence, Sissi's first encounter with adolescence is related to her body and to sex – the potentiality of sex, which is key in understanding the appeal of the Sissi figure (and consequently Schneider). Franz Joseph is first struck by Sissi's beauty: when he declares his love, he wishes his bride-to-be (Nene) looked more like this sweet stranger, saying that she should have '[her] eyes, [her] mouth, [her] hair'. Later on, when Sissi's royal identity is revealed and Franz Joseph stands up for his choice to his mother, the latter proceeds to 'examine' her niece, calling out her short stature and yellow teeth. To attack the body of young women

FIGURE 2 *Schneider bottle-feeds a fawn in* Sissi 1.

has always been part of asserting parental – and paternal – dominance, to submit them to the male's 'gentle authority' (de Beauvoir, 1997, pp. 352–5). In *Sissi 1*, while many men already praise Sissi's youthful beauty, the adults in charge (sisters Ludovika and Sophie) first try to undermine the Princess's confidence in her own body in a typical way to induce feminine passivity. Ludovika and Sophie represent the ideal 1950s housewife, dedicated to their children and their well-being (marrying them off is their duty). Fulfilment for an adult woman is to perpetuate the conventional female order of creating and maintaining a peaceful home, and Sissi is required to follow that lead.

When separated from her parents and her home by marriage, Sissi tries first to fight the rigid structures of the court with her childlike quality – her spontaneity. As Sissi, Schneider progressively loses the candour of her previous characters to grow into a more self-conscious woman, using her 'feminine charms'. She knows the effect she has on men, and the films' comic relief Gendarmeriemajor Boeckl (Joesf Meinrad), one of the men of the trilogy who falls in love with her, describes her as a 'celestial being'. Sissi becomes more influential: in *Sissi 2* she successfully soothes political tensions between Franz Joseph and Hungarian aristocrats. She is also associated with motherhood: she opposes the hold of her mother-in-law who intends to raise and educate the baby Princess, and judges the new Empress 'too young' to take care of the infant. To protest, Sissi flees Vienna and seeks refuge in her childhood home. The fact that her demand is ultimately met barely conceals her continued reliance on her parents. This example shows the ambiguity of the character: at the adolescent stage, Sissi rejects boundaries (she purchased an anniversary gift herself in the streets of Vienna), and refuses to stay put (her escape to Bavaria). Her family assumes she is inept and has a lack of interest in stately matters. Yet, at the same time, Sissi 'contains the principle of salvation' (Meyer Spacks, 1982, p. 14), especially in her royal position – that is, she is expected to give an heir. Moreover, because she acts on their behalf and believes in their cause, she is often called a 'saviour' by Hungarian characters.

Speaking of Hungarian characters, Sissi's coming-of-age is also well-illustrated in *Sissi 2* and *Sissi 3* through her chaste relationship with the dashing and former Hungarian rebel Count Andrássy (Walter Reyer), who falls desperately in love with her and becomes the principle holder of the male gaze on Sissi. Just like Franz Joseph, when Andrássy sees Sissi for the first time, he is struck by her physique. The difference between the Emperor and Elisabeth's love at first sight in *Sissi 1*, and this encounter, lies in the fact that Sissi is now a woman who carries herself with elegance and dignity (see the section on Schneider's performance). Some hints of a sexualized woman began to emerge. In *Sissi 3*, due to illness, she is recuperating in Corfu and Madera, without a man, in the sole company of her mother. There, she becomes an adult woman while rediscovering the strength of her body, regaining what she has systematically been denied since she entered her adolescent stage – her confidence in her body and in herself. However, considering the films' themes embedded in 1950s traditionalist and retrograde moral values, Sissi's next and only choice is to return to her family and to present to the Empire's people the exemplary image of the devoted wife and mother (Moeller, 1989; Krämer, 2012).

Romy's coming-of-age

Sissi's coming-of-age is not the only development charted in the films. Romy Schneider's adolescence, as an individual and as a star, was happening concomitantly. Just as with her Queen Victoria character, there was a parallel drawn by the contemporary media between Schneider's personal life and the arc of Sissi in Marischka's trilogy. The mother-daughter relationship was emphasized, as well as the rapprochement between the actress's charming and 'authentic' performance and the winsome personality of the character; with the *Sissi* films the intertwinement reached greater heights. The media discourse read that 'Romy is Sissi', and thus the star had to live the life of a fairy-tale princess. Magda Schneider, managing her daughter's career, facilitated Romy's accessibility to the press, and reporters and photographs were rarely denied (Schneider and Seydel, 1989; Krenn, 2013a). German-speaking media (quickly followed by the European press) pictured Romy as 'living every young woman's dream' (being a star), adapting the fairy-tale narrative of the films to the actress's new glamorous lifestyle. Examples of this media narrative (pushed by an intensive public relations campaign from *Sissi 1*'s distributor Herzog-Film) were numerous; they include excerpts from Schneider's own diary published every Monday during the first two months after the release of *Sissi 1* in the *Deutsche Illustrierte*, entitled 'Romy Schneider: diary of a seventeen-year-old girl', in which she mentions attending parties and premieres, meeting other stars, her mother's advice, her travels, her doubts and her sudden success (which she attributes to her good fortune and hard work); and 'My American journal' published in the *Abendzeitung* in February 1958 (and then in Dutch, Flemish and French in the Dutch-Belgian magazine *Libelle* two months later), in which she details her promotional duties for *Mädchenjahre einer Königin* in New York and Los Angeles. In all likelihood, the aim of the promotion was to give the impression of access to the 'real' life of the star. Schneider's own words had the value of authenticity and truthfulness: she was envied for her lifestyle, but equally praised for sharing it – she was accessible. She was viewed as successful, lucky and polite, the proper adolescent quietly living with her privileged family in their Bavarian home, and whose sudden popularity had not gone to her head. French reporter François Chalais in his television magazine 'Reflets de Cannes' from the Cannes Film Festival in May 1957 summarized the discourse on Schneider: she 'makes a *timid* appearance' (my emphasis), her Sissi role 'made her virtuous to all the housewives across the Rhine'. The voice-over continues: 'she is like a Maria Schell who does not think of herself as Maria Schell' – that is, Schneider is a humble, modest, well-mannered and proper young woman. The star is described as glamorous, but not a snob (her definition of glamour is understated, reasonable); she is pictured as a contemporary princess, as if Sissi had lived in the mid-1950s (*Film Revue*, 11/12/1956; *Wiener Wochenausgabe*, 29/03/1956; *Illustrierte Berliner*, 02/02/1957; Sanders, 02/02/1957; *Nous Deux Film*, 01/09/1958). Here, the emphasis on living with her parents in the countryside is primordial: whilst it connects to many aspects of Sissi in the films, it also conveys the same notions of preservation, health and simplicity that were engaging to film audiences. Indeed, the physical and visual progression towards womanhood that are at the centre of the *Sissi* films do not imply that neither Schneider nor Sissi lose their innocence. The Empress remains infantilized by adults, and she is still a romantic idealist.

Particularly telling of the Romy-Sissi conflation and their joint coming-of-age narrative was the subtle shift towards sexualization. At first, Sissi evokes virginity. She is pure and intact, a trait that influenced Schneider's star image. Between the release of *Sissi 1* and *Sissi 2*, German-speaking media dubbed the seventeen-year-old actress the 'Virgin of Geiselgasteig'[15] (*Der Spiegel*, 07/03/1956, cover), she was a 'Milchgesicht' – a 'baby face' (*Die Zeit*, quoted

---

[15]Geiselgasteig is a Grünwald's district (Munich) where are located the Bavaria Films studios.

in Sudendorf, 2008), a rosy and harmless media creation, which in turn implied the opposite of danger and called forward the concept of protection. Glamorized by costumes, Schneider was seen as perfection, a unique gem whose gentle and moral beauty must be kept away from evil. And who better than a righteous and reliable mother to ensure the safety of Germany's pristine sweetheart? Magda Schneider herself was aware of her daughter's image and of its implications: 'Why do people jump on Romy so much? Because they feel that there is finally a creature who has not come into contact with the *filth* of the world' (*Der Spiegel*, 07/03/1956, pp. 31–41, my emphasis).

Magda's protective role was further reinforced by her image of the happy mother, pleased with her daughter's success ('A mother's heart surrendered', *Film Revue*, 26/05/1956). As her daughter grew up, Magda continued to exist in the media as the voice of reason and wisdom: more than ever they were a team, elaborating strategies for Romy's future international career.[16] She also kept an eye on her daughter's suitors and when Romy began to date actor Horst Buchholz, whose image was that of the rebel who speaks his mind even if it 'displeases those dear adults' (Schneider and Seydel, 1989, p. 111), Magda intervened as the prospect of their romance (although favoured by the press) did not fit her daughter's portrayal of a proper upper-middle-class young woman. Indeed, once Schneider's image was newly defined by the concept of virginity, the next logical step in the traditional family social paradigm was marriage. Soon, the young virgin was called 'the little fiancée of Europe' (*Festival*, 01/09/1958), which definitely attests to Schneider's European star status, and indicates that a woman's value (a star is no exception) is based on her marital and maternal status: the appellation asserts that Schneider was open to marriage. Schneider was at the mercy of whoever the media decided she was 'meant to be with': more than an individual, she was part of a tandem. In a clichéd attempt to relive fictional love in real life (and in a typical star formation trait), the media paired her with her *Sissi* trilogy's co-star Karlheinz Böhm, and Horst Buchholz, her partner in *Robinson soll nicht sterben* (Josef von Báky, 1957) and *Monpti* (Helmut Käutner, 1957). With the former, the ideal matrimonial fantasy echoed the on-screen couple (in fact, Böhm was married and the father of a baby girl); with the latter, the (mostly German-speaking) journalistic discourse excitedly reported on the attraction of two opposites and the 'forbidden love' dimension that it brought. On the one hand, Buchholz

---

[16]Magda Schneider's managerial duties probably did more wrong than right for Schneider's career at the time: 'they' (i.e. Magda) refused an offer to work with Luis Buñuel, a three-year contract with Paramount, and a role in a play produced by the Burgtheater (Schneider and Seydel, 1989, p. 96). Magda's argument was that her daughter was 'not ready yet', and that she lacked experience, but the truth probably lies somewhere in the following: if Romy had left their lucrative mother-daughter duo, Magda would have lost much more than Romy, on both a professional and personal level, which is exactly what happened when her daughter moved to France in 1958.

with his 'Halbstarke' image (a bad boy, a thug) presented the possibility to soil the sweet princess, she on the other hand, as the feminine innocence, could 'tame' and 'domesticate' him with the perspective of home and family (*Bravo*, 30/12/1956, cover; Sigl, Schneider, and Tornow, 1986, pp. 130–1; Poiger, 2000, pp. 122–3). But the first romance that confirmed Schneider's sexualization was with Alpine ski champion Toni Sailer: whether their romance was real or not, what matters is the illustration that Schneider was considered 'bad juju' for the athlete's professional life (Schneider and Seydel, 1989, p. 106). The star was now allocated with sexual power: she lured him into cocktail receptions and away from his training where she distracted him with her eroticized body.

Whilst Romy Schneider's sexuality was neither outspoken nor staged, it was certainly at the core of her star image at the time, but its popular appeal was precisely its quiet and discreet nature. Other major stars of the 1950s like Marilyn Monroe, Brigitte Bardot, Jane Mansfield and Sophia Loren were celebrating sex in a more open manner – that is, it was more obviously apparent in the way they presented their either slim, curvy or busty bodies, which made their sexuality one of the most important components of their respective star images – yet Schneider was the last refuge against the looming sexual revolution. Whereas Bardot's image was modern (she was the young iconoclast woman of the time) and her films were almost all set in contemporary times, Schneider, starring essentially in historical films and often presented in the press in costume, developed an out-of-touch persona. Her erotic yet outdated image suggested the future wonders of discovering adulthood (marriage, sex, parenting) in a controlled and quiet manner. With the *Sissi* films Schneider's star image managed to fuse innocence with sexuality, but this was a carefully constructed and regulated persona (*Cinémonde* called her 'the new muse of modern romanticism', 21/11/1957).

The comparison to Bardot is here a case in point considering the French star also played a young girl (e.g. in *Cette sacrée gamine*, Michel Boisrond, 1955) whereas other popular actresses, including those of similar age (such as Sophia Loren) played more mature women. At first, at the release of *Sissi 1* in France in March 1957, French magazine *Cinémonde* labelled Schneider the 'German Brigitte Bardot' (*Der Spiegel*, 07/03/1956, p. 35; Krenn, 2013a, p. 76; Vincendeau, 2015b, p. 96). The comparison reflects the magnitude of their popularity and their similar star image at the time in one respect, that of playing the gamine and the charming adolescent. This media comparison occurred right before the release of *Et Dieu ... créa la femme* (Roger Vadim, 1956), the film that saw Bardot's superstar status 'upgraded' from gamine to sex goddess (Vincendeau, 2000, p. 93), which is considered the breaking point: while Bardot merged the 'mature sexual woman' and the gamine in the sex kitten image (p. 93), Schneider remained the 'real young girl' (*Ciné Revue*, 21/12/1956, cover; *Cinémonde*,

21/11/1957; *Nous Deux Film*, 01/09/1958). In 1958, *Le Monde* announced that 'Romy Schneider is exactly the anti-B.B. [Brigitte Bardot]. She only awakens in us notions of purity, tenderness, chaste engagement' (Jean de Baroncelli quoted in Welter, 2008).

This comparison is illustrative of two archetypes of women, with different aspirations, in mid-1950s Europe: one was the infantilized woman, whose rightful role and place were at home with her children, and the other was the sexually iconoclastic woman, representative of a new generation that was pushing against the former. If Bardot was the face of a 'new' femininity in 1950s France (the semblance of liberation, a modernity mostly confined to sexuality), Schneider's femininity was defined by the notion of potentiality within the bounds of propriety. Her sexuality was the one of a bride-to-be: it was the promise and possibility of sex (of first time sex) that transformed the star from child to prudish maiden and then finally to eroticized woman. Like Bardot, Schneider's sexuality has its roots in the natural, although their interpretations diverge. I would argue that Bardot's 'natural type of sexuality' (in opposition to Hollywood 'high glamour', Vincendeau, 2000, pp. 92–3), was not connected to simplicity to the extent it was for Schneider. Schneider's sexuality was notably defined by the natural and healthy qualities of Sissi's personality and her joie de vivre (she enjoys sports and protects animals). This is well illustrated by a performance style that essentially draws on Schneider's projection of authenticity and natural charm.[17] The two young women's sexualities differ as Schneider's on-screen persona was candid, outgoing and accessible, which forged the enticing prospect for young men to *have* her (or at least her hand in marriage), and for young women to *be* like her. This could explain women's interest in Schneider: contrary to some women who were jealous of Bardot and considered the French star a threat (Vincendeau, 2000, pp. 96–7), Schneider's potential-wife image represented the 'fulfilment of conventional maturity' (Meyer Spacks, 1982, p. 295) and offered a clear example to follow. Schneider's fairy-tale narrative made thousands of girls identify with her to accomplish what they considered their coming-of-age 'moment', that is finding their so-called independence and their 'sexual fulfilment as loved one and mother' in the arms of their husband (de Beauvoir, 1949, p. 352).

---

[17]Schneider's sexuality was imbued with the 'healthy' and the 'natural' in a similar manner to Ingrid Bergman's (Wood, 1989, pp. 303–35). Robin Wood argues that society's healthy outlook regarding nature connected with Bergman's natural beauty (attained through photographs of the star without makeup in a lifelike setting, such as an image of her with baby ducks, very similar to Schneider at the beginning of her career), which revealed a sexuality embedded in innocence.

3. Mise en scène: performance and costumes

3.1. Schneider's performance style in the *Sissi*s

Although Schneider's performance as Sissi remained within familiar territory for the actress and German-speaking audiences in the first film, it leant towards new acting registers in *Sissi 2* and *3* in which her depiction of the young Empress is both tragic and erotic. The star began to develop a repertoire of gestures and melodramatic idiosyncrasies that would become part of her performance signature. I will focus on four performance signs to illustrate this evolution: first her physique (body movements and gait), then her face (especially how she moves her chin), third her tone (voice, accent, laugh), and finally her sensual and steady gaze.

In the beginning of *Sissi 1* Schneider plays the Bavarian Princess with exhilaration. Despite imposing costumes, the actress appears at ease in her movements: her step is light, quick, even fluttering, she waves her hat, she crouches to play on the floor with her little sister, to feed the fawn or to look into a chest, she escapes through a window and climbs a roof, she slips under a fence and she runs. Her activities are athletic: she rides horses, hunts and hikes while her mother and Nene stay inside and embroider. Schneider's moving body evokes an energetic and uninhibited character, and therefore her body occupies a significant amount of space. The sequence of the family meeting in Ischl between Ludovika, her two daughters and Sophie and her son Carl-Ludwig (Peter Weck) is a great example of Schneider's performance of the young Sissi as her movements contrast with the other actors', especially Uta Franz who plays Nene. Franz is calmer and more collected than Schneider who is all over the place. She enters the frame, quickly walks towards the group, her right arms extended in anticipation of her curtsey. Because Elisabeth is her most athletic character so far, Schneider's walk becomes evident and contributes to the 'perfect fit'[18] between the character and the actress (Dyer, 1998, p. 129). Schneider's gait (straight back and pulled-back shoulders) can be considered athletic because of the position of her arms: she walks with her elbows turned outward and swings her arms in a manner that is determined and assured. Opposite her, Franz keeps her hands and arms close to her body and barely talks. Also, when Schneider delivers her lines, and despite the weight of her wig (5.5 lb), she positions her head and chest forward, inducing movements to her upper body and hair. Noticing Carl-Ludwig, for example, she waves at him in a cavalier manner, initiating a movement forward, which is immediately reprimanded by her mother who puts a hand on her arm. Ignoring her, she walks towards him,

---

[18]Richard Dyer defines the perfect fit as the way in which 'all the aspects of a star's image fit with all the traits of a character' (1998, p. 129).

crossing the frame, turns to face him and then walks out of the frame with him. These gestures make Schneider forcefully 'present' in the scene, her performance style apparently unstudied, natural. She performs an energetic girl and her moving body naturally expresses her character's enthusiasm (it leans forward). Franz's composure and stillness signify that her character knows her place in the family hierarchy, Nene fulfils everyone's expectations (she is well-educated), while Sissi is still a disorderly 'kind' (a child), as the matriarchs put it.

Sissi's coming-of-age by the end of *Sissi 1* is noticeable in Schneider's growing body (she was nineteen in the last film, and became an object of desire in part because of her physique). Once the Princess falls in love with the Emperor and realizes that her rightful place is at his side and not gambolling around in the woods, the actress adopts a more serious and composed interpretation that will continue to develop in *Sissi 2* and *3*. If Schneider's performance style is the one of the body in movement in *Sissi 1*, immobility best characterizes her acting in the next two films. Schneider adopts court mannerisms: her immobile and straight posture, often with her hands crossed in front of her, plays a significant role in her depiction of the dignified Empress, her composure carries an imposing and collected presence, making her character grow more confident and regal. The rare exceptions are a few scenes in which Schneider acts out of this newly contrived character, she is 'on edge' and reprises her performance of the passionate Sissi expressing her feelings (see below). The actress's straight posture is probably the result of her short stature: one could assume that she has to stand up as tall and straight as she could, which brings me to my analysis of Schneider's second and instrumental performance sign: her face.

Schneider's stature (she was 5 ft 3) created a recurrent acting movement that plays a part in the construction of her sex appeal. Not only did she carry her head with pride and distinction, she also had to lift her chin to look up to her partner, which sometimes she used for seductive purpose (she 'offered' her face, as if to receive a kiss). This distinctive performance sign was increasingly used by Marischka and cinematographer Bruno Mondi, especially in *Sissi 3* where Schneider was frequently filmed in profile or from an oblique angle. This lengthened her neck and enhanced her square jawline, making the movement of her head appear more delicate and sensual. The latter is particularly emphasized when she laughs: she erotically throws her head back, closes her eyes and laughs uproariously.

Schneider's laugh leads me to analyse briefly a third performance sign: her change of tone. In *Sissi 1* she smiles, laughs and talks in a girlish voice, with a cheerful, uneven tone. Schneider's first transitional phase towards womanhood remained in the domain of cuteness and for a brief moment she developed a gamine persona. This was emphasized by her comic performance in *Sissi 1*, which evolved around a mischief register: it was her character's playfulness and repartee that made her appealing. But, she abandons her smiles to, first, a range of childish, pouting faces (signalling her character's disapproval of change), and then Schneider develops a more mature tone for Sissi the woman. Her voice and accent in German are softer and a more melodic than a high German accent, which makes her sound sweeter than she probably would have otherwise. Her vocabulary and grammar were elaborate for Sissi and she employed sophisticated phrase, in line with her character's high noble rank. She laughed less and displayed a certain poise and affectation – still candid, but more demure.

From this exploration of Schneider's performing body, face and speech, we can see that their development accompanied the trilogy's narrative shift towards dramatic tonalities. Owing to her performance of the disparaged mother and of the suffering body (in *Sissi 3*), the actress's sensual aesthetics became attached to signs of tragic and melodramatic mannerism. To illustrate this evolution, I will analyse two scenes in which Schneider combined and worked these three signs. The first one is the moment Sissi discovers that her child has been removed from her care and she confronts her husband and mother-in-law. Schneider bustles about, looking nervously around the nursery for the cradle, shaking her head and losing her nerve. The movements of Schneider's hair (braids and long curls sweeping her shoulders) that I have previously mentioned were achieved by quick and sharp head turns, a performance sign that Schneider retained during her entire career and became, from her Sissi performance onwards, the bearer of a melodramatic, even histrionic tone. Schneider flares her nostrils, and talks vividly and sharply, in contrast to the Emperor whose speech tone and pace remain composed and firm, asserting his masculine, paternal and royal superiority. Schneider hastily leaves the scene with her signature walk, determined and angry.

During the scene in which Sissi overhears news of her health condition, Schneider does not speak and all the predicaments and conflicted feelings that her character experiences are translated and heightened by the many expressions of her face captured in close-up. Because Sissi has to remain quiet, hidden in the half-open door, Schneider's acting is both subtly tragic and melodramatically excessive, therefore very efficient in confronting and connecting with the spectator's empathy. Due to minimal and whitish makeup, her face is pallid, her nude lips livid. Although the character was meant to appear ill, the star had to remain beautiful: there are no bags under Schneider's eyes and they are brightened with a trait of beige eyeliner above the lashes of the lower lid, drawing attention to the intensity of her soundless performance. She first looks intrigued, then haggard, leaning her head against the wall, and desperate and shocked, widening her eyes and opening her mouth in a silent scream, inaudibly smashing the wall to finally burying her head in her hands.

Finally, the fourth recognizable sign of Schneider's acting repertoire developed over the *Sissi* trilogy is her enticing 'œillade'. Although it was

FIGURE 3 *An early sign of the seductive Schneider: her 'œillade' in* Sissi 3.

used sporadically during that period, this sidelong and frolicsome glance carried a sexual knowingness, the hint that she was aware of the power that a single teasing look can have on her interlocutors. Sissi's charm is known to be 'irresistible', and she uses it to gently coax men to bend to her will. Schneider's calculating gaze, with its insistence and shrewdness, plays an important part in this seduction technique, and she uses it more often as she comes of age. Consider the scene between Sissi and her husband in a roadside inn. In this conversation between two long-distance lovers who meet after a long time apart, Sissi has to soothe Franz Joseph, jealous of Andrássy and the time she spent in Hungary, for which Schneider had recourse to her 'œillade'. Once she has succeeded (he suggests a romantic escapade in Ischl), Schneider concludes her performance with a sigh of relief, closes her eyes and leans towards him, putting her cheek against his, caressing it, smiling and erotically opening her mouth (Figure 3). This scene illustrates an important change in Schneider's persona: she acts as a woman who purposely seduces.

My analysis shows that Sissi's appeal was in great part related to Schneider's naturalistic and spontaneous performance style that suggested authenticity. She was perceived as projecting herself into the character and, as she physically grew up, she carried Sissi within her coming-of-age. This sense of authenticity goes towards explaining her success: the young Schneider performed herself and perfectly fit the ingénue Sissi, a winsome, smiling woman whose charm remained within the limits of propriety while instilling sexual tension and a masculine desire that could never be fulfilled. Schneider's sensual acting signs remained timid; they were there nonetheless, asserting the star image of a seductive and distinguished woman, a transformation also visible through the use of costume.

3.2. An Iconographic transition: Schneider's costumes from Princess to Empress

As previously mentioned, historical costume film was very popular in 1950s Western Europe, and costumes themselves were part of the pleasure for spectators. Alongside the films' coming-of-age narrative and the star's acting repertoire, the third way Romy Schneider was 'equipped' to cross over the German-speaking borders was her appeal to European popular memory through the transition she makes iconographically via costumes. As the trilogy unfolds, an increasing number of glamorous ball gowns promote the image of an alluring young star and reinforce her princess persona that resonated with European collective memory. In this section I discuss how Sissi's costumes contributed to Schneider's performance. First, I will focus on their design in regard to their adaptation to historical reality (their authenticity), to 1950s fashion, and to Schneider's physique. Then, like the actress's performance signs partook in the character's arc, I will consider how costumes translated her narrative development.

Sissi's costumes have first to be explored regarding their degree of authenticity (Cook, 1996, p. 64; Hayward, 2010, pp. 38, 60–2). Designers Gerdago (Gerda Gottstein, who worked on the three films), Franz Szivats (*Sissi 1*) and Leo Bei (*Sissi 2* and *Sissi 3*) made sure that their creations shared similarities to their historical models, further embedding Schneider's image of the fairy-tale princess into historical reality. The dresses were loosely inspired by European royal fashion from the mid-nineteenth century and by some of Elisabeth of Austria's own ball gowns. The term 'ball' is important: there was a distinction between the Empress's daily attire and her more elaborate ball gowns for special occasions, official appearances and ceremonies. Costume designers deliberately chose the latter, a more glamorous-connoted option for Schneider's dresses, a couple of them directly quoting Elisabeth's most iconic representations. The design of the Empress's imposing gowns was particularly complicated and cluttered: in her full-length official portrait by Winterhalter she wears a creation (by Charles Frederic Worth) made of an accumulation of fluffy petticoats and tulle sewn with diamonds stars (matching the ones in her hair), and completed with a shawl. For her coronation as Queen of Hungary, she wore a silver brocade gown trimmed with lace and a midnight blue velvet bodice with pearl lacing. These dresses were already known throughout Europe in the 1950s: the reproduction of portraits and photographs of Empress Elisabeth had helped cement her popularity during the second half of nineteenth century (as did her many travels across European continent and seas) and the twentieth century with a proliferation of biographies.[19] Such representations inspired the trilogy's iconography, creating an inter-generational connection between the historical figure and her 1950s fictional embodiment: from the authentic bouffant ball gowns, Schneider's costumes kept some elements, although the choice for a more subdued style was evident. Designers respected the width of the skirts, and some of the colours (mostly whites, midnight blue, Venetian red and bottle green) worn by the Empress before she observed a mourning wardrobe. But the overall design in the films was much simpler and more delicate, especially the upper body parts where the historical swollen sleeves adorned with curlicues were replaced by smaller, ruffled, off-the-shoulder sleeves. Yet, some costumes were imitating the historical attires, such as Sissi's engagement and wedding dresses that were to become central in Schneider's 'Europe's little fiancée' image. Many magazine covers pictured the star wearing the engagement attire from the film (with the Empress's diamond stars in her hair), which was inspired by Winterhalter's portrait and the pose was replicated by Schneider in studio stills and posters. Schneider was also pictured wearing the film's wedding dress accompanied by taglines such as 'I too want my wedding gown' (*Deutsche Illustrierte*, 28/01/1956, cover), reinforcing her ideal potential-wife image. Schneider's various dresses gave the sense of a historical look, yet also fit in with 1950s aesthetics.

Equally significant to their historical references were the costumes' adaptations to 1950s fashion, especially the New Look's hyper-feminine silhouette. Aptly, the New Look itself drew inspiration from the romantic 'princess gown' style from Second Empire France (the same era of Elisabeth of Austria). Couture designers such as Charles James and Christian Dior created strict hour-glass flower shapes with wasp-waisted bodices and extravagant use of fabric for long, crinoline-like skirts. The New Look aimed to revive fantasy, luxury and the classical iconography of 'eternal beauty' after the privations of the Second World War (Steele, 1997, pp. 13–15; Hayward, 2010, p. 277), which was precisely the effect of Schneider's ball gowns that featured form-fitting bodices, a discrete emphasis on the shoulders with their dropped, short sleeves and a full skirt. Schneider's costumes went so far as to introduce fashionable 1950s colours such as soft pastels (baby pink, aquamarine, light blue, orange and purple), and patterns and accessories like polka dots, long white gloves, pearl necklaces and wide-brimmed saucer hats. The lush ball dress of the title character in Walt Disney's animation film *Cinderella* (Clyde Geronimi, Wilfred Jackson,

---

[19]One of the most 'enthusiastically welcomed' Elisabeth's biographies was Egon Caesar Conte Corti's 1934 book *Elisabeth, die seltsame Frau* (*Elisabeth, Empress of Austria*), edited many times, translated in several languages and regularly reprinted (Schraut, 2011, pp. 161–2).

Hamilton Luske, 1950) already made the synthesis of the historical princess style of the second-half of the nineteenth century with the New Look just a couple of years before the *Sissi*s, and shares a striking resemblance with Schneider's costumes. The wide cut of the dress, the small sleeves and the long gloves were reprised in most of Schneider's gowns. These might be direct quotes, as *Cinderella* came out in West Germany in December 1951 and in Austria a year later. Although *Cinderella* does not appear in Garncarz's Top Ten list for the year 1951–2 in West Germany[20] (1994, p. 124), its 13 million spectators in French cinemas (it was the second biggest success [Simsi, 2012, p. 15]) confirm the ongoing popularity of fairy-tale narratives. The film was even re-released in France in 1958, the same year *Sissi 3* and *Christine* (starring Schneider) came out, and in West Germany in 1960 at the Berlin Film Festival. Cinderella is still the princess figure par excellence, and the tale's success is bound to a specific narrative moment (the makeover, see below), and a particular body type. Indeed, Schneider's physique also participated in the popularity of her image in costumes.

The memorable visual spectacle of Schneider in her princess dress makes clear that costumes were also adapted to her physique. Enhancing her bodily transformation, they were central to the visualization of her coming-of-age. The star turned eighteen and nineteen over the filming of the trilogy, she was slim, with a small chest, and therefore departed from the fashionable fuller figure of the 1830s (sloping shoulders, rounded bust, narrow waist and full hips).[21] As previously stated, the top parts of Schneider's dresses differed from their historical references, in that they emphasized and flattered her feminine features. With a simple and form-fitting design, short sleeves and low-cut neckline, they drew the eye to the actress's juvenile aspect. We saw that it was conventionally required of Schneider to perform the fresh maiden as well as the glamorous fiancée, and therefore to induce male desire without appearing too ostensibly sexy, and her costumes did exactly that – they discretely eroticized her character. This double standard is illustrated in Schneider's skin exposure: her costumes were designed to express the Empress's dignified status, yet their cut accentuates the shape of her breasts and reveal an important amount of pale skin (neckline, shoulders, arms, hands), a complexion that carries concepts of nobility and refinement (see Dyer, 1997). The full-skirted petticoat gowns made of precious fabrics and adorned with jewels lengthened her silhouette, refined her waist (emphasized by a corset and a V-shaped waistline bodice or a tight belt) and induced a different body posture and movements as seen in the previous section

---

[20]At the time 'German-made film were more popular than American films', US films took over German film market in the 1970s (Garncarz, 1994, p. 95).

[21]In a way, Schneider tended to resemble Elisabeth of Austria herself who was famous for contrasting and outshining the conventional beauty canons of her time with her slenderness, poise and extreme thinness – it is now common knowledge that she suffered from anorexia and subjected her body to intense exhaustion (see des Cars, 1983; Clément, 1992; Schraut, 2011).

on performance (Schneider walked and moved more slowly, stood tall and straight and the corset, by constraining her breathing, emphasized the rise and fall of her chest). At first, some romantic details (such as discrete floral pattern and tiny pink butterflies and roses on the neckline) persisted on the gowns, but later the emphasis was on the dropping of the trains and the skirt lines (long strips of fabrics such as belts and shawls) to further lengthen the actress's figure. The absence of ostentatious details and ornaments on the dresses or in her hair meant that the focus stayed on the actress's performance, and the movement of her long skirts smoothly accompanied her when she walked and danced. Combined with her soft voice and thin upper body, this suggests an ambivalent image of femininity: growing elegant, graceful and confident, while also remaining delicate and fragile. How to explain the look's popularity throughout the years? The princess silhouette popularized by Schneider (and Cinderella) might function as an 'iconogramme', a visual landmark, quickly identifiable because it is monosemic and belongs to a 'shared knowledge' (de la Bretèque, 1998, p. 294). The key is that Schneider's dresses were made of simple figurative traits: the simplicity of the design and an absence of superfluous details (no excessive ruffles, laces or bows, and no additional layers of different fabrics like we see in many historical costume films) meant that the viewer was never overwhelmed by the spectacle of the costume, making it both iconic and familiar.

Like Schneider's performance signs, her costumes also participate in the character's coming-of-age. From the sporty and simple clothing of the girl frolicking in the woods, to the introduction of the fairy-tale princess gown, there is a narrative evolution of Schneider's costumes. In *Sissi 1*, the young girl wears sporty, straight-cut clothes of either warm colours (dark red, brown), or soft pinks and midnight blues, accessorized with lace pan collars and embroidery details, silk pink scarfs and aprons, neckerchieves, bottle green gloves and a felt hat. Nonetheless, her clothing gives away the character's status and already hints at a certain sophistication: hiking dresses are embellished with pearls and velvet details, and her Venetian red riding dress is heavy, with a train that Schneider has to pick up to walk, in a fashion reminiscent of royal female figures. Schneider's Bavarian dresses are usually ankle-length and her feet are visible to allow a greater freedom of movement. I have previously reflected on her performance of the girl: her character is full of energy and therefore not yet constricted by costumes, unlike those of the mother and sister whose freedom of movement was restrained by cumbersome clothing. When Schneider wore her Bavarian costumes, she had the opportunity to move her body more freely, as required for her performance of a vivid and enthusiastic girl. Progressively this casual costuming was replaced with more sophisticated attire, illustrating both Sissi's coming-of-age and the star's physical growth.

One gown in particular played a fundamental role in this: I call it 'the makeover dress'. As a trope that highlights transitions, the cinematic makeover not only maps out a female protagonist's experience of what Maryn Wilkinson (2015) calls 'becoming woman', but also rectifies the contesting notions of femininity by re-inscribing gender identity through excessive performance (here, the star's spectacularization in costume). After running away from the mesmerized Emperor who was in the midst of declaring his love, Sissi's true identity is revealed to Franz Joseph as Schneider makes a solemn entrance at his birthday ball. Her appearance is a surprise to both the imperial suitor and the spectator, who discover Schneider in the splendour of the film's first 'princess panoply'. She wears an aquamarine floor-length gown made of satin and organza, adorned with three shining stripes of floral trimming on the skirt, bodice, low-cut neckline and the short puffed sleeves that uncover her shoulders. She has bright pink lips, long curls of hair cascading down her back and she wears lace white gloves, a sparkling arrow-shaped hair jewel and a bucket clutch matching her dress. As suggested by the mise en scène, the magnificence of the dress and the spectacular effect (Figure 4) of Schneider's appearance were intended by Marischka to create a pivotal and lasting image of the young star. She enters after her mother and sister, at the centre of the frame, and when she appears at the doors (creating a frame within the frame) the music hits pompous brass notes – all enhancing her appearance as iconic. Through this makeover act, the unapologetic and free Sissi modifies her burgeoning femininity to

FIGURE 4 *Schneider's makeover princess dress and pivotal coming-of-age moment.*

create a non-threatening one (Bleach, 2010, pp. 29–32). To become a 'true woman' – that is, a feminine woman – Sissi has to appear hyper-gendered and Schneider therefore has to expose and enhance her body with her gown. We see Schneider through the eyes of her male partner Böhm: identically reproducing the Prince's reaction in *Cinderella* (reinforcing the trilogy's fairy-tale parentage), Franz Joseph is mesmerized. This was probably the same effect the producers hoped the audience would experience too, they were to be entranced by the vision of Sissi/Schneider as the pinnacle of a man's imagining of a delicate young woman: the gaze of the opposite sex validates Schneider's 'worth' inscribed onto her body. However, one should not dismiss the idea, as Rachel Moseley (2005, p. 113) astutely points out in her work on Audrey Hepburn's fashion moments, of 'an admiring gaze which is not specifically gendered male', nor heteronormative. Amongst many examples of the popularity of Sissi's costumes, there is a comedic sequence from *Les Garçon et Guillaume, à table !/Me, Myself and Mum* (Guillaume Gallienne, 2013) in which the protagonist (Gallienne, playing his younger self) portrays both Archduchess Sophie and future Empress Elisabeth in one of his enactment games, with original dialogues and identical costumes in his fantasy. The female characters' crinoline skirts are replaced by Gallienne's duvet and held at his waist by a belt (a 'trick' very familiar to me and my two younger sisters, and, I am sure, to many other boys and girls in Europe since 1956).

Conclusion

The perfect fit between Sissi and Schneider was the result of the expert blending of the character with the star's private and screen personas, creating authenticity, charisma and the sense of an intimate connection with the audience. It began with a role developed by Marischka for Schneider who was already linked to the historical imperial figure by virtue of her romantic princess image, well-established amongst domestic audiences before she embarked on *Sissi 1*. More importantly, Schneider contributed through performance and costume to the creation of the character, and she took Elisabeth from spirited youth to sensual maturity. Schneider, as Sissi, was the ever-becoming woman – that is, as much as the narrative and her costumes might have stressed ambiguous, almost hidden sexuality, the star's eyes suggested a more knowledgeable personality and seemed to have some erotic content. Her naturalistic performance, her youthful and growing body and the absence of theatrical training were all aspects that cultivated the authenticity component of her star image – the sense that she was her spontaneous self in front of the camera. Schneider's royal persona was further reinforced by her on- and off-screen relationship with Magda

Schneider, a continuous presence in her daughter's life and a constant reminder to consider the family element: Schneider was the 'crown Princess' of German-speaking cinema and its ideal and prestigious representative in Europe, as she herself came from a dynasty of actors on her father side (Schwarzenbach, 2006, p. 312). As a result, the role of Sissi and its impeccable fit with Schneider marked the star so heavily that no producer dared to delineate from this young, fresh and precious screen persona for several years.

3

Romy after *Sissi*: Transition to the 1960s

Introduction

At the age of nineteen Romy Schneider had reached trans-European stardom[1] but also had become inseparable from an image that conveyed the (sexually and racially restrictive) archetype of the ingénue. Her persona was defined to such an extent by the princess role that she faced the difficulties of typecasting and tried to move away from Sissi by changing her image. Although Sissi made Schneider a star in high demand (she made on average three films a year at the time and co-starred with the elite of European cinema) with an important media presence, her career came to a standstill – the films in which she attempted to alter her Sissi-like image were neither box-office nor critical successes.

The process of renegotiating her image involved many parties: the star herself and her (documented) wish to expand her repertoire, her mother Magda and stepfather Hans Herbert Blatzheim, producers from different film industries (Austria, West Germany, France) and French and German-speaking audiences. Many details of their respective contribution to the decision-making regarding Romy's career are imprecisely chronicled in Schneider's 'autobiography' *Ich, Romy* (Schneider and Seydel, 1988), a document that has to be considered with caution, especially since it tends to continue on a dominant discourse established a posteriori, and is contemptuous vis-à-vis the *Sissi*s.

---

[1] In the case of Schneider, and at this particular time of her career, I define trans-European stardom in terms of reception: I have examined how she was positively received by varied national audiences, even celebrated in many continental European countries for her Sissi character, and how her star image transcended the national Germanic implication of the Empress figure.

In this chapter, I track Schneider's character evolution and her unsuccessful endeavours to change into a more modern, emancipated and sexual woman on screen. The 1956–9 years are rarely taken into account in the abundant literature on Schneider, a void usually justified in journalistic rhetoric by her films' alleged lack of quality. I consider it nonetheless a crucial time in her trajectory as she continued on her trans-European trajectory by working on European co-productions, which laid the foundations of another line of discourse – her polarized reception by French and German-speaking audiences. This period of transition is complex, with many tensions between different types of film characters. As a result, I structure it into three sections: the continuity with the Sissi figure and the star's typecasting, the attempt to move away from this cumbersome image and then a suggestion for a more radical alternative – but with some unavoidable delineage away from a strict chronology, as her films did not necessarily follow such neat phases.

1. The weight of the *Sissi* legacy

Schneider's work on the *Sissi* trilogy was interspersed by other film shoots: between *Sissi 1* and *2* she did *Kitty und die große Welt/Kitty and the Great Big World* (Alfred Weidenmann, 1956), then between *Sissi 2* and *3* she filmed, amongst others, *Robinson soll nicht sterben/The Girl and the Legend* (Josef von Báky, 1957), and finally *Scampolo* (Alfred Weidenmann, 1958) right after completing *Sissi 3*. I briefly examine these three films together with *Ein Engel auf Erden/An Angel on Wheels* (Géza von Radványi, 1959) because they all typecast the star as the romantic and demure girl. I will start with her roles in the first two films as they also share other members of *Sissi* cast, and then consider *Scampolo* and *Ein Engel auf Erden*, both comedies set in southern Europe. Schneider's image of the virgin was so deep-seated in Germanic collective memory that it became untouchable in the sense that it should remain preserved from harm, hence audiences' defensive attitude towards any potential change. Heretofore the wholesome Sissi/Romy figure had proved infallible at the box office and it is not surprising that *Kitty, Robinson, Scampolo* and *Ein Engel auf Erden* exploited it, making Schneider's purity forefront.

1.1. Familiar faces

As Pamela Robertson Wojcik explains, there is a double view on typecasting (2004, pp. 169–89). On the one hand, actors subjected to typecasting resent its limitation and commercial connotation that entails lack of originality – it threatens to diminish the art of acting and deny them the exploration of their craft. On the other hand, it can provide continuous work in the industry for those who embody national and cultural stereotypes, and it is true that Schneider was very much in demand and worked continuously during those years. Sarah Thomas's study of German star Peter Lorre (2012) is enlightening in regard to typecasting. She questions the dominant views on Lorre's career by arguing how reductive the concept of an 'image' is, and its passive nature for the stars themselves (it can dispossess them of any agency as professionals). Thomas points to the decisions made by the stars themselves, and it is in this respect that Schneider's typecasting as the ingénue appears doubly imposed. The young star had almost no say in her career choices during those years – her mother and stepfather Blatzheim were still managing her career and finances. This continuous parental presence influenced Schneider's typecasting first-hand – Blatzheim received and selected the scripts sent to the family home, and forged media discourses as well, which in return contributed to maintain and propagate the national, social and sexually confined stereotype embodied by Schneider, that is, the bubbly romantic girl, ready to become a housewife.

Indeed, neither in *Kitty* nor in *Robinson* does her role depart from the maiden star image that her previous films and the media discourse had built for her so far. Both films recycle many elements associated with her romantic persona. In *Kitty*, a West German romantic comedy photographed in black and white, set in modern-times Geneva, Schneider's character (a beauty salon employee) falls in love with Karlheinz Böhm, her partner in the *Sissi*s. *Kitty* is the remake of the 1939 German comedy *Kitty und die Weltkonferenz* (Helmut Käutner's first film, he also directed *Monpti* with Schneider in 1957), and the dissimilarities between the two films are illustrative of the importance of both Schneider's ingénue persona and her typecasting. While the original Kitty (Hannelore Schroth) is more conniving and involved in a political intrigue (Geneva hosts an international conference and she charms the British Minister of Economic Affairs), Romy's Kitty has no agency. She meets the statesman (Otto Eduard Hasse in the 1956 version) in a street by chance, they bond over a lost pup (the actress is photographed cuddling a pet, a recurring sign attached to sweetness and innocence) and when she becomes prey to the tabloids the politician sends his nephew Robert (Böhm) to protect her, and the two young people fall for each other. The key here is that, exactly as in *Sissi 1*, Romy's character does not *purposely* seduce men; seduction is, for her, an 'accidental' outcome of her charming personality. Also, the reunion of the stars from the previous year's most successful film in Austria and West Germany was obviously considered a safe bet for the producers. The fairy-tale element is personified by Böhm whose actions in *Kitty* directly recall *Sissi 1*: the pair take refuge in the sunny countryside in a reference to the meeting between Sissi and the Emperor, they enjoy a stroll by the banks of Lake Geneva, they eat cheese fondue (there is a similar scene in a Tyrol inn in *Sissi 2* in which the incognito imperial couple eat an omelette) and he carries her in his arms to cross a creek.

The *Sissi*-induced fairy-tale element, at the core of Romy's popularity, is also present in *Robinson* as well as other familiar faces – Magda Schneider and Gustav Knuth – and the gentle Duke Max (Sissi's father) is now a manipulative pirate in von Báky's drama. In this costume film, which came out in West Germany a couple of months after *Sissi 2*, Magda reprised the mother role of her daughter's character, Maud. Romy inhabits for the first time a proletarian milieu (a spinning cotton factory in 1730 London) far from the lavish decors of the Vienna court, and she is dressed in rags and wears her hair parted in two short and messy plaits – the image could not be further from her pristine, sumptuous looks in *Sissi 1* and *2*. And yet her role is still that of the sweet, obliging and good girl. In *Robinson* and *Kitty* Schneider continues to personify warmth, altruism and innocence. Her first steps out of Sissi's shoes were therefore supervised by both her real-life and fictional parents, and resolutely turned towards the past. And so it continued after the completion of the trilogy.

1.2. Different settings, same girl

Scampolo, set in modern-times Ischia Island (Italy), was Schneider's first film after *Sissi 3*. She portrays the resourceful, fun-loving and vivid title character who comes to the help of the ambitious but penniless architect Costa. Her simple summer clothes (a loose red cotton skirt and a white blouse with short sleeves) and shoulder-length, untidy brunette hair fit with her performance of the flitting, outspoken (sometimes passionate, as in *Sissi 3*) Scampolo. She charms men and women with her genuine smile to encourage them to help someone in need, exactly like her role of Elisabeth of Austria. The film's sunny Ischia-location recalls its contemporary *Et Dieu … créa la femme* (Vadim, 1956) set on the Riviera and Saint-Tropez, all fashionable places on the Mediterranean coast, which gives them a modern feel. Yet, *Scampolo*'s glimpses of modernity strike a more parodic, amiable tone, as they are not transmitted by Schneider's visual representation, which remains traditional, especially in comparison to Bardot. While both stars play on the tension between the wild child and the woman, the difference in interpretation is glaring: Bardot exudes sexiness, Schneider is still a girl. The age gap may play a part (Bardot was twenty-two years old in *Et Dieu … créa la femme*, Schneider was nineteen in *Scampolo*), but their appearances, costumes and hairstyles are diametrically opposed, denoting the distance between two concurrent visual representations of femininity in 1950s Europe. Whereas Bardot swings her hips, strikes pin-up poses and wears form-fitting clothes revealing her lithe body, Schneider hops, skips and wears loose skirts and shirts (although she visibly does not wear a bra).

Schneider's costumes and performance show the character's modesty. She changes her summer attire only twice, and the reference to Sissi's free spirit is patent. First, for a dinner with Costa, she wears a lilac cotton boat-necked dress with white heels; then, at a party, she wears a delicate white lace dress offered, in fairy-tale-like fashion, by her suitor. On both occasions, Schneider shows her character's discomfort with these new outfits that do not match Scampolo's nature-loving and wild personality: she tightens her lips (Scampolo is uncomfortable wearing her first pair of pantyhose), she stumbles and traps her heel in the paving stones and takes off her shoes to slow-dance with a guest (in comparison, Bardot's torrid mambo displays sexuality through the star's lascivious dance moves), and she keeps trying to hide her décolleté with her hand. Both Bardot and Schneider convey spontaneity, youth, femininity and naturalness, but in opposing ways ('Brigitte Bardot and Romy Schneider, it's night and day', *Radio Télé Ciné*, 11/01/1959).

Two years later, in spring 1959, Schneider shot *Ein Engel auf Erden* on the French Riviera. Hitherto, Schneider's trans-European stardom has been defined in terms of reception; but progressively it began to include co-productions too, laying the groundwork for her 1960s international career. *Ein Engel auf Erden* could be considered her second French film after *Christine* (analysed later) – with the exception of Schneider (who lived in France at the time), the cast and crew were French, the capital was French-German and the script was co-written by French writer René Barjavel and Hungarian Géza von Radványi who also directed. Schneider plays a double role in the film: the guardian angel of a dashing racing driver Pierre (Henri Vidal), and Line, the stewardess desperately in love with him, of whom the angel has taken the body form in the hope of bringing them together. The film is filled with references to Schneider's generic ingénue characterization: the actress wears short blonde hair like a halo and a demure blue uniform, and she is filmed cuddling white doves; her character, who is literally an angel, advocates virtuous coupledom with a 'pure and sweet soul'. On the opposite side of the femininity spectrum is Pierre's brunette and temptress fiancée (Michèle Mercier) whom Schneider calls 'the devil' because she experiences the pleasures of sex. I close this section on Schneider's typecasting with a telling illustration. In a scene that features Pierre and his friend (Jean-Paul Belmondo) drunk, they share the vision (translated through point of view shots) of a Schneider-döppelganger mannequin (it has her facial features, blonde hair and stewardess costume) stripped of its skirt and vest to reveal white lingerie (full-cup bra, panties, garter and nylon pantyhose). What should have been the actress's body is replaced by an effigy – a frozen, unalterable version of her. The scene's surrealist and comic tone is a humorous reference to the impossibility of modifying Schneider's star persona: undressing her on camera was inconceivable at the time (although, as we shall see, it did happen on rare occasions), and here she remains literally untouchable. In spite of the playful and self-reflexive allusion to its star's typecasting, *Ein Engel auf Erden* fully embraces Schneider's ingénue character, denying this second-degree humour to the Angel/Line, who remains innocent and unaware of the metafictional joke. The film was directed by Géza von Radványi, who had made the more risqué *Girls in Uniform* the year before. The latter film illustrates Schneider's decision to take on bolder roles in an effort to alter her image.

2. Trying to leave the ingénue behind

Much has been written on and recounted in numerous documentaries about the ways in which Schneider tried to 'escape' Sissi. It is the aspect of her life and career that dominates in terms of the contemporary media reception of the star. As we shall shortly see, the event that marked considerable change for Schneider's image was her relocation from Cologne, where she lived with her family, to Paris where she moved in with her new companion Alain Delon. Focusing on the Austrian-French couple is also usually how media, then and now, frame this period. Yet, a couple of years before this rupture in her private and public life the star had already tried to expand and diversify her image, mainly by accepting more dramatic and bolder roles. Because I consider Anne-Claire in *Monpti* (Helmut Käutner, 1957) to be the first of these roles, as well as the best illustration of the conflicts inherent to Schneider's ingénue persona, I will analyse it before continuing with her more 'daring' characters and the erotically explicit presentation of her body in *Mädchen in Uniform/Girls in Uniform* (Géza von Radványi, 1958), *Die Halbzarte/Eva* (Rolf Thiele, 1959), *Die schöne Lügnerin/The Beautiful Liar* (Axel von Ambesser, 1959) and finally *Katia/Adorable Sinner* (Robert Siodmak, 1959).

2.1. *Monpti*

In this tragicomic love story set in 1950s Paris, Schneider plays seventeen-year-old Anne-Claire who falls for Horst Buchholz's character (another familiar face due to their collaboration in *Robinson* the previous year), a penniless Hungarian artist whom she calls 'my little one' ('mon p'tit' in French, hence the title). Schneider still performs the sweet girl but she is less naive than in *Sissi 1*, *Kitty* and *Robinson*; a slight change of character related to the question of sex, following her coming-of-age charted in *Sissi 2*. With *Monpti* appeared a new dichotomy between romantic ingénue and sexy young woman that informed Schneider's career and persona during the years 1956–9. Prima facie Anne-Claire is another one of Schneider's many girl characters who tells white lies (like in *Wenn der weiße Flieder wieder blüht, Mädchenjahre einer Königin* and *Sissi 1*; here she hides her precarious situation to Monpti and pretends to have a wealthy family), and wishes to marry. The desire to become a wife remained in line with Schneider's maiden figure: it drives her characters and/or closes their arcs, and it was a constant reminder of Schneider's social role model in post-war Europe – the personification of marriage, home and family unity. Yet, the role was problematic for her ingénue image, for the main conflict of the film is Anne-Claire's inner uncertainty as to whether she should yield to her urges for physical love. The FSK[2] (the regulatory organization of the German film industry) demanded cuts and amendments. In its justifications it invoked Anne-Claire's 'chastity game' (her 'fluctuating attitude between self-preservation and pre-emptive surrender'), and the tendency for sixteen-to-seventeen-year-old girls to 'identify with the main actress'. Contrary to Sissi who was celebrated for her demure attitude towards marriage and sexuality, Schneider's role as Anne-Claire and her 'willingness for pre-marital surrender' were more than discouraged, it represented a 'risk'.[3] This discussion over morality illuminates the contradictions prevailing in the late 1950s: traditional opinions and modern attitudes towards premature sexuality circulated concurrently (Wierling, 1994; Hake, 2008, pp. 112, 115; Fenemore, 2009, pp. 770–3). Schneider's presentation and performance in *Monpti* demonstrated this ambivalence: a balancing act between the virgin and the sexy young woman.

In Chapter 2, I charted the evolution of Schneider's physical appearance and acting style, as they evolved to be more feminine, and *Monpti* continues this trend. Regarding her appearance, the male voice-over narrator, setting the scene, makes a comparison between Schneider and another woman, rejecting the latter because of her mature look (a busty brunette). More credible for his 'typical love story' is the thin, blonde Schneider wearing soft pink colours (a sleeveless blouse with a Peter Pan collar, Capri pants and a neckerchief), white gloves and carrying a small white basket. Her hair is up in a ponytail, and she is carrying a book under her arm – the generic depiction of the feminine, demure and modest girl, a priori not concerned with sex. To further stress Schneider's purity and nobility, she is framed in her next shot looking with envy and wonder (she smiles, her hands crossed over her chest) at a married couple on the forecourt of Notre-Dame.

Although Schneider's facial features and performance might appear more mature (she is photographed in profile, which emphasizes her jawline, and she sometimes uses her imperious speech tone when Anne-Claire acts arrogant),

---

[2]Freiwillige Selbstkontrolle der Filmwirtschaft.
[3]Minutes of the FSK main committee, procedure 15.069, portfolio *Monpti*, Archives of the Deutsche Kinemathek (Berlin).

the film's overall tone insists on the girlish, almost childlike nature of her character, that previously appealed to audiences in *Sissi 1*. For example, Anne-Claire is afraid of thunder and snuggles in Monpti's arms, Schneider's voice is still high-pitched and soft, and when she cries she excessively lowers her head like a little girl who has done something bad. The actress was therefore balancing her character's twin desires: she performed the girl who was eager to grow up and act 'as a woman' (i.e. have a husband and thereby a sex life), while physically remaining as fresh-faced as Sissi.

Yet, *Monpti* represented a shift away from the outdated, princess imagery. She wears modern and fashionable clothing, she dances a frenzied rock and roll with Buchholz (whose teenage persona was considered very modern at the time due to his roles in *Marianne de ma jeunesse* by Julien Duvivier in 1955, and *Die Halbstarken* by Georg Tressler in 1956, for which he was nicknamed the 'German James Dean', as documented on the US film poster), and some furtive elements of physical eroticism are introduced. In a scene that shows the couple kissing on the banks of the Seine, the wind blows her skirt revealing her legs and underwear. Her legs and high heels recall the pin-up style and the moment might be a reference to the canonical image of Marilyn Monroe standing on a subway grate in *The Seven Years Itch* (Billy Wilder, 1955). Contrary to Monroe's (apparent) confidence and ownership of the instant, Schneider quickly readjusts her dress and looks embarrassed while Monpti adopts a disappointed face after she brushes off his hand coming up her thigh. Yet, her character shows sexual initiative: she decides to pose for Monpti and strips down, revealing her body covered with a towel, her bare back to the camera. Although Anne-Claire refuses to go through with posing and rushes out, the audience gets a glimpse of Schneider's naked body, particularly her back. Her straight posture and thin waist lend her an hour-glass figure – an important detail, for the exposure of Schneider's bare back will become central to her feminine identity.

Notwithstanding this significant development for her image, advertising material favoured the film's romantic angle over its sexual aspect, emphasizing Schneider's maiden role: '[She] is the lovely Anne-Claire, Monpti's innocent lover. A charming *petite Parisienne* with her despairing heart [...]. A beautiful, tender girl who hides her poverty and the depth of her feelings behind dangerous charms [...]' (Herzog Filmverleih, *Monpti* [press release]). The German-speaking media followed the trend, and did not really focus on Schneider's eroticism. They instead pointed out the romanticism of the narrative, and Schneider's 'youth', 'charm' and her 'new powerful performance' (*Der Abend*, 01/10/1957). But some noticed the star's transitional state leading towards maturity and womanhood ('The "Sissi" from yesterday is not an adolescent anymore, and not yet a woman. She stands on the edge of love, modest and desirable, ready to take the leap', *Berliner Montags Echo*, 07/10/1957; '*Monpti* demonstrates her true ability', *Süddeutsche Zeitung*, 16/09/1957). In spite of the film's ambiguous eroticism, in the end the moral status quo is restored: Anne-Claire hesitates too long and dies as a virgin following a car accident. This introduced another unprecedented dimension to her star image – tragedy.

2.2. *Girls in Uniform*

Schneider's princess image was still present in 1957 with the release of *Sissi 3* shortly after *Monpti*. Although Schneider died on screen for the first time in the latter and the theme was touched upon in the former, there is another post-Sissi role to consider: Manuela in *Mädchen in Uniform*/*Girls in Uniform* (Géza von Radványi, 1958). This drama with an all-female cast explores the topic of lesbianism and female affection as the schoolgirl Manuela, who has recently lost her mother, develops feelings for the students' favourite teacher Fräulein von Bernburg (Lilli Palmer), and openly expresses her love before attempting suicide.

One cannot document Schneider's presence in *Girls in Uniform* without mentioning its source: the German classic and (probably) first lesbian film of sound cinema *Mädchen in Uniform*[4] (Leontine Sagan, 1931), with Hertha Thiele and Dorothea Wieck in the Manuela and von Bernburg roles.[5] Contrary to its 1958 remake, *Mädchen* was a commercial and critical success at the time, in West Germany and abroad. Comparisons between the two films were drawn: in the eyes of critics, *Girls in Uniform*'s main flaw was its toned-down treatment of lesbianism and female desire. While Sagan portrays a female point of view on lesbianism (as analysed by Richard Dyer in his 1990 essay 'Less and More than Women and Men'[6]), von Radványi repressed the emotional-erotic approach to the teacher-pupil relationship, replacing it with a less subversive and clearer mother-daughter bond, and insisted on the negative view of Prussian discipline personified by the cold and rigid principal (Therese Giehse). In that regard, comparing *Girls in Uniform* to *Olivia* (Jacqueline Audry, 1950), another film set in an all-girls school (starring Edwige Feuillère, Simone Simon, and Marie-Claire Olivia),[7] is equally instructive to determine Schneider's role. In *Mädchen* and *Olivia*,

---

[4]To avoid confusion I use *Girls in Uniform* to refer to the film with Schneider and *Mädchen in Uniform* (or the abbreviated *Mädchen*) to refer to Sagan's film.
[5]All texts on historical German cinema mention the film which has been the subject of much critical and academic writing: Nancy Scholar (1975), Mädchen in Uniform, *Women and Film*, 2:7, pp. 68–72; Ruby J. Rich (1981), *Mädchen in Uniform*: From Repressive Tolerance to Erotic Liberation, *Jump Cut*, 24/25, pp. 44–50; Karola Gramann and Heide Schlüpmann (1983), 'Liebe als opposition, Opposition als Liebe', in: Hans Helmut Prinzler (ed.), *Hertha Thiele*, pp. 24–43; Richard Dyer (1990), Less and More than Women and Men: Lesbian and Gay Cinema in Weimar Germany, *New German Critique*, 51, pp. 5–60.
[6]Also reprised the same year in his seminal book *Now You See It: Studies on Lesbian and Gay Film*.
[7]See Elaine Burrows (1981), Jacqueline Audry, *Frauen und Film*, 28, pp. 22–7; and Brigitte Rollet (2015), *Jacqueline Audry: la femme à la caméra*.

the central relationship overlaps between teacher-student, mother-daughter and a lesbian romance, and it is the blurring of these lines that makes the film enjoyable. Yet, *Girls in Uniform* separates them, losing (to a large extent) the adoration and palpable desire between von Bernburg and Manuela.

Instead, the film places a strong emphasis on the missing mother. In an early scene that sets the tone (and does not exist in the previous film), Manuela visits her mother's grave to lay flowers. This absence defines the character, and is enhanced by Schneider and her mother's much publicized relationship on and off screen, and therefore pushes the idea that Manuela has to look for a substitute. A second key element is changed from *Mädchen*: the play performed by the girls for the principal's birthday is *Romeo and Juliet* (whereas it is *Don Carlos* by Friedrich Schiller in the 1931 version), and it is during a private rehearsal of Manuela's lines as Romeo that she first kisses von Bernburg (compared to a good-night kiss in the presence of the other girls in the original). Romeo is the romantic hero par excellence, and it is in his guise that Schneider and Palmer share their kiss, thus altering Manuela's homo-eroticism into hetero-romanticism. Finally, while in *Mädchen* Manuela's declaration of love inspires von Bernburg to confront the wrath of the patriarchy (embodied by the headmistress), the end of the 1958 version is more conventional: von Bernburg is reconciled with the principal. The film closes with the latter walking into the shadows of a corridor, but she is not defeated as in *Mädchen*. In the previous scene, the headmistress takes Manuela's hand as she lies in the infirmary, and looks at von Bernburg – both realize that Manuela had not been searching for an erotic or romantic relationship, but a different kind of intimate connection, to fill the maternal void. Thus, by focusing on the mother-daughter relationship, and emphasizing the romanticism of Schneider's role, the film minimizes Manuela's lesbian desire as just an adolescent phase.

That said, the dramatic tone of the film and the role of Manuela demanded a nuanced performance on Schneider's part which extended her acting repertoire with new and subtle variations. As Manuela, she has little dialogue, rarely smiles, rarely makes eye contact and adopts a distant gaze (her character is poised and calm, with an air of sobriety and fragility) – the opposite of the bubbly and energetic Sissi. She also performed more tragic emotions than she has ever done before. Although the emphasis in the film tends not to dwell on the young woman's desire, there are scenes with ambiguous moments, such as the one where von Bernburg gives her shirt to Manuela. In *Mädchen*, Manuela's ardour was expressed through substantial use of close-ups, which are very scarce in *Girls in Uniform*. Yet, rather uniquely, this defining moment for Schneider's character is captured in a close-up of her face: tears appear in her eyes, she moves her head slowly and she smiles. She is moved by von Bernburg's gentleness – there is vulnerability and sadness in Schneider's performance. Rather than Hertha Thiele's erotic anticipation or trembling adoration, at that moment Schneider expresses nonetheless Manuela's desire and makes her convey more than admiration or filial affection for her professor.

This expression of emotion and desire was new to Schneider's image, but the attempt to move beyond Sissi failed. Despite its lesbian romance, a controversial theme at a time when lesbian and gay representations on film were rare, the 1958 remake had no critical or commercial impact, and no hold on Schneider's image. The role of Manuela remained the exception in the actress's consistently light-hearted filmography at the time. She stuck to the well-established trope of the mother-daughter dyad, and continued to star as the ingénue in the romantic films that followed.

2.3. Eva, Fanny and Katia

In 1958, after *Girls in Uniform*, Schneider starred in *Christine*, met Alain Delon and moved to Paris. Still, as a compelling illustration of the extent of her typecasting, her next films remained in well-charted territories with yet more ingénue roles. Although their narratives might suggest modern and risqué topics and incorporate erotic elements, *Die Halbzarte* (Thiele, 1959), *Die schöne Lügnerin* (von Ambesser, 1959) and *Katia* (Siodmak, 1959) did not depart from the traditional and morally conservative trend posited by the *Sissi* trilogy. In the first, Schneider's character Nicole anonymously pens a racy play about sex but the film's treatment of eroticism and *grivoiserie* is misleading. It starts as a funny and open-minded representation of an unconventional family of artists (Magda Schneider appears alongside her daughter in their last collaboration, as well as Josef Meinrad and Richard Eybner from the *Sissi*s), but in the end Nicole marries the male protagonist and is co-opted into the patriarchal family as wife and future mother. In *Die schöne Lügnerin*, Schneider's Fanny is a corsetiere who charms Tsar Alexander I of Russia, Metternich and the French Ambassador (in addition to her fiancé Martin) during the congress of Vienna in 1815. And in *Katia* she plays the title character, a schoolgirl who becomes the mistress[8] and then morganatic wife of Alexander II of Russia, a few months before his assassination in 1881. *Die schöne Lügnerin* and *Katia* are historical costume films in which her characters consistently tell white lies, a formula familiar to Schneider and her audiences. The actress's comic performance around her lies projected the image of the whimsical and charming girl out to seduce the male protagonist (played by Jean-Claude Pascal and Curd Jürgens respectively, both Tsars in each film). All three love stories share an ensemble of traits already associated with Schneider, such as the light-hearted comedy aspect, the mistaken identity plot and the fairy-tale-like ascent of the heroine

---

[8]She was 19 years old, the Emperor 48.

falling in love with a man of higher social background. The novelty was
that Schneider's sexual aura and body (and the ways they were presented)
were now different: these roles meant that she had to appear seductive,
sometimes openly flirtatious, but refrain from being actively sexual within
the narrative.

Die Halbzarte is set in modern times and the attempt to further eroticize
Schneider is visible and more insistent than in her other films. She wears
modern and fashionable clothing, and displays a new dark blond hairdo:
a bouffant short bob with a fringe, whose realization by famous Parisian
maître coiffeur Alexandre was documented in the French press ('Sissi: a new
hairdo for her Parisian fiancé', *Paris Match*, 21/06/1958). Her clothes and
the framing emphasize her legs, hips and buttocks as well. She is introduced
with a close-up of her feet perched on a library ladder, with the camera
slowly traveling up her legs, and onto her tight skirt. Her glasses and her
tight bun refer to the dumb blonde stereotype (see Dyer, 1979) and iconic
representations like Marilyn Monroe, Judy Holliday and Brigitte Bardot,
with a clear reference to the latter in her secretary role in *Une Parisienne*
(Michel Boisrond, 1957). Even more daring for Schneider is a scene in
a nightclub, in which she engages in a flirting competition with another
woman, and slowly runs her tongue along her upper lip, her face close to her
dance partner, with her eyes half-closed. She repeats the suggestive gesture in
front of her bedroom mirror in a short revealing nightgown, practising her
kissing pout, and pursing her red lips. Contemporary magazines featured
the star's new look, but had difficulty connecting it to a change of image
and the Sissi tag was still persistent: 'Romy Schneider (Sissi) changes her
look in Paris' (*Marie-Claire*, 01/09/1958), 'Romy Schneider, the model girl
of German cinema' (*Elle*, 05/01/1959), 'Romy Schneider has chosen sex-
appeal' (*Ciné Revue*, 23/01/1959). Covers featured Romy wearing one of
her form-fitting dresses from *Die Halbzarte* (a top with thin straps and
a low square neck that revealed the shape of her breasts), her green eyes
slightly squinting and looking up, the shape of her lips accented by crimson
make-up (*Ciné Revue*, 23/01/1959, cover; *Revue*, 24/01/1959, cover).

In *Die schöne Lügnerin* and *Katia*,[9] other parts of Schneider's body
were the centre of attention, notably her breasts and waist. As in the *Sissi*s,
costumes enhanced Schneider's feminine body, in line with fashions of the
time. Her most noteworthy costume in *Die schöne Lügnerin* is an evening
dress inspired by the Empire silhouette: dresses were closely fitted to the
torso just under the bust, and then fell loosely below. The high waistline and
the absence of a corset display the long line of the female body, as well as
the curves of the bosom (Aaslestad, 2006). Schneider's periwinkle blue dress
was made of lightweight fabric, creating a flowing effect, with a low neckline

---

[9]*Katia* was yet another remake for Schneider. The original was the eponymous French film by
Maurice Tourneur in 1938 with Danielle Darrieux.

and short sleeves, and her bare arms are covered with long white gloves. Her chest is accentuated by her posture: the moment when she suggestively bends over was used as a production still for the film's press material. As for Katia's dresses, they remain in the same vein as Sissi's: full-skirted ball gowns that relied on crinolines and hoops, with low neckline and short off-the-shoulder sleeves which fit Schneider's petite frame. With the tight bodices emphasizing her lean waist, Schneider wears Katia's opulent gowns with the ease, poise and gracefulness inherited from Sissi. Far from erasing her princess persona, her looks in *Katia* reinforced it.

Schneider's eyebrows were also very noticeable during this period: they were shortened, arched and filled with dark brown makeup, which made them more severe, and left a large nude space at the centre of her face, enlarging her eyes. This alteration had a major impact on her coquettish 'œillade': the uncanny knowingness was reinforced, and her seductive glance, held slightly longer, became more erotically evocative (Figure 5). With this performance sign, Schneider reconciled the two opposite traits of her characters – the ingénue and the seductress. The characterization, dialogue and narrative may signify wholesomeness, but Schneider's eye performance, in tandem with her playful smile, brought a new sense of adulthood. This sidelong 'œillade' was a personal contribution that suggested she was moving towards emancipation: she began to appear provocative.[10]

I have discussed at length Schneider's recurring status as the ideal daughter figure, but in another shift toward her on-screen emancipation, her relationship with paternal figures becomes more significant. Schneider veered from being a young girl paired with a powerful mother figure (notably Magda Schneider, on and off screen), to a sexy young woman, a difference highlighted by her pairing with older father figures in many of her 1956–9 films. Her ambiguous relationship with a father figure first started with *Kitty*, in which the paparazzo's snatched picture of the young heroine with the British politician confirmed that the Schneider-Hasse couple was potentially sexual. Then, in *Scampolo*, *Die Halbzarte*, *Ein Engel auf Erden*, *Die schöne Lügnerin* and *Katia*, Schneider's love interests are all experienced men, portrayed by Paul Hubschmid, Carlos Thompson, Henri Vidal, Jean-Claude Pascal and Curd Jürgens, all ten to twenty-two years older than her. The mother figure, central to Schneider's image of the demure young woman, was progressively phased out in favour of a paternal figure, echoing the redefinition of masculine identities in German-speaking countries.[11] However, this emancipation remained limited and innocent: the play on potentially incestuous father-daughter relations was unequivocal – and

---

[10]I do not comment on Schneider's voice in *Die schöne Lügnerin* and *Katia* because she was dubbed in these two French-dominated co-productions.
[11]See Moeller, 1989 and 1993; Heineman, 1994 and 1996; Lennox, 2004; Krämer, 2012; and Fritsche, 2013.

FIGURE 5 *Schneider's more provocative glance in* Die schöne Lügnerin.

they remained overall patriarchal. Here too the comparison to Bardot is enlightening. While Bardot's characters reflected on the sexual taboo of the erotic father-daughter relationship[12] (in *Futures Vedettes*, Marc Allégret, 1955; *Cette sacrée gamine*, Michel Boisrond, 1956; *Et Dieu ... créa la femme*; and *En cas de malheur*, Claude Autant-Lara, 1958), the on-screen version suggested by Schneider was certainly playful – even rebellious and sexy – but never openly erotic. Schneider's persona was still, above all, defined by innocence and wholesomeness.

* * *

These films, often overlooked in most accounts and writings on Schneider, are in fact emblematic of a turning point in her career and life. They indicate the tension between, on the one hand, continuity with her wholesome persona, and, on the other hand, her departure towards a new era represented by her sexiness, resulting in a grey area in terms of star image definition. Indeed, too much alteration to the ingénue figure could have led to audiences turning away from Schneider's films – continuity has always been paramount for stars as it grounds their personas and solidifies their popularity; but stasis and repetition risk boring both a star and her audiences, in which case modification and variety become necessary.

---

[12]See Ginette Vincendeau (1992), Family Plots: The Fathers and Daughters of French Cinema, *Sight and Sound*, March, 3: 4, pp. 14–17.

As a continuation of what I have termed her coming-of-age over the course of the *Sissi* cycle, Schneider became a sexy young woman: as her body changed and was more exposed on camera (cleavage, legs, back), she asserted a growing sexual identity. Yet, her films' overall narratives remained conventional and normative in patriarchal terms. German-speaking and French producers and distributors wished to hang on to the success acquired with the *Sissis* (and the steady income it represented, Schneider and Seydel, 1989, pp. 108–9) so they repeated the trilogy's well-proofed formula with *Die schöne Lügnerin* and *Katia*, both historical costume films: the spectacle of Schneider's costumes, the glorious sets and the Viennese waltzes remained the central attraction. The motif of the star's *mise en abyme*, as represented by Schneider's arrival at the ball in *Sissi 1*, for example, became even more powerful considering her status in the late 1950s. Examples include when she first appears dressed in her blue gown in *Die schöne Lügnerin*; when she is framed at the top of the stairs in *Katia*; or when her character is chosen by the Tsar to open the ball and she emerges from the crowd (moments emphasized by the solemnity of the music). Schneider is singled out by a style that echoes her appearances in *Mädchenjahre einer Königin* and the *Sissis*.

Producers were still hesitant to show her engaging in explicit sexual relationships with male (or female) co-stars, and her characters' sexual desire was usually a step towards marital bliss and domestic happiness, the pillars of normative women's roles in 1950s patriarchal Europe, where women were 'seen as the foundation of reconstruction and agents of cultural stability' (Weiner, 2001, p. 6). This tension between ingénue and erotic woman reflected the tensions between tradition and modernity at a transitional time for European women's identities, especially in post-war German-speaking countries.

Indeed, the trajectory of Schneider's identity was a product of 1950s West German society, of both youth mentality and the educated bourgeoisie. Sabine Hake (2008, pp. 97, 101, 112) points out the 'narrow-mindedness of [the] emerging *Wohlstandsgesekschaft* (affluent society)', functioning 'as a protection against past trauma' and relying on social conventions, conservative family values, and a sexual repressive morality. Schneider epitomized this proclivity. The cultural imperative of her on-screen intactness (her characters remain virgins and cannot be sexually active if they are not properly married) was rooted in her Catholic, morally solid and bourgeois stepfamily, who continued to present a united front in the media: the message remained that Magda Schneider's dutiful daughter would make a desirable wife. Since Romy's first star image was defined in the early days of her career by both her relationship with her mother and her purity, finding an alternative outside of the codes that determined the 'eternal feminine' (Weiner defines the 'eternal feminine' as 'the ideology [...]

whereby women must ultimately sacrifice their individuality for the good of the family', 2001, p. 38) proved to be challenging.

Therefore, was her emerging modernity a facade? Schneider was concurrently a sentimental and erotic figure: she asserted her sexuality (a source of power and self-determination at the time), but it remained clean and safe. Her wholesomeness, to some extent, represented another facet of modernity – she became the unthreatening modern woman. As Georg Seeßlen has argued, West Germany in the 1950s 'settled for something [that] was neither new [...] nor old [...], but rather a third way in between' (1989, p. 140, quoted and translated in Bergfelder, 2006, p. 48), and Schneider bears out this argument. Like her characters, Schneider's image was suspended between the wish to move forward and the inclination to hold back. In the landscape of late 1950s European cinema and the rise of on-screen eroticism with major female stars such as Sophia Loren, Gina Lollobrigida, Diana Dors and Bardot, Schneider found herself in a delicate position with an emerging new and openly sexy image, that was still burdened by her ideal young woman status.

Thus, Schneider's personal endeavour to accept bolder and more suggestive roles such as Anne-Claire and Manuela, and to refuse the ingénue parts that were presented to her after *Katia* (interview with Schneider by François Chalais, 11/05/1962) in the hope of dismissing her good girl image, created resistance from different parties. Most significantly, the people directly concerned by her acting choices – her parents. Magda Schneider and Hans Herbert Blatzheim had both financial and creative control over Romy's career and press relations. To no longer have full control of Romy's career had consequences on their lives and finances: as we saw in Chapter 1 Magda has been relying on the 'perfect duo' dynamic with her daughter since their first on-screen collaboration in 1953 to regain her prominent star status, which she lost (again) once she stopped working with Romy. As for Blatzheim, he invested Romy's fees into his hotel and restaurant businesses (*Der Spiegel*, 07/03/1956, pp. 34–41), and he insisted that she accept *Sissi 2* and *Sissi 3* (Schneider and Seydel, 1989, pp. 108, 156) and *Katia* for financial reasons (she received the colossal amount of 750,000 Deutschmarks for her role of Katia, Krenn, 2013a, p. 128). But the media did not catch on to these disagreements: internal tensions and pressure were carefully hidden by the parents for whom it was necessary to present the picture of a harmonious family. For example, Romy and Magda attended events for the opening of Blatzheim's establishments, and appeared together at the Cannes Film Festival on several occasions (*Sissi 3* and *Die Halbzarte* were presented in competition in 1958 and 1959).[13]

---

[13]'Romy Schneider at home: at Berchtesgaden' (*Ciné Revue*, 28/03/1958); 'Romy Schneider. Berlin is still Berlin' (*Revue*, 24/01/1959); 'Romy Schneider: Cannes Film Festival' (*Zondagsvriend*, 14/05/1959); 'Alain and Romy: 15 minutes of charm at the festival' (*Paris Match*, 23/05/1959).

3. Rebellion on and off screen

This period of confusion, both for the star and the definition of her image, is well exemplified by *Christine* (Pierre Gaspard-Huit, 1958). In this French costume drama, Schneider reprised the role that made her mother famous in *Liebelei* (Max Ophüls, 1933), which stresses even further the continuity from Romy's previous ingénue roles and the importance of Magda's position in her daughter's career. Romy, due to her star status, had the prerogative to choose her partner and, based on photographs, she selected a *jeune premier* (a heartthrob), French actor Alain Delon.[14]

3.1. A Decisive encounter

Christine tells the ill-fated love story between Franz, a young Lieutenant (Delon), and Christine, an apprentice Opera-singer (Schneider) who commits suicide after he is killed in a duel. The film came out in France in December 1958, three months after *Sissi 3*, and was a great success with nearly three million spectators (Simsi, 2012, p. 23). It clearly benefitted from the highly publicized romantic relationship between its two young stars. Indeed, if *Christine* did not depart from Schneider's dominant *Sissi*-related star image (Christine is sweet, friendly, well-mannered and respectable), it marked a milestone for the continuation of her coming-of-age narrative as a star off screen. Schneider and Delon shared the same slender facial features: square jawline and cat-like green eyes for her, hollow cheeks and ironic smile for him. In the film, they echo each other physically, but also literally: they pledge their eternal love on top of a hill, loudly interlacing their words in the void, echoing one another. They had what has been called 'on-screen chemistry' (see Wright Wexman, 1993; Nochimson, 2002) reinforced by the film's narrative: Delon is as brooding and seductive (Franz has an affair with a married woman which leads to the tragic conclusion) as Schneider is luminous and positive. Christine and Franz are the romantic couple par excellence, which speaks to the hesitation behind Schneider's star image: like Romeo and Juliet, they are beautiful and tragic but do not consummate their love, and just as in many films of that period, she is still a virgin at the end of the film. The Christine-Franz couple reflected the real life couple who attracted tremendous media attention for the entire duration (and beyond) of their five-year-long relationship, one that was not to the taste of Schneider's mother.

---

[14]Delon had only worked in two French films before: *Quand la femme s'en mêle* (Yves Allégret, 1957) and *Sois belle et tais-toi* (Marc Allégret, 1957).

3.2. The rebellious daughter

As I have documented, films with settings that departed from the *Sissi*s (*Robinson*) had more demanding roles (*Monpti, Girls in Uniform*), and more suggestive bodily presentation (*Monpti*) did not truly challenge Schneider's dominant image of the ingénue. But in 1958, she then made the radical decision to cross borders: after *Christine*, her first French film, she moved to Paris with Delon, and kept her distance from the German-speaking film industry and her family. However, her on-screen image lagged behind her off-screen life. As we saw, the films that she made after this relocation (*Die Halbzarte, Ein Engel auf Erden, Die schöne Lügnerin* and *Katia*) still carried her wholesome young woman image. Her departure for Paris was widely covered by the media on both sides of the French-German border, and is still the object of journalistic examinations (documentaries *Legenden: Romy Schneider*, 1998; *Un jour, un destin*, 2010; and *Romy, de tout son cœur*, 2016). A common discourse is that the French- and German-speaking press were opposed at the time: that the first welcomed her with open arms whilst the latter insulted her. Although it is true that their opposing views had repercussions for Schneider's career, my research suggests that this chasm took a few years to take hold. I believe that this infamous Germanic trend that saw her 'rebellion' as taking aim at the nation (Schneider was Sissi and, thenceforth, a national treasure) was in fact gradually assembled around the mid-1970s and continued up to the present day (Senfft, 1992; Troller, 2007, pp. 22–32; Krenn, 2013a, pp. 141–2).

My research shows that the beginning of the polarization between German-speaking and French-speaking press and audiences had its roots in a continuous false account of the mother-daughter dynamic. Because Schneider left the family home and her 'exemplary mother' (*Elle*, 05/01/1959, pp. 48–51), and was living out of wedlock with a French man, she betrayed the motherland ('Romy Schneider: in exile for love', *Quick*, 07/10/1962; *Der Spiegel*, 13/03/1963, pp. 79–84): a line of discourse reframed in the 1970s by the French press to the benefit of Schneider who, with the help of Delon, finally 'broke free' from Germany and the malevolent Magda (Arnould and Gerber, 1986; Muscionico, 2008; Isaac, 2009; Thibault, 2010; Petit, 2014). As I shall examine later, the media turnaround on the Schneider family saga – its volume and endurance – casts a light on national, cultural and social motivations in 1970s France and West Germany. Although it is difficult to pinpoint the exact origin of such rhetoric, my investigations indicate that the depreciation of the French press for Magda do not date from her daughter's first departure for France, but later, when Romy shared with reporters how it became important for her to participate in Occupation films.

I challenge this French myth of the smothering and evil mother. Indeed, in-depth research into Romy's own writing, television appearances and press coverage shows that Magda and Romy's relationship was not as conflictual as the French media were eager to report in the 1970s. As it was later revealed (see Schneider and Seydel, 1989), there were indeed some quarrels at the time, but as far as I can tell it was not known by the French, German or Austrian audiences in the late 1950s, and in fact the press was rather cordial, and circulated an image of off-screen domestic bliss that echoed the family tropes on display in Schneider's films.[15] Some film journals even saw her engagement with Delon as positive for her career, and expressed hope for collaborations with artists of the Nouvelle Vague in Paris.[16] Romy's stepfather insisted on the couple's regard for their family's bourgeois, traditional and catholic values: 'If Romy marries, it will be announced according to all social rules' (*Bravo*, 13/07/1958). Eight months later, on 22 March 1959, he organized an engagement ceremony in the family villa in Morcote near Lugano (Switzerland) attended by the European press (print and television). Photographs show that the fiancés wear formal and fashionable clothes (a suit and a tie for him, a designer dress for her with a pendant cross around her neck) and both display fashionable hairstyles. Mother and daughter look radiant, smiling at the cameras: Romy with a large bouquet in her hands, and Magda on Delon's arm. Another photo spread (commissioned by *Bunt*, and featured in *Paris Match* too) shows the young couple spending the 1962 Christmas holidays in Lugano: they bring presents, decorate the tree, enjoy a stroll in the gardens and bake in the family kitchen wearing aprons covered in flour. Proof if any that German-speaking audiences did not hold a grudge – yet – after her departure for Paris, the popular press pleaded for her to come back to Germany after completing *Die schöne Lügnerin* and *Katia* ('Romy Schneider - Enchanting as in *Sissi*', *Österreichische Film und Kino Zeitung*, 20/06/1959). The media insisted that there was a demand from European audiences for films similar to the *Sissi*s (or better: a fourth *Sissi*) and that she had 'disappointed many fans with sex' (*Funk und Film*, 08/08/1959).

Conclusion

My analysis of Schneider's career trajectory during the 1956–9 period reflects the global and persistent 'in-betweenness' (Meyers Spack, 1982) that became characteristic of her star image after the *Sissi*s: she moved from role to role and yet remained associated with Sissi. Her typecasting

---

[15]'Romy Schneider: a wonderful fairy-tale-like career' (*Jeunesse Cinéma*, June 1958); 'For Romy "Sissi" Schneider, Alain Delon has only one face: the face of love' (*Point de vue, Images du monde*, 27/03/1959); 'Romy Schneider & Alain Delon: this spring's bride and groom' (*Bunte*, 11/04/1959).
[16]'A French-Austrian co-production' (*Österreichische Film und Kino Zeitung*, 04/04/1959).

in the post-*Sissi* years proved rather complex: she carried an image that walked a fine line between continuity and change. Schneider's box-office draw declined between 1958 and 1959, yet due to the success of the *Sissi* trilogy she remained the best paid female star of German-speaking cinema. In 1959, her fees per role ran from 500,000 to 750,000 Deutschmarks (Krenn, 2013a, p. 128), although she fell from first to twentieth place on German film theatres' popularity scale (*Der Spiegel*, 13/03/1963, p. 82; Schneider and Seydel, 1989, p. 161). Profaning her virgin persona was also an issue for French producers, who apparently could not envision the star outside of her well-established identity that had made her recognizable, and therefore profitable, in continental Europe. After *Katia*, she refused roles that appeared too similar to her ingénue image or the *Sissi* films, though it is necessary to keep in mind that the discourse of Schneider trying to 'escape Sissi' is also part of a larger and retrospective construction informed and fuelled by journalistic accounts. In spite of Schneider's audacious decision to move to Paris, and the breaking of her perfect fit with the Sissi figure, a full transformation of her on-screen image required several years in the second phase of her career, which took an international turn.

PART TWO

Romy Schneider's international career: 1960–1969

4

Negotiating an alternative image in European art cinema

Introduction

Part II focuses on the construction of Romy Schneider's persona through her film roles and media presence in the second phase of her career, which first took a wider European turn in terms of film production (and not just film reception as was the case for the *Sissi* trilogy). This new phase was, as we saw in the previous chapter, initiated in the last two years of the 1950s, and then followed an international curve. The 1960s represent a complex transition period for Schneider. Particularly in the first half of the decade, she projected a glamorous image of femininity, yet continued to present a series of paradoxes. In her career in German-speaking cinema, this tension concerned the old and the new, tradition and modernity. During this second phase, her persona oscillated between three conflicting poles: the sophisticated *bourgeoise*, the 'serious actress' of art cinema and the erotic woman. Part II is divided into three chapters, but does not necessarily follow a strict chronology, as her films of the period did not fit into neat categories and phases.

1. *Lysistrata* and *Plein Soleil*: transitional roles

Contrary to what is commonly asserted by the media, two of Schneider's roles before *Boccaccio '70* contained elements which were laying the foundations for a new haughty and erotic image. Therefore I will analyse her appearances in *Die Sendung der Lysistrata/The Expedition of Lysistrata*

(Fritz Kortner, 1960) and *Plein Soleil/Purple Noon* (René Clément, 1960) before engaging with her artistic collaboration with Luchino Visconti.

In 1958, Schneider moved in with Alain Delon in Paris. Her declarations to the press signalled her desire to be considered a serious actress by European filmmakers and critics (interview by France Roche, 1961; interview by Georges Kleinmann, 19/02/1962; Schneider and Seydel, 1989, p. 155). Schneider's first encounter with a serious drama occurred in 1960 in the controversial television play *Die Sendung der Lysistrata*, directed by Fritz Kortner and based on Aristophanes's *Lysistrata*. The TV film intertwined historical and modern settings in a self-reflexive *mise en abyme*. Agnes (Barbara Rütting, who also plays the title role) has invited a couple (Schneider in the double role of Myrrhine/Uschi Hellwig, and Karl Lieffen) to watch the broadcast of a television play in which she stars. The two female characters also appear in this TV film located in ancient Greece where Lysistrata persuades the other women to withhold sexual privileges from men as a means of forcing them to end the long and destructive war between Athens and Sparta. In the role of Myrrhine, Schneider teases her husband (Peter Arens) with the prospect of imminent intercourse; she sensually lies down on her bed and directs her husband's actions ('lie down', 'close your eyes'), but refuses him at the last minute. In another scene, she guides his hand to cup her breasts above her dress, bites her lower lip and expresses her desire to have sex. *Die Sendung der Lysistrata* had many critics in West Germany, who objected to the play's morality (*Der Spiegel*, 14/12/1960, pp. 83–4)[1] and it received negative responses in the press,[2] although Kortner toned down Aristophanes's crude dialogue.[3] Significantly, reviews were not enthusiastic over Schneider's performance, pointing out how 'strange' it was to hear 'the interpret of Sissi' delivering sexually connoted dialogue (*Der Spiegel*). Schneider's overtly sexual role and performance clashed with her sweet image, but it did not succeed in changing it. More significant in this respect is her cameo in *Plein Soleil*.

Schneider appears for a few seconds at the beginning of *Plein Soleil* – one of the films credited for turning Delon into a major international star – in

---

[1]Notably the ARD (Arbeitsgemeinschaft der öffentlich-rechtlichen Rundfunkanstalten der Bundesrepublik Deutschland, a joint organization of Germany's regional public-service broadcasters) in the states governed by the CDU (Christlich Demokratische Union Deutschlands), such as Württemberg-Baden and Bavaria.

[2]The play finally aired on 17 January 1961 at 10 pm with the exception of Bavaria (Na sowas, *Der Spiegel*, 25/01/1961, pp. 50–61) where, shortly before the broadcast, the film was released in some cinemas with an eighteen-year-old age restriction by the FSK (Lysistrata: Südlich der Gürtellinie, *Der Spiegel*, 18/01/1961, pp. 57–9). *Die Sendung der Lysistrata* aired on Bavarian television screens on 20 April 1975.

[3]Amongst other alterations, Kortner omitted a passage in which Schneider's character should lament that she has not had an 'eight-inch comforter' in a long time (*Der Spiegel*, 18/01/1961, pp. 57–9).

an uncredited and unnamed role as one of the friends of the American character Freddy Miles (Billy Kearns). She wears a chic red dress, long black gloves, a black leather handbag on one arm, a golden bangle at the other, and her chicly coiffed brunette hair is parted in the middle. The mise-en-scène deliberately highlights her cameo: she is at the centre of the frame, surrounded by Freddy and Philippe Greenleaf (Maurice Ronet). With one hand she slowly adjusts her hair to clear her face, she flares her nostrils, lifts her gaze (Kearns and Ronet are taller than her) and looks from left to right as the male characters talk to each other, then she smirks and slightly purses her lips when Greenleaf and Freddy mention Tom Ripley (Alain Delon). When the latter enters the frame she readjusts the bag on her arm, tilts her head to her left, then offers her familiar 'œillade' (she lowers her chin and looks up at him) in a subtle mix of evaluation and contempt. Before speaking her penultimate line, she moistens her lips and then she urges Freddy quite aggressively to 'Come along!'.

Schneider's brief appearance in *Plein Soleil* is more meaningful in many respects than her short time on screen would suggest. Whilst the media discourse attributed her professional reinvention to Luchino Visconti (whom she met through Delon during the shooting of *Plein Soleil*), I, on the contrary, argue that Clément's film is premonitory in terms of Schneider's new image: she speaks French for the first time on screen, looks stylish and modern and displays haughty expressions.

2. The partnership with Visconti

Visconti and Schneider's short-term collaboration (the year 1961, and their brief reunion for *Ludwig* in 1972) had a long-standing impact on her persona. Their artistic pairing was an intricate filmic and extra-filmic construction that incorporates – but is not limited to – the myth of the author as Pygmalion (a Cypriot sculptor who falls in love with the perfection of his own statue) modelling a star (Pygmalion's creation Galatea), or of the active/passive dichotomy of the muse inspiring the artist through her mere presence. In Greek mythology, Muses were the goddesses of inspiration for literature, science and the arts; this idea of muses as beautiful women providing artistic inspiration wrapped up in sexual allure has continued throughout the decades, despite its overtly sexist connotations. The notion of 'a creative man inspired by a beautiful woman' has been as prevalent in film as anywhere, not least amongst male auteur cinema. However, as Nicoleta Bazgan (2011, p. 204) points out, 'the re-evaluation of the actresses' contributions raises questions about the collaborative nature of cinema, [...] they also undermine the concept of the male auteur'. As a result, for Bazgan, female stardom 'has more recently become a potent means of escaping the

Pygmalion grasp, shifting the discussion from the cult of the author to the female star's cinematic contribution' (p. 214), which is precisely what I will demonstrate here. Visconti and Schneider, through their common work, and especially 'Il lavoro', both embraced and renegotiated the Pygmalion/muse trope, leading to a new phase in her career and star image.[4]

2.1. *'Tis Pity She's a Whore*

Their first project together was also Schneider's first stage experience in the leading role of Annabella in Visconti's stage adaptation of the Renaissance tragedy *'Tis Pity She's a Whore* by John Ford, at the Théâtre de Paris. Alain Delon co-starred. Although the production was not highly praised,[5] two decisive features in the overall development of Schneider's new image are on display – acting and eroticism. French critics and audiences were agreeably impressed by Schneider's performance (Korte and Lowry, 2000, p. 123; Violet, 2000, pp. 123–4). *Jours de France* commented: 'Romy was a lovely film actress. In a two-hour dress rehearsal Paris discovered a *comédienne*'(12/06/1963, p. 61, my emphasis). Notice the French idiom 'comédienne', a semantic particularity that distinguishes film actors from their stage colleagues who enjoy a historically superior status. It also signifies that Schneider had to earn her image of 'seriousness' through hard (stage) work, proving herself worthy of the title. Thenceforth, another layer was added to her emerging new persona – suffering. Working with Visconti was difficult, he was strict and could be abusive, and Schneider was exhausted (after the premiere she had to have an operation for acute appendicitis, but she was back on stage fifteen days later). Additional details of Visconti's treatment emerged later from various sources (Violet, p. 120) including the star herself. When evoking *Boccaccio '70* and *'Tis Pity She's a Whore*, she explained how Visconti pushed her to her limits but that his inflexible directorial approach gave her confidence and made her 'give all she had' and produce her best work (Schneider and Seydel, 1989, pp. 173–7). At the time though, the press discussed the transformation of Schneider's image into a 'serious actress' in infantilizing and condescending terms (professionally and privately, she relied on adults: her mother, Marischka and now Visconti). To some extent, she colluded in this discourse by presenting Visconti as 'her master', and 'the one who taught her everything' (interview by France Roche, 1961; she reiterated her allegiance when she dedicated her first César award in 1976 to him). Critics went even further, saying that he revealed

---

[4]For more on the Pygmalion myth and the muse, see Gayle A. Levy's book *Refiguring the Muse* (1999) and Felicity Chaplin's chapter on the muse in *La Parisienne in Cinema: Between Art and Life* (2017).
[5]'For Romy and Alain: flowers and thorns' (*Cinémonde*, 18/04/961).

her 'feminine essence': 'He teaches her how to focus, how to use every fibre of her being and thus become aware of her femininity and her real power of seduction' (Benichou and Pommier, 1981, p. 55). This derogatory (and I would argue, eroticized suffering) aspect of their Pygmalion-muse relationship was the cornerstone of the dramatic and intense actress persona for which Schneider became known in the 1970s.

Although a handful of publications praised Schneider's performance ('Romy triumphs in Paris', *Bunte*, 22/04/1961), *'Tis Pity She's a Whore* was sparsely mentioned in the German-speaking press (*Der Spiegel*, 11/01/1961, p. 63) – the reception of the play marked the starting point of the Germanic media's rejection of Schneider. I argue that this denial over Schneider's expansion of her acting register (her first stage role, and in French) was not only based on Germanic nationalistic appropriation, but on the misogynist refusal of her expressed wish to explore her acting abilities and expand her career. This is why the Pygmalion-muse relationship between Visconti and Schneider is particularly complex. As I examine it from a feminist perspective, Schneider's view on her own career through her comments in the press shows a clear case of internalized sexism. The praise over Schneider's new type of performance can therefore be traced back to her role of Annabella, but it was as Pupe in Visconti's film episode 'Il lavoro' that she reached a bigger audience and tightly intertwined her new wider acting range with her burgeoning erotic image.

2.2. *Il lavoro*

During the summer recess of *'Tis Pity She's a Whore*, Schneider went to the De Paolis Studios in Rome to shoot Visconti's segment of the anthology film *Boccaccio '70*, a programmatic title as the filmmakers (Vittorio De Sica, Federico Fellini, Mario Monicelli and Visconti) drew on the erotic aura of *Decameron* by Giovanni Boccaccio, suggesting that audiences would only be 'ready' for such a film by 1970 (Korte and Lowry, 2000, p. 123). Visconti's episode, 'Il lavoro'/'The Job' is set within a luxurious palace and tells the story of a young aristocratic couple in crisis after the husband Ottavio (Tomas Milian) is exposed in the newspapers for visiting prostitutes. He is urged by his lawyers to make amends with his wife Pupe (Schneider) as she supports the couple financially, via her rich Austrian father who has now frozen the accounts. Realizing that she has been betrayed, Pupe announces that she is planning to find a job to avoid boredom and become financially independent. At the end, she demands of her husband that he pay her to have sex. Ignorant of his wife's suffering, he writes a cheque to Pupe who lies on the bed, crying.

In the previous chapter, I examined some attempts in post-*Sissi* films to increase Schneider's erotic allure. With her first television and theatre roles, this process continued and a new persona began to emerge. Visconti's episode in *Boccaccio '70* represents a high point of this sensual evolution. Her transformation is crystallized around two points. First, there is a tension between the haughty, high-class inflected persona of Pupe (an aristocrat), and her vulnerability. Secondly, Visconti's film steps up Schneider's erotic display and aura in a number of ways: through its theme (marital prostitution), the radical reveal of the star's body, and through the ostentatious use of couture costumes designed by Coco Chanel.

Schneider's introduction in 'Il lavoro' is a classic delayed star entrance: no one in the palace knows where Pupe is, they all look for her, and she only appears after 12 minutes, lying on the bedroom floor. The palace is a jewellery box, and Schneider is the crown jewel within the lavish interiors, props and costumes. Pupe writes on a notepad, with a kitten between her elbows, a cigarette in one hand and a smooth jazz tune on the record player. She ignores her husband when he enters and tries to start a conversation, as she mouths her text and satisfyingly smiles. When Ottavio evokes the newspapers' 'lies', she slowly takes her hat off, runs her hand through her hair and casts a knowing side glance at her husband before lying back on the floor, ignoring his tirade. Ottavio talks, but the camera stays with Pupe, capturing Schneider's lack of reaction and careless attitude in a close-up. She sits up and recites her text. She slightly squints and when Ottavio asks what it is, she says: 'a poem, stupid', raising her chin and eyebrows, putting her lips forward to pronounce distinctly the word 'scemo' ('stupid'). Then she keeps her upper lips slightly raised and looks up at Ottavio with deep contempt. The camera stays on Schneider's face in close-up when she ironically asks him if he likes her poem, putting her head forward, pursing her lips and frowning, then she switches in a second to a seductive tone and presses her chin on her shoulder, looks down and says that she 'adores it' (lengthening the [o] on the Italian word 'adore'), and looks up seductively to her husband. Then, Schneider demonstrates Pupe's coldness: she mocks her husband's predicaments, walks with her hands on her hips and her cigarette in her mouth. She freely moves from one room to another, fixing her hair with a black headband as she goes (Alexandre de Paris attended to Schneider's hair), and arguing and laughing uproariously at Ottavio's remarks: she owns the space. Schneider speaks with energy, ordering her husband and the servants around, either in German, or in Italian, dragging the words out. Her elocution, along with her condescending attitude, confers class confidence to Schneider's performance.

Pupe seems to hold the upper hand over her cheating and whining husband: she decides to work to prove her independence, but she is unqualified – she is an idle, privileged woman who painfully understands that she has nothing to offer but her body. Indeed, while Schneider renders Pupe haughty, moments of vulnerability in her performance reveal that the Countess puts on a face, such as when she speaks on the phone with the lawyer. She wants Ottavio to believe that his actions do not affect her, and cynically talks about the hypocrisy of her marriage of convenience, but once he leaves the scene, her true feelings are revealed. Visconti's mise-en-scène and Schneider's performance signal this intensification and the poignant change of tone for the character: the jazzy chamber music of Nino Rota (Dyer, 2010, p. 111) grows louder and Pupe's grief is reinforced by an extreme close-up of Schneider's face and eyes, her voice breaks, her eyes start to glisten, she flares her nostrils and a single tear rolls down her cheek. The importance of Schneider's eyes is emphasized by her make-up: her double-winged eyeliner on the upper lid and a beige pencil line on the lower lid illuminate her green eyes; moreover, Schneider's eyebrows at the time are recognizable for their thickness and their lines extend towards her temples. This focus on the expressivity of Schneider's face (her character's emotional portraiture) brings forward a different articulation of desirability that displaces her feminine sensuality from her body to her face and 'feline' eyes (underlined by the kitten). Similar to the spectacular, to-be-looked-at-ness moments when the narrative is suspended and we admire the star's beauty and body (Mulvey, 1975), the close-ups of Schneider's face and eyes are moments when the narrative becomes secondary, allowing audiences to gaze at the star's beauty and 'enjoy' her performance of vulnerability.

A feminist reading of 'Il lavoro' helps analyse Schneider's ambivalent persona in the early 1960s. The segment presents a contradiction. Visconti adopts an empathetic point of view on her character (she suffers from her superficial and boorish husband) and constructs the episode's narrative around her perspective, which is rather rare in his cinema that generally presents 'a dark view on women' (Cottino-Jones, 2010, p. 85). Yet at the same time he associates his empathy with the aesthetic pleasure of exposing Pupe's vulnerability and the torment of a betrayed woman (see Clément, 1988). Visconti's mise-en-scène, Giuseppe Rotunno's cinematography and Nino Rota's music capitalize on Schneider's anguish for aesthetic purposes: the moments where she is most beautiful are framed through extreme close-ups of her green, cat-like, perfectly made-up eyes in tears, magnifying her fragility and pain. This tension underlines a certain masochism on the character's part: Pupe knows that she is in love with a worthless man, but she deliberately chooses to stay in this toxic relationship (Pupe is rich, she could therefore start a new life if she wanted to). In the end Visconti punishes Pupe: she has lost the power play in her interaction with her husband, and submits to the gender-normative organization of marital roles.

Beyond the accent on her face, the mise-en-scène of Schneider's erotic performance in this film illustrates another change of persona, by exposing her body. This process is visible in a key sequence in which Pupe takes a bath, a telling moment that presents the star as the object of a voyeuristic and fetishist male gaze. Schneider picks up the phone in the boudoir, walks with it into a vast dressing room and starts to undress; still talking on the phone she ends up in the bathroom. She speaks vividly in Italian and removes her clothes with ease. In a medium close-up in front of a mirror, she hands the phone to her maid, removes her white slip dress and examines the reflection of her face and shoulders, adjusting her hair and pearl necklaces, smiling, raising her chin, visibly content with what she sees. The pearls complement Schneider's sun-tanned skin. Her body is lithe (in another shot her arched spine and shoulder blades are visible), and only filmed from her back (the frame stops at her back dimples), as in the scene in *Monpti*. She sits on a stool and resumes her phone call. Schneider's entire naked body is filmed for the first time, but it is a small-scale reflection on the bathroom's mahogany walls, in profile, her legs crossed. Then she turns three-quarter to the camera, her breasts covered by her upper arms (she holds the phone with both hands); the camera rises slightly to leave her breasts out of frame. Schneider's erotic display is more explicit with this role, but the mise-en-scène keeps it discreet and tasteful: the context is a woman doing her toilette – a scene familiar from art history. The tone of the scene changes when the camera very briefly adopts Ottavio's point of view: we previously left Pupe to follow his narrative line, and when he re-enters the boudoir we see Schneider in the background seated on a stool, a towel loosely tied around her body. He then appears at the bathroom door and the camera rapidly zooms in for a close-up of Schneider's wet upper back, neck and hair. The narrative is built around Pupe's perspective, but here Visconti's mise-en-scène underlines male desire. In a tighter close-up, Schneider looks above her shoulder: there are drops of water on her face, her hair is tied up but wet, curly locks frame her face and fall on her forehead, her makeup is less visible and she frowns and says 'What do you want?' (Figure 6). She pretends not to understand her husband's intention (the camera cuts and zooms in on his face and he looks at her, nods with a smile, and eats a grape). He comes behind her and caresses her shoulder and neck. Schneider does not act troubled, and continues her toilette. This long (and fragmented) sequence shows Pupe/Schneider as aware of the power of her body, her eyes carry an explicit expression of both superiority and sensuality.

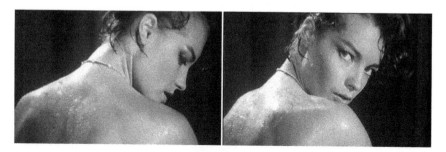

FIGURE 6 *The erotic display of Schneider's bare back in* Il lavoro.

So far, I have analysed elements of Schneider's appearance, behaviour and performance that created a new image of high class-inflected superiority coupled with vulnerability, as well as erotic attraction. Another layer is that of maturity, to which her Chanel costumes largely contributed, showcasing her move from a girl to a woman. The costumes are visually prominent in 'Il lavoro' (she changes clothes three times and makes other minor changes in-between) and they enhance the actress's erotic and vulnerable performance – as Schneider dresses down and up again she is rendered both desirable and touching. Her main costume is the signature tailored suit launched in 1954 in Paris, the embodiment of the Chanel post-war style. It is traditionally made in soft tweed, with a straight, square, collarless jacket, three-quarter-length sleeves split at the wrists, patch pockets, jewellery buttons and assembled with a lining (with visible stitching) that matches the blouse or the bodice, and a slightly flared knee-length skirt. The recognizable two-tone nude shoes with a rounded black toe-cap and a matching small tweed hat complete the look. The head-to-toe ensemble is accessorized with the characteristic Chanel assortment of ropes of pearls and camellia-shaped earrings, a gold chain and a coin belt. Throughout the episode, there is consistent coordination between her costumes and other mise-en-scène elements: the colour palette, fabrics, jewellery and accessories harmoniously echo Schneider's makeup and the colour scheme and richness of the set. Her grey suit matches her bedroom walls and velvet bed cover, and her pink blouse and jacket's silk lining complement Schneider's lip colour. The actress wears two other Chanel designs that harmonize with the set: a gold brocade ensemble with dark brown fur hat and stole, and a blue dressing gown of shimmering silver brocade on voile.

This coherent aesthetic vision reflects the perfect synergy between Visconti's idea of Pupe as a distinguished mature woman, Schneider's performance and the style of the House of Chanel, synonymous with luxury, wealth (there is a large bottle of Chanel No. 5 perfume standing prominently next to Pupe's bathtub) and a modern, privileged, kind of womanhood. Wearing Chanel was to adopt a philosophy of independence, comfort and understated elegance (Steele, 1997, p. 28; Baxter-Wright, 2012, p. 75). Chanel opposed designers such as Dior and Balenciaga who triumphed at the time with their corseted silhouettes and theatrical dresses (such as the New Look), and instead offered 'practical' fashion, better suited to active women. The tailored suit represented both the traditional *bourgeoise* and elegance associated with the image of the *Parisienne* and casual *chic à la française*[6] (Baxter-Wright, p. 89). To further illustrate how well the Chanel suit matches Schneider's persona, I will once again make a comparison between her and Brigitte Bardot. Like Bardot in *Et Dieu … créa la femme* Schneider

---

[6]Other examples include Jeanne Moreau in *Les Amants* (Louis Malle, 1958) and Delphine Seyrig in *Baisers volés* (François Truffaut, 1968).

was twenty-two when she made 'Il lavoro', but while Bardot was perceived as a *young* rebel with her tousled hair, jeans or shirt dress with rolled-up sleeves, Schneider's suit was part of her new image as a distinguished 'lady'. Even the cut of the suit affects body movement: it appears to demand a pose akin to that of a model. Vogue editor Bettina Ballard explained that Coco Chanel 'invented that famous Chanel stance that looks as relaxed as a cat and has an impertinent chic; one foot forward, hips forward, shoulders down, one hand in a pocket and the other gesticulating' (Picardie, 2011, p. 288). In Visconti's episode, we see Schneider stand with one foot and hips forward, one hand on her hip and she moves gracefully, with feline ease. Chanel herself might have taught the star this particular stance and way to walk: a photo session of the two women at Chanel's atelier for a fitting for the film shows them standing together in front of a mirror, perhaps practising? Schneider adopted the tailored suit and other Chanel designs in her everyday life and in her press appearances, thereby transferring her on-screen chic, affluent image off screen (*Jours de France*, 15/09/1962: 'Chanel, the inimitable perfection'). However, the critical reception of Schneider's role and erotic performance in 'Il lavoro' attests to patriarchal attitudes and traditional gender expectations in the early 1960s.

Media discourses privileged Visconti's influence in Schneider's professional transformation, downplaying her own agency and reducing her abilities as an actress to the erotic display of her body. *Der Spiegel* summed up the transformative process of her image and career, still referencing her past and the sweet Empress: 'Sissi became sexy' (*Der Spiegel*, 13/03/1963, p. 84; 'Adieu Sissi, Bonjour Romy', *Festival*, 01/10/1961; 'Romy Schneider writes her name with the S of Sex and Sensation', *De Post*, 28/07/1962). Critics only briefly considered her artistic agency: the reporters who focused on the collaboration between the director and the actress mentioned her contribution, but attributed the locus of power, and the paternity of her 'transformation' (Wagner, 1962) to Visconti (and Alain Delon, see later). Although she wanted to dismiss her Sissi image and she negotiated paradoxical traits in her performance of Pupe, extra-filmic texts did not valorize the star's artistic labour, culminating instead in the most literal version of the Pygmalion myth of artistic collaboration – placing the star on the celestial pedestal of pure love ('Luchino Visconti's last love', 'Luchino Visconti fell in love with her', *Mascotte spettacolo*, 28/02/1962). Even more revealing was the press's emphasis on the unthreatening aspect of her sexiness: her eroticism was glamourous and tasteful in its presentation and graceful in its performance, and therefore not subversive. As the critic from *Nouvelles littéraires* wrote: '[She] brilliantly *plays* Brigitte Bardot but she is not Bardot' (13/09/1962, my emphasis). This line of discourse was also rooted in her physique (her petite figure), while Sophia Loren and Anita Ekberg, the other female stars of *Boccaccio '70*, presented the 'abundance of their good looks' (Swamp, 1963, p. 16) and 'played their type' (Wagner, 1962). I will now further my examination of Schneider's transition in the early 1960s by considering her relationship with Delon and the couple's dynamic with respect to their careers and stardom.

3. The myth of the Schneider-Delon couple

During the period under examination in this chapter, Romy Schneider and Alain Delon influenced each other's careers and respective stardom. At the beginning of their relationship, Schneider's immense popularity undoubtedly played a part in Delon's emerging career. His seductive persona was rapidly established with *Christine*, *Faibles Femmes* (Michel Boisrond, 1959) and *Le Chemin des écoliers* (Boisrond, 1959) (Le Gras, 2015, p. 49). However, this dynamic in which Schneider had the upper hand soon went into reverse. Delon's career took off with leading roles in *Plein Soleil* and *Rocco e i suoi fratelli* (Visconti, 1961), whilst hers stagnated. Progressively, the media coverage of their relationship put his image at the forefront, and Delon's celebrity and status overtook his fiancée's. The couple first appeared together on the cover of *Cinémonde* (17/07/1958) and the magazine organized a contest to win a day with Schneider, but less than a year later Delon was pictured on his own (02/04/1959), and it was now his turn to be offered to the readers as trophy. Within six months, between June 1959 and January 1960, his fees increased exponentially, from two to thirty-five million French francs (Violet, 2000, p. 99).

Schneider's superior status and involvement in Delon's career when they first met were never acknowledged by the media, who quickly depicted her as the supportive and caring woman, proud of her man's accomplishments: 'Romy is in Milan. She is not involved in a film, but is here to comfort her "warrior" [...], holding her fiancé's hand' (*Cinémonde*, 29/03/1960). After their official engagement in Schneider's parents' villa in Morcote in March 1959, the couple was for several years the constant object of speculation from the European press regarding their prospective union,[7] to the point of being called the 'eternal fiancés' (*Paris Match*, 02/09/1961; 'Romy and Alain are tired of being the eternal fiancés: we'll get married before Christmas', *Oggi*, 13/09/1962), and the 'fiancés terribles' (echoing the French expression 'enfants terribles', *Nous Deux Film*, 09/1960), emphasizing their common disdain for the traditional marital institution. When Schneider went to the United States in 1963, the French media reported that she had been advised

---

[7] 'Alain Delon and Romy Schneider: When are we getting married?' (*Cinémonde*, 03/11/1959); *Ciné magazine*, 01/06/1960; 'Alain Delon and Romy Schneider: don't hold your breath for the wedding' (*Cinémonde*, 08/11/1960); *Ciné Revue*, 24/02/1961 (interview with Alain Delon); 'Cannes - Alain and Romy, the same mysterious ring' (*Paris Match*, 19/05/1962); 'Hey: we live!' (*Bunte*, 05/08/1961).

not to mention to the US press that she was living with her fiancé out of wedlock, but that she had nonetheless been outspoken about it, proudly stating that 'marriage [was] just a vulgar piece of paper' (Swamp, 1963, p. 16). The title 'Europe's little fiancés' ('petits fiancés de l'Europe') is also often used in the contemporary media discourse on the stars and reprised in academic and non-academic works (Haymann, 1998, p. 43; Vincendeau, 2000, p. 171; Le Gras, 2015, p. 152) while in fact, to my knowledge, it was not mentioned in the press coverage of their relationship between 1958 and 1963. 'Europe's little fiancés' is a phrase charged with the symbol of post-war reconciliation between France and Germany (the pairing of 'France's Don Juan'[8] and Germany's national treasure), and was certainly used retrospectively in that sense in the following decades and still today.

Beyond national concerns, the significance of their pairing touched upon an alliance of different classes and social types between the sweet girl and the rebellious boy. Schneider's non-marital relationship with Delon represented a departure from her Sissi persona embedded, as we saw, in the wholesomeness of marriage and family. The Schneider-Delon couple projected the fantasy image of a serendipitous match between two opposites: she was a popular star, adored all across Europe, she came from a bourgeois family where she was protected and her virtue was valued, he on the other hand was an outsider with a proletarian background, known for his insubordination in the French Indochina War, his insolence and his devilishly handsome looks (Vincendeau, 2000, p. 171; Violet, 2000, p. 98; Le Gras, 2015, p. 50). However, Schneider and Delon shared foundational elements for their star couple image: they were young and beautiful. In the previous chapter, I referred to their physical resemblance in *Christine*, and Visconti capitalized on this intriguing aspect, pushing it further by casting the couple as brother and sister and incestuous star-crossed lovers in the play *'This Pity She's a Whore*; he said:

> It is a very difficult play, and it needed young, fresh and beautiful actors for the audience to understand why they choose each other. This pair of perfect lovers had to stand out [...]. And, Alain and Romy, they look a bit like brother and sister.
>
> (*France-Observateur*, 30/03/1961)

Filmed interviews of the early 1960s show the actress in love (her eyes light up at the mention of Delon), and she insists on the important role her fiancé plays in both her career and personal life. She credits him for encouraging her to wait for 'the right parts' and 'giving her confidence' (interview by François Chalais, 11/05/1962) and for introducing her to Visconti (interview by France Roche, 1961) and allegedly giving her 'permission' to grow

---

[8]Le Gras, 2015, p. 46.

up: 'You are a woman [...]; it is time that you become a woman on screen too' (Swamp, 1963, p. 16). Indeed, Schneider's sex-appeal in *Boccaccio '70* was not only attributed to Visconti's directing, but also to Delon: because she was 'deeply in love', therefore '[expressing] so truly and evidently love [on screen]' (*Le Film Illustré*, 15/07/1962, *Ciné Revue*, 14/06/1962: 'Romy Schneider: talent is love'; Swamp, 1963, p. 16). Schneider's projection of sexuality on and off screen was thus attributed again to the influence of a man.

She also 'candidly' shared her desire to start a family:

> [...] to make a life together, a real life outside of this profession' is '[more important than her career] to me, and that was not the case before [...], because if it [her career] stops, you have nothing left. If you don't have someone, or a life, or a corner [a home] where you can go, or a child ... No, no, I have something above this profession and I hold on to it, and I want to keep it.
>
> (Interview by François Chalais, *Reflets de Cannes*, 11/05/1962)

Celebrity coupledom has always increased an audience's desire for knowledge of a couple's private life, especially matters of sex. Martha P. Nochimson (2002) explores how the great on-screen couples that show heightened attraction (she calls them the 'synergistic couple') are 'a cultural legacy of what we thought [...] about desire and love' (p. 5). In the early 1960s, the Schneider-Delon pairing engaged with the culture of marriage by reinforcing an ideal image of the heterosexual couple. Although Schneider was living with Delon out of wedlock, she continued to be seen as the paragon of traditional, patriarchal-approved femininity, and was thus presented as a model of identification for female audiences. Because her love was portrayed as 'pure' and her intentions to subscribe to domesticity and motherhood were clearly stated, she remained cemented to the foundation of her previous ideal young woman image – modern, with the right amount of sex-appeal, and submissive to the men in her life. As we saw earlier, the power relations between the two stars went into reverse: as a steady topic of the tabloid press, their coupling created and multiplied media discourses, but they also reinforced gender stereotypes and patriarchal norms. The Schneider-Delon couple – mostly constructed off-screen – already contained at this early stage the founding elements of the synergistic couple that would burst on-screen a few years later in *La Piscine*.

The French media tended to deny Schneider's agency and self-determination in her career, and yet simultaneously created a paradoxical dual narrative: she managed to rid herself of Sissi, but still remained attached to it. Moreover, at the time of the New Wave, a cultural prejudice against popular film in general, and the *Sissi* trilogy in particular, emerged amongst French critics who belittled the massive success of her ingénue character. In turn, Schneider followed this elitist line of discourse and started to deprecate her earlier Germanic career. A telling example can be found in two interviews conducted by French journalist François Chalais during the Cannes Film Festival in early May 1962, where *Boccaccio '70* was presented in competition alongside *L'Eclisse* by Michelangelo Antonioni, with Delon. In the first interview, the reporter praises her 'courage and her intelligence' and congratulates her for successfully changing her Sissi image, with a deliberately condescending attitude towards Marischka's films, but on the other hand, he takes his leave saying 'goodbye Sissi'. Chalais's second interview, featuring the star couple, illustrates Delon's blatant sexism (he cuts Schneider off, answers questions addressed to her) and the media's unequal treatment of the two actors. Beyond this particular occurrence, she was continuously asked to comment on her private life, while he shared details of his professional projects and rarely mentioned Schneider.

Schneider and Delon's breakup in December 1963 was widely reported in media.[9] The overall – frenzied and detailed – account[10] of their separation depicted Schneider as a weepy and abandoned young woman on the verge of hysteria.[11] Here too she faced a double-standard: in accordance with her persona as part of the star couple, the breakup with Delon and his subsequent marriage with actress Nathalie Barthélemy were considered both a sacrifice and a failure for Schneider, but not for him. The gossip press alleged that she could not have a child, therefore the separation was a blessing in disguise for him,[12] but an admission of defeat for her as he married his new fiancée who soon gave birth to their son: 'Nathalie, the little script-girl, succeeded where the sweet Sissi failed: she is Mrs Delon' (*Noir et blanc*, 26/08/1964).[13] The separation was met with derision in the German-speaking press that

---

[9]During the shooting of *La Tulipe Noire* (Christian-Jaque, 1964) in the summer 1963 in Madrid, Delon and Nathalie Barthélemy (who did not star in the film but was staying with Delon in his villa) began their relationship. They married on 13 August 1964 and their son Anthony was born on 30 September 1964. They separated in 1968.

[10]It is said (Schneider, Delon, and other sources have different recollection of the facts) that their friend and agent Georges Beaume went to Hollywood when Schneider was filming *Good Neighbour Sam* (David Swift, 1964) to deliver Delon's twenty-page-long breakup letter, and then she flew back to Paris to find a bouquet of red roses with a note that said, depending on the versions: 'I'm off to Mexico with Nathalie. A thousand things. Alain', or 'Romy-Schatz, I'm sorry'.

[11]'Judy Garland and Romy Schneider: their nervous breakdowns' (*Cinémonde*, 18/02/1964); 'Romy Schneider: She has been sleeping for a month to forget Alain Delon' (*Tempo*, 07/03/1964); 'Romy Schneider: I will always love Alain' (*Garbo*, 12/09/1964); 'Romy Schneider told Françoise Prévost what no actress had ever dared: "I have sacrificed the man I love"' (*Marie-Claire*, September 1964); 'Romy Schneider in loneliness hell' (*Cinémonde*, 06/10/1964); Seydel and Schneider, 1989, pp. 191–8.

[12]'One night, Romy lost Alain by telling him the sad truth … ' (*Noir et blanc*, 26/08/1964).

[13]With hindsight, we also know that Delon had an affair (amongst others) with the singer Nico, and that their son Ari was born on 11 August 1962. The affair was kept secret and, to this day, Delon never recognized his paternity.

dismissed Schneider for her (alleged) arrogance and ingratitude towards the Germanic film industry and audiences: the rumours spread that she refused to star in German-speaking films or speak in her mother tongue to reporters (*Der Spiegel*, 25/12/1963, pp. 100–1). Her years spent in Paris with Delon were associated with sex and freedom, and her abandonment was seen as a deserved punishment. She later addressed these rumours, receiving reporters in her new home in Berlin-Grunewald where she met theatre director Harry Meyen (married at the time, then divorced, and then remarried to Schneider in 1966), gave birth to their son David and put her career on hold. The return to the conventional family model and a reconnection with her previous immaculate image of the decent girl from the *Sissi* films were positively received by the media (Korte and Lowry, 2000, p. 125), but the prejudice linked to her reportedly looking down on her native cinema and audiences persisted – it would also later prove decisive in the reception of her image of her French films in 1970s German-speaking countries.

Conclusion

Romy Schneider's persona in the early 1960s was conflictual: the media presented her as still attached to traditional, moral standards, yet also yearning for defiance, transgression and change. *Boccaccio '70* marked a definitive change towards a new erotic persona, but also a different trans-European stardom. She had already crossed borders in terms of reception but she was now doing so in terms of production. By working with Visconti, a filmmaker strongly associated with Europe in terms of production, source materials, and choice of actors, Schneider became linked to her capacity to embody several nations/nationalities without every fully embracing one. In 'Il lavoro' she notably displays her (Western) trans-Europeanism through language: Pupe is an Austrian woman who speaks German, but also Italian, English and French. Moreover, as in most Visconti films, 'Il lavoro' has a European literary foundation: the episode is an adaptation of Guy de Maupassant's short story *Au bord du lit* (1883), the husband Ottavio reads in French the novel *Les Gommes* by Alain Robbe-Grillet (1953) and there is a German copy of *Der Leopard* by Giuseppe Tomasi di Lampedusa (*Il Gattopardo*, 1958) on Pupe's couch, Visconti's next film adaptation with Schneider's fiancé Delon. Through her work with Kortner, Clément and Delon, her first stage experiences, and her partnership with Visconti (an aristocratic aesthete whose oeuvre invoked highbrow cultural references), Schneider's star image became associated with high culture, auteur cinema and sophisticated eroticism, giving an alluring new singularity to a young star who already had a successful and well-defined 'first' career. These traits also promoted a cosmopolitan aspect that significantly would define the rest of her career, which was about to take an international turn. After the critical success of her performance in *Boccaccio '70*, she worked in five European countries (Austria, France, West Germany, Italy and the UK) and in the United States, and collaborated with European and American authors and directors in genres and languages (notably French and English) that were new to her, as I shall explore next.

5

The international star

After the critical success of her performance in *Boccaccio '70*, Romy Schneider's next career phase took a global turn. Over the course of the 1960s she pursued her 'metamorphosis as a serious actress' (Hanck and Schröder, 1980) with a variety of roles in various genres of European art cinema, and went on to work in Hollywood productions. I start this chapter with Schneider's presence in European films, the majority of which are French or French-dominated co-productions (such as *Le Combat dans l'île/Fire and Ice*, Alain Cavalier, 1962 and *La Voleuse/The Thief*, Jean Chapot, 1966), and/or filmed in Paris (*The Trial*, Orson Welles, 1962). The second part focuses on her participation in US runaway productions that were filmed in Europe (*The Victors*, Carl Foreman, 1963; *The Cardinal*, Otto Preminger, 1963 and *Triple Cross*, Terence Young, 1966), and her roles in two Hollywood romantic comedies (*Good Neighbor Sam*, David Swift, 1964; *What's New Pussycat?*, Clive Donner, 1965). Traits that would permanently define her persona transpired during this liminal time despite the extremely diversified nature of her films – with, first, her internationalization through multilingual performances. I follow Sabrina Yu's (2012) distinction between 'international' and 'transnational' stars; the former refers to 'a star who achieves international recognition and fame, even if he or she never makes a film outside his or her own country', while the latter is used to describe stars who 'physically transfer from one film industry to another to make films, often in a different language from his or her own' (pp. 1–2). In the films analysed in this chapter, Schneider fits the 'transnational' label as she speaks French and English, and her progress is traceable (her German accent was prominent at first, but attenuated fairly quickly); she also dubbed herself in the French, German and English versions of her films. Another defining trait was the change undergone by her on-screen sexual identity and representation of female emancipation, which brings forth a subjacent question: to what extent did her film characters problematize representations of modern womanhood, and endorse patriarchal models?

1. Schneider's European art films

Schneider's first role after completing 'Il lavoro' was on European stages when theatre director Sacha Pitoëff gave her the role of the aspiring actress Nina in his adaptation of *La Mouette* (*The Seagull*, 1896) by Anton Tchekhov for a five-month tour in France, Switzerland, Belgium and Luxembourg, that debuted in mid-January 1962. The role was previously held by Delphine Seyrig at the Théâtre Moderne in Paris, but for a European tour the Karsenty-Herbert organizers decided to capitalize on Schneider's better-known name, her enduring Sissi image and her European popularity. This choice apparently paid off as the tour was a great success (*Jours de France*, 12/06/1963, p. 61). To my knowledge, there are no video recordings of the play, only photographs that show Schneider in character, wearing a white, high-collar dress, her hair either up in a chignon with a fringe or in a wig with locks cascading down her back with a big ribbon knotted in a half-ponytail. The photos depict her declaiming her text with her chin up, maintaining her straight posture (looking up, her chest open, shoulders down, arms open on her sides with the palm of her hands facing up). Her romantic composition of Nina, an idealistic young woman who longs for a stage career echoed Schneider's first German-speaking performances back in the mid-1950s, as did the aspects of her performance pointed out by the press – the natural style and simplicity of her acting. *Jours de France* said: 'To the elaborated, cerebral, and noble performance of Delphine Seyrig, Romy opposes a performance of trembling spontaneity, her asset is sincerity' (03/02/1962).

Although Schneider was based in Paris at the peak of the movement, she never participated in nor was she identified as a star of the New Wave. However, she gravitated around the French film movement by working in two 'quasi-New Wave' films: *Le Combat dans l'île* and *La Voleuse*.[1] She shot *Le Combat dans l'île* in November 1961, before embarking on *The Seagull*'s

---

[1] I have to mention Schneider's participation in the first feature film of French director Guy Gilles, *L'Amour à la mer* (1964). Her scene was eventually cut but this romantic film might be assimilated to the New Wave in view of its formal experimentations, existentialist dialogues and its behind the scene's youthful and good-natured spirit – Juliette Gréco lent her Parisian apartment in lieu of set, friends of Gilles had minor parts (Jean-Claude Brialy, Jean-Pierre Léaud, Sophie Daumier, Alain Delon). If the film echoes the early 1960s zeitgeist with themes such as insouciance, teenage and hesitant love relations, and the Algerian War as a backdrop, Schneider's perfomance as the 'vedette' (the star) resembles more of a cameo and she appears in the film in her everyday, off-screen and elegant day-time Chanel look – not exactly the incarnation of the more casually dressed New Wave star.

European tour, but the political film came out months later in September 1962. It was the first feature of young French director Alain Cavalier, a former assistant of Louis Malle (whose *Ascenseur pour l'échafaud* in 1958 is considered a precursor of the New Wave), who supervised the film. Although *Le Combat dans l'île* is not considered part of the New Wave canon,[2] it does share a similar aesthetic, notably in terms of black-and-white photography, naturalism and location shooting, with films of the movement such as *Moderato Cantabile* (Peter Brook, 1960), or *Jules et Jim* (François Truffaut, 1962), and it makes a clear reference to *À bout de souffle* (Jean-Luc Godard, 1960) with the use of the Hôtel de Suède location. *Le Combat dans l'île* was filmed in Paris and Normandy, in the Moulin d'Andé and along the banks of the Seine. The Moulin d'Andé (a mill) was a location already seen in *Jules et Jim*, a film referenced also through the plot's love triangle, and the presence of actor Henri Serre.

Le Combat dans l'île is now one of Schneider's many forgotten films, yet her performance of her character's growth introduced French audiences to the type of women and female sexuality for which the actress would become known in 1970s France. She plays Anne, the wife of Clément (Jean-Louis Trintignant[3]), a right-wing extremist who fails to assassinate a Parisian member of parliament because of his accomplice's betrayal. Clément leaves Anne to hide with his friend Paul (Serre) and goes on a revenge mission. Anne and Paul fall in love, and she resumes her acting career on the Parisian stage, but when Clément returns he challenges Paul in a duel and dies. Made against the background of the French colonial war in Algeria, the film deals directly with political engagement by showing the contemporary French political climate. Clément is a racist, and, while it remains unnamed, his terrorist cell resembles the OAS ('Organisation Armée Secrète'), the right-wing secret army fighting against Algerian independence.[4]

Apart from its political narrative, *Le Combat dans l'île* engages with complex gender relations. Anne stands at an existential crossroads, at the centre of a love triangle between two opposite depictions of masculinity (Clément is violent, jealous, possessive and unstable; Paul is tender, supportive and understanding). In the first part of the film, Schneider represents female resilience and submission in the face of overwhelming patriarchal aggression: she is mistreated and abused by Clément who wants

---

[2]Neither Michel Marie (2003) nor Richard Neupert (2007) include the film in their discussion, only Sellier (2008) briefly considers it in regard to her analysis of New Wave films displaying a 'nostalgia for a heroic masculinity' (pp. 139–41).

[3]The original draft manuscript of the script written by Cavalier and preserved at the Cinémathèque Française indicates that the filmmaker's first choice for the role was Alain Delon.

[4]Due to this sensitive reference, *Le Combat dans l'île*'s censorship approval was delayed, which explains the film's presentation on the sidelines of the 1962 Cannes Film Festival at the cinema rue d'Antibes, and only with a special authorization (Benayoun, 1962a). It was then distributed in September 1962 (Sellier, 2008, p. 139).

to control her; he slaps her, amongst other physical and verbal brutalities. He disapproves of 'women who behave badly', that is, women who live in a modern, liberated way, which is precisely the path taken by Anne in the second part of the film when, in the absence of her husband, she falls in love with his friend. Therefore, in parallel with the political theme, *Le Combat dans l'île* is very much about its female protagonist's development towards independence. In that sense, Anne's femininity is comparable to other representations of women in early 1960s French cinema, particularly the paradoxical heroines of the New Wave who *appear* modern on the surface but are the result of misogyny (Vincendeau, 2000, p. 120), especially in the way they are relentlessly reduced to their sexuality and their love life (Vincendeau, 2000, pp. 110–35; Sellier, 2008, pp. 145–83). In the spectrum of New Wave women, Anne shares some characteristics with 'Mademoiselle Nouvelle Vague' (Cayatte, 1958; de Baecque, 1998, p. 75): she is young, idealistic and romantic ('I want to live, and you are destroying me!', she says to Clément), and the original draft manuscript of the script indicates that she is 'playful and cheerful'. However, even if Anne demonstrates a hunger for hedonistic pleasures (she likes Mozart, books, boat-party and champagne), the typical 'Mademoiselle Nouvelle Vague', as embodied by Anna Karina (*Vivre sa vie*, Jean-Luc Godard, 1962; *Bande à part*, Godard, 1964) and Jean Seberg (*À bout de souffle*), is more akin to a gamine figure (more romantic and less sexual), while Schneider and her character occupy a place closer to the chic and intellectual role developed by Jeanne Moreau in *Ascenseur pour l'échafaud* and *Jules et Jim* (see Vincendeau, 2000, pp. 121–30; Sellier, 2008, pp. 184–98). *Le Combat dans l'île* takes place in a bourgeois (Clément and Anne's richly decorated flat and their Citroën DS) and intellectual milieu (Paul's publishing house), and Schneider, even if she is young (twenty-three years old), performs a woman rather than a *jeune fille*, especially as she becomes pregnant. This is also construed through her behaviour and clothing that place her in a more 'grown-up', sophisticated idiom. Indeed, contrary to the 'sexed-up' presentations of her nude body in some of her post-Sissi films (with a sensual peak in 'Il lavoro'), Schneider's figure is downplayed by classic and elegant costumes (a black strap dress, large turtle-neck jumpers, trousers, a large camel overcoat). As is the case for the New Wave women referenced above, Schneider's beauty and erotic appeal are subtler and mainly manifested through her face rather than her body, which is not much in evidence. For instance, after Trintignant's departure, she wanders in a white nightgown in Paul's house, and with her soft voice and her natural brunette hair cut short she portrays a fragile, ethereal beauty. Then, Anne progressively comes back to her joyous self: the oval shape and whiteness of Schneider's face are emphasized by a black turtle neck, strong and dark eyebrows, and the way she combs her hair back, revealing her forehead.

Notwithstanding her overt narrative emancipation, Schneider's character considerably lacks agency: her trajectory is from abject submission to a fascist ('Without you I am nothing, I do not exist') and his abusive behaviour, for which she seems to express fascination ('I am a bitch'), to becoming a muse for an artistic/bohemian and peaceful man. Even if Anne expresses her desire by carrying on an extramarital love affair, she realizes her need for self-realization and professional emancipation only through the intervention of a man, Paul. After she expresses her lack of ambition Paul encourages her to resume the stage career she previously abandoned for Clément. Geneviève Sellier (2008, p. 141) aptly describes the process: '[the film] makes the woman's emancipation depend on her encounter with a "positive" man, after her dependence on a man who alienates her. This is a curious way to describe emancipation, which indicates a persistent suspicion regarding women's capacity for autonomy'. Anne's trajectory goes even further in her contradictory representation of modernity: her newly found independence and ambition to work are compromised by maternity. Upon discovering her pregnancy, Anne wishes to have an abortion and Paul drives her to Geneva, but out of love for him she changes her mind. Schneider's character is therefore depicted as paying the consequences for her sexual freedom. Though the film remains open-ended (it closes on Anne and Paul's embrace once he has killed Clément), the assumption is that Anne may well accept the male-constructed responsibilities imposed onto her gender and opt for motherhood and domestic life over her career.

This interpretation was reinforced when the French-speaking press conflated the character with the star, unanimously praising her portrayal of a 'free woman'. Schneider herself insisted on the term 'modern woman' when she described Anne in interviews (France Roche, 1961), and the media linked her freedom to her 'self-awareness', her 'choice' to carry on with her pregnancy now that she has found the 'right man' (Sengissen, 1962). Schneider, like Anne, was described as 'revealed' (*Candide*, 07/09/1962; *L'Aurore*, 13/09/1962; Mardore, 1962) through the star's 'radiant femininity', making her an 'accomplished *comédienne*' (Benayoun, 1962b) because of the 'free choice' her character made on-screen. Schneider's feminine identity was therefore still inscribed within traditional gender representations. Even though those New Wave's images may have appeared more tolerant to women's exploration and expression of sexual desire, they ultimately valued motherhood and romance, distancing once again Schneider from self-propelled on-screen female emancipation.

Jean Chapot's directorial debut *La Voleuse* (1966) is another of Schneider's films that may be assimilated with New Wave aesthetics: black-and-white photography, a dreary urban decor (the straight lines and whiteness of the protagonists' intellectual, bourgeois flat in a modern apartment block, in contrast with the factories, car parks, train station and wasteland depicted elsewhere), fragmented editing and modernist music (reminiscent of

Hiroshima mon amour, Alain Resnais, 1959). Furthermore, Marguerite Duras, the New Novelist whose work was associated with the New Wave, notably with her script for *Hiroshima mon amour* and her adaptation of her novel *Moderato Cantabile*, wrote the dialogue for *La Voleuse*. Focusing on the punishment of sexual emancipation and motherhood, the film is exemplary of Duras's long-standing interest in women's experience (see Hill, 1993). Set in West Germany (the film is a French-West German co-production), *La Voleuse* centres on Julia's (Schneider) torment as she steals back her young son (Mario Huth) whom she gave away in her teenage years, while her husband (Michel Piccoli, in his first of many roles alongside Schneider) tries to persuade her that the couple who lovingly raised the child have the better claim. The boy's adoptive father (Hans Christian Blech) climbs on top of a smokestack and threatens to jump if Julia insists on keeping the child. The pre-credit sequence suggests that the film will focus on its female lead and sets up Julia's state of mind: Schneider stands in front of a white background and looks astray, she speaks but is inaudible under the discordant music. The tense and anxious atmosphere created by industrial landscapes of the Ruhr region photographed in black and white echoes Julia's predicament. In reality, the film never considers the child, nor his adoptive mother, and instead stands out for its representation of a 'deranged' woman whose identity is entirely defined by dysfunctional motherhood, obsessive behaviour (Julia stalks her son's adoptive family) and her relationship to her husband. We know little of her outside of this role, she is supposed to have a job, but the film never presents what she does. It leads us to become alienated by Julia and to feel sympathy for her husband who goes to such an extent to control her that he locks her into their apartment (to 'protect her and the child from [herself]'). As the voice of reason, he has the moral high ground over Schneider's character, and when Julia surrenders, the image of Piccoli carrying the child in his arms is the last shot of the film. *La Voleuse* can be read as stemming from a position of backlash against women for their access to modernity – that is, determining their own life, and following their pleasures: Julia did what she wanted in her youth, had 'too many lovers', and chose to step away from motherhood. *La Voleuse*'s narrative offers a 'common sense morality': Julia 'steals' the child (hence the film title), so even though she is the biological mother the narrative sympathizes with the adoptive family (the original German title relates to the child's father's desperate attempt: *Schornstein Nr. 4*, meaning 'Chimney No. 4'), and her husband. Regarding Marguerite Duras's input on such a negative take on female modernity, biographer Laure Adler (1998) does not offer much insight. There is a thread in Duras's work in which she defends 'bad' mother figures and portrays them as transgressive to patriarchal norms (see her infamous text 'Sublime, forcément sublime Christine V.', *Libération*, 17/05/1985), which suggests that there could have been a more sympathetic presentation of Schneider's character at the time she gave up the child. But Adler argues that the only 'transgression' here was in Duras's intervention as a screenwriter (the way she appropriated the story), not in the narrative *per se*, given that Chapot considered that his film's viewpoint was *still* too oriented towards the female protagonist ('I wanted to show the thief and the abducted, she [Duras] dragged the film to the thief', quoted in Adler, p. 623).

Chapot's editing style consists of a series of short and fast-edited scenes without expository transitions, which strips away any affective elements in order to further enhance his star's performance. Schneider is on screen during the entire film, and her face, mostly framed in medium- and close-ups, draws all the attention. Her hairstyle, revealing her large forehead, and her pale makeup (pale lipstick) make her look older and distraught. Her performance style is, for the first time, extremely affected, and the choice of music adds to her tormented look. She appears to be languishing, as if every line (and there are not many), interspersed with long silences, demands a considerable effort. She constantly frowns, and her heavily made-up eyes express a deep sorrow. She also bursts into violent episodes in which she throws her head in all directions, her short hair brushing off her face. Piccoli's character contains her, enveloping her in his arms. In this respect, *La Voleuse* begins to consolidate the tragic dimension of Schneider's star persona that was briefly introduced in *Girls in Uniform*, *Christine* and *Le Combat dans l'île*. Her character is brittle, obsessive, melancholic and self-centred. Although the film received mixed reviews from the French-speaking press, Schneider's performance was praised. In a similar way to her work in *Le Combat dans l'île*, her representation of a dysfunctional (even potentially deadly) feminine identity was viewed as evidence of her 'intelligence' as a performer (Rabine, 1966a). Because this film, like several other of Schneider's works in the 1960s, failed commercially, her career evolution into a European auteur cinema star was largely ignored by audiences. At the time, she was a young mother living with her husband Harry Meyen and her baby son David in the posh suburb of Berlin-Grunewald. Her film career was on hold, and she was not as present in the media in either West Germany or France.

2. International co-productions

Having examined Schneider's roles in two films that illustrate ideological tensions in the representation of women in early 1960s European auteur cinema and confirm her emerging 'tragic' persona, I wish to turn to a group of films that evidence Schneider's internationalization.

At the beginning of 1962, Schneider performed in *The Trial* (1962). The film, written and directed by Orson Welles, adapted the 1925 eponymous novel (*Der Proceß* in the original German title) by Franz Kafka.

The black-and-white production is French, West German and Italian; the cast is international (with American, French, German and Italian actors); and the film was shot in Rome, Milan, Yugoslavia and Paris, at the then-abandoned Orsay station. Set in modern times and narrated by Welles, *The Trial* recounts the misadventures of Joseph K (Anthony Perkins), an ordinary man arrested, judged and condemned to death for an unspecified crime in an unnamed authoritarian country. Though innocent, Joseph K begins to feel a sense of guilt. Schneider plays Leni, the servant, nurse and mistress of the Advocate Albert Hastler, performed by Welles. The film received polarized reviews in France and English-speaking countries, but the French press unanimously acclaimed Schneider's performance. Being confined to a supporting role in a vast cast of characters, Leni's identity and personality are not particularly developed in the film. Therefore, and like the other major female characters in the film (played by Jeanne Moreau and Elsa Martinelli), she is essentially defined by her sexuality and solely intervenes in the narrative through seductive acts. Schneider is paired with Perkins who was a few years older than her, but Leni has two other older lovers – the bedridden Advocate, and Bloch (Akim Tamiroff), one of the Advocate's clients whose trial drags in length.

She wears a white nurses' uniform in a sexually suggestive way (the knee-length dress is tightened with a belt and unbuttoned at the top in a plunging V neck, similar to Brigitte Bardot's work overalls in *Et Dieu … créa la femme*), a thin gold chain and her short brunette hair is styled with curly locks down her neck and around her face. Her forehead is clear (no fringe), a detail that impacted her look by further revealing her face and drawing attention to her eyes. I have examined in previous chapters how Schneider's body was gradually revealed in films such as 'Il lavoro', which 'modernized' her erotic aura. I also pointed out how her face and her eyes, captured in close-ups, participated in building her on-screen sensuality. Her performance in *The Trial* continues in that direction. Her eyes are the first thing we see of Leni when a peephole opens, and, as in *Le Combat dans l'île*, her eyebrows are thickened and lengthened by makeup, emphasizing her gaze. Her familiar 'œillade' also comes into play in the film: while Joseph K's uncle talks to the Advocate, Leni casts insistent glances at K to attract his attention. Then she slowly walks out of the room, but stops regularly to make sure K is following her by seductively casting side glances towards him above her shoulder. The advocate explains that his nurse has a predilection for his clients, specifically the accused with whom she falls in love. Performing a character who is overtly unapologetic about her sexual desire, Schneider is constructed as desirable by Welles's camera. In a large dark room, she lies down on a pile of dossiers spilling over the entire room and presents her face to Perkins to kiss; they embrace and she pushes him down the mountains of files and papers. Perkins was a tall man and Schneider had to raise her chin, enhancing her square jawline; she pushes that movement even further by tilting her head back to expose her throat while putting her arms around Perkins's and Bloch's shoulders. Leni represents a moment of levity and peace for Joseph K in the general grim ambience of the film, but like the other female characters, she illustrates a version of anxiety – her gentleness and compassion are a source of guilt for K. She also applies lotion onto Welles's torso, their two faces are very close to one another, and her smirk and assured gestures of care create a sense of connivance between the two characters. He slaps her on the buttocks when she is done and she reacts with a smile. Schneider's coy smile, accompanied by the 'œillade', recalls her previous playful roles: these facial expressions cultivate a sense of charm and childish tenderness (a reporter called it 'her impudence', *L'Est Républicain*, 28/12/1962) but also of calculation and ambiguity. Schneider's construction of sensuality did not depend on her naked body, she used eyes and head movements to create a seductive allure. Leni wants sex and is shown as 'easy'. However, Schneider's acting and star persona bring class and a certain mystery to the character, an elusiveness that renders Leni alluring and avoids falling into vulgarity.

The Trial was released in cinemas a few months after *Le Combat dans l'île* and the press again praised Schneider's performance, confirming the critics' assessment that they were witnessing a 'transformation', and yet they still systematically referred to Sissi. Jean de Baroncelli in *Le Monde* (1962) wrote: 'It is definitely time to forget the *Sissis* and to give this actress a place worthy of her talent'. For Henry Rabine in *La Croix* (1963): '[She] confirms her performance in *Boccaccio '70*. There can no longer be any doubt: the late Sissi is a great actress. And even better, she is pretty'. Praising Schneider's acting in her 1960s films by using a language that favourably contrasts her present skills to her past work thus maintained the cultural prejudice against the *Sissis*, and Schneider's previous work in popular cinema. I shall further explore in the second part of this chapter how Schneider responded to this elitist rhetoric. Others were also prompt to notice how her subtle acting skills were beneficial for what was viewed at the time as a depiction of complex femininity ('[T]his actress seems to be promised to roles that would further enhance the psychological resources of femininity', Lovet, 1963), a type of femininity that was extoled as singular, but that fundamentally exposed the misogynist foundations of a male-constructed concept of womanhood deeply rooted in a patriarchal culture that equated femininity with sexuality.

The French-speaking press was also undivided in its assessment that Schneider distinguished herself from the other European actresses in *The Trial*. Amongst them she was often compared to Jeanne Moreau. Leaving aside the fact that Moreau was a decade older than Schneider (respectively thirty-four and twenty-three at the time of filming) and historically articulated a different type of femininity, critics praised Schneider's perennial 'sweetness' to Moreau's 'harshness' and mature look. This ageist evaluation of Schneider's romantic femininity was based on her looks in the film: because her forehead was uncovered it was described as 'honest', her 'white neck' was soft and her eyes were 'gay' (*Paris-Press-L'Intransigeant*, 30/12/1962; Capdenac, 1963). Thus, regardless of her move towards art cinema, Schneider's filmic persona retained some traces of the ingénue, and a youthful mischievousness dominated her version of sexiness – especially when seen in contrast to Moreau's 'tired' femme fatale (which Leni's dialogue defines as 'old'), and Martinelli's cool elegance. Media discourses applauded Welles's direction for the success of her performance as well as, again, the beneficial impact of Delon's love on his fiancé's beauty. Nonetheless, the star's own agency was slightly more in evidence compared to the critical reception of 'Il lavoro': progressively, the recognition of her acting skills provided her with a certain legitimacy and accomplishment. Welles's own comments were reported: 'Romy is the best actress of her generation. She soon will be the greatest' (*Paris-Presse-L'Intransigeant*, 31/05/1962).

Working with Welles brought Schneider international recognition and her international career expanded even further with a stay in Hollywood and several roles in US films. In June 1963, Schneider received an 'Etoile de Cristal de l'Académie du Cinéma' (as best foreign actress) for her performance in *The Trial*.

Schneider's performance as Leni had a lasting impact on the types of women she played on screen: sex-driven women who *appear* elusive, superior, in control of their body and desire. The actress's green, cat-like eyes accentuated by makeup, as we saw, were key in composing her elusiveness. Her 'œillade' and long static stare carried a pointed knowingness and confidence in her sensual power. The roles of Claire and Imogen in respectively *10.30 pm Summer* (Jules Dassin, 1966) and *Otley* (Dick Clement, 1969) are significant in that regard. In *10.30 pm Summer*, Schneider plays Claire, a young woman who accompanies a couple of friends (played by Melina Mercouri and Peter Finch) and their child (Isabel María Pérez) on a road trip through Spain. The film, shot on location, is an international co-production (Spain, US, France), with a script co-written by Marguerite Duras from her eponymous novel, and an international cast and crew (Dassin was an American working in France at the time, Mercouri was Greek, Peter Finch was an English-born Australian). In this ménage à trois, Maria (Mercouri) and Claire share a tacit agreement: the latter knows that the former wants her to seduce and have an affair with her husband. Schneider is both the younger rival and the friendly and caring accomplice, her character is a tool in the narrative and her body is therefore visually exploited for erotic purposes. The mise-en-scène enhances Schneider's looks in the film: she wears costumes of bright and intense colours (an electric blue A-shape knee-length dress and an orange pants-ensemble with a silk headband) on her tanned skin, which emphasize her green eyes and the coral makeup of her lips, and her hair is perfectly coiffed, clearing her face. Facing the lassitude and declining sexual prowess of the more mature Mercouri's character, Schneider is the personification of youth, beauty and temptation. Mercouri nevertheless offers a compelling, flamboyant performance as a woman who realizes that there is no love left in her marriage, and who drowns her sorrow in alcohol. Schneider's performance is more subdued. She stands still and quiet, her face and body barely move and she scarcely speaks. She displays an innocence and a youthfulness that make her character the object of sexual desire for the husband, and the friend of both the wife and the couple's daughter – almost as if she was another child herself.

Schneider's supporting role in the British spy comedy *Otley* (1969), filmed in London by Dick Clement in his directorial debut, is also that of an accessory. She plays Imogen, a foreign agent working for British Intelligence, who pops up here and there to help the title character (Tom Courtenay) to sort out the imbroglio of murder and espionage into which he has fallen. They become romantically involved along the way. The film features a range of fantastic situations (abductions, car chases) in famous London locations (Portobello Road, Cheyne Walk, Buckingham Palace). Schneider's costumes follow the fashionable Swinging London look of the late 1960s (Street, 2009, pp. 97–8): a fluid white dress with a plunging neckline made of silver sequins, a large fur coat, a mini-skirt with high boots, a pantsuit with a white turtle neck and a crimson red skirt-suit with golden buttons and black vinyl leggings. Her clothes, hairstyle (a long bob haircut with a fringe) and makeup (black eye-shadow, contoured cheeks, glossy lips) are modern but never provocative. Schneider's participation in *Otley* illustrates a stereotypical appropriation of her trans-European image, especially in the British context. She represents the sexually alluring European woman, a fantasy site of glamour and non-marital sex. Despite the absence of explicit erotic moments between Imogen and Otley, the young woman is confident in her seductive power and quickly affirms her sexual desire. Towards the end of the film, she enters Otley's room and suggests they have sex: she lies down on the bed and puts her legs clad in high black vinyl boots on Courtenay's lap. Schneider's Imogen is a legacy of the complex figure of the European woman in the late 1940s/early 1950s British films (Geraghty, 2000a, pp. 93–111),[5] for which an apt comparison is Hildegard Knef's Bettina in *The Man Between* (Carol Reed, 1953). As elusive and 'exotic' European figures, they both protect and inform the male protagonist (their mysterious pasts credit them with knowledge and experience) and they carry an air of authority and control. Schneider's performance is sober: her voice is soft with a calm intonation, and she adopts the air of class confidence

---

[5]At the time, the European woman's 'ambiguities and dilemmas come to represent those of Europe itself and the relationship between her and the protagonist parallels Britain's relationship with Europe' (Geraghty, 2000a, p. 103). The figure's maturity and political and sexual knowledge duplicated the complex politics of Europe's past.

that she displayed in Visconti's 'Il lavoro' (flared nostrils, ironic smile, chin up and straight posture). Similar to Knef, by smiling and making direct and sustained eye contact, Schneider crafted an undeniable sexual aura. This was strengthened by the myth of European society's sexual permissiveness of the 1960s that influenced films' gender dynamics: while the European woman of the 1940s–1950s was 'willing to love unreservedly and sacrifice her own interests for the male hero' (Geraghty, p. 104), Imogen at the end of the film turns down Otley's date proposal and goes on her way without looking back, turning down prospects of romance or marriage. Instead, Schneider's character embraces an aspect of modern womanhood typical of Swinging London films – mobility (Landy, 2010). Imogen is a former au pair who exiled herself by choice (her national identity is left ambiguous), which suggests subjectivity and agency (Luckett, 2000, p. 236). Furthermore, Schneider had by then made tremendous progress in English and her accent was difficult to place (and it was not distinctly Germanic),[6] increasing her alluring image of the elegant, seductive and sophisticated European woman, a figure highly exportable on foreign screens, especially in English-speaking films. Despite the failure at the box office of *10.30 pm Summer* and *Otley* (the latter was never released in France), her roles in these two films are instructive to a study of her star persona, as they progressively built up her on-screen sensuality and confidence (in this, they also paved the way for her momentous portrayal of Marianne in *La Piscine*). These two films also introduced a more international dimension to her career, something that would find a logical outcome in her move to Hollywood.

But before moving on to Schneider's US productions, it is opportune to briefly mention *L'Enfer/Inferno* (Henri-Georges Clouzot, 1964), an international film that was meant to be visually revolutionary (with many innovative lighting and editing techniques), but was shut down after three weeks of filming in July 1964 due to the lead actor's (Serge Reggiani) and the director's health issues, and was never completed.[7] US producers from Columbia, notably Carl Foreman, with whom Schneider worked on *The Victors* (1963) took interest in the project and allocated it an unlimited

---

[6]Her Austrian background and thus the softer version of German that she speaks (which is not high German nor constrained by a strong Austrian dialect/accent) is enabling rather than constraining in learning to speak English and almost omitting her accent. A counterexample would be Arnold Schwarzenegger who comes from a region in Austria that speaks a very pronounced, unique and intense type of dialect that has a vocal expression and pronunciation and is hard to mask, especially when speaking another language.

[7]In 2009 the film was presented as a full-length semi-documentary by Serge Bromberg and Ruxandra Medrea with material selected from fifteen hours of archival material and entitled *L'Enfer d'Henri-Georges Clouzot*. The film includes interviews with members of the cast and crew.

budget. Schneider was still under contract with the production company at the time (see later) and it is very likely that she played a part, if not in securing the capital, at least in bringing parties together. As we saw, by the spring and summer of 1964, she had an international art cinema reputation (having worked with Visconti, Preminger and Welles), but she was at a transitional stage, still trying to shed the Sissi image and acquire a reputation as a serious actress. She therefore had high expectations from her role in Clouzot's film in terms of what it could bring to her image. In a similar way, she had expressed an interest in working with Claude Autant-Lara at the end of 1959.[8] Both directors were credited for 'raising' Brigitte Bardot to the rank of serious actress (Autant-Lara with *En cas de malheur* in 1958 and Clouzot with *La Vérité* in 1960, which may have been on Schneider's mind in this respect, as she and Bardot had the same agent at the time). Similar to *Le Combat dans l'île*, *L'Enfer* depicts the paranoiac jealousy of hotelier Marcel (Reggiani) towards his wife Odette (Schneider). The film was shot partly in black and white, with Marcel's obsession visually translated onto the screen in the form of lurid visions shot in colours. Amongst other lightning and make-up experiments, Schneider's lips were painted blue, her face, hair and body were covered with olive oil and glitter, while rotating lighting rigs were placed in front of the camera and actors. The final effect created the illusion of their faces transitioning between emotions and personalities. In view of the film's screen tests and first rushes released in the 2009 documentary *L'Enfer d'Henri-Georges Clouzot* (Serge Bromberg and Ruxandra Medrea), in those hallucinations Schneider embodied a highly sexualized male fantasy, an inaccessible and poisonous beauty, confirming the growing sexualization of her on-screen persona.

3. The Hollywood attempt

Through her association with Visconti, Schneider was offered work with established and critically acclaimed directors (Orson Welles as we saw, Otto Preminger). She worked both *on* Hollywood films shot in Europe and made films *in* Hollywood, a career path followed by many European actors in cinema history (see Lebrun, 1987, 1992; Barnier and Moine, 2002; Phillips and Vincendeau, 2006) and 'the ultimate recognition for a star, in any case a female star' (Sellier, 2002, p. 204). She signed a seven-year contract with Columbia Pictures for seven films (Bonini, 2001, p. 23). Yet, this section is

---

[8]As attested by a telegram sent by Schneider's agent Olga Horstig to Autant-Lara and kept at the Fonds Autant-Lara (archives) at the Cinémathèque suisse in Lausanne.

called 'the Hollywood *attempt*', for Schneider belonged to the ongoing trend of European actors who were major stars in their own countries and/or across the continent, but ultimately failed to make a mark in Hollywood – other examples include prominent names such as Hildegarde Knef (who had nonetheless a successful career on Broadway), Italian stars like Isa Miranda and Marcello Mastroianni and French stars like Jean Gabin, Emmanuelle Béart and Delon[9] (see Vincendeau, 2014). Schneider made three films out of the seven planned by Columbia (*The Victors, The Cardinal, Good Neighbor Sam*), only one of which (*Good Neighbor Sam*) was filmed *on* Hollywood grounds, and she stayed in Beverly Hills for only a few months at the end of 1963. She ended up breaking her contract, returning first to Paris, and then settling with her new family in Berlin.

Except for *The Cardinal* (Otto Preminger, 1963), none of Schneider's Hollywood films had any major impact critically or at the box office. Therefore, her attempts at a Hollywood career remain, to a large extent, unknown to a European public today. This is a key point to consider in explaining the absence of Schneider's success with Anglophone audiences. Her screen time and roles in those films varied considerably, but she was on the whole overshadowed by her American and British male co-star(s), and was frequently reduced to playing incidental roles that served to highlight the masculine protagonists in male genres such as the war film (*The Victors, Triple Cross* and to some extent *The Cardinal*), the spy film (*Triple Cross*), and the comedy (*What's New Pussycat?, Good Neighbor Sam*). The lesser importance of her parts led to the oversimplification of her characters, which in turn prevented her from deploying her acting skills. All of these factors led to the diverse critical reception of her work in the United States, at home in West Germany and Austria and in France.

Schneider's failure to achieve international stardom through her short-lived Hollywood career related to some extent to the struggles she had in transferring her star persona. On the one hand, the latter was still transitioning from the Sissi character to the sophisticated woman of her European art films and, on the other, they were at odds with Hollywood genres. Schneider's representation in these Hollywood films veered between the beautiful and 'exotic' creature, the whore, the schemer and the nagging *bourgeoise*. She was mainly defined by 'her otherness' (as opposed to the hegemonic white, male and Western culture of Hollywood – in this sense fitting within Diane Negra's category of 'off-white Hollywood', 2001) and the fact that she was of foreign nationality, an unusualness that was considered exciting. Schneider's Hollywood films can be divided into two categories: runaway productions and comedies.

---

[9]They ended their relationship during her stay in Los Angeles and Delon would have his own attempt at a Hollywood career shortly after their separation.

3.1. The big runaway productions

Schneider's first experience with Hollywood was in the British-American, black-and-white war film *The Victors* (1963), which follows a group of US soldiers through Europe during the Second World War, through fighting in Italy and France, to the uneasy peace of Berlin. The film was written, directed and produced by Carl Foreman from the novel *The Human Kind* (1953) by British author Alexander Baron. The novel is a collection of short stories based on the author's own wartime experiences, some of which were selected by Foreman who developed them, added his own observations and changed the original British characters into Americans to attract US audiences. *The Victors* was shot on location in 1962 Sweden, France, Italy, Belgium and England, and features an ensemble cast of fifteen American and European actors, including six European actresses (apart from Schneider, Melina Mercouri, Jeanne Moreau, Rosanna Schiaffino, Senta Berger and Elke Sommer). Their photographs appear on the original poster with the tagline 'The six most exciting women in the world ... in the most explosive entertainment ever made!'. The film is a good illustration of a brief moment in the history of US cinema when, in the 1960s, the studio era was drawing to a close and Hollywood expanded and varied its overseas productions, especially in Europe (Betz, 2009, p. 64). European actors, as illustrated by Schneider, started working on international projects on a more fluid and temporary basis, appearing in English-language films largely financed by Hollywood but shot in Europe (the so-called 'runaway productions'). As a case in point, the actresses of *The Victors* were selected to represent an American view of Europe: a foreign place populated by beautiful women on the margins of the codes of feminine morality 'made in Hollywood'.

In her Hollywood films, Schneider's characters are explicitly foreign, a frequent narrative explanation for her slight accent, but, except for *The Cardinal*, no further precision is provided (a common feature for European actors/actresses in Hollywood) – she could be French, German, Austrian, Swiss or Swedish. In her two scenes in *The Victors* Schneider is Regine, a violinist who entertains the GIs in a bar in Oostende. It is a minor, underdeveloped part, but there are details brought through Schneider's performance that hint at the character's complexity. Regine is evidently distressed by the horrors of the war that killed her family, and Schneider's performance expresses her depression, resignation and gloominess (head down, a closed expression on her face, she speaks only a few laconic and monosyllabic words) when Georges Hamilton's character invites her to his table. But when he returns a month later he is deeply disappointed to see that Regine had become a laughing and seducing prostitute in a black lace dress. This transition is surprising for the spectator too: Schneider's character lacks such basic narrative exposition and agency (for instance, the male characters talk about her in crude terms as if she was not sitting right next to them, powdering her nose) that it is difficult to feel empathy towards her; her role as a prostitute also inhabits a space far from Schneider's usual star persona. Unsurprisingly critics deemed her 'schizophrenic' (Crowther, 1963).

Schneider had a more fleshed-out character as the young Viennese Annemarie in Otto Preminger's *The Cardinal* (1963). Schneider appears half-way through the film's lengthy 2 h 48-min running time, in the segments taking place in Vienna.[10] Based on the eponymous novel (1950) by Henry Morton Robinson, *The Cardinal* is a large-scale drama shot on location in Boston, Connecticut, Hollywood, Rome and Vienna. It features an international cast, with Tom Tryon as the title character, John Huston, Raf Vallone and Dorothy Gish, and it received six Academy Awards nominations and six Golden Globe Awards nominations in 1964 (including Best actress in a drama for Schneider), winning two (Best drama and Best supporting actor for Huston). Beginning in 1917, the film recounts the fictional life of young Irish-American Catholic priest Stephen Fermoyle (Tryon) from Boston who confronts family issues and personal conflicts as he rises to the office of cardinal, touching on various social issues such as interfaith marriage, sex out of wedlock, abortion, racial bigotry and the rise of fascism and war with the *Anschluss* in Vienna in 1938.

Following the death of his sister (Carol Lynley) after he denied a doctor the right to perform the abortion that would have saved her life, Fermoyle becomes unsure about his commitment to the clergy and is transferred to Europe where he takes a two-year sabbatical. In 1924 in Vienna he teaches an English class and enters into a relationship with one of his students, Annemarie (Schneider). Schneider plays the character with the same optimism and freshness displayed in *Sissi*. Dressed in a mid-length skirt and a Peter Pan collar shirt, she is made to look younger as she follows her professor in the streets of Vienna, while a romantic violin tune accompanies her light step. Annemarie is a modern girl (she dreams of going to America 'where people think about the future instead of always the past'): enterprising, flirtatious, cheeky (she implies to her teacher that she is free to talk all afternoon even 'an evening if needed', and she asks him to invite her for a cup of coffee). She pushes herself into Fermoyle's life and delights him with tourist attractions – some of them are well known from the *Sissi* films: Schönbrunn Palace and its Gloriette in the gardens, and a boat trip on the Danube. This decor and Annemarie's bubbly personality recall many of Schneider's 1950s roles, as do the film's conservative view of femininity and its traditional assignment of gender roles. Annemarie may display an acute and modern sense of

---

[10]The Vienna-based parts of the narrative are very much a 'Who's Who' of Austrian cinema at the time: Josef Meinrad, seen as Colonel Böckl in the *Sissi* films; Peter Weck, seen alongside Schneider in *Mädchenjahre einer Königin* and *Sissi 1* and *2*; and Vilma Degischer, famous for her role of Archduchess Sophie in the *Sissis*, are all in *The Cardinal*.

fashion, but she remains fundamentally attached to what is expected of her as a traditional young woman: 'For me, to work at a job, that is not to be a woman. I think ... there is one thing I could do well, one thing I was born for ... to love a man. To love him so much that my whole life is to make him happy'. While the film's historical context (1924 Vienna) may go some way to explaining this outdated dialogue, its blatant conservatism also relates to Schneider's late 1950s/early 1960s persona with its paradoxical depiction of femininity, and in particular the tension between modernity and tradition examined in the first part of this book. Although some aspects of Annemarie spoke of a modern feminine identity endowed with some power of self-determination (which aligned with the star's new and international career path), her image in the film was representative of a conventional bourgeois femininity more in tune with her former roles and supported by the rigid doctrine of the Catholic Church figured by Tyron's character (although *The Cardinal* was vehemently condemned by the Vatican).

Annemarie grows from a young student to a charming and passionate woman, and then finally an abandoned woman. Schneider's performance of the character's three narrative stages is constructed through acting signs that audiences had already witnessed in her collaborations with Visconti and Welles. First, she plays the young woman in love with her usual acting combination of coy smile and impish side glance. After Fermoyle tells Annemarie about his priesthood, she does not hide her romantic intentions anymore and they express their love for each other at one of the most iconic sites in Vienna, a ball (emphasizing her role as Austrian 'ambassador' in the film). Schneider's face is captured in close-up while she avows her love for Fermoyle: her expression is tense and serious, then she comforts him in a soft voice and they waltz away. Ultimately, shortly after the ball, Fermoyle does not renounce his vows and Schneider, dressed in a bright red ensemble, glimpses him in his cassock, displays an expression of mild bewilderment (her mouth slightly open), betrayal (frowning eyebrows) and deep sadness (her eyes start to water) but does not speak a word, then she turns and runs away.

She reappears in the last act of the film when Fermoyle is sent back to Vienna by the Vatican in 1938 to persuade Cardinal Innitzer (Josef Meinrad) to not cooperate with the Nazis. Annemarie is married to Kurt von Hartman (Peter Weck) who commits suicide out of fear of the Gestapo because of his Jewish parentage; then the Nazis turn on her and she is imprisoned. Behind bars, her hair loose and her face clear, surrounded by tall men, Annemarie reflects on her mistakes and regrets. Schneider's facial expressions harden to present a contemptuous and disenchanted face (obtained with her habit of raising her chin and pursing her lips) that ultimately presents all the signs of distress (tears, looking down, frowning). The camera closes in on her face framed by the prison bars and with minimal makeup, and, despite the severity of the situation, the tone of her voice remains firm, even when she

FIGURE 7 *Schneider's proud tirade in* The Cardinal.

sadly looks down, resigned, and her eyes progressively fill with tears. Her clear-eyed glance is steady, proud and insistent; she flares her nostrils with disdain and there is ardour in her tone (the way she insists on some syllable, like the [u] sound in 'fool'). The scene is an excellent example of an aspect of her acting style that would soon become characteristic: she delivers long lines of dialogue, taking her time delivering her words and refusing to be interrupted by her interlocutor (Figure 7), which contributed to her image as a proud (almost arrogant) woman, while she also demonstrates how she could span a wide emotional range, from sneering to supplication to melancholy.

And yet, despite the Golden Globe nomination and the film's box-office success in the United States and France,[11] the legacy of the demure Sissi persisted (*Libération*, 01/01/1964). Therefore, even with a challenging role like Annemarie, the European media was quick to link Schneider back to the romantic Sissi image (Chauvet, 1963). Even though Schneider made the protagonist question his priesthood – she was the female 'temptation' (Landes, 1963; *L'Aurore*, 26/12/1963; *La Croix*, 31/12/1963) – the relationship remained sexually repressed and unconsummated. Therefore, though Schneider in *The Cardinal* did not represent absolute vice (the European temptress who embodied a dangerous deviation from US patriarchal norms), her ultimate arrest is portrayed as a punishment for her vanity as a young woman and her lack of love for her husband. This fits the contemporary US rhetoric of traditional gender roles and women's domestic roles in the private sphere, at least until the mid-1960s (when it began to be

---

[11]The film ranked eleventh at the 1963 French box office with 2,520,006 spectators (Simsi, 2012, p. 28). I could not find box-office numbers for West Germany and Austria.

questioned, as signalled by the 1963 publication of *The Feminine Mystique* by Betty Friedan).

The Victors and *The Cardinal* were Schneider's first films that were, entirely for the former, and partially for the latter, set during the Second World War, and she continued her identification with the war period with the 1966 spy film *Triple Cross* (by *James Bond* director Terence Young). Her character, who goes by the vague title of 'Countess', is the first and only one to side deliberately with the Nazi regime. In this respect, the 1960s represented a decade of new on- and off-screen awareness for Schneider: she learned about her family's past sympathy for some of the Nazi party's elite and disapproved of their subsequent silence. Being acquainted with Marlene Dietrich, Lili Palmer and Otto Preminger, who took a stand against the fascist regime, Schneider progressively realized her parents' failure to take anti-Nazi positions and developed an acute sense of guilt and shame. The Countess in *Triple Cross* remained therefore an exception in her filmography. The film is a fictional account of an episode in the life of the real English spy Eddie Chapman (played by Christopher Plummer), believed by the Nazis to be their top spy in Great Britain, though he was a double agent. There is scant female presence in the film, and Schneider is marginal in a male-dominated cast. Her character is a fellow spy who interviews Chapman and participates in his training during which they become romantically involved. With her accent, her nationality and her early image as Austria's national treasure, Schneider represents the stereotype of the 'German enemy' (although the Countess's nationality is not defined), which cinematically translates as the trope of the European femme fatale, a woman of mystery and dubious sexual intent (Philips and Vincendeau, 2006, p. 268). The Countess has a high opinion of herself and is unapologetic about her work – much like Chapman, she sees to her own interests first. Her demise is nonetheless unavoidable at the end of the war (and of the film), and she accepts it with pride and a few resigned tears. Elegantly dressed in blocks of colour (blue, green, salmon, black), carefully coiffed and made-up, her look is more reminiscent of 1960s aesthetics than 1940s fashion and it is construed as the image of the sophisticated (the term 'Countess' hints at her aristocratic backgound), cold and calculating enemy spy. In this respect she contrasts with the French actress Claudine Auger (Bond girl Domino in Young's previous Bond film *Thunderball* in 1965), who plays the 'good woman' as a member of the Resistance.

During the filming of *Triple Cross* in the summer of 1966 in the studios de la Victorine in Nice, she married her first husband, German stage actor and director Harry Meyen who survived his incarceration at the age of eighteen in the Neuengamme concentration camp, and whose father was murdered by the Nazis. Meyen and Schneider, who was five-month pregnant with her son, were discretely wed in Saint-Jean-Cap-Ferrat on 15 July 1966, a day after the highly publicized wedding between Brigitte Bardot and

Gunter Sachs in Las Vegas. Schneider gave birth (in Berlin) a few days before
the film's release in early December 1966 in Paris. *Triple Cross* performed
modestly at the box office. It was distributed in the United States in July
1967, but Schneider had already put her career on hold to dedicate herself
to her son. But before examining her highly successful return to the (French)
screen with *La Piscine*, I shall examine how Schneider's performance register
shifted temporarily towards comedy during her Hollywood years. For this I
need to go back a few years.

3.2. The first comedies

Good Neighbor Sam (David Swift, 1964), filmed during autumn 1963, was
Schneider's first real comedy (as opposed to some comic episodes in her
1950s romantic films) and the only film she made in California. Schneider's
arrival in Hollywood was advertised in the US media as that of an 'exotic'
European woman coming to lighten up productions with her charm and
beauty. In *Anatomy of a movie: The Cardinal* (Jack Haley Jr.), the nineteenth
episode of the NBC television series *Hollywood and the stars*, released in
February 1964 and documenting the making of *The Cardinal*, Schneider is
all smiles, elegantly dressed in a Chanel suit with a leopard-print pillbox hat
matching her fur collar, and she kisses Preminger on the mouth (a kiss 'to
help the director' in Boston's cold winter, says the narrator).[12] Her 'exoticism'
was emphasized as a paramount aspect of her image: we hear that 'she has
come all this way [from Europe]' and she herself adds 'I was born in a
cold country'. However, like many mentions of Schneider in the mainstream
press, her birthplace was rarely specified, instead it was implied through
clichés of Viennese romanticism: her appearance is accompanied by a violin
tune reminiscent of the music in the *Sissi*s, and her scene chosen from *The
Cardinal* is the Viennese ball scene. Schneider's presence in Hollywood was
therefore one of many examples of the hegemonic film industry's strategy
to uplift its domestic productions by incorporating European 'otherness'
via national and gender stereotypes. With the European female characters
being directly contrasted with their American counterparts, this strategy
developed and cemented the foundations of North-American identity in

---

[12]Given Preminger's brutal and well-documented treatment of Jean Seberg on his films *Saint
Joan* (1957) and *Bonjour Tristesse* (1958) (Fujiwara, 2008, pp. 202–14), one could wonder
about his and Schneider's work relationship. Apparently, it was relatively harmonious despite
her recollection of the terror felt by the cast and crew during the shooting in Vienna (p. 306).
Her presence on set felt liberating for Tom Tryon who suffered from the director's 'oppressive
handling' (p. 305). This hints at Schneider's perfectionism and work ethic as she was responsive
to Preminger's precise and harsh direction, an echo of Visconti's autocratic, and occasionally
abusive, treatment and her tendency to suffer through the 'artistic' process in order to produce
her best work.

the mid-60s (Abel, 1999). This is perfectly illustrated by Schneider's looks and performance in *Good Neighbor Sam,* when compared to the blue-eyed, blonde and high-pitched Dorothy Provine in the role of the all-American and loving wife and mother.

In this comedy of manners, Schneider plays Janet Lagerlof, the recently divorced, long-time friend from Europe and new next-door neighbour of Min (Provine) whose husband Sam (Jack Lemmon) works in advertising in San Francisco. After all sorts of misunderstandings and comic imbroglios, Sam pretends to be Janet's husband in order to help her qualify for her grandfather's inheritance that stipulates that she must be married in order to receive the fortune. Janet is of foreign nationality (she also lived 'all over the world'), but she is also foreign in the sense that, being divorced, she has broken ranks, embodying a deviation from US patriarchal standards (she says that 'some girls are born to be single'). However, the perfect family picture painted by her neighbours will eventually break down her convictions, and she changes her mind at the end.

Schneider's character is introduced at her arrival at the airport in a tailored skirt-suit (that she 'just picked up from Paris') with fur coat and hat, and a three rows pearl necklace; she also speaks a few words of French with the waiter, and then she inadvertently meets Sam while she takes a shower and he walks in. These elements set up the figure of the European chic seductress, but Schneider does not seduce Sam on purpose. She may wear stunningly fashionable 1960s costumes that embrace a broad colour palette, dance the cha-cha-cha while the camera slightly zooms in to emphasize her buttocks in a tight silk dress or inhabit Sam's fantasy in his sleep, but *Good Neighbor Sam* does not depict her as a seductress, and it remains one of the very few titles in Schneider's filmography that offers the portrayal of sincere female friendship and support. If the comic situations sometimes drive Janet and Min to compete against each other, they try to make their respective husbands more responsive, which accords with the strict heteronormative morality of the film, which sees Janet and her ex-husband (Michael Connors) reconcile and remarry. Though Schneider's performance in the film is relatively naturalistic, her delivery lacks subtlety. In dramas, one can see the scope and the richness of her emotional range (as previously examined in *The Cardinal* for example), but there is no such transparency in her comedic performance. Instead she tends to call attention to her technique with histrionics such as exaggerated shrugs, dramatic head turns, overdone expressions of shock – as in the way she overplays Janet's outrageousness in reaction to her ex-husband's advances and petty jealousy. This might suggest an inept grasp of the material, but it also highlights that Schneider was uncomfortable performing in comedies.

The female characterization carried by Schneider's role in *What's New Pussycat* (Clive Donner, 1965) is equally conservative. Written by Woody Allen (who also appears in his first film role), this US slapstick comedy in the vein of the cinema of the absurd was shot in Paris and tells the story of notorious womanizer Michael James (Peter O'Toole, the title refers to his pick-up line for women) who, pressured into marriage by his fiancée Carol (Schneider), seeks counsel from a psychoanalyst (Peter Sellers) for being unfaithful. The other women (Capucine, Ursula Andress and Paula Prentiss) are presented in a misogynist way, as sex-driven creatures who cannot control their instincts in front of irresistible heartthrob O'Toole. Dressed in her now familiar Chanel suit and other classic fashion ensembles, sporting a rather unflattering permed hairstyle and heavy makeup, and with her insistent demand to marry, Schneider embodies the uptight wife against the outrageously sexy other women: Capucine as a nymphomaniac, Prentiss as an exotic dancer and Andress as a parachutist in animal-print hugging pantsuits. She defends her traditional view of marriage but is deemed 'hysterical' by Michael (she tries in vain to give him a taste of his own medicine by seducing Allen's character but she gets too drunk to sleep with him), who resists her until the last scene of the film. There, finally married to Michael, Carol rants and nags as he makes eyes at the soft-voiced city hall's clerk performed by pop singer Françoise Hardy. Playing a prudish woman in a world of farcical sex-obsessed stereotypes, Schneider is perceived as disconnected from the rest of the film in her embodiment of a 'real lady' (Rabine, 1966b), and was deemed a 'bourgeois Sissi' (Bory, 1966). Her character is not the only explanation for this negative judgement, as her performance is also in question. Her comic acting style, in *What's New Pussycat* in particular, is overly kinetic, especially in the use of her head (sharp turns), facial expressions and elocution, a register that clashes with her sophisticated, distant image in evidence in *Boccaccio '70* and other films such as *Katia* and *Plein Soleil*. Moreover, although she could convincingly perform in English, her delivery, while fluent, remains noticeably accented, clashing with the fast pace of the comic dialogues. As a result, rather than the embodiment of 'normality', she seems incongruous and self-conscious, traits that were noticed by critics of the time (Chazal, 1966; Chauvet, 1966).

Overall, Schneider's presence in Hollywood comedies was met with relative indifference from the US press, except for her self-consciousness that was viewed as a consequence of her taking her participation in every production too seriously, to the point of being nicknamed 'Miss Worry' by the US press (Benichou and Pommier, 1981, p. 69; Krenn, 2013a, p. 180). Her perfectionism and dedication, so valued in Europe, carried negative connotations in a US context – she was judged as too demanding. This sheds light on how differently Schneider's Hollywood films were perceived by various audiences. In Austria and West Germany, they illustrated the sensitive dynamic between European actors' exoticism and assimilation in Hollywood cinema. According to Vincendeau (2017, p. 367), 'too much embedding within national identity curtails the possibilities of export, too little may provoke rejection at home'. As a matter of fact, the German-speaking media's words of pride ('Romy Schneider conquers Hollywood', *Bunte*, 23/10/1963) quickly turned to bitter resentment ('Since Marlene Dietrich, no diva of German language have so profoundly avoided her place of heritage', *Der Spiegel*, 13/03/1963, p. 81). The Austrian and German press were, as we have seen, already lukewarm in their response to her break from her *Sissi*-based national treasure status. Their disgruntlement worsened when Schneider's words were (allegedly) misreported or misinterpreted regarding her relation to her native language and hometown. One example was a paper in *Look* stating she would not work with German film producers anymore,[13] and another gossipy story reported that she was refusing to speak and be spoken to in German.[14] All this prompted an 'anti-German' and 'anti-Vienna' characterization (Schneider and Seydel, 1989, pp. 188–9). This – mostly – negative reception echoes another change in the perception of the star at home. In the late 1950s, her glamourous, princess-like life was acceptable, even valorized for the traditional feminine values it carried. However, as she tried to expand her persona, she also altered her lifestyle: she acquired several properties, was associated with haute couture and travelled outside Europe's borders. For this she was condemned in media for behaving like a capricious 'diva'. Beyond criticizing Schneider for turning her back on Sissi, the media denigrated a professionally ambitious woman and her achievements.

Conclusion

Hollywood studios' main recruiting policy for signing European stars was to hire them on the basis of their image in their countries of origin (Sellier, 2002, p. 213). But while it was difficult for most European female stars (such as Michèle Morgan, Micheline Presle, Hildegarde Knef, Senta Berger) to transfer their personal, nationally anchored star identity to Hollywood film, the specific problem faced by Schneider during her Hollywood sojourn in the 1960s was that she did not have such a well-established identity. Her image of the riskily sexy European woman had not yet solidified enough for transatlantic export. The image that had proven exportable (at least on the European market) was that of Sissi – the one she vehemently rejected. Ironically it was this image of the pure maiden that first got attention from Hollywood in the late 1950s, being in line with white America's feminine

---

[13]'Ich werde [...] mit den deutschen Filmproduzenten kein Wort wechseln [...]' (*Der Spiegel*, 13/03/1963, p. 81).
[14]Schneider explained that she preferred to be addressed on film sets in the language in which she was working (in Italian and French with Visconti, in English with Welles and Preminger, etc.), and when David Swift on the set of *Good Neighbor Sam* spoke to her in German she asked him to opt for English, and the rumour spread.

codes. Walt Disney screen-tested her for the role of Lizbeth Hempel that ultimately went to Janet Munro in *Third Man on the Mountain* (Ken Annakin, 1959) (*Hollywood Reporter*, 28/01/1958; Krenn, 2013a, p. 116). Schneider had turned the offer down; she was disappointed as the role meant reinforcing the virgin stereotype and the saccharine image which she was struggling to leave behind. Her attempt at a Hollywood career and wish to secure a successful characterization in US films were therefore founded on fragile premises. Her persona was still in transition, including in Europe, and as such it failed to export to America.

As my exploration of her diverse career in the 1960s has shown, Schneider's status as an accomplished and successful international star remained problematic. Most of her US films (except *The Cardinal*) commercially failed – including in Austria, West Germany and France – and her presence in European media declined further when she retired from work and public appearances for more than a year and a half after her marriage and the birth of her son David in 1966. After the critical hit of her performances in *Boccaccio '70* and *The Trial* she did, however, achieve, if not international, at least trans-continental recognition. In addition, she was on her way to becoming a truly transnational star in the sense that she was able to act credibly in four languages (German, English, Italian and French). Despite a mild German accent, her mediocre Hollywood career was therefore not due to her language ability. Yet she seemed unable to convert these assets into a sustained form of global stardom. Instead, her career took another turn and, in its third phase, she achieved major national stardom in France.

6

The French reinvention

Introduction

The previous chapters examined Romy Schneider's uneven international career throughout the 1960s – how she built both a 'serious actress' image, notably through international art films and how she branched out into a range of film genres, from modernist European art cinema to Hollywood comedy, with varying success. Yet, despite her adopting new career strategies and following new artistic directions, Schneider stubbornly remained Sissi for the majority of the public and the press until the end of the decade. Meanwhile, as we saw, her presence in European media declined, particularly when she retired from work to concentrate on her family. There is, however, a misconception circulating in French media today: that Schneider had slowly fallen into oblivion in the 1960s, and thus that her return to French cinema screens with *La Piscine*/*The Swimming Pool* (Jacques Deray, 1969) saved her career. In fact, despite some commercial failures, she remained an important star in France throughout the 1960s, with some of her films exceeding two to three million spectators (*Katia* and *Die schöne Lügnerin* were distributed in France in 1960, *The Cardinal* in 1963; Simsi, 2012, pp. 137, 144, 204), and *Triple Cross* was successful as well with 1,718,823 spectators (p. 271).[1]

Nonetheless, *La Piscine* had a substantial impact on Schneider's career and represented a landmark in the evolution of her star image, consecrating her status as a feminine sex symbol in a *French* film. But before going into a detailed analysis of Schneider's performance and reception in *La Piscine*, I shall briefly consider a parallel media narrative built around her in the mid-

---

[1]Schneider was also named best foreign actress of the year in June 1964 by the readers of *Le Figaro* and *Cinémonde* and received the audience award 'La Victoire du Cinéma Français' (Benichou and Pommier, 1981, p. 71).

1960s – a narrative that read the star as the epitome of the unsatisfied and insecure woman with a tendency to suffer from depression.

1. The melancholy star

To fully grasp the impact of *La Piscine* on Schneider's reception in France and other European countries, it is useful to sum up her image right before the film. For this I turn to a contemporary German television documentary on the star. In the beginning of 1966, before filming *Triple Cross* and marrying Meyen, Schneider agreed to be the subject of a documentary commissioned by Hellmut Haffner, head of the *Teleclub* show on the Bavarian television's third programme. The film was directed by Hans-Jürgen Syberberg, now best known as a member of the New German Cinema movement, in particular for *Hitler, ein Film aus Deutschland* (1977).[2] Syberberg began his investigation of German culture through its popular mythology with his TV documentary on Fritz Kortner (*Fünfter Akt, Siebte Szene. Fritz Kortner probt Kabale und Liebe*, 1965), and, following the film's critical success, with *Romy - Portrait eines Gesichts/Romy - Anatomy of a Face* (aired on 21 January 1967). This 60-minute 'cinéma-vérité' (or 'cinéma direct') document (Graff, 2014, p. 412) spans over three days in February 1966 in the skiing town of Kitzbühel (Tyrol, Austria) where Schneider was spending her holidays in the house of Prince Ferdinand of Liechtenstein.

I do not have additional information about Schneider's reasons to agree to do the documentary, but her participation is in line with her strategy at the time to expand her serious actress reputation in order to distance herself from the Sissi image. The actress could have considered that a film focusing on her private life would be a good opportunity to offer her opinion on her career. Instead, it added a dark and melancholy aspect to her off-screen persona. Photographed in black and white, *Romy - Portrait eines Gesichts* is set in the privacy of her vacation, showing her skiing, walking around the Kaps castle and having an absorbed conversation with Syberberg (who stays off-camera) in an elegant living room. Due to the film's generic features, such as the use of black and white, which connotes authenticity, the image that Schneider offers in *Portrait eines Gesichts* could be interpreted by audiences as mirroring the real person, which makes the film valuable for my study concerning the emergent melancholy aspect of Schneider's persona at the time. The portrait of the star painted by the documentary is as paradoxical as Schneider's persona so far. *Portrait eines Gesichts* presents a conflicted and

---

[2]For more on Syberberg see Anton Kaez's study *From Hitler to Heimat: The Return of History as Film* (1989) on Germany's approach to its stigmatized history, and Susan Sontag's essay 'Syberberg's Hitler' in *Under the Sign of Saturn* (1980, pp. 137–65).

emotionally contradictory woman, swinging between extremes – Schneider shows a naive enthusiasm and a childish sentimentality, as well as a deep scepticism, sadness and a distance, when mentioning the commercial failures of her films and other disappointing experiences.

The feeling of having a glimpse of the 'real' Romy Schneider is notably strengthened by the film's style, and its difficult post-production history. First, the documentary departs from her other media appearances by the proximity and the openness that she seems to demonstrate. Schneider, then twenty-seven years old, presents herself as 'ordinary', wearing minimal make-up. In her soft-modulated voice she offers her perspectives on her career and craft, and how her job is affecting her private life. She recognizes her acute 'sensitivity', acknowledges her nervousness and self-doubt. Though she suffers from stage fright and fears performing in her native language, she expresses her desire to do theatre work in German, with a play 'preferably new and modern'. Adding to the authentic aspect of the portrait is Schneider's speech tone and body language. She is either assertive and confident and speaks quickly and with ease, or she speaks slowly, with long pauses, and is careful in her choice of words. At times she appears lost in her thoughts, sighs and drops her head; she nervously wrings her hands, shakes her head, clutches her hands and repeatedly moistens her lips, thus performing insecurity. This is enhanced by the many close-ups of her face showing the worry in her eyes, pensively drinking, smoking and running her hands through her hair.

The images suggest an unhappy and unsatisfied woman, an aspect of Schneider's image that started developing after her breakup with Delon, and was consolidated in the mid-1960s with several box-office failures. Schneider's projection of unhappy femininity (at such young age) and her melancholy discourse are rooted in judgements about German national identity. She refers to the so-called 'Germanic spleen', a Wagnerian and romantic notion that she discovered via Visconti who offered this explanation to her frequent mood swings (moments of euphoria followed by deep despair).[3] She therefore willingly identifies with a national trait (however stereotypical that may be), and in doing so insists on her attachment to her German origins from which she also, simultaneously, distanced herself from the French- and German-speaking press (see previous chapter). Schneider evokes the beginning of her career, with her first film by her mother's side, as well as the popular success of the *Sissi* cycle. Contrary to the French media's endorsement of Schneider's disdain towards her most successful role, the star speaks lucidly about the progress of her career and the financial and professional security and fame it gave her. When she first arrived in France she said that she 'did not want to be a princess anymore', which she repeats here in Syberberg's film, but in a more conciliatory tone. She voices her

---

[3]Notice how she again attributes the paternity of the phrase to her mentor and one of the most important male figures of her life and career.

search for happiness and simple living, and claims that she 'hates the star system' (a common discourse amongst stars). Yet she confesses to behaving like a 'diva', and the film conveys an image of leisure, with glasses of Veuve Clicquot champagne, a silver tea set, US magazines on the table, a large bouquet of daffodils and tulips and plush chairs and sofas (*Der Spiegel* pointed out that the house's 'monthly rent with butler' amounted to 8,000 Deutschmarks, 06/02/1967, p. 94). Moreover, in addition to her black wooden ring set with diamonds (a gift from Visconti), she wears an eye-catching, large pearl brooch on her simple black turtle-neck. Thus, while Schneider ostensibly aimed for the German-speaking stage, she also wished to project the image of a glamourous international star.

Finally, *Portrait eines Gesichts*'s troubled post-production, reported in the press, emphasized its 'behind the scenes' aspect, hinting at Schneider's difficult home life: before the premiere, she successfully brought an injunction preventing the film coming out. At a private screening, Meyen had objected to the superimposition of an unsavoury joke (about homesickness and Jewish people) on a Sammy Davis Jr. song. Meyen also wanted to edit out Schneider's negative comments on the German-speaking press and mentions of himself. Schneider, Meyen, Haffner and producer Rob Hower finally agreed on a single broadcast. But this was not without cost for Schneider: even before the broadcast, the press described her as a 'damaged Sissi' and quoted 'copyright expert Dr. Fromm' who said, 'You might get the impression that she is a very sad child' (*Der Spiegel*, 06/02/1967, p. 94).

After the developing melancholy aspect of Schneider's on- and off-screen persona in the late 1960s, I shall turn towards its antithesis through her performance in *La Piscine*, the film that represented a definitive turn in her career, life and persona.

2. *La Piscine* and the introduction of a sex symbol

La Piscine is a French thriller set in a grand and isolated villa in the sun-drenched hills overlooking Saint-Tropez and the Mediterranean. Jean-Paul (Delon) and Marianne (Schneider), a young, beautiful and bourgeois couple, enjoy their vacation, the hot weather and each other's bodies by lounging by the vast eponymous swimming pool. Their idle seclusion is interrupted by the arrival of their friend and record producer Harry (Maurice Ronet) and his eighteen-year-old daughter Pénélope (Jane Birkin). Marianne's decision to invite the pair to stay sets in motion a slow-burning four-way exchange of jealousy and masculine rivalry, as Marianne and Harry are former lovers and Pénélope's ingenuous charm entices Jean-Paul. The holiday ends with Jean-Paul drowning Harry in the pool and Marianne becoming his accomplice as she decides to keep his secret from the police.

The following is structured in three parts: first, the on- and off-screen reunion of Schneider and Delon and the media perception of their pairing, then Schneider's development of a sophisticated *bourgeoise* persona and finally an analysis of her haute couture costumes, which gives me the opportunity to briefly evoke the late 1960s bourgeois culture through the prism of Saint-Tropez's cosmopolitanism.

2.1. Reuniting the star couple: the myth of eternal love

For a number of reasons examined before, in the years preceding *La Piscine*, Schneider's career was at a relatively low ebb. As a result, the media narrative surrounding the film's inception, production and distribution took on a disproportionate importance in the film's marketing strategy and subsequent commercial success, and in the reshaping of Schneider's star image. The narrative went – and still goes – that Schneider had reached such a low point in her career that the French producers were reluctant to cast her in the co-starring role of Marianne alongside Delon, and it was he who suggested her name, insisted that she was cast and obtained her contract. This 'story', whether true or not,[4] was reiterated in the press and supported by the stars themselves, most notably with Schneider's staged arrival at Nice airport where she was greeted by Delon on 12 August. The media focused on their reactions as ex-fiancés meeting again after years apart – which was false as they had previously reunited at Schneider's residence in Berlin in preparation for the film. The video of this welcome party contains an interview with Delon telling the assembled journalists that he is 'a bit emotional', welcoming Schneider as it has been 'almost ten years to this day after the first time I welcomed her at an airport in 1958', when she was 'a big European *vedette* and me not at all, I was starting in the business'. Reporter Jean-Marie Molingo asks what role Schneider is set to perform in *La Piscine* and Delon's response encapsulates how Schneider's image rebranding was thought through and controlled even before filming:

> First of all, it is a woman's role. Romy is a woman, she is not a girl anymore, we must be clear about that, she is not Sissi anymore, nor the little girl with chubby cheeks, she really is a woman – besides, you will see it for yourself in a moment.
>
> (*JT 13H*, 12/08/1968)

On cue, Schneider, smiling and radiant, steps out of a plane, goes down the stairs and tightly embraces Delon. Just as in the film, they present the image of a very handsome, young, privileged and perfectly matched couple. Delon wears beige linen trousers, a black unbuttoned shirt and a leather

---

[4]Depending on the source, it was director Jacques Deray who suggested Schneider to Delon who was first inclined to cast Delphine Seyrig, Angie Dickinson, Natalie Wood or Monica Vitti.

jacket; and Schneider sports what is probably a creation by French couturier André Courrèges (he designed the film's costumes for women), an A-line 'little white dress' (in reference to Chanel's 'little black dress' but intended for the younger audience of the 1960s, Steele, 1997, pp. 52, 61, 64), white gloves and a black vinyl headband. I will return to Schneider's modern looks as they played a decisive role in propelling her towards a more mature image, that of the glamourous and distinguished woman in 1970s France.

The promotional narrative of Schneider and Delon's reunion was the reverse of the stars' first on-screen pairing in *Christine* (1958), which argued that Schneider herself had chosen new *jeune premier* Delon to co-star, based on photographs. Thus, after she helped him leap to stardom, he was returning the favour, a phrasing adopted by Delon and the French-speaking press that credited him for her 'second wind' (though I argue that it was her third). Schneider's success was, yet again, attributed to the agency of a man (Delon after Visconti and Welles), and one who had the ascendency over her in both professional and personal terms. The overwhelming presence of Delon marks the development of fundamental aspects of her image: vulnerability and dignity in the face of adversity (she had been 'abandoned' by Delon for another woman and had to put on a brave face). As already mentioned, films such as *Boccaccio '70* and *The Cardinal* reinforced her image of the beautiful yet vulnerable woman (Ginette Vincendeau phrased it as Schneider being 'shackled by beauty', 2009, p. 25). Although latent, Schneider's vulnerability also featured in *La Piscine*. The ending has her 'shackled' to Delon's character through her decision to not disclose his secret to the police, bounding them together even though they were about to breakup. The final shot shows Schneider and Delon through a window in each other's arms, a composition that signals their shared imprisonment, their poisoned love condemning them to a life of repression and guilt, a trope typical of film noir of which *La Piscine* is a descendent. As Felicity Chaplin (2015) aptly points out, the final shot might even refer to another doomed, romantic but nonetheless emblematic couple of French cinema: Jean Gabin and Michèle Morgan in *Le Quai des brumes* (Marcel Carné, 1938), similarly shot through a window frame. The end of *La Piscine* is also an allusion to Schneider and Delon's first on-screen couple in *Christine*, in which the two star-crossed lovers are reunited in a pointless death.

La Piscine was thus a vehicle[5] for the charismatic star couple, who channelled their former real-life romance into their on-screen chemistry, upon which the film largely relies.[6] They form a beautiful pair, magnified

---

[5]A vehicle is written or produced for a specific star, regardless of whether the film is to promote their career, or to capitalize on their current popularity. It is created to display that star's particular skills or personal appeal (Dyer, 1979, p. 62; Britton, 1991, p. 205).
[6]The French press also insisted on the reunion of Delon and Ronet after *Plein Soleil* (René Clément, 1960) and *Lost Command* (Mark Robson, 1966).

for audiences who had followed their relationship in the press. Their earlier romance was used to blur the line between their on-screen sexually charged embraces and what could be inferred as residual off-screen feelings. Reunited on screen, Schneider and Delon perpetuated the culturally valued image of everlasting love and youthful physical beauty ('Romy Schneider in the arms of Alain Delon', *Jours de France*, 31/08/1968).

2.2. The body on display

La Piscine reflects a new French art de vivre, a modern hedonism that started in the late 1950s and boomed in the 1960s. Parisians initiated the movement of spending expensive holidays by the sea, populating the French beaches during the summer, especially the glamorous Côte d'Azur and the fashionable village of Saint-Tropez popularized by Brigitte Bardot in 1956 (Vincendeau, 2013, p. 136). Those new types of leisure entailed physical display: bodies were exposed and taboos broken when women sunbathed topless for the first time in 1964 in Saint-Tropez (Laubier, 1990, pp. 16, 50, 66–7). Progressively, undressing became a social phenomenon and, especially via Bardot's films, songs and overall image of 'sexual liberation', a cinematographic phenomenon. If this new lifestyle was seen as evidence of progress in French society, it also represented an imposition on women's bodies, one that has moulded female beauty to this day. Revealing one's body in swimsuit became the norm, which invited a relentless gaze onto female bodies, subjecting them to objectification because of new and unrealistic social standards of physical perfection. Naomi Wolf (2002) calls this 'the beauty myth'. She explains it as the 'violent backlash against feminism that uses images of female beauty as a political weapon against women's advancement' after the latter had 'released themselves from the feminine mystique of domesticity'. According to Wolf, this pressure compromises the ability of women to be effective in, and accepted by, society: the 'ideology of beauty is the last one remaining of the old feminine ideologies that still has the power to control [women]' (pp. 10–13).[7] Thus, while women's social power increased in 1960s France thanks to changes in legislation (*La Piscine* came out a few months after the events of May 68), another way to discipline women arose – the culturally induced obligation to expose their bodies (including, particularly, for actresses), with new and stringent standards of beauty, nudity and thinness. *La Piscine* is fairly representative of this contradiction: Schneider embodies a feminine ideal of the time – a

---

[7]Although Wolf's many controversies and spread of misinformation do put into question the credibility of her work, the book *The Beauty Myth* performed an important cultural intervention in the history of popular feminist discussions.

distinguished *bourgeoise* in a luxurious setting that showcases her perfect body in a bikini. *La Piscine*'s scriptwriter Jean-Claude Carrière explained that, when casting the film, other actresses were considered for the role of Marianne, but that they all had 'a swimsuit issue' (documentary *Romy, de tout son cœur*, 2016). Putting aside the sexism of Carrière's remark, it is not clear whether other actresses were not willing to be filmed in a bikini, or whether they wanted the role but were not considered good enough. But Schneider did not have a 'swimsuit issue' as her body obviously fitted the producers' standards of perfection. The film's opening scene sets that tone.

The first shot shows a silent and sun-tanned Delon lying by the pool, one hand in the azure water, the other slowly and carefully pouring a drink into his mouth, the epitome of the ideal French *homme fatal* (Vincendeau, 2000, p. 171).[8] His idle sunbathing is disturbed by someone plunging into the pool. Schneider's head emerges from the water, she swims a few breaststrokes, catches her breath and pivots on her back, she smiles with an open mouth and offers a glimpse of her breasts in a black halter-neck bikini. She stops, lies on the pool's steps and glances over her shoulder. Her gaze is determined, Delon looks back at her and she swims backwards, glancing at him again. She climbs out of the water, sucking in her flat stomach. She slips her wet hair back and walks around the pool towards Delon, smiling. At the time of filming in August and September 1968, Schneider was turning thirty and she is stunningly beautiful on screen: her curvaceous, toned and bronzed body clad in a black bikini is overtly on display. As discussed in previous chapters, Schneider had a characteristic gait: she walked with her elbows turned outward, her hands positioned backward and swung her arms, all of which gave her a way of holding her body that was, arguably, more athletic than graceful, although her confident port de tête owed something to her ballet training.[9] She put her hips forward when walking, inducing a discreet swaying movement to her body. In this scene, this way of walking gives confidence and sensuality to Marianne who aggressively pursues Jean-Paul: she stops above him and the camera zooms in on her wet body that responds to his caresses (her stomach contracts and slightly moves), then pans down to show Delon's hands rising and touching her upper thighs. She lies down next to him and kisses him. Schneider performs a character whose sexuality is overt and confident, and her presence dominates the screen. Their embrace reveals passionate partners attuned to each other's sexual desire, enhanced by the erotic chemistry between the two stars. Their past relationship was abundantly exploited by the production ('Alain et Romy: a love as tender as the memory', *Jours de France*, 22/08/1968), as well as their

[8]This opening shot was used, amongst other shots of Delon by and in the swimming pool, in a 2011 commercial for Dior's perfume *Eau Sauvage* (Dior's first perfume for men, created in 1966), featuring the film's original music by Michel Legrand.
[9]Schneider's exercise regimen was to practice modern dance and ballet.

physical resemblance upon which Visconti had capitalized in his on-stage pairing of the young couple in 1961. The actors appear comfortable and at ease with each other's bodies, their cat-like movements and feline facial traits mirroring each other. While this magnetic opening scene can be seen as female-driven in its assertion of her desire, Schneider's erotic image in the rest of the film is exclusively defined from a heterosexual male perspective that pointedly situates her as an object of sexual fascination for the male characters. With *La Piscine*, Schneider's nude body became a new site of tension for both visual exploitation and narrative purposes, as the following analysis demonstrates.

In one significant scene, Schneider, in her black bikini, is lying on a couch in the villa's cool living room, listening to a languorous jazz tune. A sensual and silent exchange starts with Harry's perspective dictating the camera movements. Smoking a cigar, he tilts his head to have a better look at Marianne. Then, in a medium shot framing her face and breasts, Schneider smiles in his direction, turns to straighten her head on the cushion and closes her eyes as the camera slowly pans down on her body as if she could feel Harry's stare on her, with her fingers delicately brushing her left thigh (Figure 8). This shot of Schneider's body finishes on Pénélope's disapproving face, her eyes going from her father to Marianne and her father again, frowning at Harry's deceitful and intense desire for Marianne. A subsequent scene (superfluous in terms of narrative development) presents a similar composition to the film's opening scene: Schneider is lying naked on her front as the camera slowly begins panning up her body, first her calves, then her thighs, her buttocks, her back moving slightly as she breathes and finally her sleeping face, the white sheets emphasizing her tan (the display of her naked back and buttocks followed conventions of the time[10]). This image was reprised in the original poster for the film in which Delon, in a macho pose and predatory look, seems to prey above his sleeping 'victim'. This brief interlude interrupting the narrative[11] refers to a famous shot of Brigitte Bardot lying on a white pile blanket in *Le Mépris* (Jean-Luc Godard, 1963). I have mentioned Bardot several times in this book in order to better examine, through contrast, Schneider's innocent persona of the late 1950s and *bourgeoise* image of the early 1960s. *La Piscine* further developed Schneider's on-screen eroticism,

---

[10]An actress (even less a star) was rarely seen from the back: Schneider's entire nude back was filmed to show her slim and athletic figure and her tanned skin, but it was also in accordance with the French cinematographic 'code' of female nudity. *La Piscine* came out just before the early 1970s' turning point with first examples of full-frontal nudity (notably with Bardot and Birkin in Roger Vadim 1973's film *Don Juan ou si Don Juan était une femme*, Vincendeau, 2013, p. 119).

[11]In her 1975 seminal text 'Visual Pleasure and Narrative Cinema', Laura Mulvey points out an aesthetic consequence of such moments: a tension arises between the narrative course (audiences wants to know what happens next in the film), and the 'spectacle of the woman' (audiences want to stop and look at the glamorous female star).

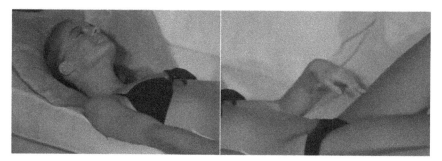

FIGURE 8 *A moment of voyeurism on Schneider's body in* La Piscine.

a primary aspect of Bardot's persona, and yet the impact of the two stars' images in this respect differs in terms of agency. Whereas Bardot raised her head and looked at Godard's camera, as if she was calling out and directly addressing the spectators caught in a voyeuristic act, Schneider remained passive and powerless in Deray's erotic mise-en-scène (contrary to Bardot's direct gaze, Schneider's eyes are shut as she appears to be sleeping).[12] In *La Piscine*, Schneider's body is highlighted, even celebrated (European film critics wrote about 'the plenitude of being in her 30s' and her 'blossoming': 'An Empress becomes a woman', 'Romy conquers men', *De Post*, 11/04/1971). Yet, she remains defined principally through her attractive physique, and her character does not exercise control over the use of her body.

Schneider's erotic characterization in *La Piscine* was the first of many that illustrated and perpetuated 'the beauty myth'. Marianne does not purposefully seduce Harry, who is arrogant enough to think that he can easily reclaim her, and yet the film's turning point (Jean-Paul's murderous act) is a direct consequence of Schneider's 'bewitching attraction' (Vincendeau, 2009, p. 25), and the overtly sexual display of her body. The two scenes described above are composed and framed to emphasize Schneider's radiant but submissive beauty. This key aspect of her persona, built through such moments of spectacle, became recurrent and anticipated Schneider's future performances from *La Piscine* onwards. Schneider's eroticism is further highlighted in contrast to Pénélope, performed by British actress Jane Birkin (who was twenty-one years old during filming). The difference between the two characters (and subsequently the impact on their star images) is observable in their respective first appearances on

---

[12]At this point of my book, one could wonder if the two knew each other and if they had an amicable relationship. According to sources, Schneider and Bardot were friends and shared a deep respect for each other's careers. Although they had the same agent (Olga Horstig) at the time of Schneider's arrival in France in 1958, they only officially met during the filming of *La Piscine* (Bardot still lives nearby Saint-Tropez), over a dinner hosted by Delon.

screen. In contrast to Marianne's confident and radiant presence, Pénélope's introduction is subdued. She sits quietly in the passenger seat of her father's car, unnoticed during the initial exchange between Marianne and Harry. Birkin is softly spoken, reserved and her long-legged, gamine appearance contrasts with Schneider's slim but womanly figure. Their respective relation to the swimming pool illustrates their different embodiment of femininity. Whereas Schneider, in the opening sequence, jumps in, Pénélope is never seen swimming, though she says that she loves to swim in the sea. Preference for the sea associates Birkin with nature (Chaplin, 2015, p. 57), connoting a youthful spirit, as opposed to Schneider's cultural allure and cosmopolitanism (seen in a number of her 1960s films discussed above). This distinction conveys another key component in the development of Schneider's French persona – her bourgeois sophistication.

2.3. The sophisticated *bourgeoise* of the 1960s

As we saw in Chapters 4 and 5, throughout the 1960s Schneider image evolved in class terms towards that of a distinguished bourgeois woman (*Boccaccio '70, The Cardinal, Good Neighbor Sam, La Voleuse*). *La Piscine* is the film that crystallized this identity and gave it a French inflexion. Three aspects form Schneider's French characterization in the film: the myth of the *Parisienne* (the elegant, chic and beautiful white woman), her elocution and accent and her costumes.

Regarding the notion of Parisian feminine identity, Felicity Chaplin (2015, 2017) argues that *La Piscine* qualifies as a '*Parisienne* film' because of its location and the presence of Schneider and Birkin, each attached to a dual *Parisienne* image – the sophisticate and the ingénue. Saint-Tropez was a favourite destination for Parisians (Chaplin, 2015, p. 49), and one could also consider *La Piscine* as a Côte d'Azur film, an unofficial subgenre of mostly thrillers that typically feature rich and beautiful protagonists in bathing suits who live in luxurious villas or hotels (Jean-Paul is a writer, Marianne a former journalist and Harry a music producer who drives a Maserati), a criminal element (Harry's murder), and a cosmopolite element (the two foreign female leads).[13] While Saint-Tropez is more associated with a carefree and bohemian attitude (at least at the time) inspired by Bardot, the French Riviera, with localitions such as Antibes, Nice, Saint-Jean-Cap-Ferrat, Cannes and Monaco, carries images of cosmopolitan glamour and French chic and luxury. Likewise, Chaplin (2015, p. 61) sees cosmopolitanism as 'one of the key motifs in *Parisienne* iconography', arguing that, despite being an emblem of French elegance and fashion flair, the Parisian woman

---

[13]The quintessential Côte d'Azur thriller would be Alfred Hitchcock's *To Catch a Thief* (1955).

is less a national figure than a universal one (2017, pp. 45–50). This means that the cultural status of the *Parisienne* is determined by taste (and wealth) rather than nationality. Chaplin also aptly remarks that Schneider and Birkin are 'part of a larger cohort of foreign actresses who have personified *la Parisienne*' on screen, pointing to Audrey Hepburn, Ingrid Bergman, Jean Seberg and Anna Karina. On and off screen, Schneider was associated with one aspect of the *Parisienne* as identified by Charles Rearick (2011, p. 34) – the 'elegant high-fashion woman' from a bourgeois upbringing (the other one being the 'sexy fun-loving young *Parisienne*', usually from the working-class). Indeed, her off-screen persona was structured around a narrative of bourgeois transformation that took place in Paris in the early 1960s when she arrived in the French capital, met Coco Chanel for *Boccaccio '70*, and was transformed from a 'plumpish Austrian beauty into a sleek *Parisienne*' (*Life Magazine*, 08/03/1963, pp. 82–3). Since then, she remained faithful to Chanel's creations off screen but at the same time cultivated other links to fashion[14] by progressively diversifying her style (for day-to-day and professional occasions) with designs by Courrèges and Yves Saint Laurent, two essential names of French haute couture who revolutionized 1960s and 1970s fashion. *La Piscine* marked a reiteration of this transformation narrative after the film's immense success, confirming her chic bourgeois *Parisienne* image and influencing her subsequent roles in French films.

Schneider's identity in *La Piscine* is also marked by her foreign-accented elocution. In the opening sequence, Marianne and Jean-Paul's embrace is interrupted by the phone ringing in the distant house. She wants to pick it up but he restrains her and the audience can distinctly hear Schneider's German accent: 'Mais attends, je vais revenir' ('I'll be back in a bit'). The way she pronounces the word 'revenir' is typical of her Germanic accent when speaking French: she had a habit of lengthening vowels and distinctly articulating each word and sound. With French being a second language to her, her pace was measured and slower than her Francophone screen partners. For instance, in a later scene, Marianne announces that it was Harry on the phone: 'Il est avec sa fille, il lui fait visiter la côte' ('He is with his daughter, he is showing her the Riviera'). There, Schneider sounds quite posh as she insists on and lengthens the phonemes [i] ('fille') and [o] ('côte') and her pronunciation is clearer and more elaborated than French natives: Delon's mumbling response, with his cigarette dangling off his mouth, offers a telling contrast. She slightly straightens her head when saying 'la côte', finishing the word by a barely perceptible pursing of her lips, followed by her signature 'œillade', gazing on the side towards Delon, looking askance with an impish, quizzical smile. This does not mean that she could not deliver a line with unstudied ease, using naturalistic performance techniques

---

[14]According to Stephen Gundle (2018, p. 172), entertainment and fashion are the two 'essential Parisian industries'.

such as interrupted speech and hesitation for instance, giving an 'an air of improvisation to the performance' (Naremore, 1988, p. 77), but this particular way of speaking contributed to Schneider's self-assured, cultured persona, that of a woman who expressed herself with refinement, exactitude and measure. Schneider's elocution also suited the film's style, based on the exchange of looks and ambiguous stares, rather than wordy dialogue. German words are mainly formed by elements either monosyllabic ('Mann', 'Mond') or disyllabic in which the second syllable has the vowel 'e' ('Vater', 'Amsel'), and this gives a particular musicality to the German, and especially the German-Austrian accent in French. Added to her round and soft voice, this musicality confers a charming and elegant quality to Schneider speaking French (see Wiese, 1996; Canepari, 2014). In that regard, she was part of a tradition in place since the beginning of French sound cinema that regularly featured French spoken by foreign actors with heavy and distinctive accents (Chion, 2008, p. 12). Films frequently made foreign actors speak with impeccable French (perfect syntax, rich vocabulary, as Schneider did) that 'the French characters themselves would fear to speak, at the risk of passing for snobs' (p. 13). Chion points out that this type of refined language is the prerogative of high society (he suggests that it might also be to add a 'touch of colour' compensating for the scarcity of regional accents in French cinema – with the notable exception of the Southern accent, pp. 13–14, 19).

Together with her identity as a *Parisienne* and as a foreigner, Schneider's sophisticated eroticism in *La Piscine* relies heavily on her costumes, designed by Courrèges, as well as her immaculate hairstyle and makeup. Schneider's fashion style is classically glamorous and mature, following an elaborate bourgeois dress code that coordinates with daily rituals (breakfast, leisure, shopping in the village and evening events); clearly Deray took every opportunity to display his star in flattering attire. Schneider's daytime costumes exude understated chic (there is a predominance of neutral colours: navy blue, white, pale blue) with dresses with modest above-the-knee hemlines. Her swimwear is seductive, chic and minimalist (either black or white to draw the eye on her body) and includes a black halter-neck bikini, a white one-piece bathing suit with thin straps and a deep back and a black one-piece swimsuit, all displaying her curvaceous figure. Marianne goes shopping in Saint-Tropez in navy flat front trousers, a tucked-in pale blue button-down shirt with turned-up collar and navy espadrilles; she carries a woven tote bag and wears tortoise-shell sunglasses, popular holiday-wear accessories, but all evidently within an affluent price range. Her evening dresses strike a more formal glamour note, with colours designed to show off her tanned skin: a floor-length gown and other dresses in vibrant nuances of greens, made from shimmering fabrics (sequins and satin). The outfits include diamond earrings and Schneider's hair, turned blond by the sun, is either worn down and meticulously swept back from her face, or tied back in a classic chignon or complicated French twist, drawing

FIGURE 9 *Two of Schneider's 'performative' dresses, designed by André Courrèges.*

attention to her bronzed face and 'striking green eyes' (Vincendeau, 2009, p. 25) often accentuated with heavy black eyeliner and, in this instance, chartreuse eyeshadow. These carefully planned ensembles compose an image of affluent and formal femininity. In contrast, Birkin's wardrobe suggests the bohemian ingénue and the *femme-enfant* with her jeans and t-shirts, mini-dresses and micro-skirts. Her white crocheted tunic over her white bikini draws attention to her long limbs, androgynous figure and connotes a more youthful style than Schneider (the tomboyish gamine) and a more veiled eroticism (Fraser-Cavassoni, 2004, p. 148; Chaplin, 2015, p. 49).

There are two scenes in which Schneider's evening dresses become the focus of the camera's attention. Two of Courrèges' designs showcase one of Schneider's best physical asset – her bare back – which helps develop her erotic aura (the designs also mean she does not wear a bra). The first one is composed of a halter-turtleneck top revealing her entire back, and she is shot in a dim light that emphasizes the lines of her spine and her lean muscles (Figure 9, left). It plays a role in a scene of sexual foreplay: Delon unties her collar, kneads her back as they passionately kiss, then cuts off a branch from a garden bush and uses it to brush and lash gently Schneider's bare back and buttocks while she moans.[15] The second 'performative' dress features in a scene in which Schneider, captured in a long shot, emerges from the villa in the twilight: she wears a floor-length sleeveless evening gown of fluid chiffon fabric featuring psychedelic swirls of various kinds of green (Figure 9, right). A large opening in the back allows Harry to slip his hand after he has expressed his admiration for the spectacular appearance of his ex-lover. Courrèges's pared-down designs, iconic of his 1960s style, combined with vivid colours (inspired by Pop Art) flatter Schneider's bronzed skin, sun-bleached hair and slim but athletic body.

---

[15]This scene was re-edited in a 2012 commercial for Dior's perfume *Eau Sauvage* and features the song 'I'm a Man' by the Black Strobe.

Conclusion

La Piscine, with 2,341,721 spectators in France in 1969 (Simsi, 2012, p. 34), was very popular and had a particularly important impact on Schneider's French star identity. Schneider could have been eclipsed by Delon and Ronet, who were two of the biggest French male stars at the time, but she so successfully embodied a winning combination of bourgeois confidence, erotic allure and Parisian chic that French audiences were ready to relinquish Sissi and embrace 'their' new female star ('Romy Schneider, in fantastic shape, makes a remarkable entrance and easily dominates her two male partners' [Martin, 1969]). The success of the film and of Schneider in particular led to the renewal of her career. Her 'second wind' would from now on be associated with French cinema, with realist and contemporary-set films featuring her as a 'modern', 'ideal' romantic partner (albeit precisely upper class); films about the German Occupation that embedded her melancholy characters into the tragic events of History; and finally an altogether more pessimistic, morbid streak. But before she reached this point, the event that changed the course of her career and moulded her French star image was meeting French director Claude Sautet during a post-synchronization session for *La Piscine* at the Boulogne-Billancourt studios. The partnership between Schneider and Sautet, which lasted over five films, changed the course of both their careers.

PART THREE

Romy Schneider's French career: 1969–1982

Introduction: Schneider and the 'long 1970s'

I now reach the third and last phase of Romy Schneider's career, which mainly took place in France and followed a successful ascending arc until her premature death at the age of forty-three in May 1982. This last phase was, and still is, considered by many (especially French-speaking audiences and critics) as the most fruitful and defining moment of her career.

This period was prolific: between 1969 and 1982, Schneider made twenty-eight films, which, unfortunately, means that I cannot deal with all of them to the same degree of detail. Three aspects emerge as particularly significant, thus the remaining chapters will follow this division: the first examines Schneider's films with Claude Sautet and the development of her 'modern woman' image; the second chapter analyses her German Occupation films that emphasized her Germanic identity; and the last chapter considers films that display her performance in an 'excessive' mode – in contrast to the more naturalistic style of her films with Sautet and her Occupation films.

The 'long 1970s' represent a complex period of change during which I track several developments in Schneider's paradoxical star image. This confirms Schneider as a star continually in transition, and this is precisely where her appeal lies. More than ever, the question of Schneider's feminine identity and what it meant in times of change in 1970s France was put to the fore.

* * *

1. The aftermath of May 68: social change

Romy Schneider's persona in the 1970s can be seen as echoing/responding to wide-scale societal shifting dynamics in the condition of women that derived from the ongoing modernization of France during the 'Trente Glorieuses' (post-war boom). This period led to a 'progressive destruction of the housewife model' (Chaperon, 1995, p. 62) with the streamlining of housework, birth control and the growth in women's paid employment. Though stemming from earlier feminist struggles, these changes benefitted from the political and cultural effervescence of the May 68 events, which is why I first consider the developments within French society throughout the late 1960s and 1970s.

Following the students and workers' demonstrations of 1968, French society experienced a destabilizing moment. Young people attacked moral and social norms and adopted new behaviours and fashions. Sexuality too became a means of revolt, breaking societal taboos. While May 68 in itself did little to advance the cause of women, the post-68 years in France were momentous, notably marked by the foundation of the Mouvement pour la Libération des Femmes, or MLF (Movement for Women's Liberation) in 1970. The Secrétariat d'État à la condition féminine was created in 1974 and numerous demonstrations in favour of equal rights for women gradually led to legislative change. On 5 April 1971, 343 women, amongst whom Simone de Beauvoir, Catherine Deneuve, Marguerite Duras, Gisèle Halimi, Françoise Fabian, Bernadette Lafont, Jeanne Moreau, Micheline Presle, Françoise Sagan, Delphine Seyrig, Nadine Trintignant and Agnès Varda, signed a manifesto publicly admitting to having broken the 1920 Law by having had an abortion, at the risk of being sentenced.[1] Women started their long fight and defended the rights to bodily autonomy and birth control, which they obtained with the reimbursement of the contraceptive pill in 1974.[2] The 'Loi Veil' (named after Minister of Health Simone Veil) legalizing abortion was voted in 1975, made permanent in 1979 and completed in 1982 with social security reimbursement. Throughout the 1970s, women fought for sexual emancipation and reached, in theory, legal foundations for equal recognition within the couple and the family, but also for professional equality, which was strengthened in the following decades.

2. French cinema: evolving genres and stardom

The revolutionary events of May 68 had a direct impact on French cinema. The 'affaire Langlois' that began in February 1968, mobilizing and uniting film professionals, predated the events of May. With the removal of Cinémathèque's co-founder Henri Langlois (later reinstated), *cinephiles* took to the streets and film became an instrument of revolt. The 1968 Cannes festival was interrupted and the venue was occupied at the initiative of filmmakers such as François Truffaut, Jean-Luc Godard, Claude Lelouch and Louis Malle. Their media intervention and political demonstration in Cannes echoed their call for a new cinema. Filmmakers called for an indefinite strike of film production in order to reform the industry and they

---

[1] In 1971, a woman who had an abortion or attempted to have one risked a prison sentence of six months to twelve years, and a penalty of 360 to 7,200 francs. In case of recurrence, women faced five to ten years in prison and a 18,000 to 72,000 franc-penalty. Pro-choice propaganda was reprimanded by a decree from 11 May 1955.
[2] The 'Loi Neuwirth' legalized the oral contraceptive pill in 1967.

attacked the abusive rules of censorship. Criticism also seized the topic of films addressing social issues and questioned the fascination that images have on audiences. Although most of these demands were not met, and none concerned women, the events had an effect on censorship.

In the 1970s, censorship considerably loosened, which led to the arrival of erotic films, from Roger Vadim's *Barbarella* (1968) to the *Emmanuelle* series (Just Jaeckin, from 1974), and the explosion of porn film. Sexuality imbued also films made by dissident and/or provocative authors, such as Nelly Kaplan with *La Fiancée du pirate* (1969), Bernardo Bertolucci with *Last Tango in Paris* (1972), Marco Ferreri and *La Grande bouffe* (1973) and Bertrand Blier with *Les Valseuses* (1974). New Wave figureheads kept working, while a few new auteurs emerged (Philippe Garrel, Maurice Pialat, Jean Eustache). The legacy of May 68 was also reflected in the *cinéma engagé* (militant cinema) including Godard and Jean-Pierre Gorin who decided to film exclusively in 16 mm (see Smith, 2005; Shafto, 2006). The decade also saw the rise of women filmmakers: Nadine Trintignant, Nelly Kaplan, Nina Companeez, Yannick Bellon, Chantal Ackerman, Coline Serreau, Anna Karina, Jeanne Moreau and women cinema's pioneer Agnès Varda put the women's movement at the centre of her film *L'une chante, l'autre pas* (1977). The (still timidly) growing feminization of cinema led to some new trends in the representation of gender relations in parallel with the expansion of feminist movements (see Rollet and Tarr, 2001). Nevertheless, French society remained strongly attached to the patriarchal status quo. French cinema mostly equated female 'modernity' with sexuality and increased on-screen nudity, frequently harnessed to misogynist stereotypes, such as the femme fatale, embodied by glamorous actresses (Jane Fonda, Brigitte Bardot, Jeanne Moreau, Stéphane Audran, Catherine Deneuve).

Beyond these changes, mainstream genres continued to flourish while adapting to new societal topics, such as comedy with the *café-théâtre* generation (more explicit humour, incisive social commentaries) (see Lanzoni, 2014, pp. 156–8), and detective films moving in the direction of political thrillers with Yves Boisset, Alain Corneau and Costa-Gavras (Guérif, 1981, p. 163). Melodrama dealt, in a classical form, with social issues such as transgressive sexual relations (*Mourir d'aimer*, André Cayatte, 1971), drugs (*More*, Barbet Schroeder, 1969) and incest (*Le Souffle au cœur*, Louis Malle, 1971). There was a renewed interest in History and the German Occupation in particular with films that were often called 'rétro' at the time and would later be termed 'heritage' films. Schneider was prominent in such films (e.g. *Le Vieux fusil*, Robert Enrico, 1975) as she was in the work of a band of post-New Wave, 'quality' auteurs, such as Bertrand Tavernier, Michel Deville and Claude Sautet who engaged, in a naturalistic style, with contemporary French bourgeois society (Vincendeau, 1996, p. 8).

In the changing landscape of French cinema in the post-68 era, female stars also evidenced a complex evolution. In 1967, 1968 and 1969, three actresses entered the 'Top 20' of the most successful films in France (Simsi, 2012, pp. 32–4): Annie Girardot at the end of 1967 with *Vivre pour vivre* (Claude Lelouch) and *Erotissimo* (Gérard Pirès, 1969); Marlène Jobert in 1968 with *Alexandre le bienheureux* (Yves Robert), *Faut pas prendre les enfants du bon Dieu pour des canards sauvages* (Michel Audiard) and *L'Astragale* (Guy Casaril), and Romy Schneider in 1969 with *La Piscine*. Other successful actresses included Mireille Darc and Jane Birkin. During this transitional period, Brigitte Bardot and Jeanne Moreau, the most popular stars of the 1960s, were on the wane. Bardot appeared in the Top 20 with *Les Novices* (Guy Casaril, 1970) and *Les Pétroleuses* (Christian-Jaque, 1971) (Simsi, pp. 35–6) but she retired from film in 1973.

While the success of *La Piscine* situated Schneider within drama, and she then became associated with Sautet's middle-class cinema, Girardot and Jobert frequently featured in comedies. The former embodied a new type of active and independent female character, and the latter played sweet, naive and scatter-brained woman. As for Deneuve, after a slump between 1968 and 1974 during which her conservative persona did not coincide with the political and naturalistic tendencies of the new French cinema, she succeeded in 'democratizing' her image with a popular role in the comedy *Le Sauvage* (Jean-Paul Rappeneau, 1975) and regained her place amongst France's most popular female stars (Vincendeau, 2008, p. 249; Le Gras, 2007b, p. 304). From Schneider's generation in France only Schneider herself, Deneuve (born in 1943) and Darc (born, like Schneider, in 1938) passed the May 68 mark, alternating roles in auteur cinema and popular genre films.

3. Schneider's eclectic, 'in-between' roles

Before Schneider's fame and popularity were re-established in France, the first years of the 1970s were marked by an erratic career path as she multiplied roles in international productions, which I will briefly examine here. None of them, however, were successful at the box office and some remained undistributed in France. Nonetheless, a particular image emerged from these diverse films: a woman fully assuming her sexuality. After May 68, traditional codes of behaviour related to sexuality and interpersonal relationships were considerably challenged and revaluated and Schneider's presence in those early 1970s films has to be considered in this light. She incarnated women who were sexually available, but not significantly emancipated in other aspects of their lives. Thus, in this respect her persona did not depart from the ones of Brigitte Bardot, Bernadette Lafont, Mireille Darc or Marlène Jobert (contrary to Deneuve whose sexuality was contained, only suggestive as in *Belle de jour* by Luis Buñuel in 1967). Their personas were, however, distinct from one another in terms of class: while

Girardot and Jobert played women from modest or 'ordinary' backgrounds, Schneider and Deneuve performed bourgeois characters.

In the London-based drama *My Lover, my son* (John Newland, 1970) Schneider plays Francesca, an older man's wealthy and unhappy wife who is devoted to her son James (Dennis Waterman) because he reminds her of her late lover. She develops feelings for him and reacts jealously when he falls in love with his girlfriend Julie (Patricia Brake). Although Schneider's previous success *Les Choses de la vie* was released in France a few months before (in March) and was still in film theatres, *My Lover, my son* failed at the box office and stayed in French cinemas for only two weeks in the summer of 1970. It also went unnoticed internationally while Louis Malle's *Le Souffle au cœur*, which had a similar topic (incest), was a success a year later. Schneider, who was thirty-one at the time, was not persuasive as Waterman's mother (he was twenty-two). Nevertheless, the role of the sophisticated rich woman, and the lavish setting (Francesca lives in a Tudor mansion with a baroque swimming pool) matched Schneider's bourgeois persona that had been very successful in *La Piscine*.

She also appeared in the French thriller *Qui?*, released in September 1970. Directed and co-written by Léonard Keigel with Paul Gégauff (who co-wrote *Plein Soleil*), the film is misogynistic in its treatment of Schneider's character, Marina – she is physically abused and, because she is presented having a mysterious and sensuous aura, the story frames her as a femme fatale who 'deserves' her punishment, as well as the obvious culprit in the murder mystery. The film failed to reach 500,000 spectators. Schneider also had a small part as the protagonist's girlfriend Nira in the British-Israeli film *Bloomfield* (Richard Harris, 1971), a Harris-vehicle shot in Tel Aviv. The film was not critically praised and failed at the box office – it was never distributed in France. Schneider later starred in *La Califfa/The Lady Caliph* (1971), the first film of Italian writer Alberto Bevilacqua adapted from his eponymous best-seller novel published in 1964.[3] The film failed in France (with 48,179 spectators it is the lowest turnout for a Schneider film in France), but was a success in Italy where it polarized critics and resonated with the country's troubled social and political climate of the 'Years of Lead' ('Anni di piombo'). The film stands out in Schneider's filmography as she performs one of her very few proletarian roles, perhaps explaining the film's failure in France. Irene Corsini, the widow of a workman killed by the police, becomes the leader of a protest movement at her factory, run by entrepreneur Doberdò (Ugo Tognazzi). Their relationship is at first belligerent (illustrated by many intense, green-eyed stares during the police charge and the riot scenes) but then develops into an affair. The role was at odds with Schneider's sophisticated bourgeois image. However, Irene's

---

[3]Schneider did not speak Italian in the film's original version.

contained fury and aggressive charm allowed Schneider to widen her acting skills, while she was made to foreground a powerful sensuality following on from *Boccaccio '70, 10.30 pm Summer*, and *La Piscine*. The erotic scenes, however, are as voyeuristic as in the above-mentioned films, and Schneider's tanned and toned body is displayed in full-figured nude scenes (the entire back and her top front).

Consolidating her sensual image, Schneider posed fully nude in the German magazine *Stern* twice in 1973: first lying on her stomach (01/03/1973) in a pose reminiscent of her nap in *La Piscine*, and then swimming in the Mediterranean Sea (16/08/1973).[4] *La Califfa* was presented at the Cannes Festival in May 1971. Joseph Losey directed Schneider the following year in her sixth and last collaboration with Delon, *The Assassination of Trotsky* (1972). Here, her supporting role of Gita Samuels (the companion of Delon as Ramón Mercader, Trotsky's assassin), was similar to Irene in *La Califfa*: she adopts a melodramatically amplified performance to convey the passionate and dedicated communist militant. As Trotsky's (Richard Burton) former secretary and friend, Gita is used and betrayed by her lover to approach and kill the former communist leader in exile in Mexico. Schneider is a stooge to Delon's laconic performance of cold elegance (in line with his then recent roles in Jean-Pierre Melville's *Le Samouraï* in 1967 and Jacques Deray's *Borsalino* in 1970), and his character constantly abuses her verbally during their few scenes together. In short, Gita merely adorned the male character's love arc and her political opinions are undeveloped, which seems implausible as she is Trotsky's assistant. In the end, Gita is too infatuated with Mercader to perceive his motives, and she proves instrumental in her leader's death, thus fitting the stereotype of a woman dominated by her emotions.

Those political roles barely left a mark on Schneider's persona (even though *The Assassination of Trotsky* was a box-office success in April 1972[5]) and she continued to build a French on- and off-screen identity by swimming against the tide of the early 1970s and identifying with upper-class characters: 'I am very *bourgeoise* you know, absolutely, I am very *bourgeoise* and very old-fashioned' (interview by Claude Couderc, 29/06/1974). And yet, in just a few years, she became the most sought-after actress of French cinema. In order to explain this paradox, I now turn towards Schneider's films and performances that attest to her return to stardom with the new French *cinéma de qualité*, notably her collaboration with Claude Sautet.

---

[4]The photos were also published in the December issue of the French men's magazine *Lui* in 1973.
[5]The film made 563,000 entries in France (Simsi, 2012, p. 128).

7

The 'Ideal French woman'*

Introduction

This chapter examines one of the most fascinating paradoxes of Schneider's star image in French cinema: her ambivalent relationship with feminism and changes in women's lives and their representation on screen. Indeed, Schneider was (and still is) praised in French-speaking media for her image of the emancipated woman in 1970s France. Yet, as we shall see, this categorization was problematic and has to be put into perspective, especially because the media discourse on Schneider has changed very little since the early 1970s. This chapter is entitled 'the *ideal* French woman' in view of the ambivalent feminine identity that she projected, worshipped by the media as 'modern', yet reactionary in gender terms.

Because Claude Sautet was the director who contributed the most to Schneider's persona in the 1970s, this chapter focuses primarily on his films. Nonetheless, I attach other Schneider films to the trend developed in his work, namely *Un amour de pluie/Love in the rain* (Jean-Claude Brialy, 1974), *Le Mouton enragé/Love at the top* (Michel Deville, 1974) and *Les Innocents aux mains sales/Dirty Hands* (Claude Chabrol, 1975).

1. The cinema of Claude Sautet

Claude Sautet, like Bertrand Tavernier and Michel Deville, is often thought of as exemplifying a new *cinéma de qualité* (quality cinema) after the innovations of the New Wave (Hayward, 1993, p. 229; Austin, 1996,

---

*Sautet said that Schneider 'perfectly answered to what [he] expected at the time of an actress regarding women' (Gassen and Hurst, 1991, p. 251).

p. 142). These directors are thereby placed within the lineage of the mainstream film-makers of the 1940s and 1950s such as Claude Autant-Lara, Jean Delannoy, René Clair and Marcel Carné who worked within the French studio system, with solid teams of craftsmen, and who were famously attacked by Truffaut in his *Cahiers du cinéma* article 'A certain tendency of French cinema' (1954). In this respect 'quality', for Truffaut, was a negative term, his critical practice a strategy that paved the way for the New Wave films. While Truffaut's argument has been very influential, Sautet and his colleagues could be seen to reclaim the values of the 1950s traditional film-making craft, while modernizing them by expressing more forcefully their own concerns and displaying a more informal visual style. Consistent features in Sautet's work, both stylistic and thematic, created an authorial signature that is now highly respected. His oeuvre reveals the significance of collective work with regular collaborators, especially with recognized screenwriters such as Jean-Loup Dabadie who wrote or co-wrote most of his films, and Claude Néron. Composer Philippe Sarde, cinematographer Jean Boffety and editor Jacqueline Thiédot were also part of the 'team', and last but not least his troupe of stars: Schneider was one of them, as well as Michel Piccoli, Lino Ventura, Yves Montand, Bernard Fresson and Jean Bouise. Sautet's films are also recognizable for their intimate realism, created through a classic, understated, mise-en-scène (shooting in colour, on location, with a discreet camerawork, except for the occasional zoom, and transparent editing – in line with the naturalistic aesthetic of his time). Finally, Sautet favoured 'modern' societal topics set in middle-class milieus. His films focus on male psychology, yet offer flattering portraits of their female stars. His 'bourgeois' cinema of the 1970s, especially the films made with Schneider, is little known outside of francophone borders, but they were successful at the French box office, which made Schneider very popular in return.

Schneider and Sautet met in the Boulogne Studios near Paris during a post-synchronization session of *La Piscine* (Schneider dubbed herself in German and English). He wished to cast Annie Girardot in the role of Hélène for his next project *Les Choses de la vie*, but she declined. Sautet apparently saw *La Piscine*'s rushes, which, according to Jean-Loup Dabadie, convinced him to cast Schneider because of her sensuality in the film (documentary *Romy, de tout son cœur*, 2016). The myth surrounding their first encounter casts it as fortuitous: Sautet either observed Schneider recording dialogues behind the sound booth's glass, or he did not recognize her in the corridor but was immediately seduced by her 'strong vivacity', her 'natural look' and her 'simplicity' (interview with Sautet by Michel Drucker, 26/11/1978). She was wearing minimal makeup and had her hair either covered by a hat or in a chignon, which he reportedly loved as it revealed her face. Although the meeting between the two was, in fact, planned (Gassen and Hurst, 1991, p. 251), the 'legend' points out key elements in the pair's working relationship and the reshaping of Schneider's persona at that time – Sautet 'discovered' Schneider and he was the director who best magnified her natural beauty.

Schneider and Sautet made five films together: *Les Choses de la vie/The Things of life* (1970), *Max et les ferrailleurs/Max and the junkmen* (1971), *César et Rosalie/César and Rosalie* (1972), *Mado* (1976) and *Une histoire simple/A Simple story* (1978). Although the media narrative framing their partnership evolved around the auteur-muse dynamic, none of those films were specifically written for Schneider, with the exception of *Une histoire simple*. The films were critical and box-office successes, all exceeding one million spectators. Moreover, they were all part of the twenty most successful films the year of their release in France. While building on her established bourgeois and sensual identity, this set of films developed for Schneider a reassuring image of vulnerable femininity, a relatively new trait of Schneider's persona that has since then defined her in the eyes of French-speaking audiences.

* * *

Sautet's films with Schneider are all set in contemporary times. Except for the thriller *Max et les ferrailleurs*, they depict the everyday life of bourgeois Parisian milieus in which Schneider performs the same type of character. Whether she is a wife, a lover, a prostitute, a divorced mother or a friend, she personifies a notion that developed from their first collaboration in 1969 to their last in 1978: the sexually emancipated, modern Parisian *bourgeoise* – or rather, the masculine vision of this '*ideal*' woman'. And yet, following May 68, French cinema experienced a period that was not favourable to bourgeois values, institutions or stars (Le Gras, 2007b, p. 303). As already mentioned, for example, most of Catherine Deneuve's films in the 1970s were unsuccessful. Schneider presented an equally conservative and traditional image as Deneuve at the turn of the 1970s. Her beauty and its presentation through grooming (makeup, accessories, hairstyle), though not as cold as Deneuve's, suggested a distance that construed her as inaccessible. Yet, she became, with Girardot, the most popular star of the decade. The work of this chapter is in part to try and understand this paradox.

The following section focuses on two complementary poles: Schneider's minimalist performance of vulnerable beauty, and her roles as the modern Parisian *bourgeoise*. For this I focus on her three most popular films with Sautet: *Les Choses de la vie*, *César et Rosalie* and *Une histoire simple*.[1]

---

[1] Respectively ranking eighth, eleventh and thirteenth in the Top 20 the year of their release.

2. Schneider's vulnerable beauty

2.1. *Les Choses de la vie*

With *Les Choses de la vie*, Claude Sautet, who until then had mostly directed thrillers, initiated a cycle of contemporary and intimate portraits of upper middle-class Parisians for which he became famous amongst French audiences. The film is based on the eponymous novel by Paul Guimard who co-wrote the screenplay with Sautet and Dabadie. The film begins with the image of a car wheel in an orchard: on a summer morning, a fancy sports car has crashed on a rural road, hurling the driver Pierre (Michel Piccoli) onto the grass. As he loses consciousness, he revisits the joys and sorrows that constitute the little but essential 'things of life': his wife Catherine (Lea Massari) from whom he is separated, his partner Hélène (Schneider), his son Bertrand (Gérard Lartigau), his father (Henri Nassiet), his friend François (Jean Bouise), his work and flashes of joy experienced whilst sailing with his family around the Île de Ré or cycling amorously with Hélène (the latter image features on the film's original poster). Pierre's inner monologue revolves around a letter that must not be found. Pierre and Hélène had quarrelled the night before the crash and, stopping at a café on his way to Rennes, Pierre writes her a letter ending their relationship, but does not post it. Driving past a wedding, he realizes that the letter was a mistake and that he should marry Hélène. Although rushed to the hospital, he does not recover and Catherine is given his belongings, including the unsent letter that she reads and tears to pieces when she sees Hélène arriving. Doing so, Catherine fulfils Pierre's ultimate wish; it also suggests that she considers Schneider's character vulnerable, as if Hélène could not handle the loss of Pierre's love and his death.

Les Choses de la vie was intended as Piccoli's star vehicle, and Schneider has a relatively small screen time. Nevertheless, her performance had a great impact on her career and persona. Schneider's presence in the film was emphasized in various media texts and promotional material: she was extensively shown in the original French trailer, she shared a co-starring credit with Piccoli (their names appearing together before the film title in the opening credits) and, amongst other examples, the Italian title of the film directly refers to her character – *L'amante* ('the lover'). She also recorded the film's theme song, a melancholy ballad entitled 'La Chanson d'Hélène' ('Hélène's song') that emphasizes her character's fragility since the lyrics evoke what Hélène and Pierre's life would have been if he had not died – as he no longer loves her he leaves her, and she is left distraught.

Hélène is not particularly developed, and her character mostly relies on Schneider's performance as a beauty and as an 'other'. It is hinted that she has a job as a German-French translator, and when she first meets Pierre she mocks her own accent ('As you can hear I'm from Paris'), referencing Schneider's Germanness, which is otherwise relatively irrelevant in Sautet's films. On the one hand, her Germanic persona contributes to the construction of her character as confident, even haughty at times; and, on the other hand, she brought with her from *La Piscine* the image of a sophisticated and chic woman. However, a new aspect of Schneider's image appeared in *Les Choses de la vie*: she started to project a fragile and victimized identity. While this was latent in a number of 1960s films, *Les Choses de la vie* crystallized an amalgam between Schneider's beauty/erotic appeal, her bourgeois register and her vulnerability, as illustrated by the scene analysed below.

After the car crash that acts as a preamble and accompanies the credits, the opening scene sets the tone. It begins with Schneider lying nude on her stomach next to Piccoli in the darkness of the bedroom; she wakes up, drapes a white towel around her body and gets up quietly. On the balcony of the Parisian apartment, she ties up her brunette hair while looking down the street. She walks back inside and greedily bites on an apple before sitting in front of a typewriter. She chews the apple and puts on reading glasses. She is filmed in profile, chin forward, emphasizing her jawline. Schneider's on-screen presence was often defined through a male character's gaze, and this film is no exception. Piccoli sits behind Schneider while she types, he smokes a cigarette and then the camera, adopting his point of view, closes in on the curve of Schneider's neck and tanned shoulders. Then the camera cuts back to Schneider who, focused on her reading and typing, softly asks: 'What are you doing?', Pierre – on behalf of the audience – responds 'I'm looking at you'. She lowers her chin slightly, the camera returns to Pierre's point of view while she turns over towards him and smiles, framed as in a painting (Figure 10). Schneider often executed her smile in two beats: first, there is a fleeting trace of a smile she appears to try and restrain, expanding her nostrils, and then she stretches her lips unreservedly, but without showing her teeth which had the particularity to put the emphasis on her eyes. Her graceful and yet hesitant smile, with its tinge of sadness, marks a defining moment for both the character and the star. Another example of this is, after Hélène has been outbid at an auction by Pierre, the fast zoom-in to an extreme close-up of her face, as she suddenly turns to the camera to react to Pierre shouting, signifying the exact moment he falls in love with her at first sight. These prolonged close-up shots of Schneider's face (during which she barely blinks) suggest a lack of distance and thus significantly favour the audience's emotional bond with her characters and with the star.[2]

Les Choses de la vie was a popular[3] and critical success: it won the Louis Delluc Prize for Best Film in 1969 and was nominated for the Palme

---

[2] Barry King calls this process 'hypersemiotization' (1985, p. 41).
[3] With 2,959,682 spectators in France, the film was the eighth highest grossing film in 1970 (Simsi, 2012, p. 35).

FIGURE 10 *Schneider's two-beat smile in* Les Choses de la vie.

d'Or at the 1970 Cannes Festival. This success revitalized the directing career of Sautet who had not directed a film since *L'Arme à gauche* in 1965 (he nonetheless participated in the writing of many scripts throughout the 1960s). The film was even more popular than *La Piscine* at the French box office. This triumph prompted their partnership and two other films quickly followed: *Max et les ferrailleurs* in 1971 and *César et Rosalie* in 1972.

2.2. *César et Rosalie*

Schneider's eponymous character in *César et Rosalie* could be an older version of Hélène from *Les Choses de la vie* as she is as sensitive and tender, yet she is more confident in her relations to others (especially men), and mature and sophisticated in her attitudes and her looks. *César et Rosalie* is one of Sautet's most appreciated and most representative films. It tells the story of a complicated love triangle. Rosalie, formerly married to Antoine (her daughter's father, Umberto Orsini), was previously also in love with handsome young artist David (Sami Frey) who let her marry Antoine and then disappeared. Now, five years later, David has returned but Rosalie is in love with César (Yves Montand), a middle-aged, rich scrap-metal dealer. Rosalie is drawn to David, then back to César and so on, in a succession of arrangements: César and Rosalie, David and Rosalie, César, David and Rosalie, and even César and David at the end. Everyone adores Rosalie: she is young, agreeable, moderately rich, accommodating and multilingual (César calls on her to do translations in English for his business).

   Schneider's performance displays a calm and easy-going composure which makes her appear, in turn, fragile and elegantly melancholy. The actress's sorrowful eyes and repressed smile inscribe a certain gravity to her face. The contrast with Montand is striking: his charm is skittish, imposing, brutish, and he displays a showman's eagerness to please (he talks fast, loudly and over people, he hums and sings, he uses a lot of onomatopoeias and hand gestures to emphasize and 'colour' his comments). César is a parvenu and Rosalie is portrayed as socially superior to him; Schneider looks at him with either contempt (with a superior and detached smirk, sometimes slightly raised eyebrows) or compassion.

In Schneider's performance panoply, now the 'two-beat smile' joins the 'œillade', as well as a pout, giving Rosalie a half-amused/half-mocking, mischievous look. Another performance sign that regularly occurs in *César et Rosalie* is a sharp turn of the head that gives a graceful swing to her bouncy curls, brushing her face. This is often seen in long or medium shots when she walks, laughs, greets people and chats in crowded scenes, to make sure viewers do not lose track of the star. Through her performance, Schneider creates an elusive and detached Rosalie: she is a woman on the move (as seen on the film's original poster), who is amused and appreciates being chased by men, but whose desire remains mysterious – she remains a male fantasy. The vitality and energy in Schneider's gait when her character is in a group are counterbalanced by her performance during more intimate scenes. Here, along with her soft voice speaking a few lines of dialogues and her sidelong and penetrating gaze, are added some relatively new motifs, such as the way she slowly and methodically carries her cigarette from her fingertips to her mouth, extensively pulling on it, suggesting a woman aware and in control of her power of seduction.

Rosalie is presented as being subjected to men's desires and inconsistencies. As the embodiment of a male fantasy, she is dispossessed of her own subjectivity, as suggested by her first appearance in the film, when spectators discover her through the eyes of César. The latter suddenly enters her bedroom without knocking. The use of a quick zoom in, scrutinizing Schneider's look, highlights César's agitation and impatience to see the woman he desires. But this process also affects our perception of Schneider's beauty as vulnerable, as her startled face occupies a growing portion of the screen. Spectators are complicit in this stolen image of Schneider and enter Rosalie's life as if by breaking in.

Indeed, because Rosalie explicitly states more than once that she is intent on keeping her free will, viewers could forget that her condition as an obliging and self-effacing woman corresponds to a very traditional role, in contradiction to women's rising demands for autonomy at the time. Despite her socially privileged status, no emotional crisis can keep Rosalie out of the kitchen: tired of attending to César's poker games, she goes to David's studio, only to serve coffee. This submissive gender configuration of Schneider's character speaks volume about her image in the 1970s. The critical consensus that saw Schneider as the 'ideal French woman' ('Romy Schneider, so beautiful, so strong, so vulnerable, is the ideal woman and a purebred actress' [Rabine, 1974]) can be seen as a backlash against women's emancipation. Overall,

Schneider's vulnerable and glamourous beauty in *César et Rosalie* created the archetype of a woman adhering to tradition under the guise of modernity. She reconciled in her persona several paradoxes: the emancipated modern woman, and the 'reassuring' – vulnerable – seductress; a woman who was respectable in class terms, an effect enshrined in her distinguished (i.e. affluent) environment and clothes, who was also sexually available.

Schneider's role as Elizabeth in the romantic drama *Un amour de pluie* (Jean-Claude Brialy, 1974) confirms this sexual aura. The film presents the simultaneous sexual awakenings of a mother (Schneider) and her teenage daughter (Bénédicte Bucher) while on vacation in the spa-town of Vittel (Vosges region). Elizabeth cheats on her husband (only present on the phone via the voice of Michel Piccoli) and enjoys a summer fling with Giovanni (Nino Castelnuovo), a dashing Italian who stays in her hotel. The same goes for her roles as Roberte in the dark comedy *Le Mouton enragé* (Michel Deville, 1974) and Julie in the thriller *Les Innocents aux mains sales* (Claude Chabrol, 1975) who both take a lover without thinking twice. Schneider's on-screen 'liberated' sexual behaviour is justified by narratives that pair her with disappointing male partners as the reason for looking elsewhere to satisfy her desire. Her characters' husbands are either absent (Piccoli in *Un amour de pluie*), insufferably pretentious (Michel Vitold as a philosophy professor in *Le Mouton enragé*) or old and impotent (Rod Steiger in *Les Innocents aux mains sales*). And yet, Schneider's characters are as docile as they are aggressive, as subordinate as they are independent, and as strong and clever as they are tender and vulnerable, and most importantly, they seek protection from men – which is often denied to them at the end (Elizabeth returns to her husband, Roberte is shot and Julie is left alone and afraid). In other words, her characters' attempts at emancipation, albeit only sexual emancipation, are punished.

To conclude, let's consider the written caption on the cover of *Le Soir Illustré* (17/01/1974): 'Romy Schneider: men are afraid of us', the boldness of this statement very much in stark contrast to the accompanying photograph of Schneider in *Le Mouton enragé*. She is beautiful, elegant (she wears couture clothes designed by Maison Torrente in the film), but also sad and fragile (her distant eyes and melancholy smile), echoing her performance in the film. Roberte represents 'love', the 'only source of happiness and of femininity' (de Baroncelli, 1974). While the caption alludes to an important anti-feminist motif at the time (that liberated women were detrimental to men; Bard, 1999), Schneider's vulnerable beauty thus became configured as a reassuring and 'ideal' representation, a soothing balm to the 'threat' of women's emancipation.

3. The Parisian *bourgeoise* look

Having examined the ideological implications of Schneider's persona in the evolving gender configurations of the time in two of Sautet's films, it is necessary to consider the spectacle of female bourgeois modernity she successfully offered on and off screen, through her clothing, makeup and hairstyle.

Schneider remained foremost a glamorous star whose fashionable appearance was fundamental. Her costume in the opening sequence of *Les Choses de la vie* (a white towel) and her mundane feminine gestures (doing her hair without the help of a mirror) are meant to signify that Hélène and Schneider are women like any others – except within a privileged social milieu. In films directed by Sautet, characters live in large, tastefully decorated, modern apartments; they regularly eat in restaurants, they drive expensive cars, they spend their vacations and weekends in pleasant country or seaside houses and they dress in couture clothes or chic ready-to-wear.

3.1. In search of a style: the turn of the 1970s

Following his work on *La Piscine*, André Courrèges designed Schneider's costumes in *Les Choses de la vie*. In the film, Schneider wears the couturier's most famous design: his A-line mini-dress, either sleeveless or with cap sleeves, and in different colours – bright white, lemon yellow and lime. The modern and minimalistic look of these dresses is sparsely accessorized. Contrary to *La Piscine*, in *Les Choses de la vie* Schneider's clothes are not the centre of attention, nor do they emphasize her figure. The line of the trapeze-shaped dresses erases the curves of her hips, and breasts; her bare legs are rarely seen and she mostly wears trousers. She wears 'casual' modern ensembles such as high-waisted, bell-bottomed jeans combined with a tucked-in, V-neck pale blue shirt. These Courrèges designs exude modernity and the androgyny of 1960s clothes; they do not overtly sexualize the woman wearing them. Courrèges's costumes discreetly flatter Schneider's beauty without being overtly spectacular.

The opposite approach was adopted for Schneider's second collaboration with Sautet in 1971 for *Max et les ferrailleurs*, in which she plays Lily, a German-born prostitute. For the part, Sautet developed a minor character into a fully fledged leading role, at the star's demand (Gassen and Hurst, 1991, p. 252). She is the girlfriend of Abel (Bernard Fresson), one of the junkmen of the title who robs construction sites with his gang in Nanterre. Undercover detective Max (Michel Piccoli) is determined to catch them in the act. Posing as a client and pretending to be a banker, he manipulates Lily and lures the gangsters into holding up a bank. Appearing 30 minutes into the film, Schneider is given a true star entrance. We see her through the eyes of Piccoli as he observes Lily and Abel leaving a restaurant from afar, in a point of view shot through his telescope. The sexual nature of Lily's work is understood because of the cliché connotations of her clothes, designed by Tanine Autré and Jacques Cottin: a fuchsia ribbon around her neck in a bow, high-heeled ankle-strapped shoes, sheer stockings and a shiny black vinyl raincoat (likely an Yves Saint Laurent creation, though the designer is uncredited). Schneider's make-up (by Jean-Pierre Eychenne) is much more pronounced than in any of her previous films, with strong lipliner giving her fuller and bigger lips, and pearly eyeshadow covering her eyelids up to the eyebrows. Her vibrantly coloured dresses are form-fitting, low-cut and conspicuously emphasize the shape of her breasts. Those elements stress the sexual nature of Lily's work, and yet there is an upper-class self-possession in the way Schneider walks, talks and carries herself (straight back, shoulders back, proud chin) that places her eroticism within the realm of fantasy and refinement rather than vulgarity. The fact that Max and Lily never sleep together (though they develop romantic feelings) is also crucial. Schneider's clothes thus signify an intense sexual aura, but without the toughness and agency that they would suggest; and with the more sordid sexual aspect of her work signified by external elements (mostly dialogue) and crucially left off screen. Despite the stated nature of her profession, the narrative, her clothes and her performance distance the star from a stereotypical prostitute role, thus retaining her aura of distinction.

3.2. Schneider and Saint Laurent

Further proof of Schneider embracing bourgeois modernity is found in her partnership with French couturier Yves Saint Laurent who designed her costumes in *César et Rosalie* and *Les Innocents aux mains sales*. In those films she is as elegant as she was in *La Piscine*, *Les Choses de la vie*, *Un amour de pluie* (in which she wears perfectly cut, cinched and single-coloured ensembles of either black or white) and *Le Mouton enragé*, yet they are distinctively more mature and emblematic of the era. According to Valerie Steele, the 1970s was a high point for Western women's fashion and Yves Saint Laurent was one of the most famous and influential designers of the time (1997, p. 99). His haute couture creations incorporated ethnic and vintage influences. Exploiting the eroticism of sexual ambiguity, he drew inspiration from menswear and created the female version of the tuxedo suit in 1966. Saint Laurent's relation with the cinema is well known and in particular he developed a close friendship and fruitful collaboration with Deneuve. Schneider never had such a strong and durable partnership with a designer, though she listed him as one of his favourite couturiers – alongside Coco Chanel. Arguably Schneider's most striking costume in *César et Rosalie* is the dress Rosalie wears at her mother's wedding at the beginning of the film. It is a long, black-and-white tartan printed chiffon dress with a slit back (a detail that surreptitiously reveals the skin) and bouffant sleeves. Through the diaphanous fabric we can glimpse that she does not wear a bra. A bow at the collar brings a flowing movement to the dress and complements her bouncy curls (Figure 11). This dress displays a great fit between the designer's flair and Schneider's sense of style and body type: through Saint Laurent's sexy and flamboyant details, Schneider imparted an erotic allure to the dress without falling into excess or vulgarity. The fact that hemlines continued to fall in the first years of the decade after the mini-skirts of the 1960s (Steele, p. 82), played in favour of Schneider who looked at her best wearing floor-length dresses.

Off screen, Schneider was fond of long and flowy dresses in the spirit of what today would be called 'bohemian chic' (adorned with yellow gold jewels), and of psychedelic-patterned or floral print caftans, echoing the late hippie style. The caftan was a staple of 1970s clothing and the ones Saint Laurent created for Schneider for *Les Innocents aux mains sales* evoke his ethnic-inspired collections of the late 1970s; it also conveys an elegant yet casual style that fits the film's luxurious setting in a villa outside Saint-Tropez with minimalist modern interiors. Analysing each of Schneider's looks from *Les Innocents aux mains sales* could fill a chapter inasmuch as they function as central aspects of the mise-en-scène (her costume changes provide a disguise for her character so that she can perform differently in relation to the men facing her), but I will focus on one attire that bears significance in the construction of Schneider's expression of the glamorous yet vulnerable woman.

Julie is a Saint-Tropez housewife married to a rich, drunken and impotent husband (Rod Steiger). The film opens with a shot of Schneider sunbathing on her stomach and wearing nothing but dark glasses and a sparkling pendant

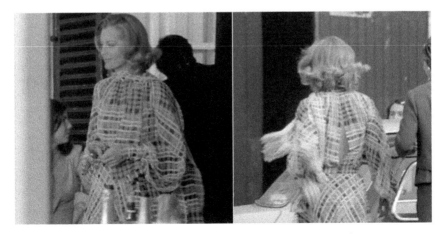

FIGURE 11 *Schneider's Yves Saint Laurent dress in* César et Rosalie.

down her back. A kite falls on her buttocks and a young man (Paolo Giusti) appears, looking for his kite. She asks him to remove it from her body in what is clearly an open sexual invitation; and despite the presence of her drunk husband they have sex in the house and then plan his murder. Leaving aside the incongruity and misogyny of this opening sequence, Schneider's clothed body has more significance. Though she suffers physical and sexual abuse, Schneider's character seems to acquire a (very) slight agency through the star's wearing of her costumes. The clothes are part of Julie's masquerade and could also be considered a defence mechanism. A moment that intertwines those two aspects is when her husband returns (she thought he was dead), rapes her and then pays her. At this point she presents herself to him with curly blonde hair and in a white, floor-length, fluid imperial-style gown. With Schneider's performance in this film based on the progression of her looks, this costume has a dramatic function: this is the character's version of the elegant 'whore' (her husband's word) who tries to regain a semblance of power. Julie has to perform marital prostitution, but she still finds a way to impose herself with exaggerated attributes (the voluminous hair, the overdone makeup, the dramatic cut and symbolic innocence of her white dress) on her abuser.

Schneider's on- and off-screen 1970s looks also included her hairstyle created by Jean-Max Guérin and Alexandre de Paris. Unlike Bardot who developed a small repertoire of spectacular and highly recognizable hairstyles (Vincendeau, 2015a), Schneider changed hers frequently, sometimes radically, going from a shoulder-length wavy cut to a shorter voluminous style with a fringe, at times using accessories (hats, scarfs, headbands), or tying it back in a ponytail or a chignon (which has the effect of clearing and framing her face, emphasizing the distinctive widow's peak on her forehead). The colour remained within a relatively natural range, from brown to honey blonde. Schneider's hairstyle in fact mirrored her star image: it was sophisticated and fashionable, but discreet and controlled. This was different to Bardot and Deneuve's evidently bleached blond hair, Jane Birkin's artfully messy hair and girly fringe and Annie Girardot's practical short haircut.

Overall, Schneider in the late 1960s and 1970s never adopted an explicitly feminist agenda, not on screen, where her bourgeois image served a conservative and male-oriented discourse, as we saw in the case of the Sautet films, nor off screen either. This somewhat changed with her fifth and last film with Sautet in 1978, *Une histoire simple*.

4. *Une histoire simple*: Schneider and French feminism

With the films mentioned above and other popular titles such as *Vincent, François, Paul et les autres* (1974) and *Mado*, Sautet became the auteur par excellence of male psychology and male friendship, exploring it in all its forms through a certain type of, usually Parisian, middle-class, man. This character is often in his forties, torn between the machismo in which he has been raised and his inability to express his feelings; he is professionally driven but sentimentally weak. Although female characters are incarnated by glamorous stars like Schneider and usually appear more assured than the men, they are never at the centre of the story. *Une histoire simple* seemed to signal a change in this respect. After her marginal role in *Mado*,[4] Schneider was 'tired' of being 'a mere presence' in Sautet's films (Delain and Heymann, 1978, p. 47). The director expressed his 'immense regret, a sort of frustration of having her only so briefly in *Mado*' (Fabre, 1978a). She asked Sautet and Jean-Loup Dabadie to 'write [her] a film about women' as a 'present for her 40th birthday' (Montaigne, 1978, p. 85; Billard, 1978, pp. 175–6). With *Une histoire simple*, Sautet agreed to produce a feminine narrative told through the eyes of Schneider who inspired the story (Billard, p. 176).

The film opens with its heroine's decision to have an abortion. Already the mother of a teenage son from a first marriage, thirty-nine-year-old Marie (Schneider) does not wish to carry the child of Serge (Claude Brasseur) whom she does not love anymore and intends to leave. Rather than the abortion, it is Marie's decision to breakup that is unfathomable to Serge because she is not leaving him for another man – a woman simply 'does not leave someone like that'. The narrative illustrates the progressive modernity of Schneider's character whose choices to be single and to have an abortion challenge male outdated visions of womanhood. *Une histoire simple* was one of the first French films to make abortion the centre of the narrative, the Veil Law had only been in place for three years. *Une histoire simple* is also notable for a scene in which Marie's female friends share their different and conflicting points of view about marriage, family and casual sex. The film suggests that men are stuck in their outdated certainties while women are able to adapt. Another rare element in Schneider's filmography is the importance of female friendship and – up to a point – their work. It is with her female colleagues, who are also her friends, that Marie finds support during difficult times. Without ever showing exactly what Marie does (she works with her friends as a designer in a large Parisian company), the film emphasizes nevertheless the tensions between work and personal life for women. The narrative is explicitly about Marie following her own desires, rejecting traditionally gendered behaviour and calmly contemplating abortion. This places it within a body of work portraying female emancipation in French society. Comparing *Une histoire simple* with other films made a few years before, such as Claude Autant-Lara's *Le Journal d'une femme en blanc* (1965) which

---

[4]Her performance of the alcoholic Hélène received ecstatic reviews: she was 'sublime' for *Le Nouvel Observateur* (25/10/1976), 'sensational' for Robert Chazal in *France-Soir* (27/10/1976), and José-Maria Bescos exclaimed admiringly 'what a Schneider!' in *Pariscope* (27/10/1976).

explores the huge difficulties faced by women's access to contraception and abortion, a milestone has been crossed: having an abortion is now depicted as a simple intervention. And, unlike the female protagonist in Nadine Trintignant's *Mon amour, mon amour* (1967), Marie does not run out of the clinic at the thought of having the abortion. A nice female doctor (Nadine Alari) gently asks Marie some personal questions without shaming her, they make an appointment for the following week and everything goes smoothly. Nor is Marie seen suffering from post-surgery complications, and the following sequence shows her in her kitchen making tea and resting in bed. She will get back to work the next day. Marie is not traumatized and no one makes her feel guilty. Yet, two things detract from this progressive view of the film.

First, Marie is shown as unhappy, underlined by Schneider's melancholy performance (as expressed through her eyes, for instance). The suggestion is that the sadness is caused by the abortion on the one hand, and by the incompleteness of female celibacy on the other. Serge, who cannot let go of Marie, is narratively framed as a loser, and Georges, the man with whom she would like to reconnect, turns her down and chooses a younger woman. Visually, *Une histoire simple* looks darker than any other Sautet film with Schneider: her make-up, hairstyle and clothes are dull and morose, a palette of greys and beiges, and Schneider's curly hair is unflattering. Her smile (except at the very end) is her characteristic weary smile of resignation, accompanied by a vulnerable look in her eyes.

Secondly, Sautet and Dabadie in the end privilege traditional representation of women and motherhood. The friends gather with their families during the weekends in Gabrielle's (Arlette Bonnard) country house near Paris. Sautet films the gatherings of the female friends with the same sensitivity and naturalness as he did for his male groups in previous films, yet he puts them in traditional domestic situations – in the kitchen and taking care of the children. None of the women talk about their jobs and, for instance, although Francine is a union representative, it is a man who we see speak at a union meeting. Although Sautet and Dabadie claimed the film turns the spotlight on a group of professionally active women, they reinforce traditional divisions, with men associated with the public sphere and women with the private sphere. Although Marie has an abortion, she is already a mother, which renders the medical act more acceptable (she has already 'fulfilled' her societal and gendered role). Additionally, all women in the film are mothers (except for Sophie Daumier's character who acts as comic relief). Finally, having briefly reconnected with her former husband, Marie is pregnant again and she decides to raise her child on her own, with the support of Gabrielle who lost her husband by suicide: the future mother is herself supported by a maternal figure. The film thereby places Marie in a 'modern' situation, opting for single motherhood, but de facto contrasts the 'sadness' of her abortion with the joy of motherhood.

The male-dominated French critics agreed with this discourse, praising the independence of Marie and her friends, yet seeing their solitude as 'the price to pay' for these victories – celibacy was an 'old privilege' so far reserved to 'the men-thinkers' (Jardin, 1978b). Moreover, Sautet, Dabadie and Schneider refused to market the film as feminist (Delain and Heymann, 1978, p. 47).[5] Critics felt that, although *Une histoire simple* presents the – white and heteronormative – couple as in jeopardy, Marie finds her 'accomplishment' (Thirard, 1978) in maternity. This is signified by the final shot of Schneider sunbathing in a chaise longue in her friend's garden: with the straps of her cream summer dress down her shoulders, she lifts her skirt up on her thighs and looks at the sun, closes her eyes, a relaxed and radiant expression across her face. Sautet abundantly shared his opinion in the press: to him, women are stronger than men because 'they have maternity', which he considered the 'raison d'être [of a woman] until her last breath' (Fabre, 1978a). He praised himself for putting women 'at centre stage', arguing that they 'carry in them, by their *biological function*, a notion of life and death that is more conscious and more fundamental' (Teisseire, 1978, my emphasis). The conservative ethos betrayed by these declarations (and the film's ending, as discussed above) must be seen as in dialogue with the fact that, at the time, many feminists contested the notion of maternity as 'destiny' for women. *Une histoire simple* therefore reflects the contradictory responses to feminism in late 1970s French society.

Schneider's performance was clearly central to this interpretation and was highly acclaimed; during the 4th César awards ceremony in February 1979, she received her second César award for Best actress for her role. That same year, she was also awarded a special David di Donatello by the Accademia del Cinema Italiano for her performance, and the film was nominated in 1980 for an Academy Award in the Best foreign film category. Significantly, many praised Schneider's performance of vulnerability, 'disarray' (Teisseire, 1978), and 'suffering' (de Baroncelli, 1978). The association between Schneider's beauty and her fragility was directly mentioned: 'the singularly perfect face of hope and destitution […] the face of all women' (Jardin, 1978b). Thus, interestingly, in her most overt 'woman's narrative', Schneider's performance in *Une histoire simple* projects an image of femininity in need of compassion and of protection. In this respect, Sautet's celebration of Schneider as his muse is disconcerting at best, and alarming at worst. The film-maker was a liberal, sophisticated and modern man in many ways (Binh and Rabourdin, 2005; Boujut, 2014),[6] yet his female characters as embodied by Schneider

---

[5]Schneider said: 'A feminist story, no. But a story about a woman entangled in the contradictions and aspirations of today' (Montaigne, 1978, p. 85).

[6]The love triangle of *César et Rosalie* was inspired by Sautet's own polyamorous relationship with his wife Graziella Escojido and another woman, was Stéphane Jardin, according to her son Alexandre Jardin who wrote about it in his book *Ma mère avait raison* (2017).

run the gamut of old-fashioned ideas of woman as mistress (Hélène), prostitute (Lily), fickle seductress (Rosalie) or mother (Marie). He claimed that Schneider was the 'synthesis of all women', praising her 'thirst for moral purity' (*Le Nouvel Observateur*, 27/11/1978). In those formative and crucial years of the women's movement, Sautet's depictions of women on a pedestal – as morally 'superior' – spoke of an outdated patriarchal ideology, while it reflected the moral panic that accompanied women's progress in society at the time, especially regarding the control of their bodies and reproduction. Schneider's star persona, in its combination of attractiveness and fragility, played a key role in this process.

Offscreen, Schneider's personal relationship to feminism was complex. She was, like many European film stars, involved, albeit discreetly, in public debates. Her only overt feminist action was when she made her position regarding abortion clear. In June 1971 and alongside 373 other German-speaking women, she acknowledged having had an abortion by adding her name to the list of signatories to the German equivalent of the French '343 Manifesto' entitled 'Wir haben abgetrieben!' ('We had abortions!') in *Stern* magazine, and she appeared on the cover. For admitting an abortion, Schneider faced criminal charges in Hamburg and risked a fine and a five-year prison sentencing. In an open letter published on 12 July in the *Nouvel Observateur*, Jeanne Moreau (who signed the French manifesto in April) supported Schneider: 'Socially, our freedom is already completely alienated and it is scandalous that the freedom to control our own bodies may expose us to legal prosecutions' (cited in Moireau, 2011). The charges against Schneider (and many other German women) were dropped – the investigation unveiled that hundreds of women sent letters admitting their own abortion to the West German seat of the pro-choice movement.

Beyond this vital question of reclaiming one's own bodily agency, Schneider had an ambiguous perspective on women's emancipation. In the mid-1960s, she constantly went back and forth between what she called her 'need for strength [in a man]': 'I need a man who is violent to, who throws me on to my knees [...], [a] stronger [man] should take care of me, bring me to heel, break me to the bone' (Schneider and Seydel, 1989, p. 206), and her own desire for independence, notably in relation to her love for her work and her personal ambition in developing a successful career. She listed 'private life, the person with whom one lives' as the very 'first condition for a woman to be happy' (interview for *Pathé magazine*, 03/02/1971) although she defended the choice for women to work (she said many times that she could not stop working). Her case illustrated the contradictions of the modern white woman in 1970s French (and European) society that demanded a feminine ideal capable of assuming multiple roles – domestic and professional. There was also a misunderstanding in terms of the vocabulary used to defend the feminist cause (it is still the case): Schneider *technically* agreed with the concept of emancipation and was, in fact, as a privileged white woman in Europe, living an emancipated life, though she always dismissed the word ('this emancipation-thing, I found it pretty false, I don't agree with it'). She insisted on the reductive and essentialist notion that 'a woman has to stay a woman', that is, 'I would not submit in matters of love, but I would answer to the man's demands, as long as they do not deteriorate into tyranny; [a] woman who loves can' (Schneider and Seydel, pp. 210–11). This was (and remains) a common position taken by many women at the time. Equality does not mean sameness but, as Christine Bard has shown (1999), the anti-feminist discourse commonly caricatured feminism as either man-hating or encouraging women to 'become men'. The evolution of French cinema over the 1970s pushed the star to change her image but also to re-evaluate her status as a woman.

When her career in France took a successful turn with *Les Choses de la vie*, Schneider continued to defend domesticity but emphasized that it had to be a woman's choice. She explained that she 'absolutely wanted [a family and home]' and that this decision was her 'real life'. She publicly admitted to not having reconciled her professional life with her private life, and that she was 'two different women' (interview by Jacques Chancel, 13/03/1970). She was considered an independent and professionally successful woman, and she personally shared her professional ambition with the press (Billard, 1978, p. 176). However, in line with Christine Geraghty's point that female celebrities are always brought back to the private sphere (2000b, p. 196), journalists tended to emphasize her vulnerable femininity that was considered 'the most beautiful virtue' (Chancel, 13/03/1970), and they asked questions indicative of the era's sexist conception of women, that is, her role as a wife and a mother. She was also relentlessly described in media as very dependent on men – her two husbands, but also her directors, whose support and approval she looked for on sets (*Le Nouvel Observateur*, 27/11/1978). As was the case for a growing number of women as the decade unfolded, Schneider was divorced and remarried by the mid-1970s. In line with her on-screen image, she continued to defend the unifying value of having a family: 'I think that [family] is the most beautiful [thing], but I refuse that women be baby-machines or just wash the dishes. I refuse it as an obligation, or a sort of function' (Fabre, 1978b). She again insisted on the importance of women's freedom to choose ('It has to be a choice'). From her film roles to her own pronouncements, Schneider's attitude to gender and feminism was thus riven with contradictions, created by a range of factors: the conflicted views of feminism in society, the rapidly changing social mores, the tensions between the stars' own views and her need to adapt to the French – largely male and often misogynist – film establishment, and the ideologically conservative media.

Conclusion

Schneider's immense popularity as a 'French' star was (and still is) rooted in her characters' apparent emancipation and independence in Sautet's films, which appears to coincide with the 1970s' progressive mentality. Hélène is ambivalent about marriage, Rosalie makes it very clear that César is no more important than any other man that she has had before, and Marie aborts without consulting her companion and she ultimately decides to go through with another pregnancy without involving the father. And yet, Schneider's characterization as a modern woman was deceptive as it was only the *semblance* of modernity that was depicted and promoted in various media texts. All in all, a soft misogyny veiled the narratives and Schneider's on-screen persona remained fairly conventional and unthreatening, offering little potential for transgression within mainstream French cinema and society.

Schneider was contemporary with the rising voice of feminism in film and with French stars such as Annie Girardot, Marlène Jobert and Miou-Miou, whose personas projected an aura of 'ordinariness', in part through their naturalistic looks and performance styles, and were very much 'of their time', offering positive visions of 'popular feminism' in their films (Jeancolas, 1979, p. 271; Vincendeau, 2008, pp. 222–35). By contrast, Schneider represented a hesitant modernity and she was more comparable to Catherine Deneuve – both of them in a way 'bypassed feminism' with their glamour and 'out of touch' upper-middle-class personas. In that sense, the 'new' Schneider in 1970s France was far from being *the* new woman. Her successful roles in Sautet's films built the feminine myth of a peaceful cohabitation between past and present, between classicism and modernity, thus following the thread that ran since the beginning of her career – her seductiveness allied with vulnerability maintained a traditional hierarchy of the sexes. These features also explain her triumph in her Occupation films that I will explore in the next chapter – whose narratives projected a resistance to women's emancipation in France's national past. They also explored Schneider's ambiguous relationship with Germany and Austria, emphasizing her Germanic identity in a way that developed a complex relationship with the memory of the Second World War.

8

Schneider's Occupation films

Introduction

This chapter analyses Schneider's roles and performances in films depicting the rise of European totalitarianism and the German Occupation of France during the Second World War. Although there are few in number, this cycle of films holds an important place in Schneider's French career as it was decisive in the shaping of her persona in the 1970s, capitalizing on her own personal life and identity being split between Berlin and Paris. They are: *Le Train* / *The Train* (Pierre Granier-Deferre, 1973), *Le Vieux fusil* / *The Old gun* (Robert Enrico, 1975), *Une femme à sa fenêtre* / *A Woman at her window* (Pierre Granier-Deferre, 1976), *Gruppenbild mit Dame* / *Group portrait with a lady* (Aleksandar Petrović, 1977) and Schneider's final film *La Passante du Sans-Souci* / *The Passerby* (Jacques Rouffio, 1982). Because these films were shaped by the larger issue of the relationship between French cinema and Western European war memory, I will first briefly focus on the broader historical and memorial shifts from 1945 to the early 1980s in the French context, before examining Schneider's romantic and tragic roles[1] in Occupation films, and how she gave them a particular 'twist' due to her Germanic origins.

---

[1]Andrea Bandhauer's chapter (2015) on Schneider in *Stars in World Cinema: Film Icons and Star Systems Across Cultures* offers useful and preliminary insights into Schneider's dramatic performance style and on- and off-screen tragic representations.

1. French cinema and memories of the Second World War

The corpus of Occupation films made in France since 1945 is substantial, and French cinema played its part in building the cultural and national memories of the Second World War. French cinematic representations of the period vary, and the changes are often significant in respect to French official discourse relating to the Second World War and national memory. It is enlightening to study the French films that achieved popular success – René Clément's *La Bataille du rail* and *Paris brûle-t-il?* (1966), Claude Autant-Lara's *La Traversée de Paris* (1956), Gérard Oury's *La Grande Vadrouille* (1966), Louis Malle's *Lacombe Lucien* (1974) and in Schneider's case, *Le Vieux fusil* and *La Passante du Sans-Souci* – as an indication of a consensus of opinion over the 'historically correct' thinking at given moments in History. Occupation films have also engendered fierce debate, suggesting that the German Occupation remains a sensitive topic long after the war. In this regard, *Lacombe Lucien*, one of the first films to deal with collaboration, is emblematic for it was subjected to violent controversies, as was *Le Vieux fusil*.

1.1. 1945–1970s: French cinema and official war memory

In the aftermath of the Second World War and until the 1970s, the memory of war in France was tied to political concerns. The French historian Henry Rousso dedicates a section of his seminal book *Le Syndrome de Vichy* (1987) to the on-screen representation of the war and Occupation, noting that nearly 200 films were made on the subject between 1944 and 1986 (many more have been made since). Statistically this represents 7 per cent of annual French film production, or about a dozen films each year during the period covered by Rousso.

Immediately after the end of the war and after the period known as 'épuration' ('purification'),[2] the issue of memory and responsibilities was replaced by the urgency of reconstruction. Amnesty laws were passed in 1947. In 1953, one law singled out Alsatians soldiers (French nationals whose region had been annexed by Germany in 1940) forced into the German army who participated in the massacre of 642 civilians in Oradour-sur-Glane in 1944, on which *Le Vieux fusil* was loosely based.[3] Charles de Gaulle,

---

[2] Also called 'legal purge', the term defines the wave of official (and unofficial) trials that followed the Liberation of France.
[3] For more on the Oradour massacre see Sarah Farmer's books *Oradour: arrêt sur mémoire* (1994) and *Martyred village: commemorating the 1944 massacre at Oradour-sur-Glane* (1999).

France's President until 1946 (and again from 1958 to 1969), and whose influence on French public opinion remained preponderant, pushed forward a narrative of national healing. According to this perspective, the Vichy regime and its collaborationist policies were a parenthesis in the history of the Republic.[4] French cinema consolidated the myth of a wholly resistant France, which Rousso calls the 'Resistancialist myth' (1987; Rousso and Conan, 1994). Subjected to multiple pressures (political, economic, social), including censorship, films had to be cautious when addressing the topic of German Occupation (Lindeperg, 1997; Jacquet, 2004).

Then, after a peak in 1946, French production dropped drastically: only eleven films about the war and the German Occupation were distributed between 1947 and 1958. Rousso calls this the 'discretion of the Fourth Republic' and explains that 'cinema [in those years] seems to be withdrawn, in reserve, avoiding the subject' (1987, p. 274). Still, French films began to make some alterations to the one-dimensional glorification of the Resistance that was seen after the Liberation, and some unsavoury characters appeared on screen.[5] In line with official war memory, however, and despite the mediatization of the discovery of the extermination camps and the Nuremberg trials, representations of the Jewish experience and persecution emerged with difficulty. The specificity of the Jewish Holocaust was muted in the global memory of the deportation, as seen in the short documentary *Nuit et Brouillard* (Alain Resnais, 1956) – although the film had the merit of showing concentration camps to the public, the role of French authorities in the deportation was censored and the word 'Jewish' is only mentioned once (Lindeperg, 2007).

When de Gaulle returned to power in 1958, the production of the Second World War films in France was at its lowest. The numbers for the following years seem to confirm that there was a 'de Gaulle effect'. According to Sylvie Lindeperg, ten Occupation films were made in 1959 and seventy films (including documentaries) in the next decade. In short, French cinema took on a more Gaullist and military tone. Two fiction films chimed particularly with the new historical doxa: Clément's *Paris brûle-t-il?* in 1966 (Schneider was part of the film's international cast, but her scene was cut; her husband Harry Meyen plays a Nazi Lieutenant), and *L'Armée des ombres* (Jean-Pierre Melville, 1969) which has given rise to much debate in terms of its Gaullism (Rousso, 1987; Lindeperg, 1997; Vincendeau, 2003).

---

[4]Historians Robert Aron and Georgette Elgey (*Histoire de Vichy*, 1954) developed the idea that Pétain did what he could to soften the condition of the French people during the war. This is the 'shield and sword' thesis that presents General de Gaulle and Marshal Pétain tacitly acting together to defend France, the latter being the shield preserving France, including with a policy of collaboration (which was, according to the thesis, simulated), until the sword (de Gaulle) was strong enough to defeat Nazi Germany. This view is widely contested (Le Groignec, 1998).
[5]*Les Portes de la nuit* (Marcel Carné, 1946), *Manon* (Henri-Georges Clouzot, 1949), *La Traversée de Paris* (Claude Autant-Lara, 1956) all include collaborators and black market traffickers.

French cinema also approached the Occupation though popular comedies in the 1960s: *Babette s'en va-t-en guerre* (Christian-Jaque, 1959), *La Vie de château* (Jean-Paul Rappeneau, 1966) and *La Grande Vadrouille* (Gérard Oury, 1966). In the 1970s the *7e compagnie* and *Bidasses* series were hugely popular.[6] These films' main characters represent the 'average French person' struggling with History, which according to Lindeperg brought 'chauvinistic satisfaction' (1997, p. 372) to French audiences. The French heroes, always resourceful and full of common sense, do not have any trouble deceiving dumb German soldiers. However, as the Gaullist period came to an end, the arrival of new generations of artists, film-makers and historians who had not experienced the war, as well as the opening of French and West German national archives[7] brought a momentous transformation.

1.2. The 1970s in France: new historical approaches and the *mode rétro*

The civil unrest of May 1968 and the arrival of a younger generation of researchers who focused more on collaboration than Resistance changed the perspective on the Second World War.[8] The ground-breaking documentary *Le Chagrin et la Pitié*, directed by Marcel Ophüls, played an influential role. Commissioned by French television in 1967, the film was interrupted by the May 68 events, then produced by French, Swiss and West German television and shot in 1969 (it was distributed in cinemas in 1971 after being banned from French television). Using interviews with collaborators and Resistance fighters from Clermont-Ferrand (Auvergne) who comment on collaboration, *Le Chagrin et la Pitié* was one of the first films to engage with French collective memory of the Occupation (Rousso, 1987, pp. 133–4). By breaking the false narrative of an entirely resistant France, it played an important role in the emergence of a new approach to the Vichy regime

---

[6]The *films de bidasses* are comedies about unmotivated and 'silly' conscription soldiers. See *Où est passé la 7e compagnie?* (Robert Lamoureux, 1973) and *Les Bidasses s'en vont en guerre* (Claude Zidi, 1974), the firsts of the genre.

[7]While the focus of this section is French cinema, other academics have expanded their study to broader contexts; see, for example, Pierre Sorlin in his *European Cinemas, European Societies 1939–1990* that has a comparative chapter on the emergence of Occupation and Resistance films in European cinema (1991, pp. 52–80).

[8]The historiographic shift in the early 1970s was partly due to foreign historians and to American Robert Paxton in particular who had access to German records and documents seized by US authorities. Paxton's 1972 book *Vichy France* (translated in French in 1973) revealed that the Vichy government was eager to collaborate with Nazi Germany and did not practise 'passive resistance'. Studies now acknowledge that the French authorities took part in the Holocaust (Jean-Pierre Azéma with *De Munich à la Libération: 1938-1944* in 1979, Henry Rousso with *Le Syndrome de Vichy* in 1987, and *Vichy, un passé qui ne passe pas* with Eric Conan in 1994).

and of a new era of Occupation memory. The film's interviewees give a strong impression of authenticity, which leads historian Annette Wieviorka to declare that France had entered the 'witness era' (1998).

The 1970s were also the time of the revival of Vichy memory, of the rise of 'négationisme' (denialism) that refuted the existence of the Shoah and of the foundation of the far-right political party the Front National (Rassemblement National now).[9] In parallel, there was a strong resurgence of Shoah memory with many French historians publishing works that centred on the Holocaust and highlighted the anti-Jewish policies of Vichy. As I shall explore, events related to 'négationisme' (and, in some cases, neo-Nazism) were of paramount importance for Schneider's decision to accept certain roles, her approach to her characters and in particular her desire to develop *La Passante du Sans-Souci*.

Then, with the re-evaluations in the 1970s of France's role in the war, a new trend in film (and literature) emerged. Rousso identifies nearly forty-five films set in, and about, the Occupation made between 1974 and 1978. He divides these into four categories: the 'prosecutors' (such as *Le Chagrin et la Pitié*), the 'chroniclers' (films that give an account of the atmosphere of the time, e.g. *Le Sauveur*, *Le Train*), the 'aesthetes' (*Lacombe Lucien* tells the enrolment of a young man in the Milice[10]) and the 'opportunists' (the aforementioned *Bidasses* series, for example). Such films – and the costume film and heritage genre at large – present an array of recurring characteristics: an historical or literary inspiration, a display of vintage costumes and decors, usually high production values, classical visual style and the presence of stars to attract a large audience (Austin, 1996, p. 142). These motifs are indeed present in Schneider's films about the German Occupation, and this chapter will endeavour to establish her personal contribution to the 'genre'. A polemical term, '*mode rétro*' (retro style), also emerged. It indicates a subgenre of heritage cinema about the German Occupation (and more generally Nazism), and it is in that sense that I use the term throughout this chapter. Its original coining in the early 1970s, notably from the *Cahiers du cinéma*'s editorial team, was meant to be derogatory (Atack, 2016, p. 336). The critics sneered at the films' glamorous and nostalgic aesthetics, which they saw as a fixation on appearance and surface, such as fashion of the 1930s and 1940s. They blamed the films' shallow revival of the past, and denounced their 'fascination for the morbid' (Domenach, 1974) – as in the discomfort caused by *Il Portiere di notte* (Liliana Cavani, 1974), a film that represents Nazism as a sexual perversion (Impey, 2011). In fact, Schneider turned down Charlotte Rampling's role in the film, as well as Cavani's

---

[9]Some RN members lay claim to the 'National Revolution' of the Vichy regime and are close to negationist and anti-Semite milieus.

[10]The Milice was a paramilitary force of the Vichy regime. For more on *Lacombe Lucien* see Harry Roderick Kedward's contribution in Ginette Vincendeau and Susan Hayward's collective book *French Films: Text and Contexts* (2000), pp. 227–39.

project of an adaptation of Frank Wedekind's *Lulu* cycle (a two-play series). These roles would have altered Schneider's persona in the direction of soft porn, and she was careful at the time to maintain her *image de marque* (her 'brand') as dignified and glamourous.

Rousso considers that particularly during these years, 'cinema precedes, anticipates and, as a result, contributes to provoking a change of mentality' (1987, p. 275). The *rétro* Occupation films challenged the heroism of the French Resistance and emphasized the ambiguity of the times (Kedward, 2000, pp. 228–9; Temple and Witt, 2004, p. 188). The persecution of the Jewish people, in particular in France, took a greater place in French cinema, appearing in popular films such as *Le Vieil homme et l'enfant* (Claude Berri, 1967), *Les Guichets du Louvre* (Michel Mitrani, 1974) and *Monsieur Klein* (Joseph Losey, 1976). Those films often insist on Vichy's role in the Nazi deportation of the Jews of France, although some highlight the actions of the French who helped the Jews. Schneider's *La Passante* is one of them.

Finally, Rousso sees in the 1980s a time of trivialization and growing consensus: '[...] cinema no longer plays, if not for a few exceptions, the role of breaking taboos' (p. 270). Occupation cinema in the 1980s instead crystallized French collective memory. *Le Dernier métro* (François Truffaut, 1981), starring Catherine Deneuve and Gérard Depardieu, is the epitome of the movement, emphasizing a consensual heritage. It was both hugely popular and critically acclaimed (with ten Césars, it was the most honoured film since the creation of the award). It is against this context that I shall now consider how Schneider's position between French cinema and her Germanic persona afforded her a special place in French film memories of the Occupation.

2. Romy Schneider's Occupation films

In the context of the debates signalled above, Schneider's decision to work in French films and live in France[11] was significant. The fact that she was German was, unsurprisingly, capitalized upon by French films about the German Occupation with characters that positioned her as a victim. This image was at times combined with her own Germanness and/or her characters' Jewishness. Invariably though, her victimhood was bound to her beauty: Schneider heightened the pathos of her performances and the tragic fates of her characters by joining Germanness, glamour and melancholy.

---

[11]Schneider definitively moved back to Paris in 1973 and separated from Harry Meyen shortly afterwards (the divorce was pronounced in July 1975); she started a new relationship with her French private secretary Daniel Biasini whom she married in Berlin in December 1975 (she was six-month pregnant but had a miscarriage shortly after the wedding). She bought a property in Ramatuelle (southern France) in 1976 and her daughter Sarah Biasini was born in July 1977.

As well as relating to the specificities of French national memory of the Occupation during the 1970s, I argue that the actress's projection of vulnerability was at least as important as her national identity in terms of her triumph in such films.

I structure the rest of this chapter in three parts, each illustrating a significant aspect of Schneider's image in Occupation cinema. I start with *Le Train* (and, to a lesser extent, on *Une femme à sa fenêtre*, both directed by Pierre Granier-Deferre in 1973 and 1976, respectively), and what I consider Schneider's most political roles. I then turn to *Le Vieux fusil* (Robert Enrico, 1975), where her role is arguably more 'passive', but it represents a turning point for Schneider's persona as an icon of beautiful suffering. I conclude with *La Passante du Sans-Souci* (Jacques Rouffio, 1982), Schneider's last film that allows me to explore her image in the West German context, along with her role in *Gruppenbild mit Dame* (Aleksandar Petrović, 1977).

2.1. Schneider's political positioning in the 1970s French cultural discourse on the Occupation

In *Le Train*, adapted from the eponymous 1961 novel by Georges Simenon,[12] Schneider is the mysterious passenger Anna on one of the last trains leaving northern France during the May 1940 exodus after the Nazi invasion. Without luggage, dressed in a below-the-knee black dress and a grey tailored jacket, she furtively boards the last cattle coach and encounters Julien (Jean-Louis Trintignant), a radio technician who has boarded the train with his pregnant wife and young daughter, seated in a passenger coach at the front of the train. As Julien is separated from his family after the convoy is halved, he and Anna begin to develop feelings for one another. After a bombing one night, they make love in the moving train amongst the other passengers. Anna tells Julien that she is German and Jewish and that she fled her country and found refuge in Belgium before having to be on the run again. She explains that the Nazis plan to 'eliminate us [the Jews] in camps, […] out of cold, hunger, and fear'. Anna's Jewishness and other allusions to the horrors to come for the Jewish people during the Holocaust were added to the script – there is no mention of her religion or culture in the original novel; moreover, no sources allow me to establish whether or not the character's Jewishness was added at Schneider's demand. This narrative element, however, strengthened Schneider's Nazi victim image. Anna and Julien part ways in La Rochelle, in the hospital where Julien's wife gives birth to a son, and only meet again three years later when he is summoned by the French police. The inspector shows him identity papers

---

[12]*Le Train* was Granier-Deferre's third adaption of Simenon's novels: he directed *La Veuve Couderc* and *Le Chat*, both released in 1971 and adapted from Simenon's eponymous novels.

in the name of his wife but with Anna's photo (arriving in La Rochelle he had registered Anna under his wife's name), but he denies knowing her. He learns her real name – Anna Küpfer – and that she is suspected of being a member of the Resistance. The inspector then brings her in to the room. At first, Anna and Julien remain silent, giving the impression that they do not know each other, but when Julien is about to leave, cleared of all suspicion, he changes his mind, approaches her and tenderly caresses her cheek. Doing so, he implicitly recognizes her and condemns them both to death.

This epilogue is significant as it deviates from the source material. At the end of Simenon's novel, Julien re-encounters Anna, who asks refuge for a British pilot and herself for a few days as they are being pursued by the Gestapo; Julien hesitates and Anna does not insist. A month later, he reads her name on a list of spies who have been shot. Simenon's more cynical ending thus has Julien betray Anna and survive, whereas in the film he remains faithful to their love and signs his own death warrant. Opportunely, this presents a more romantic but also an upstanding and heroic French male character to audiences; Gilles Jacob in *L'Express* praised this decision, calling the finale 'exemplary' (05/11/1973).

There are two possible interpretations (and competing evidence) of the motives underlying this change. Screenwriter Pascal Jardin, the son of notorious collaborationist politician Jean Jardin, may have wished to absolve his name of the taint of collaboration[13] (and possibly of association with Simenon's anti-Semitic and collaborationist activities[14]). On the other hand, it was reported in the press that no one from the crew knew for sure the end of the film until shooting it, and that it was Trintignant, deeming his role thankless, who opted for his character's more noble behaviour. Either way, this change inscribes the film more fully within a Resistancialist narrative, and places Trintignant in the favourable light of projecting a chivalric masculinity. Pierre Granier-Deferre claimed to be uninterested in making sociopolitical cinema; he argued that his principal subject was 'a love story', a couple, with the sociopolitical element functioning merely as 'background' (*Le Quotidien de Paris*, 05/11/1976), but *Le Train* is in effect a political and partisan film. Granier-Deferre personally experienced the May 1940 exodus and his film shows the contrast between the dramatic events of

---

[13]See Pascal Jardin's novel *Le Nain Jaune* (1978), and Pierre Assouline's 1986 biography of Jean Jardin *Une éminence grise: Jean Jardin (1904–1976)*.

[14]During the war and while he was staying in Vendée (western France), Simenon was a representative of the Belgian State for Belgian refugees, but he refused to help those who were Jewish. The agreements he made with the German-controlled French film production company Continental Films came back to haunt him at the Liberation. He fled to Canada, avoiding French justice and the National Committee of purification of literary men in Paris that was investigating his literary and film successes during the Occupation. See Pierre Assouline (1992), *Simenon: biographie*, and Michel Carly (2005), *Simenon, les années secrètes: Vendée, 1940–1945*.

the war and the daily life of the escapees. He also interposed news archive material of the time that showed Nazi attacks and bombings, without any comment, but with a distressing and ominous music (composed by Philippe Sarde), enhancing the horror and the misery of the war.

This solemn tone, as well as the significantly different ending, were also related to the casting of Schneider and reflected in her subdued performance. In Simenon's novel, Anna is Czech, but in Granier-Deferre's film she is German and her accent is recognized by the passengers, raising suspicions that do not last long – the men are busy noticing Anna's beauty and propositioning her. Almost a decade after her Hollywood films, Schneider performs again the mysterious and alluring foreign woman who alters the course of the male protagonist's life. Indeed, the novel and the film's central theme, more than the war itself, is a man's expectation of an event that would change the course of his monotonous life (a recurrent Simenon theme) – here the encounter with Anna, set in motion by the Nazi invasion.

While Schneider's Germanness was largely irrelevant to her success in the Sautet films (it was occasionally mentioned), it played a central role in her Occupation films. Although it was relatively rare for a Germanic actor to perform the 'good German' in French films, there are examples that include Marlene Dietrich, Hildegard Knef, Curd Jürgens and Hardy Krüger; although those last two, like many German-speaking actors in foreign productions, were also at times assigned antagonistic roles, that is, Nazis (see Phillips and Vincendeau, 2006, p. 268).[15] *Le Train* was not Schneider's first World War II film: she had previously appeared in *The Victors* (Foreman, 1963), *The Cardinal* (Preminger, 1963), and *Triple Cross* (Young, 1966). But her characters do not suffer in the hands of the Nazis. They suffer from the war (Régine in *The Victors* becomes a prostitute, Annemarie in *The Cardinal* ends up in jail and the Countess in *Triple Cross* has to flee to Portugal), but their national, ethnic or religious identity is not specifically targeted – and crucially, they are not Jewish.

Schneider's characters in her 1970s Occupation films are, by contrast, victims of the Nazi – they are either Jewish or part of the Resistance and, for the most part, are brutally murdered. These deliberate career choices, in addition to events in her private life (her husband's ancestry and camp imprisonment, her children's Hebrew names David and Sarah), positioned Schneider as a redemptive figure for both German- and French-speaking audiences. On and off screen she embodied the 'perfect' victim, disapproved of by the former and celebrated by the latter. The reasons for this are to be found in the historical relationship between Germany and France,

---

[15]As ironically illustrated by Harry Meyen's case, Schneider's Jewish husband, who survived deportation in a concentration camp during the war and performed a Nazi Lieutenant in two of Schneider's films: *Paris brûle-t-il?* and *Triple Cross*. For more on the 'good German' characterization see Pól Ó Dochartaigh and Christiane Schönfeld (2013), *Representing the 'Good German' in Literature and Culture after 1945: Altruism and Moral Ambiguity*.

which echoed Schneider's personal relation to the two nations and to these roles in particular. For centuries, France and Germany were nations and cultures engaged in a dialectic marked by aggression and distrust, but also by cultural fascination and mutual respect (Gassen and Hurst, 1991, p. 5; Hawes, 2017, pp. 80–1). With regard to the French-German military conflicts of the two World Wars (as well as the 1870 Franco-Prussian War), the relationship between the neighbouring nations was (and still is) often reduced to interaction between victory and defeat, humiliation and revenge, and deeply embedded historical fears. The French and West German cultural amity was slow to be restored after 1945, yet both nations aimed for reconstruction under the European Union project. Schneider, as an Austro-German émigré in Paris, situated herself as a paradigmatic example of this charged relationship between the two countries, and notably as a focal point regarding the tragedy of the Holocaust. The Franco-German memorial discourse merged with her off-screen persona, intertwining Schneider's own trajectory as a woman with a controversial family history and her native country's difficult recent past. Speaking of her role in *Le Train* in an interview with the *Deutsches Allgemeines Sonntagsblatt*, she explained: 'In all of my recent films, this is the role with which I agree the most. [This] woman acts, thinks and loves as I would have. I accepted the role to send a message to the Nazi guys who still have a say in Germany [...]. I identify with the role' (15/12/1974).

The rest of this chapter elucidates the complex cultural, social and personal dynamics to which Schneider refers, in particular her comments on her roles in which she represents the Jewish people. Although raised a Catholic, Schneider never expressed nor shared any religious conviction. She began developing political opinions in the 1960s when she worked with and met people who influenced her political consciousness. Lilli Palmer, Schneider's co-star in *Girls in Uniform* in 1958, had to flee Germany for Paris and London with her family in 1934 after Hitler's rise to power because of their Jewish heritage (she returned to Germany in 1954). In France, Schneider met Marlene Dietrich through Orson Welles in 1962. Dietrich was an outspoken critic of the Nazis; she refused to return to Germany to become a film star of the Third Reich. She applied for US citizenship in 1937 and was a fervent supporter of the Allied troops during the war. It is said (documentary *Un jour, un destin*, 2010) that she revealed to Schneider the horrors committed by the Nazi regime to which Schneider's parents and paternal grandmother were close and even benefitted from. The next year, Schneider met Otto Preminger who allegedly helped her better comprehend the rise of fascism in Europe. Thus, through personal and professional contacts and through her film roles in the 1970s, Schneider became more politicized regarding German fascism, and she broadcast her opinions through the press. In doing so, she added her voice to the chorus of a younger and so-called 'second generation' (the children of Nazi perpetrators and sympathizers) who experienced difficulties with *Vergangenheitsbewältigung*. As we shall see, her voice in this respect would only grow louder as the decade unfolded.

Three years after *Le Train*, Schneider worked again with Granier-Deferre in *Une femme à sa fenêtre*, in which she performed the title character, Margot Santorini. Set in 1936 Athens, the film paints Margot as a wealthy and beautiful Austrian-born Marquise, cynical and idle, married to the penniless playboy and Italian diplomat Rico (Umberto Orsini, already seen alongside Schneider in *César et Rosalie* and *Ludwig*). They feel affection for each other but the romantic Margot expects more from life than a string of suitors, amongst whom is rich French industrialist and her friend Malfosse (Philippe Noiret). While her husband does not hide his extramarital affair, Margot remains faithful, but bored and without purpose amongst her peers who enjoy the privileges of their class, until she passionately falls in love with the fugitive Michel Boutros (Victor Lanoux), who takes refuge in her room at dawn on 5 August, after the coup of General Metaxas, who declared martial law and established the totalitarian '5th of August regime' in Greece (1936–41). Boutros is a dashing communist activist pursued by the police. His bravery and idealism seduce Margot. Rico is tolerant of her attachment to the rebel and they plan to help Boutros escape and after a few days, Margot decides to escape with him. At the end, the narrative jumps to 1945 France after the Liberation when Rico and Malfosse try to find Margot who had disappeared after entrusting Rico with her daughter. They discover that she was deported and probably assassinated. In 1967, the daughter of Boutros and Margot (also performed by Schneider dressed in 1970s clothes), returns to Greece where her parents met. Like *Le Train*, *Une femme à sa fenêtre* is a literary adaptation. The eponymous novel by Pierre Drieu la Rochelle was written in 1929; his story was therefore set during the Second Hellenic Republic, a period in which he leant towards socialism (he published his political essay *Socialisme fasciste* in 1934), although he is remembered as the fascist and collaborator that he became in occupied France.

Une femme à sa fenêtre contains much more resonant political undertones than its source material. The screenwriter, Spanish left-wing writer Jorge Semprún, intentionally modified the time setting of Drieu La Rochelle's novel to bring his narrative closer to the rise of European fascisms and the Second World War. Added to the film was Austria's fascism, directly related to Schneider's identity. Margot shares with Rico the reason why she feels so drawn to Boutros: she recalls that two years earlier, when she was in Vienna, 'the troops of Engelbert Dollfuss crushed the workers' militia … I didn't understand, but I was horrified. Now this story makes sense'. Schneider's character also makes narrative use of her Germanic origins with the film's references to the Austrian Civil War, also known as the February Uprising, four days of skirmishes between socialists and the Austrian Army in February 1934. Schneider also speaks a few words of German, which are chosen to dismiss Nazi politics. To a German diplomat (Carl Möhner) who raises his glass to her in honour of the forthcoming *Anschluss*, she coldly and loftily responds that she does not find this perspective desirable. Moreover, the disappearance and death of Margot depart from the source material to bolster Schneider's Nazi victim image (the ending of Drieu la Rochelle's novel remains open and hopeful as the lovers promise to meet in Patras).

Une femme à sa fenêtre was in line with Schneider's image of glamorous upper-class sophistication, but critics were divided regarding its visual style. Some considered that the film's impressive collection of historical costumes, fancy cars, immaculate tennis courts and its ornamental quality detracted from its political message, and others saw it as a betrayal of Semprún's politics ('it is a right-wing film [made] to seduce left-wing intellectuals', *Politique Hebdo*, 22/11/1976). The tension picked up by critics had its source in the film's inception: as for *Le Train*, Granier-Deferre denied making a political film,[16] while it was clear for Semprún and producer Albina du Boisrouvray that he was writing a political story (Chazal, 1976b).

Drieu la Rochelle makes a brief appearance as a character (played by Jean Martin) at the end of the film when Rico and Malfosse investigate Margot's whereabouts. He informs them that Margot has been arrested and they come to the conclusion that she has probably died. Drieu's comments on Schneider's character are significant. Immediately after he pronounces the words 'deported in a camp somewhere in Germany', he continues: 'She was beautiful, wasn't' she? I remember a sort of inner flame, a stubborn, almost desperate, *joie de vivre*. What a waste'. Here, a character impersonating a man known in mid-1970s France for his sympathy for the Nazi regime makes a direct association between Schneider's character's tragic fate and the actress's beauty. This is paramount in understanding Schneider's image of the vulnerable woman: the beautiful body was never very far from the body brutalized by Germany.

Regardless of how unchallenging those two political roles were to any 'historically correct' French narrative about the memory of the Occupation, the Jewishness (in *Le Train*) and Austrianness (in *Une femme à sa fenêtre*) of Schneider's characters clearly associate her with the figure of the victim, turning her into an alluring icon of suffering. Pursuing her work in Sautet's films, Schneider's image in Occupation films continued to build on her physical beauty, this time closely related to a cinematic treatment of the star, in particular a pervasive use of prolonged facial close-ups, starting with *Le Vieux fusil*.

2.2. The beautiful a-temporal victim

Le Vieux fusil was Schneider's biggest success of her French career: with 3,365,471 spectators, the film ranked fifth at the French box office in 1975

---

[16]'What interested me foremost is the couple's love story [...]' (Pérez, 1976).

(Simsi, 2012, p. 40), consolidating Schneider's star status in France. With hindsight, and comparing the numbers of French filmgoers in the mid-1950s (398 million in 1956) and in the 1970s (181 million in 1975), the success of *Le Vieux fusil* was about equivalent to *Sissi*, until that point Schneider's most successful film at the French box office. The film divided French critics at the time but nonetheless won the César award for Best Film, Best Actor (Philippe Noiret) and Best Music (awarded posthumously to François de Roubaix) at the first César awards ceremony in April 1976. Schneider was not nominated for her part in *Le Vieux fusil* – perhaps unsurprisingly in view of her relatively small screen time – but she won the César for Best Actress for her role in *L'Important c'est d'aimer* (see next chapter), so she was very much part of *Le Vieux fusil*'s 'victory lap'. The film received a 'César des Césars' in 1985 (an 'ultimate' César award voted by the public, the only other film having received one is Jean-Paul Rappeneau's 1990 *Cyrano de Bergerac*).

Schneider plays Clara, a young woman married to Julien Dandieu (Noiret), a surgeon in the local hospital in Montauban (south-western France). As for Clara's national identity, the film remains elusive: she is neither German nor Austrian, nor even Alsatian (as Schneider's character in Henri-Georges Clouzot's unfinished *Inferno* was, for example), but it does not say that she is French either. As we shall see, the character's identity does not really matter: what is instead foregrounded is Schneider's glamour and atemporal suffering. During the German retreat in June 1944, Dandieu fears for his family's safety (he '[doesn't] do politics' but treats members of the Resistance and is threatened by the Milice) and asks his friend François (Jean Bouise) to drive his wife and their daughter Florence to La Barberie, a remote village where he owns a château, for them to wait there until the Liberation. A week later, Dandieu sets off to join them for the weekend, but he discovers that the villagers have been shot in the church, and that his château is occupied by the SS. He sees Florence lying dead in the grass, shot, alongside another charred body. A flashback shows Clara being violently raped by Nazis in front of Florence and immolated with a flamethrower. The rest of the film follows Dandieu's revenge: he kills every Nazi one by one with his old shotgun (as in the film's title), taking advantage of his knowledge of the secret passages in his château. While he progresses through the château and the village, the familiar place awakens Dandieu's memory, and he periodically remembers tender and everyday moments with his late family.

Le Vieux fusil was one of the first French 'rape revenge' films. It was released a few months after *Death Wish* by Michael Winner (1974), the US reference for the genre, and *L'Agression* (1975) by Gérard Pirès, with Catherine Deneuve.[17] It was also loosely based on the massacre at

---

[17]Robert Enrico had thought of Deneuve for the role of Clara (Moriamez, 2000).

Oradour-sur-Glane in June 1944, during which the first Battalion of the 4th SS Panzer Grenadier Regiment assassinated 642 civilians gathered in the village church and burned down the village. Set in the aftermath of D-Day, the film's fictional time coincides with the June 1944 date. At the beginning of the film, Nazi soldiers drive by two hanged men, referencing hangings in Tulle (ninety-nine deaths) on 9 June 1944, and Montauban (four deaths) on 24 July 1944.

   Le Vieux fusil's screenwriter was Pascal Jardin, who also wrote *Le Train*. Whereas the latter film alluded to the cowardice of some French people, Jardin here took the opposite route. Enrico too seemed inclined to celebrate the courage of modest and brave French heroes; he would later direct the first (*Les années lumière*) of the two-part film *La Révolution française*, a colossal international production celebrating the bicentenary of the French Revolution in 1989. *Le Vieux fusil,* however, divided French critics at the time of its release. *Cahiers du cinéma* (October and November 1975, pp. 1–96) dedicated an entire issue to it despite its journalist Jean-Pierre Oudart blaming Enrico for an 'abject discourse on the last war, Nazism and Vichy, [that] tries to give pleasure with a manhunt that lasts three quarters of an hour'. Overall, French critics deplored the film's Manichaeism (*Politique Hebdo*, 21/09/1975) – '[T]hese are the enemies from the outside, the eternal *Boches*, not the Militia that we saw at the beginning of the film and quickly forgot' (Oudart, 1975). Some denounced a form of emotional blackmail (*France Nouvelle*, 08/09/1975) by a 'revengeful' director, while other critics saw a beautiful love story thwarted by the course of History ('a tragic tone for a hymn to happiness' [Rabine, 1975]).

   The film's originality is that it visually pairs these two extremes, being both classic in its narrative structure and mise-en-scène, and offering an experience of rare psychological violence. Regarding the film's violence, the role of Dandieu was originally offered to Lino Ventura who had worked three times with Enrico, but he refused due, allegedly, to the scenario's brutality (Dandieu executes the Nazis with impressive composure). On the surface, Ventura would have made a more credible tough hero, but Noiret's casting proved key to the film's success because of his 'debonair' aura and soft physique, which makes the bitter pill of the apolitical and non-violent French doctor's fall into barbarism somehow easier to swallow. Alongside Noiret, Schneider's character represents lost happiness. The sequence in which Clara is raped and then murdered is memorable and shocking. It is set 31 minutes into the film and devoid of dialogue, with only François de Roubaix's menacing music and the horrific sound of the flame-thrower on the soundtrack. It was rumoured in the press that Schneider's performance during the scenes was so credible that the actors who performed the Nazi soldiers felt extremely uncomfortable; Enrico also mentioned her heart-breaking cries and agonizing screams, which he later decided to mute for dramatic purposes (Benichou and Pommier, 1981, p. 112). But beyond these sensationalist details, there is a fascinating aspect scarcely discussed – Clara's rape is *imagined* by Dandieu: what we see is what he assumes has happened. This situates Schneider's performance in the domain of prurient fantasy. In Enrico's film, there are at least two pasts: the violent past of the rape and a pre-war past in which Schneider represents a prelapsarian ideal of beauty and happiness. It is precisely at the intersection of these two moments that Schneider's narrative construction as Clara is overtaken by Schneider's presence as star. One famous scene perfectly encapsulates this construction.

As Dandieu kills the SS one by one and remembers happy moments with his family, the film goes further back in time to the origins of his family and finally his first encounter with Clara. Julien and Clara meet in what I call the 'veil scene', which presents Schneider's face in close-ups as she performs a coquettish flirtatious routine. Set in a Parisian brasserie (shot in the well-known La Closerie des Lilas in Montparnasse), it shows Noiret's character mesmerized by Clara's appearance. She walks in through a revolving door, smiling and laughing at the sound of a classical piano tune. Julien notices her from afar. She wears a long black dress with long sleeves and a 'sweetheart' neckline, her hair is styled up into a bun surmounted by a small black hat adorned with pink flowers and a net veil that covers her features with discreet, dark flecks.[18] The image created here projects the 'ideal' and atemporal (the scene is literally outside the 'present' diegesis of the film) femininity associated with Schneider's beauty in which the veil plays a significant role. Its main purpose, with its game of concealing and revealing, is to suggest a 'mysterious' and seductive femininity, but also to showcase the face of the star. Shortly after Schneider's entrance, the camera zooms in on to her face, which fills the whole screen when Clara is introduced to Julien by François. Her face is discreetly made up[19] and lit, filmed in soft focus to reinforce her glamourous quality. Clara is radiant and confident as she sits down, puts her arms on the table, getting closer to Julien. From now on the scene is filmed in a shot-reverse-shot with their faces in close-up. He looks dazed, longingly gazing at her. Champagne arrives, she sits up straight and gracefully follows the bottle's pouring movement with her head. She then lifts her veil and brings her glass to her lips with her right hand. She takes a sip while glancing sideways at Julien on her right (her familiar 'œillade'). She swallows the champagne, replaces her veil, pinches her lips together, runs her tongue on her lower lip, then clicks her tongue and smiles contentedly (Figure 12).

---

[18]The hat was a creation of French milliner and hat maker Jean Barthet, famous for his collaborations with stars (Sophia Loren, Catherine Deneuve, Maria Callas, Brigitte Bardot and Jacqueline Kennedy). He also made Schneider's hats in *Une femme à sa fenêtre* and *La Banquière*.

[19]Schneider's makeup artist for most of her French career was Didier Lavergne, notably known for his work with Marion Cotillard for *La Môme* (Olivier Dahan, 2007).

FIGURE 12 *Schneider's courtship routine shot in close-up in* Le Vieux fusil.

If her costume evokes pre-war fashion in line with the character, Schneider's glamour is so carefully constructed by the mise-en-scène described above that the scene exists almost separately from the film, which indeed has propelled it to cult status. The close-ups of Schneider make the moment both central to the narrative and atemporal – a moment where the star is celebrated beyond the character and becomes an object of spectacle (Mulvey, 1975) and of viewers' desire. This romantic scene occurs at the end of the film, *after* the rape and death of Clara, strengthening its impact on audiences that already know the fate of the character. Her youthfulness and her beauty are destroyed and yet continue to exist: Schneider's radiant, beautiful face highlights the Nazi horror while it 'justifies' Dandieu's revenge and by extension French righteous outrage. Thus isolated and intensified, Schneider's face offers itself to contemplation and immersion, and *transcends* the narrative (Noa Steimatsky evokes the notion of transfiguration, 2017, p. 4; Roland Barthes speaks, about Greta Garbo's face, of 'mystical feelings of perdition', 1957, p. 65), situating the star as an ahistorical icon of suffering.

Schneider's physical attractiveness, her charismatic performance and the close-up were key to the *photogeny* of the veil scene. In her mid-thirties, her face was characterized by regular and smooth features (short, thin and straight nose, square jawline, green almond-shaped eyes, arched and thin eyebrows, a full and delicate mouth with a marked cupid's bow) not unlike Garbo's symmetrical and angular features, but with more warmth and roundness. The veil scene accentuates Schneider's own photogeny as a star: it invests her face with intensity and power (Aumont, 1992, p. 92; Driskell, 2015, pp. 65–7, 88), inscribing it into the spectators' memory, allowing them to become attuned to the story told by the incremental movements of her face (Aumont, p. 88). There is a gravity in Schneider's eyes, a melancholy charged with sensuality, empathy and compassion.

Other close-ups in other films show that French cinema was fascinated with Schneider's 'sculptural' face (in May 1980 *Paris Match* named her 'the most beautiful woman of the post-war period', Cau, 1981, pp. 68–71). In *Le Train*, the camera is absorbed by her visage's oval shape and weary expression, focalizing Trintignant's gaze. In one significant scene, he takes off his glasses to have a better look at Schneider, seated right next to him; the camera scrutinizes every part of her profile in extreme close-ups, slowly moving downward to stop on her mouth. Many of Schneider's films, from all the different phases of her career, end on a freeze-frame of her face in close-up, crying or not, as was the case from her first role in *Wenn der weiße Flieder wieder blüht* in 1953. This framing and editing technique underlines the role of her face in enhancing the pathos of a given narrative, while sustaining the star's glamorous persona. *Une femme à sa fenêtre* ends on a freeze-shot of Schneider's face in close-up, reaching sexual climax. A similar technique is used at the end of *Le Train*: Trintignant puts his hand on her cheek, then the camera stays on her as she slowly frowns in anguish, closes her eyes and stretches her mouth in a painful wince and then drops her face against his arm. The shot freezes on Schneider's agonized face, and slowly fades. Schneider does not utter a word in this final sequence. The emphasis on her silent performance heightens our perception of the nuances of melancholy and misery crossing her face. This configuration echoes formalist film theorist Béla Balázs's observation about the 'polyphony' of facial expressions ('a face can display the most varied emotions simultaneously') that is richer than the 'succession of words' (2010, p. 34). Barthes also evoked the exaltation and idealization of a 'beauty who do not speak' (1957, p. 24).

Schneider's silent performance of pathos magnified in repeated close-ups of her face (some of them in freeze-frame), rather than on her body, on the one hand signalled a move away from the traditional eroticism of films like *Boccaccio '70* and *La Piscine*. On the other hand, it foregrounded an affecting image of pervasive suffering – a visual clue to her ahistorical persona in the 1970s, detached from the social changes taking place, as signalled in the previous chapter. Schneider's characters in these films were systematically depicted as women who suffered intense emotional pain, illustrating what Catherine Clément (1988), in her seminal study of opera, calls the 'undoing' of women, where narratives almost systematically feature the literal or metaphorical death of female characters.

There is an array of factors explaining Schneider's winning combination of suffering and beauty in Occupation films; some are generic, some are cultural and some are personal. Firstly, there is the tremendous interest in the topic of the Occupation in general. Henry Rousso identifies 1974, the year Schneider made *Le Vieux fusil*, as the strongest moment in the *mode rétro*: 'Three years after *Le Chagrin [et la Pitié]*, France is "occupied" again' (1987, p. 149). Schneider's films' success was therefore not solely due to her presence – her co-leads' star status (Trintignant, Noiret, Piccoli) also ensured large audiences. However, Schneider was the only female star to feature prominently at the time in a genre that was overwhelmingly male. To name a few, *L'Armée des ombres*, *Le Chagrin et la Pitié*, *Lacombe Lucien* and *Mr. Klein* focus almost entirely on men. Nor do other popular Occupation films made in 1970s France present central female characters; female roles tend to be underwritten and secondary, usually relegated to the love interest. Schneider's major female roles, albeit as victim, were thus unique in their importance and visibility, attesting to her privileged star status in France. Secondly, broad cultural reasons in relation to West German public discourse of nation-building shed light on Schneider's victim figures. For this, I turn towards her last film *La Passante du Sans-Souci* (1982), and a film that remains little known – *Gruppenbild mit Dame* (1977), both allowing us to consider the personal reasons explaining Schneider's success in the Occupation genre.

2.3. Schneider's tense relationship with Germanic culture

Schneider's roles in *La Passante du Sans-Souci* and *Gruppenbild mit Dame* and her positioning in West German cultural memory of the Second World War both prolong and depart from her beautiful victim figure. The female repression and vulnerability that informed Schneider's Occupation roles have been illuminated by larger feminist discussions with regard to German fascism, and more specifically about German women of the post-war generation (Schneider's generation) and how they relate to the generation of their fathers. Susan Linville notably, in her in-depth study *Feminism, Film, Fascism* (1998), shows that feminist and autobiographical German films of the 1970s and 1980s by Marianne Rosenbaum, Helma Sanders-Brahms, Jutta Brückner and Margarethe von Trotta, amongst others, are instilled with female victimhood and that a whole post-war generation of German women both claimed a status as victims and opposed the patriarchal and authoritarian nature of post-war German culture. Alice Schwarzer, a prominent but controversial figure in the West German women's movement, who met Schneider and published a biography of the star (1998), shares the view that there is an intimate relationship between post-war patriarchy and German fascism. She suggests that Schneider's roles in Occupation films bound the star's personal history to Germany's political past in very specific ways. She contends that the misogynist abuse of women in Schneider's films (such as the rape scene in

Le Vieux fusil) merges with Nazi war crimes and the Holocaust. Schwarzer also draws a parallel between Schneider's alleged 'quest' for roles that include such abuse and suffering, and her personal life. Thus, what the French tend to perceive as redemption, Schwarzer sees the star as symbolically taking revenge on a generation of men represented by her stepfather Blatzheim (Schneider allegedly confided to Schwarzer that he tried to 'sleep with her several times' [p. 80] and that she was sexually abused by a neighbour during a bombing nearby her childhood house when she was six years old).[20] In short, Schneider chose to perform Jews and/or suffering women during the war because she personally identified with their pain. However, it has to be pointed out that the abuses Schneider may have suffered in her private life were not known by her audiences and therefore could not have influenced the reception of her roles at the time of the films' distribution. Apart from Schwartzer's allegations, there is no substantial evidence of these abuses, nor of their connection to Schneider's choice of parts. However, in the section below I bring some nuance to Schwarzer's – at times far-fetched – argument by exploring how personal motivations and tragic events lent added poignancy to the perception of Schneider, especially amongst French audiences, as the embodiment of atemporal and eternal female suffering.[21]

Since the early 1980s, the reception of Schneider's persona has been very much marked by the last year and a half of her life, a period that unfolded miserably from one traumatic event to another. The main event was the tragic death of her son David on 5 July 1981 at the age of fourteen. He fatally injured himself climbing his former step-grandparents' entrance gate at their house in Saint-Germain-en-Laye, near Paris (Schneider and Biasini separated in February and the divorce was pronounced in June). He slipped and fell on the gate's metal spikes, piercing his femoral artery. Although David died during surgery at the hospital, the shocking image of the boy impaled remains one of the most vivid memories associated with Schneider. She herself also went through health-related ordeals shortly before her son's fatal accident: in April, she broke her left foot during a stay in a spa at Quiberon (Brittany), and on 23 May she had her right kidney removed following the detection of a tumour. This is the context against which to consider Schneider's performance in *La Passante du Sans-Souci*. Moreover, Schneider asked the director, Jacques Rouffio, to dedicate his film to Harry Meyen (who had committed suicide in 1979) and her son, insisting that the film's opening credits read, under her name, 'to David and his father'. Audiences knew that a close relationship united mother and son: she had

---

[20]Michael Jürgs had mentioned the alleged abuse of Schneider by her stepfather before in his 1991 biography of the star.

[21]It is important not to equate the dehumanization and threat of annihilation of the European Jews with the lack of empathy for women as subjects and the trivialization of their experiences. The two phenomena are disparate, but they are related in symptomatizing patriarchal society's tendency to play down the realities experienced by groups defined through difference.

paid Meyen a fortune to obtain her son's custody after the divorce and it
was reported in the press that David accompanied Schneider on film sets
and that she valued his appreciation and his help (notably with French
pronunciation) despite his young age.

The film's release and distribution were therefore intertwined with
Schneider's personal hardship. This tended to eclipse *La Passante du Sans-
Souci*'s pre-production and narrative choices, that are nonetheless of interest
with regard to her political position in this phase of her career and amongst
cultural memories of war. The project was initially developed by Schneider
herself, who had read the eponymous novel by Joseph Kessel (1936) while
filming *Une histoire simple* (Siclier, 1982; Schneider and Seydel, 1989,
p. 302). She insisted on playing the lead and double role of Elsa Wiener
(the adoptive mother of the protagonist as a child, in the 1930s) and Lina
Baumstein (the wife of the protagonist as an adult, in the 1980s), and
suggested Rouffio as director to the producers. With Jacques Kirsner, Rouffio
developed a script that expanded the frame of Kessel's original story into the
Second World War and then the Paris of the 1980s. *La Passante du Sans-
Souci* starts in the 'present', the early 1980s, with Max Baumstein (Michel
Piccoli), the respected president of the humanitarian organization Solidarité
Internationale, shooting dead the ambassador of Paraguay in Paris. On
the stand at his trial, Max reveals that the man was a former Nazi officer,
responsible for killing his adoptive family, the Wieners. He goes on to testify
in front of the court – and this is a cue for several flashbacks – about his life
as a Jewish boy and how he had to flee Germany for Paris with his guardian
Elsa Wiener, who saved his life when he was beaten up by SA brownshirts.
Elsa's husband Michel (Helmut Griem), an anti-Nazi book publisher, was
deported to a camp. Elsa drowned her sorrows in alcohol and drugs, singing
in a Parisian cabaret and prostituting herself to a Nazi officer in a desperate
attempt to help liberate her husband. Michel was released, but then he and
Elsa were both assassinated in front of the café Sans-Souci in Pigalle by
Elsa's former Nazi lover.

One scene in particular has been much discussed (it almost invariably
figures in all documentaries and biographical books about the star, in
any language) in terms of Schneider's legacy as a glamorous icon of
female suffering and resilience. Again, her face plays a significant role. On
Christmas Eve in the 1930s past, Elsa and young Max have dinner in an
upscale Parisian restaurant. She is dressed in a long, form-fitting, sequined,
pale blue gown with a train and covered with a fluid colour-matching shawl
in organza forming a large corolla collar attached with a precious glittering
brooch – clothes that visually translate the combined notions of beauty,
luxury and fragility associated with the star's persona. She is sad because
they have not heard from Michel who stayed behind in Germany. Elsa asks
Max to play the violin and, while he does, Schneider is filmed in medium
close-up, her eyes filling progressively with tears. The emotion grows, she

FIGURE 13 *The suffering mother in* La Passante du Sans-Souci.

closes and opens her eyes and mouth several times, a tear rolls down her left cheek and she trembles as she smiles (Figure 13). The actor who plays Max (Wendelin Werner) was about the same age of Schneider's late son at the time of shooting the scene, which led many to assume that Schneider was not performing but genuinely crying over David in front of the camera. On-set rumours spread, adding potency to this painful mingling between fictional on-screen narrative and private off-screen sphere (a particularly emotional version of a typical feature of stardom): the intense moment was allegedly captured in one take, crew members were crying on set and after the scene Schneider ran off to her dressing-room, which she had previously turned into a 'mausoleum' in memory of her son by pinning dozens of photographs of him on the walls (Guillou, 2006; documentary *Un jour, un destin*, 2010). This clearly increased the overwhelming impact of Schneider's performance of the grieving mother. Her role in the film was made even more poignant by her own death a few weeks after its release. With time, audiences, media outlets and fans alike made *La Passante du Sans-Souci* a film entirely dedicated to Schneider, the cinematic proof of, and testimonial to, her personal pain.

While in Kessel's novel the Sans-Souci is the place where the narrator observes Elsa passing by the street, the cafe has a more substantial and political significance in the film, condemning more explicitly, with a plaque, the French involvement in war exactions and the repression of memories of the war. During her testimony in the 1980s trial, Charlotte (Dominique Labourier), Elsa's friend and fellow prostitute from Pigalle, explains that she affixed a commemorative plaque to Elsa and Michel on the cafe's wall when she herself returned from the camps and realized that their bodies had been disposed of by the 'Vichy people'. Charlotte continues by saying that the sign displeased some back in 1945: '[Elsa and Michel were] German resisters, it was the least we could do, they were the first ones to fight against Hitler'. But this is not the biggest alteration from the source material: in the novel, the Wieners are not assassinated, but Elsa kills herself after Michel ceases to love her. Thus, Elsa's personal suicide in the book is turned into a political murder by the film. The enduring consequences of fascism are emphasized in the film through Max's flashbacks to his childhood in 1930s Paris, from the vantage point of the 1980s, especially since he is himself assassinated with his wife Lina six months after his trial. The last shot of the film shows the couple in the Sans-Souci with a text band informing the viewer about their imminent death. We are not told who murdered the Baumsteins, but the film, via Max's humanitarian activities ('against repression and for the defence of liberties'), draws a link between old and rampant, contemporary fascism. The film points to the neo-Nazis though, as two men verbally assault Lina at the end of the film when she learns that Max is condemned to a mere five-year suspended prison sentence: one spits in Lina's face, adding 'that's for your Jew, you whore!'.

Mentioning the murder of Max and Lina allows the film to suggest a critique of both German and French politics in the early 1980s – notably the rise of neo-fascist movements, which were loudly denounced at the time by Rouffio, Piccoli and Schneider who said: 'Nazism is still everywhere, every day' (interview by Michel Drucker, 14/04/1982; Chevillard, 1982). However, the last sequence where Max and Lina meet at the Sans-Souci was altered when the film was broadcast on German TV (Bayerischer Rundfunk) on 15 December 1999. The text band announcing the murder of the Baumsteins at the end was cut – in the German version Schneider's character lives. The now reconfigured 'happy end' allows the resurrection of Elsa as Lina in a classic redemption fantasy. Through the double role, Schneider reconciled history and memory, past Elsa and contemporary Lina merging as the promise of a successful *Vergangenheitsbewältigung*. By contrast, in the French version Schneider solidified her role as glamorous Nazi victim.

Because of her sudden death in May 1982, Schneider was unable to synchronize her part for the German version of *La Passante* which came out in West German cinemas in October; actress Eva Manhardt stepped in. But whether Schneider would have actually done it is up to debate, especially given the West German censorship of *La Passante*. Schneider previously refused to dub herself for the German version of *Le Vieux fusil* in protest against the West German censorship of (amongst other minor cuts and edits) the infamous rape scene; Manhardt replaced her voice for this version as well. This example is one of many illustrating the conflictual relationship between Schneider and the German-speaking press, in particular in West Germany where her French Occupation roles were perceived as Francophile and therefore either ignored or frowned upon (Wild, 1975, p. 156). By contrast, *Gruppenbild mit Dame* in 1976 was her first and sole German-speaking role in a predominantly West German production about the rise of Nazism, the war and the post-war years.

When Schneider went to Berlin for three months at the end of 1976 to film *Gruppenbild mit Dame*, it marked her return to West Germany, solely for work, for the first time in ten years (the last was for *La Voleuse* in 1966). The film is an adaptation of the eponymous novel (1971) by German author Heinrich Böll who carried a reputation as the 'conscience of the nation' and was a fervent moral critique of West German society since the foundation of the Federal Republic (Uecker, 2013, p. 98). It was directed by Aleksandar Petrović, a French-born and acclaimed Serbian/Yugoslav film-maker who was one of the major figures of the Yugoslav Black Wave (Goulding, 2002; Kirn, Sekulić and Testen, 2011). Through an array of characters (friends, family, colleagues) all connected to the protagonist Leni Gruyten (Schneider), *Gruppenbild mit Dame* depicts everyday life in West Germany from the late 1930s to the late 1960s, showing ordinary people's perception of the Nazi era (though with a major omission, as the Holocaust is not evoked). Schneider portrays Leni, an uncompromising woman who intends to live the way she wants – but this solely applies to the romantic life of the character, a generous, altruistic woman defined through her ability to love. We see Leni at four different ages: she first has an intellectual friendship with a Jewish woman disguised as a Catholic nun at her school; second, she falls in love with her cousin, a Nazi officer critical of fascist ideology and murdered along with Leni's brother in their attempt to defect and flee to Sweden. Third, towards the end of the war, she is employed by a florist (Michel Galabru) to make wreaths in company of Boris (Brad Dourif), a Russian prisoner of war with whom she has a baby. Boris dies at the end of the war. Fourthly, in the 1960s, Leni, pregnant again, refuses to concede to the new consumerism of West Germany's capitalist society, and rather than give her apartment to her greedy relatives she prefers to shelter Turkish immigrants. The time structure of this dense narrative is fragmented, moving back and forth through the years in a way that many critics found confusing (*L'Humanité*, 25/05/1977; *Le Figaro*, 25/05/1977).

It is striking that Schneider who, as I shall develop, had had such a contentious approach to West German culture and identity, was cast as Leni, a character who is, according to Matthias Uecker (2013), Böll's ideal embodiment of the 'good German' from a West German perspective. I will not dwell on comparing Leni from the novel and Leni from the film for she is, in Böll's book, largely (physically) absent and only represented indirectly through the stories collected by the narrator to the point that she has been described as an immaterial 'Kunst-Figur' ('artificial figure'; Schnell and Schubert, 2005, pp. 434, 445). In both versions though, Leni is more of a 'utopian wish-fulfilment that represents everything Germans *ought to be*, inspiring admiration and partial imitation in some and violent rejection in

others' (Uecker, p. 99, my emphasis, see also Bernhard, 1973, pp. 365–7)
– she exists in contrast to the others, her main function within the novel is
to inspire them and remind them of their own humanity (Uecker, p. 108).
Through Leni, Schneider embodies both political criticism (denunciation
of the Second World War and of the desolation in which the war left
Germany) and social protest. Her character is shown to stand apart, usually
in opposition to the mainstream of German society. Leni gives and loves
while people around her take, destroy or kill. Schneider's impassive face or
tender, vulnerable expressions are used to express small acts of resistance
(befriending a Jew, giving her coffee to Boris, loving a person of colour
at a time when this was frowned upon). Leni's marginalization echoes
Schneider's own conflictual positioning within West German culture.

Schneider explained that she agreed to do the film because it finally
showed 'a Germany that we've rarely seen before, from the defeated side,
and not from the victorious side' (interview by Michel Drucker, 07/11/1976).
Although she tended to avoid any press, French and West German alike, she
gave a rare, extended interview with French TV personality Michel Drucker
in Berlin during the shooting of *Gruppenbild* in which she stressed her
attachment to France and probed her ambiguous relationship with Germany,
and Berlin in particular, in ways that were both critical and appreciative. At
one point in the interview, Schneider's voice breaks and she excuses herself
for being emotional:

> I feel like doubly a stranger here […]. I am more foreign in this city than
> our French crew members. My homesickness is for Paris, for France. I
> play a German woman, but I have chosen France. I am married to a
> Frenchman, I am fully French, and perfectly happy with that. But […]
> Berlin and Berliners will always move me, because of their strength. It is
> not a city any longer, it is an island. Some Berliners pretend that there is
> no Wall, and Böll – and this is why I find him sympathetic – denounces
> how this country and this city failed to seize their chance after the total
> collapse [of World War II]. I want to say that Leni is a woman with whom
> I identify: she learned how to love amongst ruins, she is a true German,
> very strong, like the people [of Berlin], which is why she was able to
> survive the hell of 1945, the hell of the war.
>
> (*Les rendez-vous du dimanche*, 07/11/1976)

She would nonetheless, a few years later, contradict herself by going
further in her criticism of West Germany's politics during the promotion
of *La Passante du Sans-Souci* by saying, in reference to the Berlin Wall, that
'[the city] is a shame for the entire world, a shame that *we* have carried for
30 years' (interview by Michel Drucker, 14/04/1982). The French-speaking
media, not without chauvinism, portrayed her as a historical victim of the
war whose perspicacity in choosing later to stay in France situated her

amongst the 'good Germans' (*L'Express* reported that the rise of Nazism 'forced her to leave Vienna for a small Austrian village where she spent part of her childhood' [Delain, 1977], which was incorrect). French director Bertrand Tavernier, with whom Schneider worked on *La Mort en direct* in 1980, even argues that Claude Sautet 'de-Germanised her' (documentary *Romy Schneider à fleur de peau*, 2013).

The amalgam went so far that Schneider was recently described – by a notoriously provocative broadcaster – as 'a collaborator with the French' (Yann Moix, *On n'est pas couché*, 09/06/2018). Although in the late 1970s/ early 1980s she situated herself on the French side of the Franco-German cultural dyad, Schneider was torn between her two identities. Arguably she was both French *and* German at the same time, but she herself could not contemplate that idea. At times, she claimed that she was French; at others, she emphasized her Germanic origins by identifying with national stereotypes. Those included the 'Germanic spleen' which Luchino Visconti said she was prone to, and a 'strong' Germanic femininity. Here, I use 'strong' in the sense that Schneider meant it when speaking of Leni, that is, resilience and forbearance rather than power and strength (Schneider evoked the idea of self-reliance and resourcefulness: 'Leni is very German. She just "gets out of herself". In that sense, I would call myself very German', *Der Spiegel*, 22/11/1976, p. 219).

Schneider belonged to the generation of Germans whose parents had experienced the war, and to question them and their lives meant to interrogate Germany's past. For many years, 'no one had dared to ask their parents what they did during the war, how they lived under Hitler, and to what extent they collaborated with the regime, unwittingly or not' (Kaes, 1989, p. 140). In the mid-1970s, the post-war generation looked back at their childhood and became introspective about the psychological trauma impacted by National Socialism on their country. As Angelika Bammer pointed out – without mentioning *Gruppenbild* nor *La Passante* though – many West German films of that period were the products 'of [late 1950s] West German cultural and political history [...] marked by the struggle of a new generation of German artists – writers, painters, poets and filmmakers – to find words and images with which to understand and articulate their experience as Germans, an experience passed on to them by the generation of their parents whom denial and shame had, for the most part, rendered silent' (1985, p. 95). So, like many other German artists born with the anguish of the collectively given shame and pain, Schneider made an attempt to understand her parents' generation by facing the truth of the history of that period, rather than accusing them – which was promptly ignored by the French-speaking media at the time.

Gruppenbild mit Dame represented West Germany at the Cannes Film Festival in May 1977 but the press's response was lukewarm and the film fell short of European box-office expectations (Helmut Karazek in *Der*

Spiegel argued that it pales in comparison to Böll's novel and he blamed the film for being Petrović's 'vanity project' and the film-maker for 'constantly communicating his own showmanship', 1977, p. 198). Despite a Best Actress award at the German Film Awards in June (her pregnancy prevented her from attending the ceremony), Schneider returned to France, where she gave birth to her daughter Sarah and took some time off before starting *Une histoire simple*. It had been difficult to keep the German-speaking press at bay during her presence in Berlin, and the star was aggressively scrutinized and smeared by the tabloid press for weeks. Notwithstanding a small participation, a minute of screen time in the TV film *Tausend Lieder ohne Ton* by Claudia Holldack (the first and only time Schneider worked with a female director, which was the reason for her cameo, Schneider and Seydel, 1989, p. 278) and two more co-productions, of which only *La Passante du Sans-Souci* was partially shot in Berlin, Schneider would not work in West Germany anymore.

This is a convenient place in the progress of my analysis to pivot and discuss Schneider's reception in the German-speaking media. More than her decision to live in France and to uphold her attachment to Frenchness, it was her reported views on Germany that antagonized her German-speaking audiences. Schneider had been suspicious of West German reporters since they had misconstrued her words in the early 1960s (see Part II, Chapter 5) and she called herself 'a renegade in the eyes of Germany' (Schneider and Seydel, 1989, p. 243). Overall, her films were slightly less successful in West Germany than in France, but unsurprisingly, her Occupation films were even less popular. Many times, she complained of the critical reception she received in West Germany ('all I do is treason', p. 259) and of the West German film industry's 'lack of imagination' (p. 248).

There are several underlying reasons for this tension, some of which have to do with Schneider's relationship with Austrian theatre and German cinema in the 1970s. According to Austrian novelist and playwright Peter Handke, Schneider appreciated Thomas Bernhard's oeuvre (Schimmelbusch, 2014). Bernhard was critical of, and even hostile towards, the Austrian nation, and was often called a 'Nestbeschmutzer' (literally 'someone who fouls his/her own nest'), a derogatory term used to describe people who badmouth their own country. He was nonetheless an important theatrical figure: his most famous work was the play *Heldenplatz* (published in 1988, after Schneider's death). The title refers to the square where Austrians celebrated the arrival of Hitler after being annexed by Nazi Germany in the *Anschluss*, and the play problematizes the lingering anti-Semitism in Austria (Daviau, 1991). Many of Bernhard's plays met with criticism from many Austrians, who claimed they sullied Austria's reputation (Mitgang, 1989). Schneider was comfortable with Bernhard's criticism of the Austrian past and she attempted to work with him, or at least to have Harry Meyen direct one of his plays. But the playwright always categorically refused. Like Heinrich

Böll, whose first reaction to the casting of Schneider for *Gruppenbild* was to try and prevent it (Benichou and Pommier, 1981, p. 115), Bernhard could not go beyond the conflation of Schneider with Sissi (Schimmelbusch, 2014). New German Cinema film-maker Rainer Werner Fassbinder made the same judgement, and their projects together (an adaptation of Theodor Storm's novella *Immensee*, and then *Die Ehe der Maria Braun* in 1979, for which he cast Hannah Schygulla) never came to fruition. German producer Hanns Eckelkamp explained that 'She did not belong to his "clan"' (2007, p. 2).[22]

Schneider was therefore overlooked by the New German Cinema of the 1970s and by Germanic auteur theatre alike.[23] In part this may have had to do with her broadcasting (perhaps tactlessly) the idea that her Germanic heritage was somewhat inferior to French culture. But we need also to place her in the context of actors arising from the popular cinema of the 1950s who were shunned by auteur cinema. Schneider similarly 'missed' the French New Wave in the 1960s for reasons I have developed in Part II, Chapter 5. Her former screen partner in the 1950s Horst Buchholz experienced a similar situation. After a career in popular German films of the 1950s and in Hollywood, he only made only two West German films in the 1970s, both by popular German film directors (Alfred Weidenmann and Rolf Thiele). So, when Schneider said that she was not accepted in West Germany (or Austria), she did not mean German-speaking audiences but rather the West German film industry, and the auteur film and theatre communities that failed to recognize her as the 'perfect *comédienne*' as she was then saluted in France (Billard, 1977, p. 5). Generally speaking, and though there were exceptions ('Our best ambassador', *Jede Woche*, 11/10/1979), the Germanic media were more interested in the string of failures in her personal life ('How Romy loves and suffers', *Bunte*, 01/07/1976) than in her professional accomplishments. As we will see in the general conclusion on Schneider's legacy, the French press and fan literature were not that different in this regard, with a tendency to concentrate on her as a celebrity rather than a professional actress.

---

[22]Fassbinder's specialist Thomas Elsaesser claims, without referencing his source though, that the director's rejection had to do with 'Schneider's [excessive] demands, her indeciveness and heavy dependence on alcohol' (2001, p. 154).

[23]Andrea Bandhauer (2015) suggests instead that the dismissal of Schneider from 'serious' German directors was linked to her family background to which she was still 'connected' – that is, the mark 'left by her parents' absolute refusal to acknowledge their involvement in the Nazi regime' (p. 219). I distance myself from that argument that tends to suppress Schneider's own self-agency in the shaping of her career.

Conclusion

Schneider's roles and performances in Occupation films situated her at the centre of the complex relationship between West Germany and France and the memory of the Second World War. These films, their success in France and lack thereof in West Germany, constructed a persona polarized between two national receptions, oscillating between the two poles of her double identity, a liminal position that she occupied since the massive success of the *Sissi* cycle. On the French side, her choice of roles represented an active and redemptive voice for Germany's violent past and implicitly a vindication of her choice to work in France. On the West German side, her reception was unsurprisingly more ambivalent – as she was frequently perceived as a 'traitor' – and she was not only criticized by the media but also shunned by avant-garde Austrian theatre and New German Cinema. This further complicated her conflictual relationship with Germanic cultures as she struggled to occupy, in the West German film *Gruppenbild mit Dame,* the ethical victim that she embodied in her French roles.

Schneider's vulnerability, an aspect of her conservatively feminine persona already familiar to French audiences, and her characters' suffering, melancholy and ultimately tragedy, set her films apart from others within the Occupation genre in French cinema. They also stood out in their unique featuring of a major female star, within a genre dominated by male characters and actors. The films deployed her physical beauty, notably through a pervasive use of prolonged close-ups of the actress's face, and the period costumes of the *mode rétro* were particularly suited to a star known for her costume films since the beginning of her career. This chapter also showed that, with her projection of traditional feminine vulnerability, the German Occupation films Schneider made in France enabled her to add a darker side comprised of violence and tragedy, echoing off-screen events in her private life that were widely circulated in the media. This brings me to the next and last chapter of this book in which I am concerned with Schneider's performances in an 'excessive', melodramatic mode in a set of increasingly morbid films.

9

Pathos and hysteria

Introduction

This final chapter considers films made towards the end of Romy Schneider's career that display new types of roles for the star – more sombre and more within the sphere of hysteria (defined as spectacular emotional manifestations, histrionics).[1] On the one hand, I explore the relationship between those roles and Schneider's roles in Occupation films, and on the other hand I consider how Schneider's evolution towards sombre and victimized roles relate to the status of women in French society in the second half of the 1970s and the early 1980s. I am also interested in the way these films draw on Schneider's acting skills in a more overt way, leading the media to construct a dichotomy between the accomplished actress and the unhappy woman.

I look at those films through a thematic lens rather than following a strict chronology, dividing them in three groups. The overall trajectory of this chapter is a tragic one, Schneider's vulnerable persona begins to veer towards a more pathetic one, and I begin with the 'retro aesthetics' films as they use similar aesthetics to the *mode rétro* films previously examined, but are not thematically concerned with the German Occupation. Then I move on to *L'Important c'est d'aimer* / *The Most Important Thing: Love* (Andrzej Żuławski, 1975), focusing on Schneider's performance as a turning point in her career where she becomes associated with excess. I conclude this book with Schneider's series of particularly sombre films with roles connoted with morbidity.

---

[1]I am aware that the term 'hysteria' is, in common usage, loaded with anti-feminist sentiment (see *Hysteria beyond Freud* by Sander L. Gilman et al. (1993), and 'Hysteria, Feminism, and Gender Revisited: The Case of the Second Wave' by Cecily Devereux (2014) in *ESC: English Studies in Canada*, 40:1, pp. 19–45).

1. Retro aesthetics films

Ludwig (Luchino Visconti, 1973), *Le Trio infernal / The infernal trio* and *La Banquière / The Lady Banker*, both directed by Francis Girod in 1974 and 1980, respectively, belong to a broader 'retro aesthetics' trend in West-European cinema, and with which Schneider was familiar as they share a similar visual style, notably with *Le Vieux fusil* and *Une femme à sa fenêtre*. Regarding the two Girod films I was very fortunate to meet and interview journalist and filmmaker Anne Andreu, Girod's widow, at the Cinémathèque française on 2 December 2016. She gave me rare insight into her husband's work with Schneider (she also co-directed with Francesco Brunacci a documentary about Romy Schneider in 2002).

With the exception of *Ludwig*, shot outside of France, the aesthetic continuity can mostly be attributed to the French team that created Schneider's costumes (Jacques Fonteray), hats (Jean Barthet), hair (Jean-Max Guérin) and makeup (Didier Lavergne), as they had in her Occupation films. However, the narratives cover different topics: *Ludwig* recounts the reign of King Ludwig II of Bavaria in the second half of the nineteenth century, and the Girod films are set in 1920s–1930s France. I will not dwell for long on the Visconti film because Schneider's role as Elisabeth of Austria is a minor one. Although the European marketing of the film drew on the fact that she reprised the iconic regal role for the fourth time, she only agreed because of her friendship with Visconti whom she trusted to create an 'historical authentic portrayal of Sissi', Schneider and Seydel, 1989, p. 245). She was given a co-starring credit alongside star of the film, German actor Helmut Berger.

Ludwig was a project that Visconti had long contemplated, and no expenses were spared to produce what he considered his masterpiece. However, the film, deemed too long and some scenes too suggestive regarding the King's homosexuality, was drastically shortened by distributors twice without his consent (Visconti suffered from a stroke during filming and was not healthy enough to prevent a first one-hour cut, and then a second 55-minute cut after the premiere in Munich in January 1973).[2] Although the film was a critical and commercial success (especially in France and Italy),[3] due to the major editing, it is difficult to evaluate its impact on Schneider's career at the time. Several versions of the film have been available at different times, and as I have not been able to view them all, I cannot assess what scenes include Schneider in these versions, which is why I proceed with care in my analysis.

---

[2]*Ludwig* was restored to its four-hour original running time by *Ludwig*-scriptwriter and Visconti's long-time collaborator Suso Cecchi d'Amico and *Ludwig*-film editor Ruggero Mastroianni in 1980.
[3]1,390,846 viewers went to see the film in France (Simsi, 2012, p. 208), and it is estimated that around 3,165,000 spectators saw it in Italy.

What is certain though is that Schneider wears several imperial costumes designed by Visconti's regular collaborator Piero Tosi, and that imagery from the film's promotion mostly centred on her presence in these costumes, featured in many European outlets and magazine covers (*The Sunday Times Magazine*, 10/09/1972). The delicate, pastel-coloured dresses and hour-glass silhouettes that she wore in the mid-1950s in Marischka's trilogy were replaced by lavish, heavy,[4] and highly detailed designs (brocade, lace, ruffles, beads, jewels, feathers). These more historically accurate costumes are designed in a mostly dark palette of black, burgundy, blue and grey, and include a range of hats, black veils of various laceworks and lengths, many furs and a lace umbrella. The Austrian Empress's much celebrated locks of hair are also on full display. Schneider wears the iconic tresses styled in heavy and complicated crowns down her neck or loosened, the gigantic wig forming a cape from her head down to her ankles. The development of Schneider's acting style since her Sissi years is noticeable: she has lowered her voice (as suggested by Claude Sautet a couple of years before in order to attenuate her German accent, a habit that she applied to the other languages she fluently spoke, French and English), her tone is more assured and controlled, which makes her acting appear more cerebral and sophisticated, less impulsive and 'natural'. There are nonetheless traces of the sensual Sissi from the third instalment of the series in Visconti's film. The equestrian top hat that she wears in her first appearance in the film is reminiscent of Schneider's costume in *Sissi 3*. Schneider embodies the Empress/horse-riding woman with pride and the sense of entitlement that she showed in 'Il lavoro' – chin up, straight back, determined speech, air of superiority. If Schneider's smile and laugh were perceived as natural and 'authentic' in the 1950s – the expressions of an ingénue, incarnated in this version in the role of Sophie-Charlotte (the Empress's younger sister performed by Sonia Petrovna) – she now opts for a derisive smile. Schneider's flared nostrils are unerring indicators of this sarcastic expression. She sometimes laughs, throwing her head back, but in a spirit of mockery, not of gaiety. In this way, Visconti (and Schneider who rallied up to his idea) wished to 'set the record straight' and offer a glimpse of the 'real' Elisabeth (Schneider and Seydel, 1989, p. 245; Bonini, 2001, pp. 153–6). In her few scenes, Schneider's portrayal of the Empress is that of a cynical, disillusioned and melancholy woman, speaking sharply, gazing away or frowning, deep in her thoughts. She feels misunderstood by the court and her entourage (in that sense, Ludwig and Elisabeth share a bond, which briefly brings them together in an incestuous moment), closer in personality to the historical figure described by contemporaries and historians, than the gentle young woman imagined by Marischka.

---

[4]Schneider's scenes take place in winter and were shot on location (Bavaria and Austria) in January and February 1972.

To consider *Ludwig, Le Trio infernal* and *La Banquière* solely through the lens of the French debates about the *mode rétro* evoked in the previous chapter would be restrictive, as these debates tend to highlight the conservative ideology of the films and are, for that period, mainly aimed at the German Occupation films. The discussions around heritage cinema in an Anglo-American context, however, allow me to expand my perspective on those three films by arguing that Schneider's roles and performances took full advantage of retro aesthetics in order to convey potentially progressive gender and sexual politics (or appear to do so, as we shall see for *Le Trio infernal*). This is the argument advanced by scholars such as Richard Dyer (1995), Claire Monk (1995a, 1995b, 2002) and Belèn Vidal (2012b) from a feminist and pro-LGBTQ[5] stance. They purport that, beyond the costume genre previously criticized for presenting the past (the English past, in that context) in a nostalgic and lavish fashion which detracts from historical or critical understanding (Higson, 2003, 2006), period films instead offer a more progressive stance, and enable the films to talk about issues that contemporary-set films could not address, notably by depicting the personal struggles, social position and the rights of women and LGBTQ individuals.

Ludwig, Le Trio infernal and *La Banquière* belong to the heritage genre in terms of their setting in the past, their adaptation of literary texts, their high-quality visual production values and their depictions of high-class (even royal) lifestyles with luxurious settings and clothing, but also, to some degree, for their progressive stance on sexual politics. *Ludwig* was penalized by heavy cuts for its queerness for several years. In that regard, moving on to a comparison between *Le Trio infernal* and *La Banquière* is a fruitful task as the latter suggests a more enlightened position, one that is in addition mirrored by the greater star power that Schneider had gained by the beginning of the 1980s. I will start with *Le Trio infernal* in order to contrast the agency gained by Schneider with her starring role in *La Banquière*.

The dark comedy *Le Trio infernal* was adapted from the eponymous novel (1972) by French author Solange Fasquelle, who was inspired by real-life, sordid events that made headlines in the 1930s in the Marseille region, when lawyer and assassin Georges-Alexandre Sarret was put on trial, condemned for double murder and guillotined. In the film version, set in 1920s Marseille, Schneider performs Philomène Schmidt, a German émigré who forms a dubious alliance with Georges Sarret (Michel Piccoli, who was also executive producer and a significant influence on Schneider accepting to co-star). They become lovers and Georges elaborates a plan to swindle ailing men out of their life insurance: Philomène marries the men (on the first occasion becoming a French citizen) and then makes them take out a contract for life insurance that she and Sarret cash in once they

---

[5]I am aware that it is anachronistic to label 'LGBTQ' what was 'Gay and Lesbian' in the mid-1990s.

die. Philomène's sister Catherine (Polish actress Mascha Gonska) arrives in France and becomes Sarret's mistress and their new partner in crime. The 'infernal trio' murder their accomplice who has been pretending to be the husbands in the medical examinations conducted by the insurance companies, as well as his mistress, and dissolve their corpses in bathtubs filled with acid. They then plot to contract life insurance for Catherine and pretend that she has died, and to substitute the body with that of Magali (Monica Fiorentini), a young woman suffering from tuberculosis. But the plan backfires when Magali recovers and Catherine dies by falling from a window – it is not clear if she committed suicide or if Magali pushed her. Upon her sister's death, Philomène forces Georges to marry her, which he does, looking utterly unhappy.

Le Trio infernal came out in France in May 1974, a year that witnessed important cultural and sexual shifts within the film milieu: censorship had considerably loosened since the events of May 68 and was practically abolished in 1974; the soft-porn film Emmanuelle (Just Jaeckin) with Sylvia Kristel came out in cinemas in June that same year, and porn cinema was generally booming. The depiction of bold sexuality (polyamorous relations, including incestuous ones) in the film therefore conforms to wider trends in the French film industry, and might even appear 'transgressive'. However, the film's sexual politics are situated in a sensationalist and mercantile register. Indeed, the sex relations in Le Trio infernal may be located outside of Western society's hetero-patriarchal norms, but they do not veil the film's misogyny and homophobia. The women (including the sisters) in Le Trio infernal are rivals and replaceable with one another as suggested by the ending (Magali will take Catherine's place in the scheme), all for Sarret's personal satisfaction and sexual gratification. Though every character is malevolent, especially Piccoli's dubious solicitor and evil mastermind, it is the women who are depicted as having 'perverse morals' (i.e. lesbian relations). Homosexuality as represented in Le Trio infernal is far from being subversive (or simply normal): as Sarret forces Catherine to play the role of Magali's nurse, he suggests that she goes further by exhausting the young woman sexually, pushing her to have sex with the convalescent. Catherine expresses her opposition but grudgingly obeys him. Sarret and Philomène later spy on the two women having sex through the bedroom's keyhole, reinforcing the exploitative and sensationalist aspect of the lesbian pairing.

In spite of its sensationalism, with just over 600,000 spectators Le Trio infernal was not a success at the French box office (Simsi, 2012, p. 270). Although it is difficult to point out the exact reasons for this lack of popularity, we can consider the fact that many critics expressed their annoyance at the film's polished retro look (Siclier, 1974), and their disgust at the gratuitous 'provocation' (Le Quotidien de Paris, 21/05/1974) of the long and detailed sequences showing the acid baths in which bodies are dissolved (Les Echos, 31/05/1974; La Croix, 01/06/1974; Le Canard *enchaîné*, 05/06/1974). Schneider's performance drew mixed reviews, a few journalists found her 'amazing' (Douin, 1974) and 'dazzling' (*Les Echos*, 31/05/1974); Philomène was 'one of her best roles so far' (*France-Soir*, 22/05/1974), while others brushed over her presence in the film, simply mentioning her impressive collection of hats (Pantel, 1974), in other words dismissing her character and performance by pointing to the shallowness of the *mode rétro*. Those critics had a point, and I will now examine in what way Schneider's persona fits the visual aesthetic of the film, but rings false with the characterization and tone of her role.

As part of the *rétro* trend, the film deploys a luxurious 1920s iconography, notably through costumes – *Le Trio infernal* was the most expensive debut film by a new director in French cinema history at the time (*L'Aurore*, 21/05/1974). I have already analysed how historical costumes fitted Schneider well – in that regard, *Le Trio infernal* was no exception. The film explicitly foregrounds fashion. Schneider, as its leading female star, strikes an alluring silhouette, especially once the trio's scam starts paying off and she becomes rich. More than her chic dresses (loose and knee-length designs, with straight-lines and a dropped waist), sheer evening gowns (low-cut and form-fitting lines, embellished with feathers) and fur coats and capes, her cloche hats of various colours and fabrics, adorned with rhinestones, feathers and veils, take centre stage (Figure 14). The hats showcase her prominently made-up face. Schneider had a facial structure well suited to vintage looks and the soft lines of the hats enhanced the glamorous spectacularization of her face: the lines of her cheekbones and jawline were accentuated with blushes and shadows, the contours of her lips outlined in crimson red and her eyes were accentuated with dark eyeliner. Arguably, Schneider's image being once again associated with period fashion, and her silhouette in historical costumes, acted as a nostalgic reminder to the viewer, and thus a reinforcement of her stardom. And yet Schneider's persona did not fit the dark comedic tone of the film and of her character. Piccoli, on the other hand, was famous for his roles as perverse and shady bourgeois men, thus the character of Sarret was a 'perfect fit' for him, in Richard Dyer's terms (1998, p. 129) – reminiscent of his earlier cynical and sarcastic types, notably in *Belle de jour* (Buñuel, 1967). Schneider on the contrary struggled to provide the ironic distance[6] necessary to perform the chilling but comic character of Philomène; the latter was too different from either her chic bourgeois persona (as in the Sautet films) or her vulnerable roles in the Occupation films. Philomène was Schneider's last comedic role in a filmography that does not include many.

---

[6]Unlike, for instance, Mireille Darc whose persona developed an amalgam of blond glamour and comic farce such as in *Elle boit pas, elle fume pas, elle drague pas, mais … elle cause* (Michel Audiard, 1970), or Jeanne Moreau in *Le Journal d'une femme de chambre* (Luis Buñuel, 1964), whose erotic persona included an important sardonic dimension.

FIGURE 14 *Schneider's makeup and hat accentuating the spectacle of her face in* Le Trio infernal.

And yet, despite being a 'problematic fit' (Dyer, p. 129), Philomène exhibits some affinities with Schneider's tragic image because of her deadly nature; she does not pull the trigger herself, but she gets rid of the bodies and manipulates the dying Magali. It is in that sense that the role began to situate the star within morbidity, an aspect that would become important to her roles in the late 1970s and the early 1980s. I will now move on to Francis Girod's second film with Schneider, *La Banquière*, and explore how, this time, her role as the treacherous but powerful Emma Eckhert represented a 'perfect fit' with Schneider's persona.

Made six years after *Le Trio infernal*, *La Banquière* (1980) focuses on the complex character of Emma Eckhert, inspired by the Parisian businesswoman Marthe Hanau (1886–1935). She was a controversial figure implicated in a major financial and political scandal in 1928 – in the film as in real life, her profits are based on insider trading and on her construction of what we now call a Ponzi scheme. Her role as an independent woman in a position of economic and political power is unique in Schneider's filmography – and it also stands out in French cinema history as one of the very few featuring a woman banker in a leading role or simply progressing in the world of high finance (another rare exception is Pascal Bonitzer's *Tout de suite maintenant*, with Agathe Bonitzer in 2016). *La Banquière* is a biopic that oscillates between fiction and the reality of a historical figure who famously defrauded many small investors. Very well known in the 1930s, Hanau was less so at the end of the 1970s when the film was made (which may have enabled the filmmakers to take liberties with Hanau's biography).

The role was offered to Schneider by Girod a couple of years after *Le Trio infernal*. He created the Hanau-inspired character for her (Gabrysiak, 2015, p. 235). Despite the critical and commercial failure of his second film *René la Canne* in 1977, Schneider reiterated her support to Girod, and *La Banquière* was funded and produced because of her presence in the cast (interview with Anne Andreu, 2016). The film was an expensive production (16 million francs, according to Catherine Hermary-Vieille, 1988, p. 207), and it benefitted from a huge promotional campaign (Douin, 1980b, cover and pp. 70–3; *Elle*, 25/08/1980, cover and pp. 14–15; *Première*, 08/1980, cover and pp. 14–19; *Libération*, 02/09/1980). Many French critics disapproved of the 'American-like' scale of the film and Girod's continuing allegiance to the *mode rétro* with the film's lavish visual style (sets, costumes, furniture, vintage cars, *Libération*, 02/09/1980). With nearly 2.5 million spectators in France, the film was a success and the fourteenth most successful film the year of its release (Simsi, 2012, p. 45).

Emma Eckhert crystallizes Schneider's 1970s French persona: she is beautiful and imperial, she appears modern and sophisticated, she is feminine and seductive, and yet she ultimately meets a tragic end and is depicted as a victim.[7] The scenario, written by Girod and novelist Georges Conchon, was mostly developed from a biography of Hanau by Dominique Desanti, entitled *La Banquière des années folles* (1968). Desanti's perspective on Hanau's life and career is positive; she praises her trail-blazing approach to savings and investments. This is understandable in terms of her political views: Desanti was a feminist, a former member of the Resistance and of the French Communist Party. Girod and Conchon adopted a similar standpoint and the film therefore differs from historical facts in several ways, including (important with regard to Schneider's image) a conclusion that is more favourable to the protagonist, rendering her almost heroic.

At first, the narrative seems analogous to Hanau's life: Emma is Jewish with Alsatian origins, her French is slightly German-accented, she has a

---

[7]In 1979, Schneider played a similar character in her second film with Terence Young, *Bloodline*. The film stars Audrey Hepburn amongst an international cast (James Mason, Ben Gazzara, Omar Sharif, Maurice Ronet) but failed at the box office, was lambasted by critics and rapidly fell into oblivion, leaving no mark on Schneider's persona. Schneider's few scenes show her character Hélène as a powerful, ambitious and greedy woman. Alongside her husband (Ronet), she manages the French branch of her family's pharmaceutical company. She wins a racing car, showing no remorse for a fellow contestant who died in the race. She is, however, ultimately the deceived party in her husband's financial scheme.

tense relationship with her mother, and she is a lesbian but agrees to marry out of convenience with a man, Moïse (Jacques Fabri), who becomes her friend and her first business partner. These details are presented in the first minutes of the film, with the help of intertitles, and shot in black and white. The main narrative is in colour and begins in 1929, a time characterized by a buoyant stock market (though the October crash is not mentioned, nor does it appear to have any effect). Back then, women were barred from the Paris Stock Exchange, yet Emma is a prosperous banker. She is the founder and president of a lucrative savings bank bearing her name, and the owner of two financial newspapers. Emma's professional and private lives are interlaced, she flirts and teases and falls in love while developing her business organization. Yet, her immense triumph causes her defeat, plotted by her opponent Vannister (Jean-Louis Trintignant), who represents the conservative establishment and would rather not see a Jew ('a foreigner', he says), let alone a woman, defy him. He helps the authorities to put Emma behind bars, close down her company and ruin her and her clients. Then, he plans her assassination at a public meeting, held soon after she escapes from prison and during a rallying speech to her friends and supporters.

The biopic distances itself from historical reality early on in the narrative and in several respects which, for the most part, have to do with sexuality and gender relations. Emma lives in a virtually all-male world, as Hanau did in the 1920s as the sole woman in a milieu reserved for men. Judging by photographs of her and descriptions by Desanti, the real-life Hanau had a quasi-manly physique. Emma, in this respect, was adapted to Schneider: beyond her professional achievements, the film foregrounds the character's femininity, her sophisticated clothes and her delicate makeup. Schneider's beauty, the foundation of her star identity, was explicitly used to 'elevate' the original character to the rank of 'myth' (Douin, 1980b, p. 71). Hanau was known for being tough and cynical, and Schneider sometimes delivers her lines in a rapid and aggressive manner, or in a slow, condescending vocal tone. Her drawl is linked to her German accent and often goes with a disdainful expression of the mouth. But those scenes are rare and Schneider frequently appears more seductive and gentle than what would normally be expected of characters (male or female) in the same position of decision-making and power. And while Hanau disguised herself as a bearded man to enter the Palais Brongniard (where the stock exchange was located at the time) (Desanti, 1968, pp. 13–18), Schneider instead sends her male employees to the stock exchange and is never seen wearing men's clothes except once, in an attire reminiscent of Marlene Dietrich's tuxedo and white tie in Josef von Sternberg's 1930 film *Morocco,* with her hair short and slicked back.

Hanau was known for being a lesbian: she had affairs with women, including a long and scandalous (for the time) relationship with a woman named Josèphe. In the film, Josèphe is renamed Camille (Noëlle Châtelet), and she is described as a rich heiress and the very first person with whom Emma falls 'really in love'. Marthe and Josèphe had a relationship until Marthe's death, but in the film Emma soon establishes a distance and falls out of love with Camille after the first ten minutes. She proceeds to have an affair with the promising male politician and brilliant orator Rémy Lecoudray (Daniel Mesguich). After their first night together, he says that he thought that she 'only liked women'; she responds that she 'thought so too'. Emma's lesbian sexual orientation is therefore shown to be a phase, and somewhat used in an exploitative manner (the original poster shows her wearing an androgynous outfit) to instil a semblance of modernity to the film: Emma's homosexuality is quickly erased from the narrative to leave room for a more normative heterosexual relationship. There are remaining traces of Emma's queerness in the form of a lasting bond with Camille and a meaningful friendship with Colette Lecoudray (Marie-France Pisier), the wife of Emma's lover who, horrified at the prospect of his own downfall, kills himself.

Although I did not find documents that confirm or refute that those narrative choices in La Banquière were deliberately made to fit Schneider's persona, another significant change from historical facts brings further support to this argument – the manner of Emma's death. While Hanau committed suicide in her prison cell in 1935, Emma dies publicly in a spectacular ending, so theatrically staged and excessively performed that it verges towards Grand Guignol. Emma is shot by one of Vannister's acolytes while she gives a passionate speech: in slow motion, Schneider throws her head back and opens her mouth widely, raising her arms, before awkwardly collapsing onto the floor. This scene is the pinnacle of a narrative that has led the viewers to side with the protagonist and see the cruel Trintignant and his clique as misogynistic, anti-Semitic, jealous villains who plot the defeat of a 'visionary' and modern woman – even though we are aware of Emma's misdemeanours and fraud. In comparison, male characters in similar films about the world of high finance either lose their job (L'Argent des autres, Christian de Chalonge, 1978), end up ruined (Le Sucre, Jacques Rouffio, 1978), start their career all over again or go to prison (Mille milliards de dollars, Henri Verneuil, 1981) – except for Stavisky in Alain Resnais's 1974 eponymous film, who dies a suspicious death. Thus, the fate of Schneider's characters at the end of the 1970s and beginning of the 1980s is invariably tragic. Showing a proud, ambitious, intelligent and successful woman banker as the prey of the patriarchal establishment and toning down the fact that Hanau was a crook serves to emphasize the victim status of the character, in line with the vulnerability at the core of Schneider's star image.

2. Valorizing hysteria: Schneider's melodramatic performance in *L'Important c'est d'aimer*

When Schneider filmed *L'Important c'est d'aimer* in the second half of 1974, it was her fourth film of that year after *Un amour de pluie*, *Le Mouton enragé*, and *Le Trio infernal*. She was approaching the peak of her French career (the success of *Le Vieux fusil* and *Une femme à sa fenêtre* would shortly follow) and was the most sought-after actress at the time in the French film industry (Couderc, 1974; interview by France Roche, 12/02/1975). She was paid 1 million francs for her role in *Le Trio infernal* and obtained 200,000 more for her staff, that is, babysitter, secretary, chauffeur and personal assistant, according to *Le Nouvel observateur* (10/06/1974). Her fame enabled her to choose her projects, the directors with whom she wanted to work and she was able to influence some aspects of the production of her films (character development, casting and very occasionally cinematography and editing,[8] Benichou and Pommier, 1981, p. 103). Polish film-maker Andrzej Żuławski was one of the filmmakers Schneider wished to work with. He had previously written and directed the critically acclaimed *Trzecia część nocy* (1971) and *Diabeł* (1972); upon its theatrical release the latter was banned by the Communist government in Poland until 1988. Following this experience with censorship, Żuławski came to work in Paris. He had been there before, at the end of the 1950s when he was exposed to the New Wave[9] and studied at the IDHEC[10] film school. He also worked as a script-doctor for Philippe de Broca and Louis Malle, amongst others.

L'Important c'est d'aimer is the adaptation of Christopher Frank's novel *La Nuit américaine* (1972).[11] Frank was already associated with Schneider's career as he wrote the script for *Le Mouton enragé*, a film produced by Léo L. Fuchs[12] who suggested Frank's novel to Żuławski to adapt for his first 'French' film. With Schneider, the German Klaus Kinski, the Italian Fabio Testi, the Polish director and crew and funds from Paris, Rome and

---

[8]As stipulated in her contract, Schneider demanded that most of the close-ups of Gisela Hahn, her co-star in *César et Rosalie* in the role of Rosalie's sister Carla, be cut (Steinbauer, 1999, pp. 108–10).

[9]As a film about an actress at work, *L'Important c'est d'aimer* shows parallels to *Le Mépris* (Jean-Luc Godard, 1963), notably in the dynamic relationship between the three leads set against the film industry world, Georges Delerue's melodramatic music and the misogyny shown towards the female protagonist (Loshitzky, 1995, pp. 138–41; Vincendeau, 2013, pp. 102–6).

[10]Institut des hautes études cinématographiques (now called La Fémis).

[11]The novel's original title *La Nuit américaine* was left aside early in pre-production in order not to be confused with François Truffaut's 1973 film of the same name. The title *L'Important c'est d'aimer* was chosen by producer Albina Du Boisrouvray against Żuławski's (and Schneider's) wish (interview with Żuławski by Christian Defaye, November 1981).

[12]Not to be confused with Leo Fuchs (1911–1994), the Polish-born American actor.

Munich, *L'Important c'est d'aimer* is a transnational film made in France (Goddard, 2014, p. 250). Frank and Żuławski co-wrote the scenario from *La Nuit américaine* and Albina Du Boisrouvray, who owned the rights to the novel and had a contract with Schneider, stepped in as producer (Fuchs is credited as associate producer). Sources differ as to whether Schneider herself suggested the name of Żuławski to Fuchs or Boisrouvray, or simply agreed to work with him after she saw *Trzecia część nocy* (telling her agent Jean-Louis Livi that she would like to collaborate with the auteur) – in any case Schneider's stardom was a determining factor in the film's existence and Żuławski credits her for making the project possible (Grassin, 2012). However, we should be wary of attributing too much agency to the star, as media discourse on Schneider frequently leans towards hagiography and tends to give her more decision-making power than she had. An oft-repeated refrain at the time (and ever since) suggested that Schneider 'took risks' in putting her fame at the service of film-makers seen as 'underdogs', such as Żuławski, Girod, Costa-Gavras and Claude Miller, and that agreeing to star in their films was a 'leap of faith' for her career and her image (Benichou and Pommier, 1981, pp. 130–4). The reality is more nuanced: Żuławski already had international critical recognition for his first film before working with Schneider, and Costa-Gavras had made the hugely successful *Z* (1969) and *L'Aveu* (1970) before collaborating with Schneider. As for Girod, even though *Le Trio infernal* was indeed his first film, he was steeped deep into the French film industry as an assistant director, screenwriter and producer (it was Piccoli, as executive producer, who took a financial risk). It is true that Miller represented more of a risk for Schneider's career: his last film *Dites-lui que je l'aime* (1977), made four years before *Garde à vue*, failed at the box office, but Schneider loved it and she wished to work with the 'promising' director (Benichou and Pommier, p. 139). The presentation of Schneider as a champion of auteur cinema and a risk-taker tells us instead that the star was eager to diversify her career by accepting challenging roles that would bring her artistic legitimacy. The reference to Sissi still remained persistent in the mid-1970s and in the 1980s (even if it was to emphasize that she was 'becoming the film actress of the century', *Minute*, 31/01/1980; and in her last two interviews in *Stern* and *Paris Match* the topic of Sissi takes up a third of the articles, 23/04/1981 and 08/05/1981, respectively), and can still explain her choice of certain roles, such as in *Le Trio infernal*, for which Girod said to her 'it would be the suicide of Sissi' (*Télérama*, 14/10/1987). However, the diversification of films and characters, if it indeed left behind the 'innocence' of Sissi, did little to steer her persona away from vulnerable femininity; on the contrary, each role in the films under discussion in this chapter reinforced the tragic aspect of Schneider's image further into pathos (as well as misogyny), starting with a bang in *L'Important c'est d'aimer*.

Żuławski's work is mostly known for its excess: the narratives are confusing at times (with an absence of conventional explanation), but consistently about characters torturing themselves and each other, with displays of hostility, horror and violent clashes of emotions underlined by music. Most films centre on a female character performed by a young, beautiful star (after Schneider came Isabelle Adjani, Valérie Kaprisky and Sophie Marceau) who suffers greatly and displays neurosis and hysteria – the first retrospective of Żuławski's films in 2012 in the United States was entitled 'Hysterical excess'. *L'Important c'est d'aimer*, Żuławski's first film in France, is narratively and visually dark (with murky and unflattering colours and lighting). It inaugurates the dour and tortured emotional landscapes that Żuławski would further explore in his French career.

Żuławski changed Frank's original material to concur with his cinematic vision of decay: instead of the novel's artistic and intellectual milieu, he set his film in the seedy pornographic film business in contemporary Paris. Beginning with the encounter between photographer Servais (Testi) and Nadine (Schneider), an 'aging' actress who is reduced to appearing in lurid, soft-core B-movies, *L'Important c'est d'aimer* charts their destructive and toxic relationship by showing her descent in a brutal and extreme way. Servais becomes obsessed with Nadine, resulting in a love triangle between them and Nadine's husband Jacques (pop singer Jacques Dutronc in his first dramatic film role). In an effort to revive Nadine's sagging career and get in her good graces, Servais borrows money from a dubious underworld boss, Mazelli (Claude Dauphin), to fund a theatre production of Shakespeare's *Richard III* staged by an eccentric German director (Klaus Kinski). Meanwhile he continues his regular job which consists of taking pornographic photographs. When Nadine realizes that Servais was behind the play, she offers to sleep with him in order to 'pay off her debt'. Although he rejects her, Jacques commits suicide out of jealousy. Jacques's death separates Servais and Nadine who feels responsible, while Servais refuses to comply with the degrading demands of Mazelli who beats him. In the final scene that echoes the beginning of the film (which I analyse below) and brings some cyclical unity to the narrative, she finds him badly hurt and she expresses her love for him.

Żuławski's move to France coincided with a shift from male romantic protagonists to female performers who became central to his themes and visual style (Goddard, 2014, p. 248). Cinematographer Ricardo Aronovich uses slow zooms that end in tight close-ups of Schneider's face, whose tortured expressions suggest a fractured mind and unbalanced emotional state. Although it features several brutal altercations between characters, *L'Important c'est d'aimer* concentrates on Nadine's violent emotional pain, expressed through her intense performance. Schneider's character and acting are situated within the melodrama register.

In a first example, I examine an internalized, toned-down aspect of Schneider's acting, and in a second example, a feverish, externalized and physical expression. Both instances relate to the complex phenomenology of the melodrama genre – that is the emphasis on 'the inner emotional states of the characters' (DeCordova, 1991, p. 121), which requires, argues Christine Gledhill, an 'excess of expression' such as 'hyperbolic emotions, extravagant gesture, high-flown sentiments, declamatory speech [...]' (1991, p. 212). One of *L'Important c'est d'aimer*'s first scenes illustrates this concept of melodramatic performance, as well as functioning as a narrative element (a performance-within-the-performance). Performance inflections typical of melodrama to convey emotions such as hysteria, madness or suffering, as in this scene, are used to display acting skills by providing moments 'exhibiting high degrees of expressive incoherence' as James Naremore puts it (1988, p. 76). As Servais sneaks onto a film set to take illicit photos of her, Nadine struggles to act in an intimate and emotional scene – saying 'I love you' to her lover lying in a pool of blood. She is directed aggressively by a female director (Nadia Vasil). Naremore adds that 'in such moments, the actor demonstrates *virtuosity* by sending out dual signs, and the vivid contrast between facial expressions gives the "acted image" an emotional richness, a strong sense of dramatic irony' (p. 76, my emphasis). This intense scene shows Schneider-the-star and her character as an emotional performer, expressing an affective inner life. When she becomes aware of Servais's camera and presence, she softly pleads with him to stop, extending her arm towards him, her hand covered with fake blood. She is straddling a bloodstained body, in a silk nightie and heavy, smudgy makeup with fake long eyelashes and streams of tears on her cheeks. She justifies her poorly convincing performance by saying that she is 'an actress [*comédienne*], you know, I can do good stuff and that, that here, it was just for nothing' (Figure 15). We are meant to understand that Schneider's 'bad' acting in the soft-porn film, and the signs of her character's struggle to emote, are marks of her 'good' performance in Żuławski's film. Her delivery is hesitant, she stumbles on 'I love you', then she says it without emotion nor meaning, sighing out of despair, and shaking her head and tearfully responding to the tyrannical director that she 'can't do it'. At the end of the film, Schneider mouths 'I love you' to Testi: she is in tears again, but her character is overwhelmed with 'real' emotion – Nadine means it this time, and the scene shows that Schneider can act

FIGURE 15 *Schneider's pathetic plea in* L'Important c'est d'aimer.

both emotional sides of the same phrase. She can show that her character cannot feel powerful sentiment (in the opening scene), and she can show that Nadine is finally in love.

The opening scene, which initiates the contact between the two protagonists, also shows Żuławski appealing to cinematic elitism by emphasizing the gap between his auteur film style and the 'idea of porn' used to illustrate the 'exploitative dynamics of Western media culture' (Goddard, 2014, pp. 250–1). The importance of pathos to the scene is reinforced by Georges Delerue's music that begins the moment Schneider sees Servais (their faces filmed in alternating close-ups), developing a romantic theme that is used each time Schneider's character experiences pain. This sequence conflates the screen exploitation of female emotions with devotion as it instils in Servais the desire to photograph her 'properly', to find a suitable artistic role worthy of her, and to become her lover. In other words, his desire is rooted in the pathos and abasement of Schneider's character that he somewhat manipulates from 'behind the scenes'. We could also point to Żuławski's posture of hypocrisy here: through Servais, the director appears to denounce the vulgarity and the exploitative nature of the pornographic industry, and yet his own mise-en-scène uses the same exploitative tropes. As in this scene, his female performers are often naked or scantily dressed. There also follows a gratuitous scene (i.e. that does not advance the narrative) in which Schneider begins to touch her genitals over her silk nightgown, suggesting masturbation.

The misery of Nadine culminates in Schneider performing an extravagant meltdown in a cafe when she and Jacques breakup (he kills himself shortly after, ingesting pills in the bathroom). In this scene as in many others, Schneider lays herself bare emotionally, making her performance the focal point of narrative *and* style. She begins by making her character ostensibly fight against an outbreak of emotions: she cries softly and tries to conceal her tears by grabbing her head with her hands, progressively building the intensity of the exchange from minimal facial movements, overall body-control and poise, to violent head movements and shaking, screams and smashing her hands onto the table. The violence and the physicality of Schneider's performance give the impression of a woman on the edge now losing control over herself; and yet her movements are so well orchestrated, albeit in an exaggerated way, that her acting reaches old-fashioned melodramatic eloquence as defined by Gledhill above, an acting style that creates a tension between naturalness and strangeness. This is also noticeable in the dialogue: although Schneider's German accent was considerably softened over the decade, she kept a distinct elocution and diction, particularly noticeable when she raises her voice. Her verbal flow never gets rushed in angry scenes so that each sound comes out clearly (still with a light insistence on the [k] sound and on vowels). Such scenes, during which Schneider displays histrionics, call attention to her technique and make the audience more mindful that they are watching a performance (Naremore, 1988, p. 139). Her acting style creates a theatrical effect, which increases her *value* as a performer, but paradoxically connotes authenticity (she is blurting out emotions she cannot contain).

With Nadine's melodramatic descent, Żuławski added a new leaf to the book of feminine stereotypes embodied by the star – an unbalanced woman, dominated by her emotions, who has no control nor power, and is afraid of aging. Nadine is only thirty years old (Schneider turned thirty-six during filming) but she is made to appear 'too mature' and terrified of aging: the industry rejects her and she feels 'tired and lost', as she says. She lacks self-confidence, as displayed on Schneider's face. It is telling that Schneider's most critically valued performance so far, in a film that was commercially successful, was that of a damaged, neurotic and fragile woman – another 'defeated' figure, in Catherine Clément's terms. In April 1976, Schneider received the first César award ever for Best actress for her performance as Nadine. This acknowledgement by her peers is not surprising when one contemplates the track record of such trophies in Western film cultures: awards tend to go to roles in which acting is apparent, even ostentatious, hence the received idea in the film industry that actors are rewarded for excessive and violent performances (historical roles in period dramas also offer a great exposure for actors' performances, Vidal, 2014, p. 2; Moine, 2017, p. 10). The other explanation has to do with the character of Nadine. Contrasting with the momentum of the women's movement and the fight for equality between the sexes in mid-1970s France and Western Europe, images of feminine hysteria that had connotations of morbidity represented a striking backlash against notions of female independence and strength. Considering the context for her César, it is also revealing that the strongest competition for Schneider that year was Isabelle Adjani, nominated for *L'Histoire d'Adèle H.* (François Truffaut, 1975), also a melodrama of excess – Adjani's character ends up mad in an asylum after a life of passion and drama. Such bias is confirmed by the fact that Adjani received her first César for Best actress in 1982, for another Żuławski film, *Possession* (1981), a particularly misogynistic role which also demanded a hysterical performance.

The vulnerability of Schneider's character in *L'Important c'est d'aimer* was also constitutive of her on- and off-screen star persona, in different ways: at a professional level, with her approach to acting; and at a more intimate level with her personal behaviour. Schneider became known for her intense working method in approaching and impersonating characters. She liked 'immersing herself' in a part, building background stories for the women she performed, and finding details that would trigger emotions. From the mid-1970s onwards, she was held in high regard by French-speaking journalists and her colleagues for her perfectionism. They praised Schneider's dedication to her roles – a recurrent cliché was that she 'gave herself' completely to them (*Première*, 08/1980, pp. 18–19) and that she summoned her feelings from deep inside, giving the impression that she was revealing something about herself through her acting (the term 'intensity' recurrs in reviews). This applies particularly to her dramatic, physically and emotionally demanding performances, such as that of Clara in *Le Vieux fusil* (with the rape scene), Nadine in *L'Important c'est d'aimer* and Katherine in *La Mort en direct* (discussed below).

Although it is difficult to judge private behaviour in the absence of precise documentation, the filming of *L'Important c'est d'aimer* brought out, by all accounts, a pattern of personal behaviour that became known about Schneider and that can be connected to her working method. Schneider's technique was to research the role through long discussions and rehearsals with the screenwriter(s) and the director, with whom she demanded to have an exclusive relationship (asking him to reassure her, comfort her on set, exchanging notes about the role). She often expressed in interviews her 'need' to be guided and told exactly what to do. In some cases, it appears this need for reassurance took the form of amorous relations with directors (as with Claude Sautet, although this persistent rumour has never been conclusively verified). Rumours of liaisons with co-stars (Horst Buchholz, Serge Reggiani, Jean-Louis Trintignant, Sami Frey) are persistently circulated, and an affair during the shooting of *L'Important c'est d'aimer* was recently confirmed in an interview with Jacques Dutronc in *Vanity Fair* (Denisot and Douin, 2015). Because Schneider's 'need to fall in love', as singer Françoise Hardy (Dutronc's partner) puts it in her memoirs (2008), was known and discussed by journalists, it became part of her star 'myth', reinforcing her persona as that of a woman who is needy and vulnerable, seeming to echo the nature of her characters. In some cases, commentators did not hesitate to qualify this feature with misogynistic remarks ('Romy Schneider, a girl not so sure of herself who desperately needs love', *Paris Match*, 05/09/1980).

After the turning point of *L'Important c'est d'aimer* in terms of Schneider's melodramatic, 'hysterical' role and performance, I move on to her roles in even more sombre films in order to determine in what ways and to what extent they contributed to her overall 'tragic' persona.

3. The last sombre films

The last three years of Schneider's life and career were marked by morose, even depressing, films. In *Clair de femme / Womanlight* (Costa-Gavras, 1979), *La Mort en direct / Death Watch* (Bertrand Tavernier, 1980) and *Garde à vue / Under Suspicion* (Claude Miller, 1981), she performs characters with direct associations with sadness, despair and death.

Clair de femme is the adaptation of the eponymous novel by French writer Romain Gary (1977). Director Costa-Gavras explains in his memoirs (2018) that he was often asked at the time when he would make a romantic film (p. 283), as he had so far mainly written and directed political action films, with great success. When he came across *Clair de femme*, he immediately thought of Yves Montand (a long-time collaborator: they made four films together) and Romy Schneider (whom he 'admired') for the lead roles – before writing a script. Producer Georges-Alain Vuille, who owned the rights, wanted to cast Capucine instead of Schneider for the role of Lydia Tovalski, but he was convinced by Costa-Gavras's choice. If the film-maker remains elusive in his book about the exact reasons behind his casting (he evokes 'the good atmosphere of a film shoot with [Montand]' and that Schneider 'would be perfect', p. 283), he was uncompromising. Two reasons might explain his choice. First, Schneider's romantic, vulnerable and tragic image fitted the description of her character, Lydia. Secondly, although Costa-Gavras does not mention this, a Schneider-Montand reunion, seven years after the success of *César et Rosalie*, was an undeniable commercial argument. The pairing of two of the biggest stars of French cinema indeed paid off as *Clair de femme* was a success with nearly two million tickets sold in France, making it the seventeenth most successful film to come out in the country that year (Simsi, 2012, p. 44).

Costa-Gavras's script is a close adaptation of the original material with most of the dialogue taken from Gary's prose. At the last minute, Michel (Montand) refuses to embark on a plane to Caracas and takes a taxi from the airport to Paris where, opening the car's door, he bumps into Lydia and spills her groceries in the gutter. He insists on repaying her and they exchange contact information. He meets her at her apartment in the first of several encounters over the course of two days and two nights, while he goes back and forth between the airport and Paris, changing his mind about leaving. Both characters look unhappy – for reasons as yet undisclosed – and console each other. Their background unfolds as they learn about one another and become lovers. Lydia's husband had a car accident in which their daughter died and he suffered a severe brain injury. Michel's wife Yannick was incurably ill and they had agreed that she would commit suicide the day before, after Michel's had left for Caracas. Yannick is now dead and Michel confesses to Lydia that, before he left for the airport, she had said that she would take on the form of the next woman he would meet. At the end of the film, Lydia phones Michel and explains that she cannot deal with him in his present emotional state, but invites him to live in her apartment while she goes away, leaving open a possibility of a relationship when she returns.

As Lydia, Schneider impersonates death: she replaces a dead woman in the life of a widower.[13] This key narrative trope is mentioned early on in the

---

[13]In a similar way, she incarnates death in the Italian film *Fantasma d'amore* (Dino Risi, 1981) as Anna, a revengeful ghost visiting her past lover performed by Marcello Mastroianni.

novel, but it is not revealed until much later in the film, creating dramatic suspense. Schneider performs a woman who is visibly depressed, exhausted and suicidal. She wears unflattering clothes (loose lines, muddy and dull colours) and barely any make-up, and her hair hangs down flatly on her shoulders, which emphasizes her overall air of fatigue and gloom. There are similarities to her earlier roles in Claude Sautet's films: Lydia's appearance resembles that of her character in *Une histoire simple*, pushed to an even duller register, and the Lydia-Michel couple could be a drearier version of Rosalie and César. The psychological suffering, however, unfolds in a world of privilege: as in the Sautet films, the characters in *Clair de femme* are from backgrounds where money is irrelevant (Lydia's husband comes from a wealthy aristocratic Russian family, Michel is clearly well off – he is a former airline pilot in the book).

Although Schneider's presence is central to *Clair de femme*, Lydia is merely used as an emotional support to Michel. Her suffering adds layers to the character, but in many ways she is mirroring Michel's pain, whose wandering leads the narrative. Her subordinate role, slowly revealed throughout the film, is made clear early in the book: Lydia is the 'femininity' without which it would be 'impossible [for Michel] to live', says Yannick (Gary, 1977, p. 28). Lydia is viewed as a lifeline. However, at the end, she realizes that Michel's love is misguided (he is too unhappy, too desperate) and she insists on delaying their reunion. This last-minute epiphany acts as a burst of self-determination for Schneider, but barely cancels out the 100 minutes' duration of the film during which she looks utterly miserable and is exploited to make Montand's character feel better.

Schneider never explained why she accepted the role of Lydia, given her reticence about working with Montand a second time – she had expressed her irritation at the star's attention-grabbing personality and acting style during the shooting of *César et Rosalie* (Bonini, 2001, pp. 165–6). But the two actors were friends nonetheless and Schneider, true to her reputation, obtained Costa-Gavras's undivided attention during filming and held equal ground with Montand (Costa-Gavras, 2018, pp. 286–7). Given Costa-Gavras's track record and status, *Clair de femme* had the potential to bring success, prestige and artistic legitimacy to her and it did – she was nominated for her third César in five years, but lost to Miou-Miou for her role in *La Dérobade* (Daniel Duval, 1979).

A similar situation occurred the following year with the international science fiction film *La Mort en direct* directed by Bertrand Tavernier, in which Schneider performs the role of Katherine Mortenhoe, diagnosed with an incurable disease. Set in Glasgow in a near future where death from illness has become rare, Katherine is approached by a television company offering her a large sum of money to film her last days for a reality show. She agrees but then runs away at the prospect of being followed everywhere. She is helped by Roddy (Harvey Keitel) but Katherine does not know that he was 'planted' by the television company. He has cameras implanted in his eyes and his mission is to follow Katherine and film her. When he catches the show playing in a pub, Roddy takes pity on his subject, yet a short-circuit in his eyes causes his blindness. He reveals who he is and they continue on their way to her ex-husband Gerald (Max Von Sydow) in rural Scotland, where she wishes to spend her last days, but are chased by a television crew now that Roddy's blindness has stopped the feed. We learn that the doctor and the television company were conspiring together: Katherine is not ill and the pills that she is taking to relieve her symptoms are in fact causing her pain for more sensational televised entertainment. The producer explains that she is not dying and must stop medicating. Instead, and because 'this is the only way [she] can win' (against the evil producer), she decides to kill herself and ingests the rest of her pills.

Contrary to *Clair de femme* in which Schneider's character was used by a man in pain until the very end, but where there is a glimpse of a hopeful, 'normal' future, *La Mort en direct* presents Schneider seemingly taking matters into her hands for the entirety of the film, only to see her being manipulated and tragically die at the end. Katherine's suicide is treated as a last heroic moment of pride. She dies right before the arrival of the television crew: this is presented as her having the last word, exacting a revenge against the televised exploitation of her death. The fact remains that she is dead. The film does not end there but continues to show Roddy (still blind) and his wife reconciling. Schneider's tragic death is therefore again exploited for the benefit of a male character: Roddy has changed thanks to Katherine and he is gratified with a happy ending, while she is gone. The tragedy of Schneider's characters always serves a double purpose – valorizing the leading man at the level of the character, but showcasing her tragic performance at the level of the star.

Continuing the trend we observed, Schneider was highly praised for her performance in *La Mort en direct*. The result was a persistent conflation between the pathos of her role in the film, the 'virtuosity' of her acting style and her overall star persona. Katherine's death is not seen by critics as a tragedy but as a 'triumphant ending' that mirrored Schneider's acting process (de Gasperi, 1980). Tavernier mentioned several times Schneider's 'lyricism', calling her a 'tragedian' who 'gave herself whole-heartedly [to her role]' (de Gasperi, 1980; Bauby and Rémond, 1980, p. 38). When Tavernier was trying to secure funds for his film, American producers wanted Jane Fonda or Diane Keaton for the role of Katherine (and a bigger star such as Robert de Niro in lieu of Keitel), but Tavernier vehemently refused, citing the lack of depth, purity and sincerity in the American actresses' performances (de Gasperi). Very noticeable in this last period of her career is the evolution in the language used to describe Schneider's performance: she went from *comédienne* (actress) in the 1960s, an appellation that signified that she had already climbed an important step in the European

cinema hierarchy since *Sissi*, to *tragédienne* (tragedian), the latter clearly
reinforcing Schneider's association with classical theatre and pathos. When
Katherine radiantly smiles and gazes up intensely at her ex-husband while
she tells him about her forthcoming suicide, she is described in the press as
a woman 'bearing life within herself' (*Télérama*, 30/01/1980, p. 88), and
Schneider as an actress who is 'more and more beautiful as she disintegrates'
(Bouteiller, 1980). The choice of words reveals misogynistic views of women
being aligned with death and self-oblivion rather than agency and strength.
L'Humanité, for example, argues that Katherine rebels against 'the violation
of her personality and her intimacy' and that she 'fights with *the only* means
she has', flight, then death, a *'healthy and successful* fight' (my emphasis,
23/01/1980). In the voyeuristic world denounced by Tavernier, Schneider
is adulated for embodying a woman who holds the high moral ground, yet
this is achieved through the sacrifice of her own life. I previously referred
to Catherine Clément's demonstration of the 'rule' in opera, according to
which women must be tragic and preferably die to be valued in our culture
(1988). Tavernier, though he might have been unaware of this reference,
equated Schneider to 'an opera actress' (de Gasperi) and more precisely –
although never naming the character – to Violetta, the tragic heroine of
Giuseppe Verdi's *La Traviata* (1853) by which he was 'inspired in writing
and filming' *La Mort en direct* (Douin, 1980a).

The synthesis epitomized by *La Mort en direct*, but evident in *Clair de
femme* too, between Schneider's tragically suffering and dying characters,
and the 'luminosity' and 'radiance' that the press assigned to her looks and
performance, constitutes her legacy. Although the reifying discourse about
the tragic Schneider stems in significant part from her own death at a young
age (forty-three) and that of her son, and other unhappy events unravelling
at a fast pace towards the end of her life (Meyen's suicide, major surgery,
divorce from Biasini), my analysis of her films from the mid-1970s onwards
shows that assigning Schneider a tragic image was an ongoing process that
started long before her death, via on-screen roles that started to merge with
her off-screen persona. This amalgam was also due to her working method
that projected the image of an intense woman-on-the-edge, on the verge of
breaking. As *Paris Match* put it, 'Cinema's good little girl [...] does not know
where cinema ends and where her life begins' (*Paris Match*, 08/05/1981).

In this respect, *Garde à vue* is situated at the extreme end of the tragedy
continuum for Schneider, although the film had little impact over her image
because, as a chamber piece vehicle for two major French male stars, Lino
Ventura and Michel Serrault, it leaves little room for Schneider's role.[14] Her
presence is nonetheless essential to the film's gender dynamics for she is

---

[14]*Garde à vue* was a critical and commercial success (with 2,100,865 spectators it was the
seventeenth most successful film in France in 1981, Simsi, 2012, p. 46). It was awarded four
Césars out of eight nominations in 1982.

mainly present to enhance the character of Serrault, Jérôme Martinaud, called in to a Cherbourg police station during New Year's Eve. He is first named as a witness, then suspected and held in custody by Inspector Antoine Gallien (Ventura) for the rape and the murder of two girls, one of whom he knew personally. Gallien is doubting the guilt of his suspect though, and lacks concrete evidence. The arrival of Chantal (Schneider), Martinaud's wife, instils trouble in Gallien's mind. According to her, Jérôme has an inappropriate penchant for young girls; she asserts that she could provide the Inspector with a clue that would link her husband to the murders. Martinaud then breaks down and confesses to the murders. But the real murderer is caught at the end, and Martinaud leaves the station to find his lifeless wife in their car: she shot herself in the head after witnessing the discovery that clears her husband (a body is found in the murderer's car). The producers had doubts about casting Schneider for they feared that adding her to the Ventura-Serrault duo would be 'too much' in terms of star quota. Despite the slight implausibility of her accent (Chantal is a very French name), her presence in the film is used by the director precisely for her star persona, which is the raison d'être of Chantal's intervention (Dumont, 1981).

Schneider's role draws on misogynistic clichés in its opaqueness. She is a deceitful woman who apparently attempts to bring her husband's downfall by wrongly accusing him, and tries to make him pay for their unhappiness. Yet, although Martinaud is not guilty of the rapes and murders of which he is accused, her testimony suggests he is morally guilty of amorous feelings for their young niece. The narrative presents Schneider as a jealous, sad, 'frigid' and castrating woman. According to Gallien, her refusal to execute her 'marital duties' means she is 'failing' her husband. *Garde à vue* is a particularly sexist film: the sympathy and the solidarity developing between the two male characters (enhanced by their charismatic performances) are ironically reinforced by Schneider's intervention, as she renders the character of Serrault more likable. She performs Chantal with cold arrogance, elegant and solemn in her long, tailored black dress. This image, like Schneider's performance, was inspired by the femme fatale from post-war Hollywood cinema as impersonated by Jean Simmons and Gene Tierney to cite Miller's examples (Dumont, 1981; Durante, 1981, p. 79). Schneider says her lines throughout her scene in a flat tone: she never raises her voice and the intonation is mostly kept at a whispering, calm level. This mode of delivery emphasizes the mysterious and dangerous aspect of her character. Embodying such a baleful character, Schneider is used to justify Serrault's cynicism – it is *her* fault if he developed inappropriate desires for a girl. Martinaud asks Gallien if he would have called his niece as a witness, but the policeman pretends not to understand the insinuation. This is male solidarity upholding patriarchy in its most toxic form: by refusing to address (or at least verify) Martinaud's predatory behaviour, Gallien further casts doubt on Chantal's testimony and enables him, potentially, to continue his possibly abusive behaviour.

Mental instability, emotional excess and morbidity were key components of Schneider's persona in these last films. Though these aspects remain under the same banner of 'vulnerability', they differ from Schneider's tragic *fate* in Occupation films, where her downfall is at the hands of History, in this case Nazism and/or French collaboration. This nuance further reinforces the notion of a backlash against women in such films as *Clair de femme*, *La Mort en direct* and *Garde à vue*, and the film-makers' retrograde concept of femininity. The films indicate that their female protagonists' personalities and aspirations are the real problem – and they bring their own misfortune upon themselves.

Conclusion

In the introduction to Part III, I briefly compared Catherine Deneuve's and Annie Girardot's career paths in the 1970s to Schneider's, in order to bring out the specificity of her star image. The present conclusion is a good point to reflect upon and further contrast the images projected by these three stars at the turn of the 1980s, against the backdrop of a cultural backlash against feminism and progressive representations of womanhood that started at the beginning of the decade (Frischer, 1997; Bard, 1999; Badinter, 2003).

As the three most popular female stars of the 1970s, Girardot, Deneuve and Schneider exhibit different levels of engagement with contemporary roles that reflect changes in women's lives. During the 'long 1970s', Girardot's films – beyond their consensual aspect – offered the rare on-screen representation of joyful and positive womanhood with a degree of sexual satisfaction, gender equality and professional authority. She fitted the cinematic naturalism of the period (the same aesthetic seen in Sautet's films), making her an emblem of the modern, yet 'ordinary' woman. Because of this accessible, 'ordinary' dimension, her star image normalized the transformations within patriarchal status quo, negotiating a transition between traditional and emancipated womanhood. Meanwhile, as said in the introduction, Deneuve's sophisticated and conservative persona was at odds with the naturalism and more overtly politicized narratives seen in French cinema at the time, which explained her films' relative lack of success at the box office. In the 1970s, her career split into two directions: she turned towards European auteur co-productions on the one hand, and French comedy on the other. As we saw, the quasi-absence of comedies in itself is an aspect that singles out Schneider from her two colleagues at the height of her French career. I have extensively talked about Schneider's on- and off-screen chic, bourgeois persona and, in this respect, she and Deneuve shared the same template. Deneuve's imagery of refined glamour was 'colder' though (the 'icy' blonde, Le Gras, 2010) and more distanced than Schneider who projected a warmer and touching vulnerability. Moreover, Deneuve (unlike Schneider) benefitted from an off-screen image as an autonomous, committed and 'pioneer' woman; she represented a 'timeless' elegance *à la française* (notably in her collaboration with Yves Saint Laurent), while simultaneously advocating feminism (she signed the 343 Manifesto in April 1971 and claimed to be a feminist in September 1975). Comedy exploited Deneuve's chic and independent persona to poke fun at the star, and in doing so, films such as *Le Sauvage* (Jean-Paul Rappeneau, 1975) implicitly questioned the hard-won emancipated status acquired by women and denounced the 'moral failure' of the women's movement – in *Le Sauvage* Deneuve is characterized as indomitable and domineering, but ultimately unable to manage her autonomy. Because Girardot best personified the strong woman archetype, she was gradually sidelined, as she played roles that fit into the popular representative of feminism and women who 'went too far' (Burnonville, 1992), an ideological backlash that hardened over the years and overthrew the image of the sexually liberated, independent, working and often single woman of the 1970s. Girardot's last on-screen success was *La Clé sur la porte* (Yves Boisset) in 1978, based on the novel by the feminist author Marie Cardinal. She then worked in different media (radio, theatre) with varying degrees of success. While Girardot's film stardom declined, however, 1981 marked Deneuve's 'come-back' to the forefront with the success of *Le Dernier métro* (Le Gras, 2007a). The film and Deneuve's leading role present good comparison points to Schneider in *La Banquière*, as both films came out a year apart and share a similar retro aesthetic. Although their narratives are set in the past (Occupation of France for the former, the 1920s for the latter), the two films speak of gender dynamics that were taking a retrograde turn in the early 1980s. Schneider and Deneuve perform active, working women who are celebrated for their wit, charisma and resourcefulness throughout the films, yet masculine domination is strongly reinstated at the end in both cases. But while Deneuve's character offers a reassuring representation of female emancipation and presents a vision of femininity that is both modern and traditional (after taking over her husband's professional duties during the war, she reinstates him to his role during the epilogue), Schneider's character is vehemently depreciated (Emma is imprisoned and murdered). After *Le Dernier métro*, Deneuve's persona continued to embody female emancipation with a 'reassuring' form of seduction that suggested the safe-keeping of traditional values – as 'officialized' in 1985 when she modelled for the bust of Marianne, the national emblem of the French Republic. Schneider's on-screen persona expressed the exact same social contradictions regarding femininity, only in a more conservative fashion, and with the added morbid dimension of her vulnerable and tragic image. Gwénaëlle Le Gras (2005, p. 33) argues that the image of Deneuve presents a morbid aspect as well in combining eroticism and death, especially in *Tristana*, but while this dimension intensified for Schneider, it waned for Deneuve. Moreover, and unlike Deneuve, Schneider expressed inconsistent opinions in various media outlets with regard to the changes in women's lives. In fact, my research shows that her views on feminism and women's autonomy tended to espouse the latest societal trend of the moment. Thus, even though she signed the German equivalent of the 343 Manifesto in June 1971, which corresponded to her most feminist period, and she voiced her support for the women's movement on occasion, her stance at the turn of the 1980s corresponded to the resistance against feminism. Remarkably, her position was linked to what is still at the core of her French persona – vulnerability. However, by this she meant not her own (on- or off-screen) vulnerability, but that of men, whose 'fears and problems' called for 'a men's day' as she said in reaction to the formalization of International Women's Day in France in March 1982 (Schneider and Seydel, 1989, p. 309); in other words, at that point she endorsed one of the key anti-feminist points of the period – that feminism was damaging men.

Conclusion: The legacy of Romy Schneider

Two concepts best describe Schneider's trajectory: consensus and paradox. Throughout this book, I have demonstrated that her image, though constantly developing, was defined by recurring opposing poles – tradition/modernity, past/future, obedient child/hopeful young woman, arrogant *bourgeoise*/erotic woman, vulnerability/sophistication, beauty/morbidity. It was Schneider's ability to embody such strong oppositions and reconcile such contradictions that made her an object of both fascination – verging on the cultish – and popular affection. She was both endowed with a fixed identity, yet she also evolved over time, *balancing between extremes*, as her persona encompassed a wide range of female representations. In other words, there always was something for every member of her vast and diverse audiences to look for in terms of representation. While this explains her popularity at the time, this also begs the question of her legacy in terms of feminine image. There is an abundance of examples showing that Schneider is still 'present' in European popular culture forty years after her death. In what ways is she remembered in the media today?

That Schneider still generates a devoted following is illustrated in a number of ways. Every five years or so brings a new anniversary or a 'would-have-been' birthday: celebrations marked by the publication of new coffee-table books on her life and career, the production of documentaries, biographies, DVD releases and the programming of her films on television. The broadcasting of the three *Sissi* films is a quasi-religious observance over the holiday period in many continental European countries. Small towns and large cities in Germany, Austria, France, Belgium, the Czech Republic and Turkey regularly organize exhibitions, and retrospectives in Film Institutes abound. The most attentive visitors at the Cinémathèque française in Paris will recognize her image on one of the entrance pillars, looking for a book in a library, from *What's New, Pussycat?* (1965). Schneider's face is one of the first pictures welcoming visitors at the Sissi museum at the Hofburg palace in Vienna. The European film industry celebrates the star too, with the Prix Romy Schneider in France, established in 1984, the most prestigious award for upcoming actresses in French cinema. And since 1990, the Austrian newspaper *Kurier* has organized the annual Romy Awards at the Hofburg in Vienna, to celebrate Austrian television and film. The trophy – named a Romy – is a gilded statuette of Schneider. In 2010 Schneider was part of the first group of forty German-speaking celebrities to have their stars on the Boulevard der Stars in Berlin (the German version of the Hollywood Walk of Fame). Furthermore, she has inspired two biopics: the TV film *Romy* (Torsten C. Fischer, 2009) was broadcast on German public television (and in 2012 on French public television), and the recent German-Austrian-French co-production *3 Tage in Quiberon* (Emily Atef, 2018), a critical and commercial success especially in Germany where it received seven Lola awards at the Deutscher Filmpreis in 2018 (including Best film and Best actress for Marie Bäumer in the role of Schneider). In France, however, the film provoked controversy as Schneider's daughter Sarah Biasini and her father Daniel (Schneider's second husband) objected to the star's portrayal in the film – pointing to discrepancies in the construction of the star's image between her screen persona and her celebrity based on the more salacious aspects of her private life (Biasini, 2020, pp. 143–5).

What *3 Tage in Quiberon* also shows is the consensual hindsight view of Schneider as imbued with 'tragedy', a theme that informs most press discourse, especially in France. Alain Delon famously presented her with a posthumous Honorary César in 2008 (he led the audience to a standing ovation to celebrate what 'should have been' Schneider's seventieth birthday that year), and continues to speak publicly about their relationship, their pairing in *La Piscine* and his overall 'pain' at her evocation (interview by Laurent Delahousse, 11/12/2016). The eternal love myth is thus still alive through Delon who took on the role of Schneider's widower. A typical comment from *Le Figaro* describes her as unhappy and ultimately 'stricken by destiny' (15/09/2018).[1] Brigitte Bardot equally adopted this particular bias. In 2012 she referred to her own decision to stop her film career back in 1973 as influenced by her not wanting to experience a tragic ending like Schneider, a historically inaccurate point, since Schneider's career was very successful at that time, and the star's image was not marked by tragedy (*7sur7*, 21/02/2012; interview by Vincent Niclo, 01/01/2019). Further sealing Schneider as a tragic myth, Bardot brings forth a comparison with another star with a tragic aura, calling Schneider the 'Marilyn Monroe of Europe' (*Moustique*, 02/11/2015). Schneider and Monroe share an unexplained death at a young age (Monroe was thirty-six), which means

---

[1] The love myth was recently and briefly revived again when their respective daughters, Sarah Biasini and Anouchka Delon, both actresses based in Paris, met (allegedly) for the very first on live television (interview by Laurent Delahousse, 10/01/2021).

that their images froze, gaining more potency over time, an image preserved and cherished by the media and cohorts of fans[2] (I shall come back to Schneider's fandom below).

The legacy of Schneider as a tragic figure that dominates French media allies this tragic aspect with her 'radiant femininity', fashioning a particular version of the 'eternal feminine'. Many illustrations could be cited here. In the summer of 2018 the radio station France Inter broadcast a series fronted by film critic Guillemette Odicino placing Schneider within a cohort of 'great tragic stars' (Odicino, 14–15/08/2018). In 2018 too, the cinema chain Pathé-Gaumont ran an ad featuring the soundtrack of the dialogue between Schneider and Philippe Noiret from the cult 'veil scene' in Le Vieux fusil, in which the Noiret character declares his love for her at first sight, a scene that comes as a flashback, once the spectator knows she was horrendously raped and killed by Nazi soldiers. These various retrospective manifestations reinforce the construction of an atemporal image of Schneider, whose photogeny and erotic power are equated with vulnerability and tragedy. The media in France have thus construed the memory of Schneider as a timeless ideal of beautiful, suffering femininity.

Besides the print and audio-visual media, the memory of Schneider has been kept alive by masses of fans of all nationalities and generations, from distant admirers to the hard-core fans who started organizing into regional groupings as early as 1955 with the European-wide distribution of Sissi. Announced in the French magazine Jeunesse Cinéma, the 'Club Romy Schneider-Sissi', the first official French fan club, was founded in Paris in January 1960, followed by a provincial branch in Lyon. The members (male and female) gathered to go and see Schneider's films, discuss them, write to her for autographs and dance together (according to the club's secretary Jacqueline Demanest, some members met their life partners at the club, Bonini, 2001, p. 70). Two years later, the club started publishing a journal in order to keep its members informed about Schneider's and Delon's activities through diverse rubrics such as 'letters', 'opinions', 'humour', 'recipes' and 'latest news'. To my knowledge there was no German-speaking equivalent of such dedicated gathering. The club ceased to exist in 1965, coinciding with Schneider's return to Berlin.

Like all fans, Schneider's fans over the decades collected memorabilia associated with her career and private life – lobby cards, cinema programmes, original film posters, photos and interviews in magazines. Since Schneider's death, they have organized outings to her grave in Boissy-sans-Avoir (a village west of Paris, where she bought a house shortly before her death). In Bavaria, there are trips to her childhood home in Schönau am Königssee (where in the

---

[2]For more on a star's image youthfulness and its potency beyond death see Heather Addison (2005), Transcending Time: Jean Harlow and Hollywood's Narrative of Decline, Journal of Film and Video, 57:4, pp. 32–46.

past some went to meet Magda Schneider who lived there until her death in 1996), and where there has been, since 2015, the only permanent exhibition about the Schneider mother and daughter – with items assembled from a fan's collection. Several postage stamps have been issued since the 1990s (in Austria, Germany, France, Belgium, Gibraltar, Senegal, Netherlands) with Schneider's image on them, and streets in France, Germany and Austria are named after her, the result of fan campaigns (Beaugrand, 2002). The arrival of the internet launched a plethora of websites, amateur montage videos and, most recently, multi-language Facebook groups dedicated to Schneider.

From these eclectic manifestations of fandom, a few themes emerge from the star's legacy. First and foremost, they preserve her dual image of 'luminous beauty' and vulnerability. Schneider's fans, principally those of Germanic and French backgrounds who largely outnumber other nationalities, are eager to share photographs that show Schneider at her best. For the fan community, this means favouring the French part of her career over the earlier two phases, including the Sissi period. Interestingly, although the trilogy is extremely popular amongst fans, and photographs of Schneider in costumes and anecdotes of that time are posted and widely shared, there are variations in this respect. The specific types of fandom branching out from the *Sissi* films' reception remain unexplored territories. As discussed, there have been studies of the queer reception of the trilogy, but the young female audiences who seem particularly appreciative of the films would require an empirical and systematic study in itself – I have only been able to touch on this here, but this topic could provide a fruitful subject for further study. My chapter on the *Sissi* films has shown that the Sissi/Romy figure had a greater success on the Germanic side during the 1950s. This appears to have endured over time, albeit slightly sliding towards the former Eastern block (Hungary, Czech Republic), whose audiences only discovered Schneider after 1989 through the *Sissi* cycle. On the other hand, French fans are adamant that they 'stay true' to Schneider by honouring what they see as her 'aspiration' to move away from the Sissi image, by not dwelling on those films. Hence the overwhelming presence on French internet sites of Schneider's French period from *La Piscine* onwards. The core of Schneider's fan base is also on the lookout for any sensationalist output that might 'disrupt' the memory of the star, that is, any new information likely to detract from the beautiful/vulnerable narrative. The latest example concerns German journalist and feminist Alice Schwarzer's French translation and edition of her biography of Schneider (2018). Schwarzer adopts a provocative position by 'sharing' new facts about Schneider's life and career, notably her alleged bisexuality. Schwarzer's 'revelations' caused an uproar amongst fans of Schneider in France,[3] not so much because of their nature, but because

---

[3]The impact of such revelations was less important in Germany when the original German edition came out in 1998, mostly because Schwarzer's book on Schneider draws on the biography written by Michael Jürgs in 1991 (in which he already alluded to the star's sexuality).

she 'betrayed' Schneider's memory by going against her 'last wish' to be 'left alone' (interview by Michel Drucker, 14/04/1982) – as the star said in her last memorable TV appearance after the death of her son, in which she forcefully denounced the intrusion of the paparazzi who infamously dressed up as nurses to photograph David's body in the hospital.

The 'tragic mother' image is thus a particular subtheme that most deeply affects Schneider's fans of all nationalities, and the impulse to read her persona retrospectively is probably what best defines her fandom today – the most dedicated fans are up in arms against those they view as 'responsible' for Schneider's life-long misery. In this respect, while there seems to be a negative consensus around her second husband Daniel Biasini, Delon remains a highly controversial, polarizing figure amongst fans of Schneider, as is her mother Magda. What Romy Schneider's fans see in these three individuals is, respectively, a breach of trust,[4] abandonment and exploitation, all three elements foretelling the final tragedy – the death of her son, precipitating her own. The case of Magda Schneider also illustrates the complicated relationship experienced by her daughter between France and West Germany. While Magda embodies the misogynistic stereotype of the powerful and abusive mother who used her daughter's fame to her own advancement, she also brings in a difficult political issue. In the French media and parts of the German-speaking media, Magda is portrayed as a Nazi sympathizer (I have argued that her involvement with the Nazi elites – rather than politics – was more ignorant and self-interested than ideology-driven). As the history of the Nazi era continues to dominate views of Germany, in France as elsewhere, the negative and accusatory discourse on Magda impacts on the legacy of her daughter, painting her as the victim of a mother demonized by her association with the historical arch-enemy.

The relationship between France and Germany leads me to the more paradoxical aspects of the star's legacy. Indeed, Schneider's representation of gender in her roles spoke to different national audiences at different times (hearty and demure femininity for Germanic cultures during the 1950s, glamorous eroticism in the 1960s, vulnerable sophistication in 1970s France). Her success in Occupation films in France, and lack thereof in West Germany, created a persona polarized between two national receptions, enhancing and capitalizing on her Germanness on the French side. Her roles in Occupation films represented a redemptive way to atone for Germany's violent past, through her embodiment of glamorous suffering. This is certainly an important part of her persona that is still held up in

---

[4]Schneider's fans consider that he married her for financial reasons and her film business connections, that he did nothing to help her when her alcohol consumption allegedly turned into an addiction in the mid-to-late-1970s, and that he did not protect their daughter Sarah from the press after Schneider's death (he shared private photographs with popular outlets, organized photoshoots with Sarah who was pictured on the covers of several magazines, and they appeared together on television until her late teens).

French media today, since these roles in Occupation films made it especially clear that she *chose* France for 'freedom', for love and to lead her adult life, as well as for her career (Morice, 15/09/2018; even Sarah Biasini echoes this perspective in her 2020 memoirs, saying that she herself 'rejects the German language', p. 127). They also represent the moment in the 1970s when Schneider sparked the interest of feminist journalists and scholars in continental Europe, although their analyses differ by some degree.

Two positions emerged. For some, Schneider was a victim of the patriarchy both in her private life and in her on-screen identity. I have discussed this view in Chapter 5 of Part II about Schneider's Occupation films. In her chapter about the construction of the Schneider myth in 1970s West Germany, Nina Zimnik (2005) argues that her star persona was instrumentalized by West German feminists as being both representative of the feminist movement and an example of patriarchal victimization. A notable example of the latter representation is Schwarzer's biography of Schneider entitled *Romy Schneider: Mythos und Leben* (1998, translated into French in 2018). Seeing Schneider as a victim of the patriarchy is one way to defend her as a feminist, but yet again, she is a tragic figure. Other feminist critics claimed, on the contrary, that Schneider was an example of a woman who followed her desires and thrived in a male-dominated environment by being determined and committed enough to build a new identity, without regard for repercussions (Jürgs, 1991), and who exhibited honesty and hypersensitivity in performances and interviews. This (minority) view sees a strength in Schneider's personality, which it is argued is also shared, to some extent, by contemporary actresses, including recipients of the Prix Romy Schneider such as Vanessa Paradis, Audrey Dana, Julie Gayet or another successful German 'export' Diane Kruger (as is claimed in the documentary *Romy Schneider, eine Frau in Drei noten, une femme en trois notes*, 2008). A number of working actresses today cite Schneider as their model, mentioning how inspired they are by the star's acting style, and in particular how Schneider 'went beyond her beauty' to deliver energetic and sincere performances (interview with Julie Gayet by Claire Chazal, 11/02/2019). But mostly, they praise Schneider for her 'eternal quest for perfection' that they view as both an asset (perfection here meaning ambition), and a typically *female* quality. Others, such as Isabelle Huppert, value how unapologetic and demanding Schneider came across, as she expressed her disapproval at male directors who mistreated her and her female colleagues on set (*Vanity Fair*, 13/12/2018). Although they acknowledge the excesses of celebrity culture, including the intrusive media presence, these actresses fail to recognize the authoritarian dimension of some film-makers Schneider worked with (such as Visconti, Preminger and Żuławski), and the hostile climate they contributed to the film world, which we would in some cases call abusive today – something we are more aware of in the post-#*metoo* era. In the French context though, such oblivious reactions to Schneider can be read as symptomatic of the greater reluctance to embrace certain feminist struggles and in particular the controversies sparked in the wake of the #*balancetonporc* campaign.[5] Commentators tend to brush such power relations aside and focus instead on her *emotional* performance style, consequently trivializing Schneider's suffering, seen as essential to her approach to roles and acting.

One major paradox of Schneider's career and legacy is that, despite her success as a trans-European star, she has been largely absent from English-speaking film culture. While there is no single, conclusive, reason to explain this phenomenon, I wish to offer some tentative thoughts to address this question. First of all, Schneider's biggest success and for a significant part of her audience and fans, her most cherished work, the *Sissi* films, did not export to English-speaking countries. This was partly because the historical figure on which the title character is based is largely unknown in Anglo-American culture, where British monarchy figures are the subject of much literary and film fiction. By contrast, both Elisabeth of Austria and her screen embodiment by Schneider are popular not only in continental Europe, but also in Latin America and parts of Asia. Secondly, it seems fairly clear that the *Sissi* cycle did not export across the English Channel and the Atlantic because of the Anglo-American construction of post-war Austrian identity. The intention to distance Austria from its Nazi past was also, ostensibly, in evidence domestically, yet the execution differed. In fact, as Hametz and Schlipphacke point out, many Americans shared the European adoration for Elisabeth of Austria in the first years of the twentieth century (p. 21), but the two World Wars changed Anglo-American perspectives regarding the Habsburgs and the 1950s 'Habsburg nostalgia' (Fritsche, 2013, p. 71) never took off as it did in Austria. *The Emperor Waltz* (Billy Wilder, 1948), for example, is almost forgotten, and the condensed English-language version of the three *Sissi* films entitled *Forever My Love* released by American distributors in 1962 went practically unnoticed (the critic from *The New York Times* called the film 'visually striking', yet 'simple-minded', and dismissed the – dubbed – 'kindergarten dialogue' as 'plain ludicrous', 28/03/1962). Three years later, *The Sound of Music* (Robert Wise, 1965), on the other hand, offered a more acceptable version of Austrian identity for global audiences. First of all, it provided concrete evidence to support the 'portrayal of Austria as Hitler's "first victim" and as a site of anti-Nazi resistance' (Hametz and Schlipphacke, 2018, p. 22), and on the other hand it was in English, with a British-born Hollywood star, Julie Andrews. Thus, Schneider as a star was not able to capitalize on the success of the *Sissi* compilation film in the way

---

[5]See Christine Bard (2018), La tribune signée par Deneuve est l'expression d'un antiféminisme, *Le Monde*, 11 January.

Julie Andrews was with *The Sound of Music*, and her subsequent 'export' to English-speaking countries suffered from this.[6]

As for Schneider's post-Sissi period, I discussed in Part II how and why her career in Hollywood and Britain never really took off – a combination of several factors such as her films' lack of distribution overseas, even though, contrary to many French or Italian stars in Hollywood, language aptitude was not the issue. Schneider successfully toned down her German accent, as can be heard in the films, and it was noticed by US critics. In addition, other events kept her out of the Anglo-American film market. Following her separation from Delon she broke her contract with Columbia and returned to Europe to be with her family. Then, after the triumph of *La Piscine*, she was content with the success of her career in France, where she had become a major figure. She also yearned for home and family stability, and thus did not wish to travel (her regular round trips between Berlin and Paris before her definitive resettling in Paris in 1973 took a toll on her personal life). Finally, her 1970s French films, especially the persona-defining works directed by Sautet, did not export to Anglophone markets either, as they presented a social dimension finely embedded in their French context, and they foregrounded French-language performances around Schneider, by the likes of Yves Montand, Michel Piccoli and Philippe Noiret.[7] Schneider's own eloquent use of French enabled her to attain trans-European stardom, but this did not translate into transnational success. This missed opportunity on the international art cinema market was matched by a trend in popular cinema which saw, in the 1970s, the increasing hold of Hollywood stars across the globe. Schneider's at first surprising absence from Anglo-American film culture is thus understandable through a combination of cultural, political, personal and industrial factors.

Fortunately, a few contemporary factors are beginning to paint a different picture. First, having worked with international auteurs of the calibre of Visconti, Welles and Preminger, Schneider's reputation as an art cinema actress, built at the beginning of the 1960s, has endured, just like the films of these directors – *Ludwig*, *The Trial*, *The Cardinal*. Moreover, since 2007, an original, restored version of the *Sissi*s has become available in the United States (along with *Mädchenjahre einer Königin* and *Forever My Love*). The

---

[6]Following in the footsteps of successful historic dramas and royal television shows such as *The Crown* (Netflix, 2016–), a new six-hour series focusing on the relationship between Sissi and Franz Joseph has been announced by German broadcaster RTL for a late-2021 release on its subscription streaming service TVNow. Producer Beta Film is also handling world sales and, in our current world of global TV, the story of Sissi might find an anglophone audience this time (Roxborough, 2021).

[7]By contrast, later Sautet films lost their social anchorage and focused on characters' interiority. His last two films *Un cœur en hiver* (1992) and *Nelly et Monsieur Arnaud* (1995) were art-house hits that did a lot for the international career of Emmanuelle Béart.

trailer for the Film Movement Classic DVD collection puts Schneider centre stage, reading: 'featuring Romy Schneider in the role that made her a star'. If Schneider remains known in the United States and Great Britain mostly to an eclectic niche of art film *cinephiles*, as well as scholars and aficionados of popular historical cinema, the enhanced distribution of films through digitalization can only bring better exposure to the films and talent of Romy Schneider. I hope that this book contributes to this process.

I started this book by wishing to show the singularity of Romy Schneider's star persona and to connect her trajectory to the mechanics of trans-European and transnational stardom. As scholarship on German, French, trans-European and transnational stardom and star systems continues to grow, I hope that my study also contributes useful material to these areas, with its consideration of a popular and prolific European actress. Beyond the necessity to examine Schneider with regards to her absence in scholarly studies, this book has demonstrated how a star comes to embody changing and complex depictions of femininity through several post-war European cinemas. It has also shown that examining the larger social and cultural implications of such representations underlines the important place of European female stars as a record of the history and experiences of women in Western European cultures.

APPENDIX 1: ROMY SCHNEIDER'S TIMELINE

1938   Born 23 September in Vienna. Moves to Schönau am Königssee, Bavaria

1941   Birth of her brother Wolf

1944   Starts school in Schönau am Königssee

1945   Divorce of Magda Schneider and Wolf Albach-Retty

1949   Starts school at Goldenstein boarding school near Salzbourg

1953   First film. Her mother remarries to Hans Herbert Blatzheim

1955   'Sissi mania' starts in December

1958   First audition in Hollywood. Meets Alain Delon and moves to Paris

1959   German Film Awards nomination (Best actress for *Mädchen in Uniform*). Official engagement with Delon in front of the press

1960   Meets Luchino Visconti

1961   First theatre play *'Tis Pity She's a Whore*, directed by Visconti, Théâtre de Paris

1962   European tour with *La Mouette*, directed by Sacha Pitoëff

1963   Breakup with Delon. Etoile de Cristal de l'Académie du Cinéma (Best foreign actress for *The Trial*)

1964   Golden Globe nomination (Best actress for *The Cardinal*)

1966   Moves to Berlin, marries Harry Meyen, birth of David Haubenstock

1967   Death of Wolf Albach-Retty

1968   Death of Blatzheim. *La Piscine*

1969   Meets Claude Sautet

1971   Signs the petition 'Wir haben abgetrieben!' in *Stern* magazine

1973   Moves to Paris, separation from Meyen

1975   Divorces Meyen, marries Daniel Biasini

1976   Best actress at the César Awards for *L'Important c'est d'aimer*

1977   Best actress at the German Film Awards for *Gruppenbild mit Dame*. Birth of Sarah Biasini

1979   Suicide of Meyen. Best actress at the César Awards and special David di Donatello award for *Une histoire simple*

1981   Divorces Daniel Biasini. Right kidney removed. David Haubenstock dies on 5 July

1982   Schneider dies the night of 28–9 May

APPENDIX 2: THE *SISSI* FILMS ACROSS CONTINENTAL EUROPE

	RS films prior releases to Sissi 1	Release dates			Box office		
		Sissi 1	*Sissi 2*	*Sissi 3*	*Sissi 1*	*Sissi 2*	*Sissi 3*
Austria	*Wenn der weiße Flieder wieder blüht* (December 1953), *Mädchenjahre einer Königin* (December 1954), *Die Deutschmeister* (September 1955)	21.12.1955	December 1956	1957	10 million at the premiere (unconfirmed)	Bigger success than the first film	No data available
West Germany	*Wenn der weiße Flieder wieder blüht* (November 1953), *Feuerwerk* (September 1954), *Mädchenjahre einer Königin* (December 1954), *Die Deutschmeister* (August 1955), *Der Letzte Mann* (October 1955)	22.12.1955	19.12.1956	18.12.1957	12 million, 1st place (1955–6)	Second place (1956–7)	Third place (1957–8)
Belgium	*Mädchenjahre einer Königin* (December 1955), *Der Letzte Mann* (February 1956)	30.03.1956	29.03.1957	18.04.1958	No data available	447,000 Bfr (Brussels only: 337,000 Bfr)	No data available
Denmark	*Mädchenjahre einer Königin* (March 1956)	31.08.1956	24.04.1957	18.04.1958	No data available		
Finland	*Feuerwerk* (February 1956), *Mädchenjahre einer Königin* (July 1956)	28.09.1956	22.03.1957	21.03.1957			

Country	Films	Release date 1	Release date 2	Release date 3	Admissions 1	Admissions 2	Admissions 3
France	*Feuerwerk* (May 1956), *Mädchenjahre einer Königin* (May 1956 + re-release in March 1957 in Paris), *Die Deutschmeister* (January 1956)	01.03.1957	16.08.1957	10.09.1958	6,497,043	1,275,021	5,149,522
Greece	No data available	No data available					
Italy	No data available	Christmas 1956	No data available				
Netherlands	*Wenn der weiße Flieder wieder blüht* (March 1954)	18.05.1956					
Norway	No data available	01.04.1956	01.08.1957	No release	No data available	No data available	no release
Portugal		2.10.1956	23.04.1957	No data available	85,000		No data available
Spain		28.04.1956	24.06.1957	1974 (re-release?)	1,527,872	890,835	
Sweden	*Feuerwerk* (February 1955), *Mädchenjahre einer Königin* (October 1955)	12.03.1956	4.02.1957	10.03.1958	No data available		

BIBLIOGRAPHY

Books, chapters and academic articles

Aaslestad, Katherine B. (2006). 'Sitten und Mode: Fashion, Gender, and Public Identities in Hamburg at the Turn of the Nineteenth Century', in: Gleixner, Ulrike, and Gray, Marion W. (eds.), *Gender in Transition: Discourse and Practice in German-Speaking Europe 1750–1830*, Ann Arbour: University of Michigan Press, pp. 282–318.

Abel, Richard (1999). *The Red Rooster Scare, Making American Cinema*, Berkeley and Los Angeles: University of California Press.

Addison, Heather (2005). Transcending Time: Jean Harlow and Hollywood's Narrative of Decline, *Journal of Film and Video*, 57:4, pp. 32–46.

Adler, Laure (1998). *Marguerite Duras*, Paris: Gallimard ('Folio').

Albrecht, Gerd (ed.) (1985). *Die großen Filmerfolge: vom Blauen Engel bis Otto*, Ebersberg: Edition 8 1/2.

Altman, Rick (1987). *The American Film Musical*, Bloomington and Indianapolis: Indiana University Press.

Altman, Rick (1999). *Film/Genre,* London: British Film Institute.

Arnould, Françoise, and Gerber, Françoise (1986). *Romy Schneider: princesse de l'écran*, Paris: France Loisirs.

Aron, Robert, and Elgey, Georgette (1954). *Histoire de Vichy: 1940–1944*, Paris: Fayard ('Les grandes études contemporaines').

Assouline, Pierre (1986). *Une éminence grise: Jean Jardin (1904–1976)*, Paris: Balland.

Assouline, Pierre (1992). *Simenon: biographie*, Paris: Julliard.

Atack, Margaret (2016). Performing the Nation in the Mode Rétro, *Journal of War & Culture Studies*, 9:4, pp. 335–47.

Aumont, Jacques (1992). *Du visage au cinéma*, Paris: Éditions de l'Etoile.

Austin, Guy (1996). *Contemporary French Cinema: An Introduction*, Manchester and New York: Manchester University Press.

Azéma, Jean-Pierre (1979). *De Munich à la Libération: 1938–1944*, Paris: Éditions du Seuil ('Nouvelle histoire de la France contemporaine').

Badinter, Élisabeth (2003). *Faire fausse route*, Paris: Éditions Odile Jacob.

Balázs, Béla (2010). *Béla Balázs: Early Film Theory. 'Visible Man' and 'The Spirit of Film'*, edited by Erica Carter and translated by Rodney Livingstone, New York and Oxford: Berghahn Books.

Bammer, Angelika (1985). Through a Daughter's Eyes: Helma Sanders-Brahms' 'Germany, Pale Mother', *New German Critique*, 36 (special issue on Heimat), Autumn, pp. 91–109.

Bandauer, Andrea (2015). '"I Cannot Live Without Performing". Romy Schneider's On- and Off-Screen Embodiments of the Tragic', in: Bandauer, Andrea, and Royer, Michelle (eds.), *Stars in World Cinema: Film Icons and Star Systems across Cultures*, London and New York: I.B. Tauris, pp. 213–25.

Barbier, Philippe, Dureau, Christian, and Pommier, Sylvie (2009). *Delon-Romy. Ils se sont tant aimés*, Paris: Didier Carpentier ('Stars de l'écran').

Bard, Christine (ed.) (1999). *Un siècle d'antiféminisme*, Paris: Fayard.

Barnier, Martin, and Moine, Raphaëlle (eds.) (2002). *France-Hollywood: échanges cinématographiques et identités nationales*, Paris: L'Harmattan ('Champs visuels').

Baron, Alexander (1953). *The Human Kind*, London: Cape.

Barthel, Manfred (1986). *So war es wirklich. Der deutsche Nachkriegsfilm*, Berlin: Herbig.

Barthes, Roland (1957). *Mythologies*, Paris: Éditions du Seuil.

Baxter Wright, Emma (2012). *The Little Book of Chanel*, London: Carlton Books.

Bazgan, Nicoleta (2011). From Bardot to Binoche: The Pygmalion Myth and Artistic Collaboration in French Cinema, *Contemporary French Civilization*, 36:3, pp. 201–18.

Benichou, Pierre JB, and Pommier, Sylviane (1981). *Romy Schneider*, Paris: PAC.

Bergfelder, Tim (2006). *International Adventures: German Popular Cinema and European Coproductions in the 1960s*, New York and Oxford: Berghahn Books.

Bernhard, Hans-Joachim (1973). *Die Romane Heinrich Bölls: Gesellschaftskritik und Gemeinschaftsutopie*, Berlin: Rütten & Loening.

Bernon, Marcel, Knibiehler, Yvonne, Ravoux-Rallo, Elisabeth, and Richard, Eliane (1983). *De la pucelle à la minette. Les jeunes filles de l'âge classique à nos jours*, Paris: Messidor.

Bessen, Ursula (1989). *Trummer und Traume. Nachkriegszeit und funfziger Jahre auf Zelluloid: deutsche Spielfilme als Zeugnisse ihrer Zeit, eine Dokumentation*, Bochum: Dr. N. Brockmeyer.

Betz, Mark (2009). *Beyond the Subtitle: Remaping European Art Cinema*, Minneapolis: University of Minnesota Press.

Biasini, Sarah (2020). *La beauté du ciel*, Paris: Stock.

Bigelow, Marybelle S. (1979). *Fashion in History: Western Dress, Prehistoric to Present*, Minneapolis: Burgess.

Binh, Nguyen Trong, and Rabourdin, Dominique (2005). *Sautet par Sautet*, Paris: Éditions de la Martinière.

Bischof, Günter (1997). 'Founding Myths and Compartmentalized Past: New Literature on the Construction, Hibernation, and Deconstruction of World War II Memory in Postwar Austria', in: Bischof, Günter, and Pelinka, Anton (eds.), *Contemporary Austrian Studies*, vol. 5, Austrian Historical Memory and National Identity, University of New Orleans Press, pp. 302–41.

Bleach, Anthony C. (2010). Postfeminism Cliques? Class, Postfeminism, and the Molly Ringwald-John Hughes Films, *Cinema Journal*, 49:3, Spring, pp. 24–44.

Bliersbach, Gerhard (1985). *So grün war die Heide. Der deutsche Nachkriegsfilm in neuer Sicht*, Weinheim and Basel: Beltz.

Bloch- Dano, Évelyne (2007). *La Biographe*, Paris: Grasset.

Böll, Heinrich (1971). *Gruppenbild mit Dame*, Cologne: Kiepenheuer & Witsch.

Bonini, Emmanuel (2001). *La véritable Romy Schneider*, Paris: J'ai lu.

Boujut, Michel (2014). *Conversations avec Claude Sautet*, Lyon and Arles: Institut Lumière, Actes Sud.

Boym, Svetlana (2001). *The Future of Nostalgia*, New York: Basic Books.

Britton Andrew (1991). 'Stars and Genre', in: Gledhill, Christine (ed.), *Stardom: Industry of Desire*, Abingdon and New York: Routledge, pp. 198–206.

Bruckmüller, Ernst (1985). *Sozialgeschichte Österreichs*, Vienna: Herold.

Burnonville, Francine (1992). *Les femmes sont-elles allées trop loin? De la citoyenneté au pouvoir politique*, Montréal: Le Jour.

Burrows, Elaine (1981). Jacqueline Audry, *Frauen und Film*, 28, pp. 22–7.

Canepari, Luciano (2014). *German Pronunciation and Accents*, Munich: Lincom.

Carly, Michel (2005). *Simenon, les années secrètes: Vendée, 1940–1945*, Le Château-d'Olonne: Éditions d'Orbestier.

Carnes, Mark C. (ed.) (1995). *Past Imperfect: History According to the Movies*, New York: Henry Holt.

Carter, Erica (1997). *How German Is She? Postwar West German Reconstruction and the Consuming Woman*, Ann Arbor: University of Michigan Press.

Carter, Erica (2010). 'Sissi the Terrible: Melodrama, Victimhood, and Imperial Nostalgia in the *Sissi* Trilogy', in: Cooke, Paul, and Silberman, Marc (eds.), *Screening War: Perspectives on German Suffering*, New York: Camden House, pp. 81–101.

Chaperon, Sylvie (1995). La Radicalisation des mouvements féminins Français de 1960 à 1970, *Vingtième Siècle. Revue d'Histoire*, 48, October–December, pp. 61–74.

Chaplin, Felicity (2015). The Sophisticate and the Ingénue: Two Visions of *La Parisienne* in Jacques Deray's *La Piscine, Colloquy: Text Theory Critique*, 29, pp. 48–65.

Chaplin, Felicity (2017). *La Parisienne in Cinema: Between Art and Life*, Manchester: Manchester University Press.

Chion, Michel (2008). *Le complexe de Cyrano: la langue parlée dans les films français*, Paris: Cahiers du cinéma ('Essais').

Clément, Catherine (1988). *Opera, or the Undoing of Women*, translated by Betsy Wing [1979], Minneapolis: University of Minnesota Press.

Clément, Catherine (1992). *Sissi, l'Impératrice anarchiste*, Paris: Gallimard ('Découvertes Gallimard', 148).

Cobb, Shelley, and Ewen, Neil (eds.) (2015). *First Comes Love: Power Couples, Celebrity Kinship and Cultural Politics*, New York and London: Bloomsbury Aacdemic.

Conan, Eric, and Rousso, Henry (1994). *Vichy, un passé qui ne passe pas*, Paris: Fayard ('Pour une histoire du XXᵉ siècle').

Cook, Pam (1996). *Fashioning the Nation: Costume and Identity in British Cinema*, London: British Film Institute.

Costa-Gavras (2018). *Va où il est imposible d'aller: Mémoires*, Paris: Éditions du Seuil.

Cottino-Jones, Marga (2010). *Women, Desire, and Power in Italian Cinema*, New York: Palgrave Macmillan.

Custen, George Frederick (1992). *Bio/Pics: How Hollywood Constructed Public History*, New Brunswick: Rutgers University Press.

Dalsmier, Katherine (1986). *Female Adolescence: Psychoanalytic Reflections on Works of Literature*, New Haven: Yale University Press.

Daviau, Donald G. (1991). Thomas Bernhard's 'Heldenplatz', *Monatshefte*, 83:1, Spring, pp. 29–44.

Davidson, John, and Hake, Sabine (eds.) (2007). *Take Two. Fifties Cinema in a Divided Germany*, New York and Oxford: Berghahn Books.

Davis, Natalie Zemon (2000). *Slaves On Screen: Film and Historical Vision*, Cambridge: Harvard University Press.

de Baecque, Antoine (1998). *La nouvelle vague: portrait d'une jeunesse*, Paris: Flammarion.

de Beauvoir, Simone (1958). *Mémoires d'une jeune fille rangée*, Paris: Gallimard.

de Beauvoir, Simone (1997). *The Second Sex*, translated and edited by Howard Madison Parshley, London: Vintage [Gallimard, 1949] ('Vintage Classics').

DeCordova, Richard (1991). 'Genre and Performance: An Overview', in: Butler, Jeremy (ed.), *Star Texts: Image and Performance in Film and Television*, Detroit: Wayne State University Press, pp. 115–24.

De La Breteque, François Amy (1998). 'Le regard du cinéma sur le Moyen Age', in: Le Goff, Jacques, and Lobrichon, Guy (eds.), *Le Moyen Age aujourd'hui. Trois regards contemporains sur le Moyen Age: histoire, théologie, cinéma. Actes de la rencontre de Cerisy-la-Salle (juillet 1991)*, Paris: Le léopard d'or, pp. 238–301 ('Cahiers du léopard d'or', 7).

Desanti, Dominique (1968). *La Banquière des années folles: Marthe Hanau*, Paris: Fayard.

Des Cars, Jean (1983). *Elisabeth d'Autriche, ou la fatalité*, Paris: Perrin.

Devereux, Cecily (2014). Hysteria, Feminism, and Gender Revisited: The Case of the Second Wave, *ESC: English Studies in Canada*, 40:1, March, pp. 19–45.

Drieu La Rochelle, Pierre (1929). *Une femme à sa fenêtre*, Paris: Gallimard.

Drieu La Rochelle, Pierre (1934). *Socialisme fasciste*, Paris: Gallimard.

Driskell, Jonathan (2015). *The French Screen Goddess: Film Stardom and the Modern Woman in 1930s France*, London and New York: I.B.Tauris.

Dureau, Christian (2010). *Romy Schneider. Des lilacs blancs en enfer*, Paris: Éditions Didier Carpentier ('Stars de l'Écran').

Dyer, Richard (1979). *The Dumb Blonde Stereotype*, London: British Film Institute.

Dyer, Richard (1990). Less and More than Women and Men: Lesbian and Gay Cinema in Weimar Germany, *New German Critique*, 51 (special issue on Weimar mass culture), pp. 5–60.

Dyer, Richard (1991). '*A Star Is Born* and the Construction of Authenticity', in: Christine (ed.), *Stardom: Industry of Desire*, Abingdon and New York: Routledge, pp. 132–40.

Dyer, Richard (1995). 'Heritage Cinema in Europe', in: Vincendeau, Ginette (ed.), *The Encyclopedia of European Cinema*, London: British Film Institute and Cassell, pp. 4–5.

Dyer, Richard (1997). *White*, Abingdon and New York: Routledge.

Dyer, Richard (1998). *Stars*, new edition [1979], London: British Film Institute.

Dyer, Richard (2003). *Now You See It: Studies on Lesbian and Gay film*, 2nd edition [1990], Abingdon and New York: Routledge.

Dyer, Richard (2010). *Nino Rota: Music, Film and Feeling*, London: British Film Institute.

Eckelkamp, Hanns (2007). *Rainer Werner Fassbinder und Atlas 1976–1982. Eine Liebe im Zwiespalt*, Berlin: Hanns Eckelkamp Filmproduktion.

Elley, Derek (1984). *The Epic Film: Myth and History*, Abingdon and New York: Routledge.

Elsaesser, Thomas (2001). *Rainer Werner Fassbinder*, Berlin: Bertz Verlag.

Evangelischer Presseverband München (1955), Kritik Nr 23, *Evangelischer Filmbeobachter*.

Farmer, Sarah (1994). *Oradour: arrêt sur mémoire*, Paris: Calmann-Lévy ('Essai Histoire').

Farmer, Sarah (1999). *Martyred Village: Commemorating the 1944 Massacre at Oradour-sur-Glane*, Berkeley and Los Angeles: University of California Press.

Fasquelle, Solange (1972). *Le Trio infernal*, Paris: Presses de la Cité.

Fehrenbach, Heide (1995). *Cinema in Democratizing Germany*, Chapel Hill and London: University of North Carolina Press.

Fenemore, Mark (2009). The Recent Historiography of Sexuality in Twentieth-Century Germany, *The Historical Journal*, 52:3, pp. 763–79.

Feuer, Jane (1993). *The Hollywood Film Musical*, 2nd edition [1982], Bloomington and Indianapolis: Indiana University Press.

Friedan, Betty (1963). *The Feminine Mystique*, New York: W. W. Norton.

Frischer, Dominique (1997). *La revanche des misogynes. Où en sont les femmes après trente ans de féminisme?*, Paris: Albin Michel.

Fritsche, Maria (2013). *Homemade Men in Postwar Austrian Cinema: Nationhood, Genre and Masculinity*, New York and Oxford: Berghahn Books ('Film Europa' series, vol. 15).

Fujiwara, Chris (2008). *The World and Its Double: The Life and Work of Otto Preminger*, New York: Faber and Faber.

Gabrysiak, Diane (2015). A Woman in a Man's World: 'La Banquière', Money, Transgression and the World of High Finance, *Studies in French Cinema*, 15:3, pp. 225–36.

Garncarz, Joseph (1994). 'Hollywood in Germany: The Role of American Films in Germany, 1925–1990', in: Ellwood, David W., and Kroes, Rob (eds.), *Hollywood in Europe: Experiences of a Cultural Hegemony*, Amsterdam: VU University Press, pp. 94–135 ('European Contributions to American Studies', 28).

Gary, Romain (1977). *Clair de femme*, Paris: Gallimard ('Folio').

Gassen, Heiner, and Hurst, Heike (eds.) (1991). *Tendres ennemis: cent ans de cinema entre la France et l'Allemagne*, Paris: L'Harmattan.

Geraghty, Christine (2000a). *British Cinema in the Fifties: Gender, Genre and the 'New Look'*, Abingdon and New York: Routledge.

Geraghty, Christine (2000b). 'Re-examining Stardom: Questions of Texts, Bodies and Performance', in: Gledhill, Christine, and Williams, Linda (eds.), *Reinventing Films Studies*, London: Arnold, pp. 183–201.

Gledhill, Christine (1991). 'Signs of Melodrama', in: Gledhill, Christine (ed.), *Stardom: Industry of Desire*, Abingdon and New York: Routledge, pp. 207–29.

Gilman, Sander L. et al. (1993). *Hysteria beyond Freud*, Berkeley and Los Angeles: University of California Press.

Giloi, Eva (2011). *Monarchy, Myth, and Material Culture in Germany 1750–1950*, Cambridge: Cambridge University Press.

Goddard, Michael (2014). 'Beyond Polish Moral Realism: The Subversive Cinema of Andrzej Żuławski', in: Mazierska, Ewa, and Goddard, Michael (eds.), *Polish Cinema in a Transnational Context*, Rochester: University of Rochester Press, pp. 236–57.

Goulding, Daniel J. (2002). *Liberated Cinema: The Yugoslav Experience, 1945–2001*, 2nd edition [1985], Bloomington and Indianapolis: Indiana University Press.

Graff, Séverine (2014), *Le cinéma-vérité. Films et controverse*, Rennes: Presses Universitaires de Rennes.

Gramann, Karola, and Schlüpmann, Heide (1983). 'Liebe als opposition, Opposition als Liebe', in: Prinzler, Hans Helmut (ed.), *Hertha Thiele*, Berlin: Deutsche Kinemathek, pp. 24–43.

Guérif, François (1981). *Le cinéma policier français*, Paris: Éditions Henri Veyrier.

Guillou, Sophie (2006). *Romy Schneider*, Paris: Libretto.

Gundle, Stephen (2011). *Bellissima: Feminine Beauty and The Idea of Italy*, New Haven: Yale University Press.

Gundle, Stephen (2018). 'The Enduring Glamour of the Parisienne', in: Philips, Alastair, and Vincendeau, Ginette (eds.), *Paris in the Cinema: Beyond the Flâneur*, London: British Film Institute, pp. 166–76.

Hanck, Frauke, and Schröder, Pit (1980). *Romy Schneider und ihre Filme*, Munich: Goldmann.

Hanisch, Ernst (1994). *Der lange Schatten des Staates. Österreichische Gesellschaftsgeschichte im 20. Jahrhundert*, Vienna: Ueberreuter.

Hake, Sabine (2008). *German National Cinema*, 2nd edition [2002], Abingdon and New York: Routledge (National Cinemas Series).

Hametz, E. Maura, and Schlipphacke, Heidi (eds.) (2018). *Sissi's World: The Empress Elisabeth in Memory and Myth*, New York and London: Bloomsbury (New Directions in German Studies).

Handyside, Fiona, and Taylor-Jones, Kate (eds.) (2016). *International Cinema and the Girl: Local Issues, Transnational Contexts*, New York: Palgrave Macmillan.

Hardy, Françoise (2008). *Le désespoir des singes et autres bagatelles*, Paris: Robert Laffont.

Harper, Sue (1994). *Picturing the Past: The Rise and Fall of the British Costume Film*, London: British Film Institute.

Hawes, James (2017). *The Shortest History of Germany*, Devon: Old Street Publishing.

Haymann, Emmanuel (1998). *Alain Delon, splendeurs et mystères d'une superstar*, Lausanne: Favre.

Hayward, Susan (1993). *French National Cinema*, Abingdon and New York: Routledge.

Hayward, Susan (2010). *French Costume Drama of the 1950s: Fashioning Politics in Film*, Bristol: Intellect.

Heineman, Elizabeth D. (1994). *What a Difference a Husband Make? Women and Marital Status in Nazi and Postwar Germany*, Berkeley and Los Angeles: University of California Press.

Heineman, Elizabeth D. (1996). The Hour of Women: Memories of Germany's 'Crisis Years' and West German National Identity, *American Historical Review*, 101:2, pp. 354–95.

Hennessy, Peter (1992). *Never Again: Britain 1945–1951*, London: Penguin Books.

Hermary-Vieille, Catherine (1988). *Romy*, Paris: Éditions Olivier Orban.

Hickethier, Knut (1993). 'Die Bedeutung regionaler Filmforschung für die überregionale Filmgeschichte', in: Poch, Bernd, Steffen, Joachim, and Thiele, Jens (eds.), *Spurensuche: Film und Kino in der Region: Dokumentation der 1. Expertentagung zu Fragen Regionaler Filmforschung und Kinokultur in Oldenburg*, Oldenburg: Bibliotheks- und Informationssystem der Carl von Ossietzky Universität Oldenburg, pp. 32–48.

Higson, Andrew (1991). 'Film Acting and Independent Cinema', in: Butler, Jeremy (ed.), *Star Texts: Image and Performance in Film and Television*, Detroit: Wayne State University Press, pp. 155–81.

Higson, Andrew (2003). *English Heritage, English Cinema: Costume Drama since 1980*, Oxford: Oxford University Press.

Higson, Andrew (2006). 'Re-Presenting the National Past: Nostalgia and Pastiche in the Heritage Film', in: Friedman, Lester (ed.), *Fires Were Started: British Cinema and Thatcherism*, 2nd edition [1993], London: Wallflower, pp. 91–109.

Hill, Leslie (1993). *Marguerite Duras: Apocalyptic Desires*, Abingdon and New York: Routledge.

Impey, Nick (2011). Ideas of Sex: Discourses on Sexuality in Liliana Cavani's 'The Night Porter' and Cesare Canevari's 'The Gestapo's Last Orgy', *Alphaville: Journal of Film and Screen Media*, 1, Summer, pp. 1–13.

Innocenti, Marco (2009). *La malattia chiamata Donna. Erano belle, famose e depresse*, Milan: Mursia.

Jacquet, Michel (2004). *Travelling sur les années noires. L'Occupation vue par le cinema français depuis 1945*, Paris: Alvik.

Jardin, Pascal (1978a). *Le Nain Jaune*, Paris: Éditions Julliard.

Jardin, Alexandre (2017). *Ma mère avait raison*, Paris: Grasset.

Jary, Micaela (1993). *Traumfabriken made in Germany. Die Geschichte des deutschen Nachkriegsfilms 1945–1960*, Berlin: edition q, pp. 143–52.

Jeancolas, Jean-Pierre (1979). *Le cinéma des français: la Ve république (1958–1978)*, Paris: Stock.

Johnson, Lesley (1993). *The Modern Girl: Girlhood and Growing Up*, Buckingham: Open University Press.

Jürgs, Michael (1991). *Der Fall Romy Schneider: Eine Biographie*, Munich and Leipzig: List.

Kaes, Anton (1989). *From Hitler to Heimat: The Return of History as Film*, Cambridge: Harvard University Press.

Kedward, Harry Roderick (2000). 'The Anti-Carnival of Collaboration. Louis Malle's *Lacombe Lucien* (1974)', in: Vincendeau, Ginette, and Hayward, Susan (eds.), *French Films: Text and Contexts*, 2nd edition [1990], Abingdon and New York: Routledge, pp. 227–39.

Kessel, Jospeh (1936). *La Passante du Sans-Souci*, Paris: Gallimard.

King, Barry (1985). Articulating Stardom, *Screen*, 26:5, pp. 27–51.

Kirn, Gal, Sekulić, Dubravka, and Testen, Žiga (eds.) (2011). *Surfing the Black: Yugoslav Black Wave Cinema and Its Transgressive Moments*, Maastricht: Jan van Eyck Academie.

Knef, Hildergarde (2011). *Romy Schneider. Betrachtung eines Lebens*, 2nd edition [1983], Edel: Funkturm.

Korte, Helmut, and Lowry, Stephen (2000). *Der Filmstar. Brigitte Bardot, James Dean, Götz George, Heinz Rühmann, Romy Schneider, Hanna Schygulla und neuere Stars*, Stuttgart: Metzler.

Kramer, Thomas, and Prucha, Martin (1994). *Film im Lauf der Zeit: 100 Jahre Kino in Deutschland, Österreich und der Schweiz*, Vienna: Ueberreuter.

Kraemer, Olaf (2008). *Ende einer Nacht*, Munich: Blumenbar.

Krämer, Nadja (2012). 'Models of Masculinity in Postwar Germany. The *Sissi* Films and the West-German Wiederbewaffnungsdebatte', in: Ginsberg, Terri, and Mensch, Andrea (eds.), *A Companion to German Cinema*, Chichester: Wiley-Blackwell, pp. 341–78 ('Companions to National Cinema').

Krenn, Günter (2013a). *Romy Schneider. Die Biographie*, 3rd edition [2008], Berlin: Aufbau Taschenbuch.

Krenn, Günter (2013b). *Romy & Alain. Eine Amour fou*, Berlin: Aufbau.

Landy, Marcia (2010). 'Swinging Femininity, 1960s Transnational Style', in: Bell, Melanie, and Williams, Melanie (eds.), *British Women's Cinema*, Abingdon and New York: Routledge, pp. 111–23.

Lanzoni, Rémi Fournier (2014). *French Comedy on Screen: A Cinematic History*, New York: Palgrave Macmillan.

Laubier, Claire (ed.) (1990). *The Condition of Women in France, 1945 to the Present: A Documentary Anthology*, Abingdon and New York: Routledge ('Twentieth century French texts').

Lebrun, Dominique (1987). *Paris-Hollywood: les Français dans le cinéma américain*, Paris: Hazan.

Lebrun, Dominique (1992). *Trans Europe Hollywood. Les Européens du Cinéma Américain*, Paris: Bordas.

Le Gras, Gwénaëlle (2005). Soft and Hard: Catherine Deneuve in 1970, *Studies in French Cinema*, 5:1, pp. 27–35.

Le Gras, Gwénaëlle (2007a). 'L'Ambivalence de Catherine Deneuve au service du *Dernier Métro* (Truffaut, 1980). Perception, recomposition et utilisation de sa *persona*', in: Amiel, Vincent, Nacache, Jacqueline, Sellier, Geneviève, and Viviani, Christian (eds.), *L'Acteur de cinéma: approches plurielles*, Rennes: Presses universitaires de Rennes, pp. 205–16 ('Le Spectaculaire').

Le Gras, Gwénaëlle (2007b). 'Remise en cause et mutation de l'idéal féminin dans le cinéma français des années 1970. Catherine Deneuve dans *Touche pas à la femme blanche* (Marco Ferreri, 1974)', in: Bertin-Maghit, Jean-Pierre, and Sellier, Geneviève (eds.), *La Fiction éclatée. Petits et grands écrans français et francophones, volume 1: études socioculturelles*, Paris: L'Harmattan, pp. 303–13 ('Les Médias en actes').

Le Gras, Gwénaëlle (2010). *Le mythe Deneuve, une 'star' française entre classicisme et modernité*, Paris: Éditions du Nouveau Monde ('Histoire et cinéma').

Le Gras, Gwénaëlle (2015). 'France's "New Don Juan": The Representation of Delon's Youth', in: Rees-Roberts, Nick, and Waldron, Darren (eds.), *Alain Delon: Style, Stardom and Masculinity*, New York and London: Bloomsbury Academic, pp. 43–58.

Le Groignec, Jacques (1998). *Pétain et de Gaulle*, Paris: Nouvelles éditions latines.

Lelait-Helo, David (2017). *Romy*, Paris: Télémaque.

Lennox, Sarah (2004). 'Constructing Femininity in Early Cold War Era', in: Mueller Agnes C. (ed.), *German Pop Culture: How 'American' Is It?*, Ann Arbor: University of Michigan Press, pp. 66–82.

Lévi-Strauss, Claude (1958). *Anthropologie structurale*, Paris: Plon.

Levy, Gayle A. (1999). *Refiguring the Muse*, New York: Peter Lang.

Lewandowski, Elizabeth J. (2011). *The Complete Costume Dictionary*, Lanham: Scarecrow Press.

Lindeperg, Sylvie (1997). *Les écrans de l'ombre: la Seconde Guerre mondiale dans le cinéma français*, Paris: CNRS Éditions.

Lindeperg, Sylvie (2007). *Nuit et Brouillard, un film dans l'histoire*, Paris: Éditions Odile Jacob.

Linville, Susan E. (1998). *Feminism, Film, Fascism: Women's Auto/Biographical Film in Postwar Germany*, Austin: University of Texas Press.

Loshitzky, Yosefa (1995). *The Radical Faces of Godard and Bertolucci*, Detroit: Wayne State University Press.

Luckett, Moya (2000). 'Travel and Mobility. Femininity and National Identity in Swinging London films', in: Ashby, Justine, and Higson, Andrew (eds.), *British Cinema Past and Present*. Abingdon and New York: Routledge, pp. 233–45.

Majumdar, Neepa (2009), *Wanted Cultural Ladies Only! Female Stardom and Cinema in India, 1930s–1950s*, Urbana and Chicago: University of Illinois Press.

Marie, Michel (2003). *The French New Wave: An Artistic School*, translated by Richard Neupert, Oxford: Blackwell.

Marschall, Susanne (1997). 'Sissis Wandel unter den Deutschen', in: Koebner, Thomas (ed.), *Idole des deutschen Films. Eine Galerie von Schlüsselfiguren*, Munich: edition text + kritik, pp. 372–83.

McBride, Will (2002). *Romy. Fotografische Erinnerungen Paris 1964*, Munich: Knesebeck.

Meyer Spacks, Patricia (1982). *The Adolescent Idea: Myths of Youth and the Adult Imagination*, London: Faber and Faber.

Moeller, Robert G. (1989). Reconstructing the Family in Reconstruction Germany: Women and Social Policy in the Federal Republic, 1949–1955, *Feminist Studies*, 15:1, pp. 137–69.

Moeller, Robert G. (1993). *Protecting Motherhood: Women and the Family in the Politics of Postwar West Germany*, Berkeley and Los Angeles: University of California Press.

Moine, Raphaëlle (2017). *Vies héroïques. Biopics masculins, biopics féminins*, Paris: Librairie philosophique J. Vrin ('Philosophie et cinéma').

Moireau, Jean-Claude (2011). *Jeanne Moreau, l'insoumise*, Paris: Flammarion.

Monk, Claire (1995a). Sexuality and Heritage, *Sight and Sound*, 5:10, October, pp. 32–4.

Monk, Claire (1995b). The British 'Heritage Film' and Its Critics, *Critical Survey*, 7: 2, pp. 116–124.

Monk, Claire (2002), 'The British Heritage-Film Debate Revisited', in: Monk, Claire, and Sargeant, Amy (eds.), *British Historical Cinema: The History, Heritage and Costume Film*, Abingdon and New York: Routledge, pp. 176–98.

Moseley, Rachel (ed.) (2005). *Fashioning Film Stars: Dress, Culture, Identity*, London: British Film Institute.

Mulvey, Laura (1975). Visual Pleasure and Narrative Cinema, *Screen*, 16:3, pp. 6–18.

Naremore, James (1988). *Acting in the Cinema*, Berkeley and Los Angeles: University of California Press.

Negra, Diane (2001). *Off-White Hollywood: American Culture and Ethnic Female Stardom*, Abingdon and New York: Routledge.

Neupert, Richard John (2007). *A History of the French New Wave Cinema*, 2nd edition [2002], Madison: University of Wisconsin Press.

Nolan, Mary (1994). *Visions of Modernity: American Business and the Modernization of Germany*, Oxford: Oxford University Press.

Nochimson, Martha P. (2002). *Screen Couple Chemistry: The Power of 2*, Austin: University of Texas Press.

Ó Dochartaigh, Pól, and Schönfeld, Christiane (eds.) (2013). *Representing the 'Good German' in Literature and Culture after 1945: Altruism and Moral Ambiguity*, New York: Camden House ('Studies in German Literature, Linguistics, and Culture', 132).

Pascuito, Bernard (2002). *La double mort de Romy*, Paris: Albin Michel.

Paxton, Robert (1972). *Vichy France: Old Guard and New Order, 1940–1944*, New York: Knopf.

Picardie, Justine (2011). *Coco Chanel: The Legend and the Life*, London: Harper Collins.

Pidduck, Julianne (2004). *Contemporary Costume Film: Space, Place and the Past*, London: British Film Institute.

Phillips, Alastair, and Vincendeau, Ginette (eds.) (2006). *Journeys of Desire. European Actors in Hollywood: A Critical Companion*, London: British Film Institute.

Poiger, Uta G. (2000). *Jazz, Rock, and Rebels: Cold War Politics and American Culture in a Divided Germany*, Berkeley and Los Angeles: University of California Press.

Rearick, Charles (2011). *Paris Dreams, Paris Memories: The City and Its Mystique*, Stanford: Stanford University Press.

Rich, Ruby J. (1981). *Mädchen in Uniform*: From Repressive Tolerance to Erotic Liberation, *Jump Cut*, 24/25, pp. 44–50.

Robertson Wojcik, Pamela (2004). 'Typecasting', in: Robertson Wojcik, Pamela (ed.), *Movie Acting: The Film Reader*, Abingdon and New York: Routledge, pp. 169–89.

Rollet, Brigitte (2015). *Jacqueline Audry: la femme à la camera*, Rennes: Presses Universitaires de Rennes ('Archives du féminisme').

Rollet, Brigitte, and Tarr, Carrie (2001). *Cinema and the Second Sex*, London and New York: Continuum.

Rosen, Philip (2001). *Change Mummified: Cinema, Historicity, Theory*, Minneapolis: University of Minnesota Press.

Rousso, Henry (1987). *Le Syndrome de Vichy de 1944 à nos jours*, Paris: Éditions du Seuil ('Points Histoire. XXᵉ siècle').

Santner, Eric L. (1990). *Stranded Objects: Mourning, Memory, and Film in Postwar Germany*, Ithaca: Cornell University Press.

Schlipphacke, Heidi (2010). Melancholy Empress: Queering Empire in Ernst Marischka's *Sissi* Films, *Screen*, 51:3, Autumn, pp. 232–55.

Schneider, Romy, and Seydel, Renate (1988). *Ich, Romy: Tagebuch eines Lebens*, Munich: Langen Müller Herbig.

Schneider, Romy, and Seydel, Renate (1989). *Moi, Romy. Le journal de ma vie*, Paris: Presse Pocket.

Schnell, Ralf, and Schubert, Jochen (2005). Ästhetik der Moderne: 'Gruppenbild mit Dame', in: Böll, Heinrich, (ed.), *Gruppenbild mit Dame: Werke (Kölner Ausgabe)*, vol. 17, Cologne: Kiepenheuer & Witsch, pp. 417–49.

Scholar, Nancy (1975). Mädchen in Uniform, *Women and Film*, 2:7, pp. 68–72.

Schraut, Sylvia (2011). 'Sissi: Popular Representations of an Empress', in: Paletschek, Sylvia (ed.), *Popular Historiographies in the 19th and 20th Centuries: Cultural Meanings, Social Practices*, New York and Oxford: Berghahn Books, pp. 155–71.

Schwarzenbach, Alexis (2006). 'Imagined Queens between Heaven and Hell: Representations of Grace Kelly and Romy Schneider', in: Schulte, Regina (ed.), *The Body of the Queen: Gender and Rule in the Courtly World, 1500–2000*, New York and Oxford: Berghahn Books, pp. 306–26.

Schwarzer, Alice (1998). *Romy Schneider: Mythos und Leben*, Cologne: Kiepenheuer & Witsch.

Schwarzer, Alice (2018). *Romy Schneider intime*, translated by Jean-Marie Argelès, Paris: l'Archipel.

Schygulla, Hanna (1988). *Romy Schneider: Portraits 1954–1981*, Munich: Schirmer/Mosel.

Seeßlen, Georg (1989). 'Durch die Heimat: und so weiter. Heimatfilme, Schlagerfilme und Ferienfilme der fünfziger Jahre', in: Berger, Jürgen, Reichmann, Hans P., and Worschech, Rudolf (eds.), *Zwischen Gestern und Morgen. Westdeutscher Nachkriegsfilm, 1946–1962*, Frankfurt-on-Main: Deutsches Filminstitut, pp. 139–61.

Seeßlen, Georg (1992a). Eine Geschichte vom Mädchen, das Frau werden wollte. Zum 10. Todestag von Romy Schneider am 29. Mai, *Epd Film*, 5, pp. 10–14.

Seeßlen, Georg (1992b). 'Sissi – Eine deutsches Orgasmustrauma', in: Marsiske, Hans-Arthur (ed.), *Zeitmaschine Kino. Darstellungen von Geschichte im Film*, Marburg: Hitzeroth, pp. 65–79.

Seidl, Claudius (1987). *Der deutsche Film der fünfziger Jahre*, Munich: Heyne.

Sellier, Geneviève (2002). Danielle Darrieux, Michele Morgan and Micheline Presle in Hollywood: The Threat to French Identity, *Screen*, 43:2, pp. 201–14.

Sellier, Geneviève (2008). *Masculine Singular: French New Wave Cinema*, translated by Kristin Ross, Durham and London: Duke University Press.

Seydel, Renate (1987). *Romy Schneider: Bilder ihres Lebens*, Munich: Schirmer/Mosel.

Shafto, Sally (2006). *Zanzibar: les films Zanzibar et les dandys de mai 1968/The Zanzibar Films and the dandies of May 1968*, Paris: Éditions Paris Expérimental ('Classiques de l'Avant-Garde', 13).

Sigl, Klaus, Schneider, Werner, and Tornow, Ingo (1986). *Jede Menge Kohle? Kunst und Kommerz auf dem deutschen Filmmarkt der Nachkriegszeit. Filmpreise und Kassenerfolge 1949–1985*, Munich: Filmland Presse.

Simenon, Georges (1961). *Le Train*, Paris: Presses de la cité.

Simsi, Simon (2012). *Ciné-passions. Le guide chiffré du cinéma en France*, Paris: Dixit (Ciné Passions).

Smith, Alison (2005). *French Cinema in the 1970s: The Echoes of May*, Manchester and New York: Manchester University Press.

Sobchack, Vivian (ed.) (1996). *The Persistence of History: Cinema, Television, and the Modern Event*, Abingdon and New York: Routledge.

Sontag, Susan (1980). *Under the Sign of Saturn*, New York: Farrar, Straus and Giroux.

Sorlin, Pierre (1980). *Film in History: Restaging the Past*, Oxford: Backwell.

Sorlin, Pierre (1991). *European Cinemas, European Societies 1939–1990*, Abingdon and New York: Routledge.

Steele, Valerie (1997). *Fifty Years of Fashion: New Look to Now*, New Haven: Yale University Press.

Steimatsky, Noa (2017). *The Face on Film*, Oxford: Oxford University Press.

Steinbauer, Marie L. (1999). *Die andere Romy*, Hamburg: Marion von Schröder Verlag.

Street, Sarah (2009). *British National Cinema*, 2nd edition [1997], Abingdon and New York: Routledge.

Thomas, Sarah (2012). *Peter Lorre: Face Laker. Constructing Stardom and Performance in Hollywood and Europe*, New York and Oxford: Berghahn Books.

Traubner, Richard (2007). 'Der deutsche Operettenfilm vor und nach 1933', in: Schaller, Wolfgang (ed.), *Operette unterm Hakenkreuz. Zwischen hoffähiger Kunst und 'Entartung'*, Berlin: Metropol, pp. 147–69.

Troller, Georg Stefan (2007). *Lebensgeschichten: Die Stars, Die Heiligen, Die Poeten, Die Sünder, Die Autoren, Die Künstler*, Düsseldorf: Artemis und Winkler.

Uecker, Matthias (2013). 'Saints and Sinners: The Good Germans and Her Others in Heinrich Böll's *Gruppenbild mit Dame*', in: Ó Dochartaigh, Pól, and Schönfeld, Christiane (eds.), *Representing the 'Good German' in Literature and Culture after 1945: Altruism and Moral Ambiguity*, New York: Camden House, pp. 98–110 ('Studies in German Literature, Linguistics, and Culture', 132).

Uhl, Heidemarie (2011). Of Heroes and Victims: World War II in Austrian Memory, *Austrian History Yearbook*, 42, pp. 185–200.

Vidal, Belén (2012a). *Figuring the Past: Period Film and the Mannerist Aesthetic*, Amsterdam: Amsterdam University Press.

Vidal, Belén (2012b). *Heritage Film: Nation, Genre and Representation*, New York: Columbia University Press.

Vidal, Belén (2014). 'Introduction', in: Brown, Tom, and Vidal, Belén (eds.), *The Biopic in Contemporary Film Culture*, Abingdon and New York: Routledge, pp. 1–32.

Vincendeau, Ginette (1992). Family Plots: The Fathers and Daughters of French Cinema, *Sight and Sound*, March, 3:4, pp. 14–17.

Vincendeau, Ginette (1996). *The Companion to French Cinema*, London: British Film Institute.

Vincendeau, Ginette (2000). *Stars and Stardom in French Cinema*, London and New York: Continuum.

Vincendeau, Ginette (2003). *Jean-Pierre Melville: An American in Paris*, London: British Film Institute.

Vincendeau, Ginette (2008). *Les stars et le star-système en France*, Paris: L'Harmattan.

Vincendeau, Ginette (2009). Shackled by Beauty, *Sight and Sound*, 19:12, p. 25.

Vincendeau, Ginette (2013). *Brigitte Bardot*, London: British Film Institute.

Vincendeau, Ginette (2014). The Perils of Trans-National Stardom: Alain Delon in Hollywood Cinema, *Mise au point*, 6 (http://map.revues.org/1800, last accessed: 11 September 2017).

Vincendeau, Ginette (2015a). And Bardot ... Became a Blonde: Hair, Stardom and Modernity in Post-War France, *Celebrity Studies*, 7:1, pp. 98–112 (https://doi.org/10.1080/19392397.2016.1104898, last accessed: 15 December 2018).

Vincendeau, Ginette (2015b). A Star is Torn (To Pieces): Brigitte Bardot Seen through Readers' Letters in Cinémonde, *Contemporary French and Francophone Studies*, 19:1, pp. 90–105.

Vincendeau, Ginette (2017). 'Stars across Borders: The Vexed Questions of Stars' 'Exportability', in: Cooke, Paul, Dennison, Stephanie, Marlow-Mann, Alex, and Stone, Rob (eds.), *The Routledge Companion to World Cinema*, Abingdon and New York: Routledge, pp. 359–68.

Violet, Bernard (2000). *Les mystères Delon*, Paris: Flammarion.

Von Molke, Johannes (2002). 'Evergreens: The Heimat Genre', in: Bergfelder, Tim, Carter, Erica, and Göktürk, Deniz (eds.), *The German Cinema Book*, London: British Film Institute, pp. 18–28.

Von Molke, Johannes (2005). *No Place Like Home: Locations of Heimat in German Cinema*, Berkeley and Los Angeles: University of California Press.

Wauchope, Mary (2002). 'Sissi Revisited', in: Lamb-Faffelberger, Margarete (ed.), *Literature, Film and the Culture Industry in Contemporary Austria*, New York: Peter Lang, pp. 170–84 ('Austria culture', 33).

Wauchope, Mary (2007). 'The Other German Cinema', in: Davidson, John, and Hake, Sabine (eds.), *Take Two. Fifties Cinema in a Divided Germany*, New York and Oxford: Berghahn Books, pp. 210–22.

Weiner, Susan (2001). *Enfants Terribles: Youth and Femininity in the Mass Media in France, 1945–1968*, Baltimore and London: Johns Hopkins University Press.

Wierling, Dorothee (1994). 'Die Jugend als innerer Feind: Konflikte in der Erziehungsdiktatur der sechziger Jahre', in: Kaelbe, Hartmut, Kocka, Juanrgen, and Zwahr, Hartmut (eds.), *Sozialgeschichte der DDR*, Stuttgart: Klett-Cotta, pp. 404–25.

Wiese, Richard (1996). *The phonology of German*, Oxford: Oxford University Press.

Wieviorka, Annette (1998). *L'ère du témoin*, Paris: Plon.

Wilkinson, Maryn (2015). The Makeover and the Malleable Body in 1980s American Teen Film, *International Journal of Cultural Studies*, 18:3, pp. 385–91.

Wolf, Naomi (2002). *The Beauty Myth: How Images of Beauty Are Used against Women*, reprint edition [1990], London: Chatto & Windus.

Wood, Robin (1989). *Hitchcock's Films Revisited*, revised edition [1965], New York: Columbia University Press.

Wright Wexman, Virginia (1993). *Creating the Couple: Love, Marriage, and Hollywood Performance*, Princeton: Princeton University Press.

Yu, Sabrina Qiong (2012). *Jet Li: Chinese Masculinity and Transnational Film Stardom*, Edinburgh: Edinburgh University Press.

Zimnik, Nina (2005). 'Romy Schneider, *La Passante du Sans-Souci*: Discourses of *Vergangenheitsbewältigung*, Feminism, and Myth', in: Brueggemann, Aminia M., and Schulman, Peter (eds.), *Rhine Crossings: Germany and France in Love and War*, Albany: State University of New York, pp. 251–71.

Zipes, Jack (2002). *The Brothers Grimm: From Enchanted Forests to the Modern World*, 2nd edition [1988], New York: Palgrave Macmillan.

Press articles and film reviews

Adieu Sissi, Bonjour Romy, *Festival*, 1 October 1961.

Alain et Romy: un amour tendre comme le souvenir, *Jours de France*, 22 August 1968.

Alain et Romy: un quart d'heure de charme au Festival, *Paris Match*, 23 May 1959.

Bard, Christine (2018). La tribune signée par Deneuve est l'expression d'un antiféminisme, *Le Monde*, 11 January.

Bauby, Jean-Dominique, and Rémond, Alain (1980). Bertrand Tavernier: autocritique, *Paris-Hebdo*, 23–9 January, pp. 37–8.

Beaugrand, Véronique (2002). Fidèle sà la mémoire de Romy Schneider, *Le Parisien*, 8 August (http://www.leparisien.fr/yvelines/fideles-a-la-memoire-de-romy-schneider-08-08-2002-2003306410.php, last accessed: 27 February 2019).

Benayoun, Robert (1962a). Un bon point, *France Observateur*, 17 May.

Benayoun, Robert (1962b). Ce combat dans l'île qui nous concerne, *France Observateur*, 20 September.

Bertrand, Olivier (1998). Portrait: Laurent Davenas, 54 ans, procureur d'Evry, magistrat réputé docile, subit les foudres du RPR depuis qu'il s'est attaqué à Xavière Tiberi. L'ivresse des cimes, *Libération*, 20 May (https://www.liberation.fr/portrait/1998/05/20/laurent-davenas-54-ans-procureur-d-evry-magistrat-repute-docile-subit-les-foudres-du-rpr-depuis-qu-i_236547, last accessed: 23 March 2021).

Bescos, José-Maria (1976). *Pariscope*, 27 October.

Billard, François (1977). La paix sera terrible, *Le Point*, 23 May, p. 5.

Billard, François (1978). Le bel âge des femmes libres. Romy Schneider à son zénith, *Le Point*, 27 November, pp. 175–81.

'Boccace 70', *Nouvelles littéraires*, 13 September 1962.

Bory, Jean Louis (1966), Un vaudeville à la française, *Arts*, 2 February.

Bouteiller, Pierre (1980). 'La mort en direct'. Voyeur non-stop, *Le Quotidien de Paris*, 26 January.

Bravo, 30 December 1956, cover.

Brigitte Bardot et Romy Schneider, le jour et la nuit, *Radio Télé Ciné*, 11 January 1959.

Candide, 7 September 1962.

Capdenac, Michel (1963). *Lettres Françaises*, 2 January.

Cau, Jean (1981). Alain Delon et Romy Schneider: ils crèvent l'écran, *Paris Match*, 9 January, pp. 68–71.

Cayatte, André (1958). *L'Express*, 30 October.

Ciné Revue, 21 December 1956, cover.

Chanel, l'inimitable perfection, *Jours de France*, 15 September 1962.

Chauvet, Louis (1963). 'Le Cardinal', *Le Figaro*, 20 December.

Chauvet, Louis (1966). Les films par Louis Chauvet. 'Quoi de neuf, Pussycat?', *Le Figaro*, 1 February.

Chevillard, P.-B. (1982). Jacques Rouffio, un ami qui vous veut du bien, *La Croix*, 15 April.

Chazal, Robert (1966). 'Quoi de neuf Pussycat?' (six personnages en quête d'ardeur), *France-Soir*, 2 February.

Chazal, Robert (1976a). 'Mado' … et Simon, Pierre, Hélène et les autres, *France-Soir*, 27 October.

Chazal, Robert (1976b). 'Une femme à sa fenêtre', *France-Soir*, 15 November.

Cinéma: 'Le Cardinal', *La Croix*, 31 December 1963.

Cinémonde, 17 July 1958, cover.

Cinémonde, 2 April 1959, cover.

Cinémonde, 3 November 1959.

Cinémonde, 29 March 1960.

Cinémonde, 8 November 1960.

Cinémonde, 18 February 1964.

Cinémonde, 6 October 1964.

Couderc, Claude (1974). Romy Schneider: une actrice qui sait dire non, *Le Quotidien de Paris*, 9 July.

Crowther, Bosley (1963). Screen, The Grim Message of War: Foreman's 'The Victors' at Two Theaters, *The New York Times*, 20 December (http://www.nytimes.com/movie/review?res=9501E6DA1F30EF3BBC4851DFB4678388679 EDE, last accessed: 12 October 2017).

de Baroncelli, Jean (1962). 'Le Procès', *Le Monde*, 25 December.

de Baroncelli, Jean (1974). *Le* Monde, 18 March.

de Baroncelli, Jean (1978). *Le Monde*, 24 November.

de Gasperi, Anne (1980). Romy mise à nu, *Le Quotidien de Paris*, 24 January.

Delain, Michel (1977). Cinéma. Romy Schneider, Galabru et Petrovic, *L'Express*, January 17, p. 10.

Delain, Michel, and Heymann, Danièle (1978). Sautet, Romy et les autres, *L'Express*, 18 November.

Denisot, Michel, and Douin, Jean-Luc (2015). Exclusif: Romy Schneider, son histoire d'amour avec Jacques Dutronc, *Vanity Fair*, 28 April (https://www.vanityfair.fr/pouvoir/politique/articles/romy-schneider-et-jacques-dutronc/13853, last accessed: 7 December 2018).

Der Abend, 1 October 1957.

Der Spiegel, 11 January 1961, p. 63.

Deutsches Allgemeines Sonntagsblatt, 15 December 1974.

Deutsche Illustrierte, 28 January 1956, cover.

Die Jungfrau von Geiselgasteig, *Der Spiegel*, 7 March 1956, cover.

Die Romy-Schneider-Story, *Wiener Wochenausgabe*, 29 March 1956.

Domenach, Jean-Marie (1974). Les ambiguïtés de la mode 'rétro', *Le Monde*, 18 April (http://www.lemonde.fr/archives/article/1974/04/18/les-ambiguites-de-la-mode-retro_2523719_1819218.html#Wl1mXfec4x20UpU6.99, last accessed: 8 June 2018).

Douin, Jean-Luc (1974). *Télérama*, 25 May.

Douin, Jean-Luc (1980a). Bertrand Tavernier. 'Tant de beauté à côté de la mort', *Télérama*, 23 January.

Douin, Jean-Luc (1980b). La Banquière, *Télérama*, 25 June, pp. 70–3.

Dumont, Etienne (1981). '*Garde à vue* est avant out pour moi une histoire de visages' dit Claude Miller au sujet de son dernier film, *La Tribune de Genève*, 3 October.

Durante, Christan (1981). 'Garde à vue': un petit chef-d'oeuvre français, *Figaro Magazine*, 17 September.

Duras, Marguerite (1985). Sublime, forcément sublime Christine V., *Libération*, 17 July.

Een keizerin werd vrouw, *De Post*, 11 April 1971.

Ehestreik gegen Atomtod, *Der Spiegel*, 14 December 1960, pp. 83–4.

Ein Mütterherz kapitülierte, *Film Revue*, 26 May 1956.

Eine französisch-österreichische Gemeinschaftsproduktion, *Österreichische Film und Kino Zeitung*, 4 April 1959.

Elle, 25 August 1980, cover, pp. 14–15.

Elle s'appelle Leni, *L'Humanité*, 25 May 1977.

Ente für Romy, *Bravo*, 13 July 1958.

Es weihnachtet sehr – Film Revue fotografierte Romy Schneider bei ihren Vorbereitungen für das Fest, *Film Revue*, 11 December 1956.

Et si la mort c'était encore la vie!, *Télérama*, 30 January 1980, pp. 88–9.

Fabre, Maurice (1978a). *France-Soir*, 11 July.

Fabre, Maurice (1978b). *France-Soir*, 30 November.

France-Observateur, 30 March 1961.

France Nouvelle, 8 September 1975.

France-Soir, 22 May 1974.

Fraser-Cavassoni, Natasha (2004). Secrets of French Style, *Harper's Bazaar*, p. 148.

Fernsehen. Romy Schneider: Beichte am Berg, *Der Spiegel*, 6 February 1967, p. 94.

Garbo, 12 September 1964.

Girod et Pasolini: enfer et paradis, *L'Aurore*, 21 May 1974.

Grassin, Sophie (2012). Andrzej Zulawski: 'Mes films ne veulent pas mourir', *Le Nouvel Observateur* (https://teleobs.nouvelobs.com/actualites/20160217. OBS4842/andrzej-zulawski-mes-films-ne-veulent-pas-mourir.html, last accessed: 23 November 2018).

Heißa, wir leben!, *Bunte*, 5 August 1961.

Herzog Filmverleih (n.d.). *Monpti* [press release], Munich: Herzog-Filmverleih, Central-Press and advertising department.

'Im Moment bin ich ganz kaput ...', *Stern*, 23 April 1981.

Isaac, Anéma (2009). Romy Schneider: elle a grandi à l'ombre noire d'Hitler, *France Dimanche*, 13 March (http://www.francedimanche.fr/infos-people/cinema/romy-schneider-elle-grandi-lombre-noire-dhitler/, last accessed: 19 March 2017).

'J'aurais pu finir comme Marilyn Monroe ou Romy Schneider', *7sur7*,
    21 February 2012 (https://www.7sur7.be/7s7/fr/1527/People/article/
    detail/1397976/2012/02/21/J-aurais-pu-finir-comme-Marilyn-Monroe-ou-
    Romy-Schneider.dhtml, last accessed: 1 February 2019).
Jacob, Gilles (1973). 'Le Train', *L'Express*, 5 November.
Jardin, Pascal (1978b). Concerto pour une âme solitaire, *Le Matin*, 24 November.
Karazek, Helmut (1977). Film. Im Rasierspiegel, *Der Spiegel*, 6 June, p. 198.
Kehr Zurück, Romy!, *Funk und Film*, 8 August 1959.
L'Aurore, 13 September 1962.
L'Est Républicain, 28 December 1962.
La Croix, 1 June 1974.
Landes, Marie-Gisèle (1963). Arts, 19 December.
La vie et les amours de Romy Schneider, nouvelle muse d'un romantisme moderne,
    Cinémonde, 21 November 1957.
'Le Cardinal', *L'Aurore*, 26 December 1963.
Le fric de 'La Banquière'. Portrait d'un parvenu artiste, *Libération*, 2 September
    1980.
Le match Jeanne Moreau-Romy Schneider, *Paris-Press-L'Intransigeant*, 30
    December 1962.
Le Nouvel Observateur, 5 April 1971 (http://tempsreel.nouvelobs.com/
    societe/20071127.OBS7018/le-manifeste-des-343-salopes-paru-dans-le-nouvel-
    obs-en-1971.html, last accessed: 11 February 2018).
Le Nouvel Observateur, 10 June 1974.
Le Nouvel Observateur, 27 November 1978.
Le Quotidien de Paris, 21 May 1974.
Le Soir Illustré, 17 January 1974, cover.
'Le Trio infernal', *Le Canard enchaîné*, 5 June 1974.
'Le Trio infernal', *Les Echos*, 31 May 1974.
'Le Trio infernal', L'humour monstre, *France-Soir*, 22 May 1974.
Les Cahiers du cinéma, October–November 1975, pp. 1–96.
Les fiancés terribles, *Nous Deux Film*, September 1960.
Les médias en question, *L'Humanité*, 23 January 1980.
Libération, 1 January 1964.
Lovet, Marcel (1963). *Le Soir de Bruxelles*, 8 March.
Lui, December 1973.
'Lysistrata': Südlich der Gürtellinie, *Der Spiegel*, 18 January 1961, pp. 57–9.
'Mado', *Le Nouvel Observateur*, 25 October 1976.
Mardore, Michel (1962). 'Le combat dans l'île', *Lettres Françaises*, 19 September.
Marie-Claire, September 1964.
Martin, Marcel (1969). 'La Piscine' de Jacques Deray, *Lettres Françaises*, 5
    February.
Mascotte spettacolo, 28 February 1962.
Mein Film, 25 December 1953.
Minute, 31 January 1980.
Mitgang, Herbert (1989). Thomas Bernhard Is Dead at 58; His Last Play Enraged
    Austrians, *The New York Times*, 17 February, p. 19.
Montaigne, Pierre (1978). Romy Schneider: la grâce inflexible, *Le Figaro*, 18
    November, p. 85.

Moriamez, Stefan (2000). *Le Vieux fusil*: film de Robert Enrico tourné à Montauban, *Arkheia*.

Morice, Jacques (2018). Romy Schneider, l'Allemande amère, *Télérama*, 15 September (https://www.telerama.fr/television/sur-arte-romy-schneider,-lallemande-amere,n5799543.php, last accessed: 15 February 2019).

Moustique, 2 November 2015 (https://www.moustique.be/14349/romy-schneider-fleur-de-peau, last accessed: 15 February 2019).

Muscionico, Daniele (2008). Die Jägerin als Beute, *Die Weltwoche* (http://www.weltwoche.ch/ausgaben/2008-29/artikel-2008-29-die-jaegerin-als.html, last accessed: 19 March 2017).

Na sowas, *Der Spiegel*, 25 January 1961, pp. 50–61.

Noir et blanc, 26 August 1964.

Pantel, Monique (1974). *France-Soir*, 21 May.

Paris actualités. Romy et Anna Karina couronnées par l'Académie, *Jours de France*, 12 June 1963, pp. 60–2.

Pariser Leben, *Der Spiegel*, 25 December 1963, pp. 100–1.

Paris Match, 19 May 1962.

Paris-Presse-L'Intransigeant, 31 May 1962.

Paris-Press-L'Intransigeant, 30 December 1962.

Petit, Olivier (2014). Romy Schneider: qui était vraiment Magda, sa mère tyrannique?, *Téléstar*, 31 december (http://www.telestar.fr/article/romy-schneider-qui-etait-vraiment-magda-sa-mere-tyrannique-diapo-66915, last accessed: 19 March 2017).

Pérez, Michel (1976). 'Une femme à sa fenêre', *Le Quotidien de Paris*, 12 November.

Politique Hebdo, 21 September 1975.

'Portraits de groupe avec dame', *Le Figaro*, 25 May 1977.

Pour l'amour d'Alain Delon, Romy Schneider a tué 'Sissi', *Le Film Illustré*, 15 July 1962.

Pour Romy et Alain, des fleurs et des épines, *Cinémonde*, 18 April 1961.

Pour Romy Schneider 'Sissi', Alain Delon n'a qu'un visage: celui de l'amour, *Point de vue, Images du monde*, 27 March 1959.

Première, August 1980, cover, pp. 14–19.

Rabine, Henry (1963). *La Croix*, 15 January.

Rabine, Henry (1966a). 'La Voleuse', *La Croix*, 5 December.

Rabine, Henry (1966b). 'Quoi de neuf Pussy Cat?', *La Croix*, 5 February.

Rabine, Henry (1974). 'Le mouton enragé', *La Croix*, 19 March.

Rabine, Henry (1975). 'Le Vieux Fusil'. 'Oradour' sur bonheur, *La Croix*, 1 September.

Romantische Romy, *Illustrierte Berliner*, 2 February 1957.

Romy e Alain sono stanchi di fare gli eterni fidanzati: ci sposeremo prima die natale, *Oggi*, 13 September 1962.

Romy Schneider: 'À 42 ans, après tant d'épreuves, je veux enfin vivre', *Paris Match*, 8 May 1981.

Romy Schneider a choisi le sex-appeal, *Ciné Revue*, 23 January 1959, cover.

Romy Schneider at home: à Berchtesgaden, *Ciné Revue*, 28 March, 1958.

Romy Schneider & Alain Delon: Das brautpaar dieses frühlings, *Bunte*, 11 April 1959.

Romy Schneider et Alain Delon: ces photos démentent la brouille des éternels fiancés, *Paris Match*, 2 September 1961.

Romy Schneider. Berlin bleibt doch Berlin, *Revue*, 24 January 1959.

Romy Schneider – bezaubernd wie in *Sissy*, Union-Film Verleihprogramm 1959–1960, *Österreichische Film und Kino Zeitung*, 20 June 1959.

Romy Schneider dans les bras d'Alain Delon, *Jours de France*, 31 August 1968.

Romy Schneider. Die Tocher-Gesellschaft, *Der Spiegel*, 7 March 1956, pp. 34–41.

Romy Schneider, en demeurant tout simplement une vraie jeune fille, elle a conquis le monde entier, *Nous Deux Film*, 1 September 1958.

Romy Schneider erobert Hollywood, *Bunte*, 23 October 1963.

Romy Schneider: Filmfestival te Cannes, *Zondagsvriend*, 14 May 1959.

Romy Schneider, la jeune fille modèle du cinema allemand, *Elle*, 5 January 1959, cover.

Romy Schneider, la nouvelle petite fiancée du monde n'a pas le temps de songer au mariage, *Festival*, 1 September 1958.

Romy Schneider: le talent, c'est l'amour, *Ciné Revue*, 14 June 1962.

Romy Schneider. Sachte, Mausi!, *Der Spiegel*, 13 March 1963, pp. 79–84.

Romy Schneider schrijft haar naam met de S van Sex en Sensatie, *De Post*, 28 July 1962.

Romy Schneider (Sissi) change de visage à Paris, *sou*, 1 September 1958.

Romy Schneider, une actrice fascinante au destin tragique, *Le Figaro*, 15 September 2018 (http://www.lefigaro.fr/cinema/2018/09/15/03002-20180915ARTFIG00053-romy-schneider-une-actrice-fascinante-au-destin-tragique.php, last accessed: 18 February 2019).

Romy Schneider: une carrière merveilleuse comme un conte de fées, *Jeunesse Cinéma*, June 1958.

Romy Schneider, une jeune fille presque modèle, *Elle*, 5 January 1959, pp. 48–51.

Romy triumph in Paris, *Bunte*, 22 April 1961.

Romy verovert de mannen, *De Post*, 11 April 1971.

Roxborough, Scott (2021). RTL, Beta to Reboot Royal Classic 'Sisi' (Exclusive), *The Hollywood Reporter*, 24 March (https://www.hollywoodreporter.com/tv/tv-news/rtl-beta-to-re-boot-royal-classic-sisi-exclusive-4155249/?utm_source=facebook&utm_medium=social&fbclid=IwAR0l8Ig9cWQyU4tHlxsmgtgteggD6AYl227f_iJmA50G5IWrvADnT_gtdsY, last accessed: 1 July 2021)

Sanders, Claudia (1957). Kleines Mädchen – Großer Star. Die Geschichte der Romy Schneider, *Libelle*, 2 February.

Screen: Royal Romance: Austrian 'Forever My Love' at 72d Street, *The New York Times*, 28 March 1962.

Schimmelbusch, Alexander (2014). Thomas Bernhard gegen Peter Handke, *Die Zeit*, 12 February (https://www.zcit.dc/kultur/literatur/2014-02/peter-handke-thomas-bernhard-vergleich/seite-4, last accessed: 31 May 2018).

Senfft, Heinrich (1992). Die Hatz war unerträglich, *Die Zeit/Magazin*, 29 May.

Sengissen, Paule (1962). *Télérama*, 29 September.

Siclier, Jacques (1974). 'Le Trio infernal' de Francis Girod, *Le Monde*, 27 May.

Siclier, Jacques (1982). Contre l'oubli, *Le Monde*, 17 April.

Sissi: coiffures nouvelles pour son fiancé Parisien, *Paris Match*, 21 June 1958.

Stars. Gruppenbild mit Romy, *Der Spiegel*, 22 November 1976, p. 219.

Stars Pick the Paris Plums, *Life Magazine*, 8 March 1963, pp. 82–3.

Stern, 1 March 1973.

Stern, 16 August 1973.

Sudendorf, Werner (2008). Wie Deutschland Romy Schneider vertrieb. *Die Welt*, 22 September (http://www.welt.de/kultur/article2469284/Wie-Deutschland-Romy-Schneider-vertrieb.html#, last accessed: 1 May 2016).

Swamp, J. M. (1963). Romy a séduit et scandalisé l'Amérique, *Ciné Revue*, 18 April, p. 16.

Teisseire, Guy (1978). Les femmes de Sautet, *L'Aurore*, 18 November.

Tempo, 7 March 1964.

The Hollywood Reporter, 28 January 1958.

The Sunday Times Magazine, 10 September 1972.

Thibault, Régis (2010). Romy Schneider: Spoliée par sa mère !, *France Dimanche*, 3 September (http://www.francedimanche.fr/infos-people/cinema/romy-schneider-spoliee-par-sa-mere/, last accessed: 25 March 2021).

Thirard, Jean-Louis (1978). *Rouge*, 1 December.

Truffaut, François (1954). Une certaine tendance du cinéma français, *Cahiers du cinéma*, January, pp. 15–29.

'Une femme à sa fenêtre', film français de Pierre Granier-Deferre, *Politique Hebdo*, 22 November 1976.

Wagner, Friedrich (1962). Erotische Episoden. 'Boccaccio 70' mit Anita Ekberg, Romy Schneider und Sophia Loren', *Frankfurter Allgemeine Zeitung*, 7 August.

Wie Romy liebt und leidet, *Bunte*, 1 July 1976, cover.

Wild, Dieter (1975). Barbaren am Werk, *Der Spiegel*, 22 September, p. 156.

Wir haben abgetrieben!, *Stern*, 6 June 1971, cover, pp. 16–23.

Wonder Woman. Le jour où Romy Schneider a pris la défense d'Isabelle Huppert sur le tournage d'un film, *Vanity Fair*, 13 December 2018 (https://www.vanityfair.fr/actualites/articles/le-jour-ou-romy-schneider-a-pris-la-defense-disabelle-huppert-sur-le-tournage-dun-film/71274, last accessed: 1 February 2019).

Website

Welter, Julien (2008). *Romy, Delon et les brûmes de l'Allemagne*, Arte TV (http://www.arte.tv/fr/mouvement-de-cinema/Romy-Schneider/1345568.html, last accessed: 1 May 2016).

Audio and television interviews and journalistic documents

Reflets de Cannes, François Chalais, 17 May 1957.

Interview with Romy Schneider by France Roche on the set of *Le Combat dans l'île*, 1961.

Interview with Romy Schneider by Georges Kleinmann for the television magazine *Carrefour*, 19 February 1962.

Interview with Romy Schneider by François Chalais for the television magazine *Reflets de Cannes*, 11 May 1962.

Interview with Romy Schneider and Alain Delon by François Chalais for the television magazine *Reflets de Cannes*, 11 May 1962.

Hollywood and the Stars. Anatomy of a Movie: The Cardinal, Dir: Jack Haley Jr., NBC, 12 February 1964.

Interview with Romy Schneider and Alain Delon by Jean-Marie Molingo for the news show *JT 13H*, 12 August 1968.

Interview with Romy Schneider by Jacques Chancel for the radio show *Radioscopie*, France Inter, 13 March 1970.

Interview with Romy Schneider for the television magazine *Pathé magazine*, 3 February 1971.

Interview with Romy Schneider by Claude Couderc for the television magazine *Midi trente*, 29 June 1974.

Interview with Romy Schneider by France Roche for the news show *Le Journal A2 20H*, 12 February 1975.

Interview with Romy Schneider by Michel Drucker, 'Rencontre avec Romy Schneider à Berlin' for the television show *Les rendez-vous du dimanche*, 7 November 1976.

Interview with Claude Sautet, Romy Schneider, Jean-Loup Dabadie, and Bruno Crémer by Michel Drucker for the television show *Les rendez-vous du dimanche*, 26 November 1978.

Odicino, Guillemette (2018). *Romy Schneider, premier volet*, 'On s'fait des films', France Inter, 14 August (https://www.franceinter.fr/emissions/on-s-fait-des-films/on-s-fait-des-films-14-aout-2018, last accessed: 24 March 2019).

Odicino, Guillemette (2018). *Romy Schneider, deuxième partie*, 'On s'fait des films', France Inter, 15 August (https://www.franceinter.fr/emissions/on-s-fait-des-films/on-s-fait-des-films-15-aout-2018, last accessed: 24 March 2019).

Interview with Andrzej Żuławski by Christian Defaye for the television show *Spécial Cinéma*, November 1981.

Interview with Romy Schneider by Michel Drucker for the television show *Champs-Elysées*, 14 April 1982.

Legenden: Romy Schneider, 1998, Dir: Michael Strauven, Germany.

Romy Schneider, étrange étrangère, 2002, Dir: Anne Andreu and Francesco Brunacci, France.

Romy Schneider, eine Frau in Drei noten, une femme en trois notes, 2008, Dir: Frederick Baker, Austria.

Un jour, un destin. Romy Schneider: ange et démons, 2010, Dir: Serge Khalfon, France.

Romy Schneider à fleur de peau, 2013, Dir: Bertrand Tessier, France.

Interview with Alain Delon and Patrice Lecomte by Laurent Delahousse for the news show *JT 20H*, France 2, 11 December 2016.

Romy, de tout son cœur, 2016, Dir: Pascal Forneri, France.

On n'est pas couché, TV talk show (produced by Catherine Barma and Laurent Ruquier), France 2, 9 June 2018.

Interview with Brigitte Bardot by Vincent Niclo for the radio show *Carte Blanche*,
   BBC2, 1 January 2019 (https://www.bbc.co.uk/programmes/m0001ttm, last
   accessed: 1 February 2019).
Interview with Julie Gayet by Claire Chazal, *Entrée libre*, France 2, 11 February
   2019.
Interview with Sarah Biasini, Anouchka Delon, and Khatia Buniatishvili by Laurent
   Delahousse for the news show *20h30 le dimanche*, France 2, 10 January 2021.

FILMOGRAPHY

Romy Schneider's filmography

Wenn der weiße Flieder wieder blüht, 1953, Dir: Hans Deppe, West Germany
Feuerwerk, 1954, Dir: Kurt Hoffmann, West Germany, Switzerland
Mädchenjahre einer Königin, 1954, Dir: Ernst Marischka, Austria
Die Deutschmeister, 1955, Dir: Ernst Marischka, Austria
Der letzte Mann, 1955, Dir: Harald Braun, West Germany
Sissi, 1955, Dir: Ernst Marischka, Austria
Kitty und die große Welt, 1956, Dir: Alfred Weidenmann, West Germany
Sissi, die junge Kaiserin, 1956, Dir: Ernst Marischka, Austria
Robinson soll nicht sterben, 1957, Dir: Josef von Báky, West Germany
Monpti, 1957, Dir: Helmut Käutner, West Germany
Sissi, Schicksalsjahre einer Kaiserin, 1957, Dir: Ernst Marischka, Austria
Scampolo, 1958, Dir: Alfred Weidenmann, West Germany
Mädchen in Uniform, 1958, Dir: Géza von Radványi, West Germany, France
Christine, 1958, Dir: Pierre Gaspard-Huit, France, Italy
Die Halbzarte, 1959, Dir: Rolf Thiele, Austria
Ein Engel auf Erden, 1959, Dir: Géza von Radványi, West Germany, France
Die schöne Lügnerin, 1959, Dir: Axel von Ambesser, West Germany, France
Katia, 1959, Dir: Robert Siodmak, France
Plein soleil, 1960, Dir: René Clément, 1960, France, Italy
Die Sendung der Lysistrata, 1961, Dir: Fritz Kortner, West Germany (TV film)
Boccaccio '70, 1962, Dir: Vittorio De Sica, Federico Fellini, Mario Monicelli,
    Luchino Visconti, Italy, France
Le Combat dans l'île, 1962, Dir: Alain Cavalier, France
The Trial, 1962, Dir: Orson Welles, France, West Germany, Italy
The Victors, 1963, Dir: Carl Foreman, UK, USA
The Cardinal, 1963, Dir: Otto Preminger, USA
L'Amour à la mer, 1964, Dir: Guy Gilles, France (scene cut)
Good Neighbor Sam, 1964, Dir: David Swift, USA
L'Enfer, 1964, Dir: Henri-Georges Clouzot, France (unfinished)
What's New Pussycat?, 1965, Dir: Clive Donner, USA
10:30 p.m. Summer, 1966, Dir: Jules Dassin, Spain, USA, France
Paris brûle-t-il?, 1966, Dir: René Clément, France, USA (scene cut)
La Voleuse, 1966, Dir: Jean Chapot, France, West Germany
Triple Cross, 1966, Dir: Terence Young, UK, France

Romy – Portrait eines Gesichts, 1967, Dir: Hans-Jürgen Syberberg, West Germany (TV film)
Otley, 1968, Dir: Dick Clement, UK
La Piscine, 1969, Dir: Jacques Deray, France, Italy
My Lover, My Son, 1970, Dir: John Newland, UK
Les Choses de la vie, 1970, Dir: Claude Sautet, France, Italy
Qui?, 1970, Dir: Léonard Keigel, France, Italy
Bloomfield, 1971, Dir: Richard Harris, UK, Israel
La Califfa, 1971, Dir: Alberto Bevilacqua, Italy, France
Max et les ferrailleurs, 1971, Dir: Claude Sautet, France, Italy
The Assassination of Trotsky, 1972, Dir: Joseph Losey, Italy, France, UK
César et Rosalie, 1972, Dir: Claude Sautet, France, Italy, West Germany
Ludwig, 1973, Dir: Luchino Visconti, Italy, West Germany, France
Le Train, 1973, Dir: Pierre Granier-Deferre, France, Italy
Un amour de pluie, 1974, Dir: Jean-Claude Brialy, France, Italy
Le Mouton enragé, 1974, Dir: Michel Deville, France, Italy
Le Trio infernal, 1974, Dir: Francis Girod, France, Italy, West Germany
L'Important c'est d'aimer, 1975, Dir: Andrzej Żuławski, France, Italy, West Germany
Les Innocents aux mains sales, 1975, Dir: Claude Chabrol, France, West Germany, Italy
Le Vieux Fusil, 1975, Dir: Robert Enrico, France, West Germany
Mado, 1976, Dir: Claude Sautet, France, Italy, Germany
Une femme à sa fenêtre, 1976, Dir: Pierre Granier-Deferre, France, Italy, Germany
Tausend Lieder ohne Ton, 1977, Dir: Claudia Holldack, West Germany (TV film)
Gruppenbild mit Dame, 1977, Dir: Aleksandar Petrović, West Germany, France
Une histoire simple, 1978, Dir: Claude Sautet, France, West Germany
Bloodline, 1979, Dir: Terence Young, West Germany, USA
Clair de femme, 1979, Dir: Costa-Gavras, France, Italy, West Germany
La Mort en direct, 1980, Dir: Bertrand Tavernier, France, West Germany
La Banquière, 1980, Dir: Francis Girod, France
Fantasma d'amore, 1981, Dir: Dino Risi, Italy, West Germany, France
Garde à vue, 1981, Dir: Claude Miller, France
La Passante du Sans-Souci, 1982, Dir: Jacques Rouffio, France, West Germany
L'Enfer d'Henri-Georges Clouzot, 2009, Dir: Serge Bromberg, Ruxandra Medrea, France

Other films cited

3 Tage in Quiberon, 2018, Dir: Emily Atef, Germany
À bout de souffle, 1960, Dir: Jean-Luc Godard, France
Alexandre le bienheureux, 1968, Dir: Yves Robert, France
Ascenseur pour l'échafaud, 1958, Dir: Louis Malle, France
Babette s'en va-t-en guerre, 1959, Dir: Christian-Jaque, France
Baisers volés, 1968, Dir: François Truffaut, France

Bande à part, 1964, Dir: Jean-Luc Godard, France
Barbarella, 1968, Dir: Roger Vadim, France, Italy
Belle de jour, 1967, Dir: Luis Buñuel, France
Bonjour Tristesse, 1958, Dir: Otto Preminger, USA, UK
Borsalino, 1970, Dir: Jacques Deray, France, Italy
Cette sacrée gamine, 1955, Dir: Michel Boisrond, France
Cinderella, 1950, Dir: Clyde Geronimi, Wilfred Jackson, Hamilton Luske, USA
Cyrano de Bergerac, 1990, Dir: Jean-Paul Rappeneau, France
Death Wish, 1974, Dir: Michael Winner, USA
Der Feldherrnhügel, 1953, Dir: Ernst Marischka, Austria
Der Letzte Mann, 1924, Dir: Friedrich Wilhelm Murnau, Germany
Diabeł, 1972, Dir: Andrzej Żuławski, Poland
Die Ehe der Maria Braun, 1979, Dir: Rainer Werner Fassbinder, West Germany
Die Halbstarken, 1956, Dir: Georg Tressler, West Germany
Die Sterne lügen nicht, 1950, Dir: Jürgen von Alten, West Germany
Dites-lui que je l'aime, 1977, Dir: Claude Miller, France
Don Juan ou si Don Juan était une femme, 1973, Dir: Roger Vadim, France
Elle boit pas, elle fume pas, elle drague pas, mais... elle cause, 1970, Dir: Michel Audiard, France
Emmanuelle, 1964, Dir: Just Jaeckin, France
En cas de malheur, 1958, Dir: Claude Autant-Lara, France
Erotissimo, 1969, Dir: Gérard Pirès, France
Et Dieu... créa la femme, 1956, Dir: Roger Vadim, France
Faibles Femmes, 1959, Dir: Michel Boisrond, France
Faut pas prendre les enfants du bon Dieu pour des canards sauvages, 1968, Dir: Michel Audiard, France
Forever My Love, 1962, Dir: Ernst Marischka, Austria
Fünfter Akt, Siebte Szene. Fritz Kortner probt Kabale und Liebe, 1965, Dir: Hans-Jürgen Syberberg, West Germany
Futures Vedettes, 1955, Dir: Marc Allégret, France
Gone with the Wind, 1939, Dir: Victor Fleming, USA
Hiroshima mon amour, 1959, Dir: Alain Resnais, France
Hitler, ein Film aus Deutschland, 1977, Dir: Hans-Jürgen Syberberg, West Germany, France, UK
Jules et Jim, 1962, Dir: François Truffaut, France
Kaisermanöver, 1954, Dir: Franz Antel, Austria
Kaiserwalzer, 1953, Dir: Franz Antel, Austria
Katia, 1938, Dir: Maurice Tourneur, France
Kitty und die Weltkonferenz, 1939, Dir: Helmut Käutner, Germany
L'Agression, 1975, Dir: Gérard Pirès, France
L'Argent des autres, 1978, Dir: Christian de Chalonge, France
L'Arme à gauche, 1965, Dir: Claude Sautet, France
L'Armée des ombres, 1969, Dir: Jean-Pierre Melville, France, Italy
L'Astragale, 1968, Dir: Guy Casaril, France, West Germany
L'Aveu, 1970, Dir: Costa-Gravas, France
L'Eclisse, 1962, Dir: Michelangelo Antonioni, Italy, France
L'Histoire d'Adèle H., 1975, Dir: François Truffaut, France
L'Une chante, l'autre pas, 1977, Dir: Agnès Varda, France

La Bataille du rail, 1946, Dir: René Clément, France
La Clé sur la porte, 1978, Dir: Yves Boisset, France
Lacombe Lucien, 1974, Dir: Louis Malle, France
La Dérobade, 1979, Dir: Daniel Duval, France
La Fiancée du pirate, 1969, Dir: Nelly Kaplan, France
La Grande bouffe, 1973, Dir: Marco Ferreri, France, Italy
La Grande Vadrouille, 1966, Dir: Gérard Oury, France
La Môme, 2007, Dir: Olivier Dahan, France, UK, Czech Republic
La Nuit américaine, 1973, Dir: François Truffaut, France
La Révolution française, 1989, Dir: Robert Enriro (Part 1: *Les années lumières*),
    and Richard T. Heffron (Part 2: *Les années terribles*), France, Germany, Italy,
    UK, Canada
Last Tango in Paris, 1972, Dir: Bernardo Bertolucci, Italy, France
La Traversée de Paris, 1956, Dir: Claude Autant-Lara, France
La Tulipe Noire, 1964, Dir: Christian-Jaque, France, Italy, Spain
La Veuve Couderc, 1971, Dir: Pierre-Granier-Deferre, France
La Vérité, 1960, Dir: Henri-Georges Clouzot, France
La Vie de château, 1966, Dir: Jean-Paul Rappeneau, France
Le Chagrin et la Pitié, 1971, Dir: Marcel Ophüls, France, West Germany,
    Switzerland
Le Chat, 1971, Dir: Pierre-Granier-Deferre, France
Le Chemin des écoliers, 1959, Dir: Michel Boisrond, France
Le Dernier métro, 1981, Dir: François Truffaut, France
Le Journal d'une femme de chambre, 1964, Dir: Luis Buñuel, France, Italy
Le Journal d'une femme en blanc, 1965, Dir: Claude Autant-Lara, France, Italy
Le Mépris, 1963, Dir: Jean-Luc Godard, France, Italy
Le Quai des brumes, 1938, Dir: Marcel Carné, France
Le Samouraï, 1967, Dir: Jean-Pierre Melville, France
Le Sauvage, 1975, Dir: Jean-Paul Rappeneau, France
Le Sauveur, 1971, Dir: Michel Mardore, France
Le Souffle au cœur, 1971, Dir: Louis Malle, France
Le Sucre, 1978, Dir: Jacques Rouffio, France
Le Vieil homme et l'enfant, 1967, Dir: Claude Berri, France
Les Amants, 1958, Dir: Louis Malle, France
Les Bidasses s'en vont en guerre, 1974, Dir: Claude Zidi, France
Les Garçon et Guillaume, à table !, 2013, Dir: Guillaume Gallienne, France
Les Guichets du Louvre, 1974, Dir: Michel Mitrani, France
Les Novices, 1970, Dir: Guy Casaril, France
Les Pétroleuses, 1971, Dir: Christian-Jaque, France, Italy, Spain, UK
Les Portes de la nuit, 1946, Dir: Marcel Carné, France
Les Valseuses, 1974, Dir: Bertrand Blier, France
Liebelei, 1933, Dir: Max Ophüls, Germany
Lost Command, 1966, Dir: Mark Robson, USA, France
Mädchen in Uniform, 1931, Dir: Leontine Sagan, Germany
Manon, 1949, Dir: Henri-Georges Clouzot, France
Marianne de ma jeunesse, 1955, Dir: Julien Duvivier, France
Mille milliards de dollars, 1982, Dir: Henri Verneuil, France
Moderato Cantabile, 1960, Dir: Peter Brook, France, Italy

Mon amour, mon amour, 1967, Dir: Nadine Trintignant, France
Monsieur Klein, 1976, Dir: Joseph Losey, France
More, 1969, Dir: Barbet Schroeder, West Germany, France, Luxembourg
Morocco, 1930, Dir: Josef von Sternberg, USA
Mourir d'aimer, 1971, Dir: André Cayatte, France
Nelly et Monsieur Arnaud, 1995, Dir: Claude Sautet, France
Nuit et Brouillard, 1956, Dir: Alain Resnais, France
Olivia, 1950, Dir: Jacqueline Audry, France
Où est passé la 7e compagnie?, 1973, Dir: Robert Lamoureux, France
Possession, 1981, Dir: Andrzej Żuławski, France, West Germany
Quand la femme s'en mêle, 1957, Dir: Yves Allégret, France
René la Canne, 1977, Dir: Francis Girod, France, Italy
Rocco e i suoi fratelli, 1961, Dir: Luchino Visconti, Italy
Romy, 2009, Dir: Torsten C. Fischer, Germany
Saint Joan, 1957, Dir: Otto Preminger, USA, UK
Sois belle et tais-toi, 1957, Dir: Marc Allégret, France
Stavisky, 1974, Dir: Alain Resnais, France
To Catch a Thief, 1955, Dir: Alfred Hitchock, USA
The Emperor Waltz, 1948, Dir: Billy Wilder, USA
The Man Between, 1953, Dir: Carol Reed, UK
The Seven Years Itch, 1955, Dir: Billy Wilder, USA
The Sound of Music, 1965, Dir: Robert Wise, USA
Third Man on the Mountain, 1959, Dir: Ken Annakin, USA
Thunderball, 1965, Dir: Terence Young, UK
Tout de suite maintenant, 2016, Dir: Pascal Bonitzer, France, Belgium, Luxembourg
Tristana, 1970, Dir: Luis Buñuel, France
Trzecia część nocy, 1971, Dir: Andrzej Żuławski, Poland
Un cœur en hiver, 1992, Dir: Claude Sautet, France
Une Parisienne, 1957, Dir: Michel Boisrond, France
Vincent, François, Paul et les autres, 1974, Dir: Claude Sautet, France
Vivre pour vivre, 1967, Dir: Claude Lelouch, France
Vivre sa vie, 1962, Dir: Jean-Luc Godard, France
Z, 1969, Dir: Costa-Gravas, France, Algeria

INDEX

Milton Keynes UK
Ingram Content Group UK Ltd.
UKHW021850210824
447180UK00009B/181